Scotland, England, and the Reformation
1534–61

CLARE KELLAR

CLARENDON PRESS · OXFORD

OXFORD
UNIVERSITY PRESS

Great Clarendon Street, Oxford OX2 6DP

Oxford University Press is a department of the University of Oxford.
It furthers the University's objective of excellence in research, scholarship,
and education by publishing worldwide in

Oxford New York

Auckland Bangkok Buenos Aires Cape Town Chennai
Dar es Salaam Delhi Hong Kong Istanbul Karachi Kolkata
Kuala Lumpur Madrid Melbourne Mexico City Mumbai Nairobi
São Paulo Shanghai Taipei Tokyo Toronto

Oxford is a registered trade mark of Oxford University Press
in the UK and in certain other countries

Published in the United States
by Oxford University Press Inc., New York

British Library Cataloguing in Publication Data

Data available

Library of Congress Cataloging in Publication Data

Data applied for

ISBN 0-19-926670-0

1 3 5 7 9 10 8 6 4 2

Typeset in Ehrhardt
by Regent Typesetting, London
Printed in Great Britain
on acid-free paper by
Biddles Ltd,
Guildford and King's Lynn

For

DAD, JAMES,
and SUSANNAH

PREFACE

This book started life as a D.Phil. thesis on the interactions between English and Scottish religious reformers in the mid-sixteenth century. Its essential theme is that the period from 1534 to 1561, opening with England's Act of Supremacy and ending with the return of Mary Queen of Scots to her newly Protestant realm, saw fascinating and sometimes very unexpected associations between the English and Scots in the name of religion. The choice of this timescale, not a conventional one for the subject of Anglo-Scottish reforming links, reflects the fact that many of these connections have in the past been overlooked. Episodes such as England's Rough Wooing of Scotland in the 1540s, and its support for Scotland's religious revolution of 1559–60, are well known, but further light may be shed upon them, and upon the whole process of reform in each country, by examining a far wider range of religious interactions. In 1534 a confessional distinction between the countries was set in place, but far from creating a rigid divide between two religious regimes it instead focused attention on the border, as a source either of exciting possibilities or pressing dangers, according to individual persuasions. The interconnectedness both of reforming endeavours, and efforts to resist reform, was continually apparent, as clergymen and laypeople, government officials and notorious rebels, all came to realize the import of the Anglo-Scottish religious division. Their attempts to come to terms with it, eliminate it, or else turn it to their advantage, would leave indelible imprints upon each Church. The process would also have a profound and lasting effect on English and Scottish perceptions of one another.

In arriving at these conclusions I have received enormous help and encouragement from many areas, not least from Dr Jenny Wormald who supervised my thesis and who has assisted me ever since in revising it for publication. I am very grateful for her lively criticism, interest, and support, all of which helped to ensure that it finally reached this point. I would also like to thank Mr Christopher Morgan, who first sparked my interest in the religious troubles of this period, and Professor John Morrill, whose teaching later inspired me to examine the interrelatedness of religious change across the border. Professor Morrill's work and helpful criticism have, I hope, had a lasting impact on my own thinking on the reformations in England and Scotland. I have been fortunate to receive further advice and guidance from Professor Michael Lynch and Fr Allan White OP, and from Dr Felicity Heal and Dr Roger Mason whose comments at my viva led me into some useful new areas. I am grateful to Dr Lucy Wooding for her opinions on my work, and to Dr Pamela Ritchie for her generosity in providing me with extracts from her thesis. I have been glad to receive the efficient assistance of staff at the National Library of Scotland, Scottish Record Office, Bodleian Library, British Library, and other institutions visited in the course of writing this book; and my research has also benefited from travel grants from the British Academy and from Jesus College, Oxford. My greatest thanks, however, are to my family: to my father and husband for being endlessly patient and encouraging, and to my daughter, who, though her arrival nearly brought everything to a halt, inspired me to continue.

C. K.

CONTENTS

Abbreviations   x

Introduction: Reform in an Anglo–Scottish Context   1

1. England's Break with Rome and the Scottish Dimension   11

2. Anglo–Scottish Diplomacy and Europe, 1534–1542   46

3. The Pursuit of a Godly Conjunction   78

4. Humanism and Reform   113

5. Protestant Alliances: The Privy Kirks and the Marian Exile   149

6. 'This Common Cause of Christ and Liberty?'   184

Conclusion: 'To Enrich with Gospel Truth the Neighbour Realm'   220

Bibliography   229

Index   245

ABBREVIATIONS

Place of publication is London unless otherwise stated

APC	*Acts of the Privy Council of England*, ed. J. R. Dasent et al., 46 vols. (HMSO, 1890–1964)
APS	*The Acts of the Parliaments of Scotland 1124–1707*, ed. T. Thomson and C. Innes, 12 vols. (Edinburgh, 1814–75)
BL	British Library
Calderwood	David Calderwood, *History of the Kirk of Scotland*, ed. T. Thomson and D. Laing, 8 vols. (Edinburgh: Wodrow Society, 1842 9)
CSP Dom.	*Calendar of State Papers, Domestic, Edward VI, Philip and Mary, Elizabeth*, ed. R. Lemon, M. A. E. Green, et al., 9 vols. (HMSO, 1856–72)
CSP Dom. Edw. VI	*Calendar of State Papers, Domestic, of the Reign of Edward VI*, ed. C. S. Knighton (HMSO, 1992; replacing older Calendar for 1547–53)
CSP Dom. Add.	*Calendar of State Papers, Domestic, of the Reign of Elizabeth 1601–1603; with Addenda 1547–1565*, ed. Mary Anne Everett Green (HMSO, 1870)
CSP For.	*Calendar of State Papers, Foreign*, ed. W. B. Turnbull, J. Stevenson, et al., 23 vols. (HMSO, 1836–1950)
CSP Scot.	*Calendar of the State Papers relating to Scotland and Mary Queen of Scots, 1547–1603*, ed. J. Bain et al., 14 vols. (Edinburgh: General Register House, 1898, 1969)
CSP Span.	*Calendar of State Papers, Spanish*, ed. P. de Gayangos, G. Mattingly, M. A. S Hume, and R. Tyler, 15 vols. in 20 (HMSO, 1862–1954)
CSP Ven.	*Calendar of State Papers, Venetian*, ed. R. Brown, C. Bentinck, and H. Brown, 9 vols. (HMSO, 1864–98)
DNB	*Dictionary of National Biography*, ed. Leslie Stephen and Sidney Lee, 63 vols., with supplements (Smith Elder, Oxford University Press, 1885–1990)
EHR	*English Historical Review*
EUL	Edinburgh University Library
Foxe	John Foxe, *Acts and Monuments*, ed. S. R. Cattley, 8 vols. (R. B. Seeley, W. Burnside, 1837–41)
HJ	*Historical Journal*
HP	*The Hamilton Papers: Letters illustrating the Political Relations of England and Scotland in the Sixteenth Century*, ed. Joseph Bain, 2 vols. (Edinburgh: General Register House, 1890–2)

JEH	*Journal of Ecclesiastical History*
Knox	*The Works of John Knox*, ed. D. Laing, 6 vols. (Edinburgh: Bannatyne Society, 1846–64)
LP	*Letters and Papers, Foreign and Domestic, of the Reign of Henry VIII 1509–1547*, ed. J. S. Brewer et al., 21 vols. and 2 vols. addenda (HMSO, 1862–1932)
NLS	National Library of Scotland
PRO	Public Record Office
RPC	*Register of the Privy Council of Scotland, 1545–1625*, ed. J. Hill Burton and D. Masson, 14 vols. (Edinburgh: General Register House, 1877–98)
RSCHS	*Records of the Scottish Church History Society*
RSTC	*A Short Title Catalogue of Books printed in England, Scotland, and Ireland and of English Books Printed Abroad before the Year 1640*, ed. A. W. Pollard and G. R. Redgrave, rev. W. A. Jackson and F. S. Ferguson, completed by K. F. Pantzer, 3 vols. (Bibliographical Society, 1967–91)
SHR	*Scottish Historical Review*
SHS	Scottish History Society
SP	*State Papers Published under the Authority of His Majesty's Commission, King Henry VIII*, 11 vols. (Record Commission, printed by G. Eyre and A. Strahan, 1830–52)
SRO	Scottish Record Office
SSP	*The State Papers and Letters of Sir Ralph Sadler, Knight-Banneret*, ed. Arthur Clifford, 2 vols. (Edinburgh: A. Constable, 1809)
STS	Scottish Text Society
TA	*Accounts of the Lord High Treasurer of Scotland*, ed. T. Dickon and Sir James Balfour, 12 vols. (Edinburgh: General Register House, 1877–1916)
TRHS	*Transactions of the Royal Historical Society*
TRP	*Tudor Royal Proclamations*, ed. P. L. Hughes and J. F. Larkin, 2 vols. (New Haven: Yale University Press, 1964, 1969)

Introduction: Reform in an Anglo-Scottish Context

The reformations in the kingdoms of England and Scotland might seem, on the face of it, to have had few common features. The official beginnings of reform in each country were separated by almost thirty years, during which time the English embarked hesitantly on the path towards a Protestant Church, while the Scottish Kirk's official stance was of resolute opposition to reformed doctrines. If the new teachings actually elicited a more ambivalent response in Scotland, they were still denied formal countenance until almost a generation after the English alteration. In addition to the simple fact of timing, the two reformations appeared fundamentally different in character. The rebellion initiated by Scottish reformers in 1559 would transform the theology and polity of the Kirk. The emphatic proceedings of the 1560 parliament stood in marked contrast to England's protracted and controversial experience of magisterial reform, with its wholesale reversals of religious policy in 1553 and 1558. Any association between the reformations in the two realms seems difficult to detect.

This impression owes much to contemporary interpretations of events, and has persisted in subsequent historiography. In the years immediately following the completion of Scotland's religious revolution, members of the Kirk began to develop the theory that their actions had set in place a uniquely pure brand of worship. The notion of Scottish singularity captured imaginations, and became a firm conviction of reformers by the early seventeenth century.[1] There was, at the same time, a tendency towards stubborn insularity among certain leading English churchmen, for whom internal religious affairs were all-consuming.[2] The conjunction of these trends created an inclination to view the reformations as entirely separate occurrences, even if the Calvinist-informed tenets they set forth were broadly similar. English self-absorption in consideration of the

---

[1] S. A. Burrell, 'The Apocalyptic Vision of the Early Covenanters', *SHR* 43 (1964), 3, 8–11; John Row, *The Historie of the Kirk of Scotland*, ed. D. Laing (Edinburgh: Wodrow Society, 1842), 12–13; John Forbes, *Certaine records touching the estate of the Church of Scotland*, ed. D. Laing (Edinburgh: Wodrow Society, 1846), 345.

[2] This attitude, though far from universal, was exhibited by leading clerics such as John Aylmer and John Whitgift: see Aylmer, *An Harborowe for Faithfull and Trewe Subiectes . . .* (Strasbourg, 1559; *RSTC* 1005), fo. Piv ; John Strype, *The Life and Acts of John Whitgift* (Oxford: Clarendon Press, 1822), i. 296–7.

religious estate was matched by Scottish pride in the Kirk, which, though merely one member of the universal Protestant communion, seemed marked out for especial divine favour.

Such diverging strands of thought are also a feature of more recent works. The English reformation remains a perpetual focus of interest, with studies of the social and cultural aspects of reform, and increasing numbers of biographies and local investigations rounding out our knowledge of the period.[3] The total volume of work on the Scottish reformation is smaller, but it, too, has received comprehensive treatment from historians such as Gordon Donaldson, James Kirk, and Michael Lynch.[4] Explicitly Anglo-Scottish perspectives on the religious developments of the period are less common, though, and many of these focus on the second half of the sixteenth century. Donaldson's theory of 'virtual unanimity' between the English and Scottish Churches after 1559 has been convincingly challenged by Kirk, who identifies links between two diverging Protestant parties within each establishment, while Stephen Alford has illuminated the politics of Anglo-Scottish reform during Elizabeth's reign.[5] For the years prior to 1559, Roger Mason has demonstrated the religious component to developing unionist thought, drawing attention to the differing political ideologies underwriting reform in the two countries, while Jane Dawson has highlighted the origins of an emerging Anglo-Scottish Protestant culture.[6] Despite such important investigations, little attention

---

[3] Amid the countless contributions to English reformation historiography, recent titles with particular relevance for this book include Eamon Duffy, *The Stripping of the Altars: Traditional Religion in England c.1400–c.1580* (New Haven: Yale University Press, 1992); Andrew Pettegree, *Marian Protestantism: Six Studies* (Aldershot: Scolar Press, 1996); Diarmaid MacCulloch, *Thomas Cranmer: A Life* (New Haven: Yale University Press, 1996); and Andrew D. Brown, *Popular Piety in late Medieval England: The Diocese of Salisbury, 1250–1550* (Oxford: Clarendon Press, 1995).

[4] Donaldson, *The Scottish Reformation* (Cambridge: Cambridge University Press, 1960); Kirk, *Patterns of Reform: Continuity and Change in the Reformation Kirk* (Edinburgh: T. & T. Clark, 1989); Michael Lynch, *Edinburgh and the Reformation* (Edinburgh: John Donald, 1981). Many more studies shed important light on the 16th-cent. Kirk: Jenny Wormald, *Court, Kirk and Community: Scotland 1470–1625* (New History of Scotland, 4; Edinburgh: Edinburgh University Press, 1991); David McRoberts (ed.), *Essays on the Scottish Reformation, 1513–1625* (Glasgow: John S. Burns & Sons, 1962); and Margaret H. B. Sanderson, *Ayrshire and the Reformation: People and Change, 1490–1600* (East Linton: Tuckwell Press, 1997) are just a small sample.

[5] Donaldson, 'The Relations between the English and Scottish Presbyterian Movements to 1604', Ph.D. thesis (London, 1938), 1, 71; Kirk, '"The Politics of the Best Reformed Kirks": Scottish Achievements and English Aspirations in Church Government after the Reformation', *SHR* 59 (1980), 26–30, 51–3; Stephen Alford, 'Knox, Cecil, and the British Dimension of the Scottish Reformation', in Roger A. Mason (ed.), *John Knox and the British Reformations* (Aldershot: Ashgate Publishing, 1998), 201–19.

[6] Mason, 'The Scottish Reformation and the Origins of Anglo-British Imperialism', in id.

has been directed towards even earlier cross-border exchanges, and to the implications that continuing religious interactions would have for both realms.

The years following England's rejection of papal authority and prior to the Scottish revolution in church and government offer a compelling picture of the complicated relationship between closely related realms of differing confessions. A more detailed examination of the period 1534 to 1561 reveals, moreover, that the English and Scottish experiences of reform were more thoroughly intertwined than traditional accounts might imply, even if the broad characterization of Scottish vitality as opposed to English circumspection might not be altogether misplaced. This is not to suggest that Scotland's acceptance of Protestant reform was the inevitable outcome of associations with England during these transitional years. It does seem clear, however, that interactions between Scottish and English reformers and laypeople had important mutual influences upon the proceedings of both Churches. England evidently did not remain unbendingly committed to Protestant doctrines from 1534, and neither did the people of Scotland shun all contacts with the unorthodox opinion of their English neighbours before 1559. Their associations with one another in this time irrevocably shaped their attitudes both to the old religion and the new learning.

Henry VIII's break with Rome may have redefined the Anglo-Scottish border as a religious frontier, but there was no rigid separation between the populations of the two countries, any more than there had been before the confessional split. Cultural and linguistic similarities were most marked among borderers, but correspondences also extended further into lowland Scotland and England, if not to the Highlands and the most southerly parts of the English realm. Cross-border associations of all descriptions, encompassing bonds of kinship, trading contacts, social ties, and, inevitably, religious discussions, were the result.[7] After 1534 there developed a complex pattern of interaction on religious grounds, some of it favouring the new doctrines, but equally some tending to the defence of traditional practices. There was ample evidence of collaboration, imitation, and assistance

(ed.), *Scots and Britons: Scottish Political Thought and the Union of 1603* (Cambridge: Cambridge University Press, 1994), 161–86; id., 'Knox, Resistance, and the Royal Supremacy', in id. (ed.), *John Knox and the British Reformations*, 154–75; Dawson, 'Anglo-Scottish Protestant Culture and Integration in Sixteenth Century Britain', in Steven G. Ellis and Sarah Barber (eds.), *Conquest and Union: Fashioning a British State 1485–1725* (Longman, 1995), 87–114.

[7] Thomas I. Rae, *The Administration of the Scottish Frontier, 1513–1603* (Edinburgh: Edinburgh University Press, 1966), 10–11, 67, 175–6.

between the English and Scots, as well as some aversion, hostility, and distancing. Furthermore, at a time when no reforms seemed irreversible, and doctrinal distinctions were not yet irretrievably entrenched, there were more similarities than might be expected between the religious practices and opinion of two nominally opposing churches. England's return to Rome at the accession of Mary Tudor affirmed the unpredictability of religious trends, adding to pervading uncertainties among the laity of the two countries. The midyears of the century demonstrated that the English and Scottish reformations involved not single events, but gradual and long-term changes, with a redefinition of religious stances, both internally and in relation to one another.

Throughout Europe the consolidation of nation–states, through assimilation of territory and extension of royal control, could be closely linked to the requirements of reform. Whether in support of orthodox religious loyalties or aiming to promote Protestant doctrines, such governmental activity encouraged the re-examination of relations with neighbouring realms. This was especially necessary if it appeared that there would be a conflict of reforming opinions, and it quickly became clear that England and Scotland would come into this category. Henry VIII and James V, both energetic statesmen with a keen interest in asserting unchallenged princely authority, were set at odds by their contrasting religious views. Their concerns over the loyalties of their subjects, together with their differences on reform, served to focus attention ever more closely on Anglo–Scottish relations, and specifically on the border between the realms.

The variety of cross-border exchanges in the mid-century could not help but have some impact upon attitudes towards reform within each country, although it is evident that such contacts were only one element in the shaping of contemporary religious opinion. The well-documented differences between the formal reformations in England and Scotland suggest that mutual influences between the countries were not the conclusive ones in determining the final appearances of the reformed establishments: the European context was all-important, and the churchmen of both countries looked to the continent for inspiration and support. Anglo–Scottish associations were, however, an essential determining factor in the evolution of the reformed churches in both realms. Recent studies in British history have drawn attention to the vital significance of this 'layer of explanation'. John Morrill argues, 'The relations between the peoples of these islands need to be seen in terms of their interactions. It is not the only way in which they need to be seen; but it is *an* essential way of making sense of their history.'[8]

[8] Morrill, 'Introduction', in Brendan Bradshaw and John Morrill (eds.), *The British Problem, c.1534–1707: State Formation in the Atlantic Archipelago* (Basingstoke: Macmillan,

Certain historians have questioned the usefulness of such a British perspective, with Nicholas Canny, for instance, highlighting the danger of imposing potentially artificial constructs on the study of the past.[9] Though the concern is justifiable it does not seem to apply in this instance, as the inescapability of the Irish role in Scottish religious affairs, and vice versa, together with English concerns over the affairs of both, created a genuine three-kingdom mentality. Against a background of ancient bonds between the Scottish Highlands and the north of Ireland, the varied responses to English reforming initiatives throughout Britain gave rise to potent connections between the realms.

The focus of this study is consciously an Anglo-Scottish one. The reformation changes initiated by England from 1534 produced a dynamic interplay between two autonomous kingdoms sharing a single island form, making the northern border an immensely significant flashpoint for religious tensions. The resulting interactions between the countries were profoundly important in shaping contemporary religious and political thought. This said, the English and Scottish experiences of reform clearly cannot be studied in isolation. The dealings of the English crown's subjects in Ireland had an inescapable influence upon religious developments, and, as such, they are an important feature of many of the events described. The impact of reform upon Wales is also impossible to ignore, and the interweaving of the religious affairs of all areas of the British Isles forms a recurring theme of this work. A concentration on the particular interactions between England and Scotland, however, aims to offer one means of making sense of the evolution of reform in each country.

Although the religious climates of England and Scotland remained in a continual state of flux during this period, the simple fact of the proximity of the countries was a constant in the considerations of policymakers and reformers. The geographical conjunction of the realms, combined with their physical separation from the rest of Europe, made English and

1996), p. viii. The current interest in British history, denoting a pluralistic approach to the national histories of England, Wales, Scotland, and Ireland, has been inspired principally by two articles of J. G. A. Pocock: 'British History: A Plea for a New Subject', *Journal of Modern History*, 47 (1975), 601–29; and 'The Limits and Divisions of British History', *American History Review*, 87 (1982), 311–36. Among many articles and collections of essays on this theme, the most useful for Anglo-Scottish religious relations in this period include Mason (ed.), *Scots and Britons; id.* (ed.), *John Knox and the British Reformations*; Jenny Wormald, 'The Creation of Britain: Multiple Kingdoms or Core and Colonies?', *TRHS*, 6th ser. 2 (1992), 175–94; and Jane E. A. Dawson, 'William Cecil and the British Dimension of Early Elizabethan Foreign Policy', *History*, 74 (1989), 196–216.

[9] Canny, 'Irish, Scottish and Welsh Responses to Centralisation, c.1530–c.1640', in Alexander Grant and Keith J. Stringer (eds.), *Uniting the Kingdom? The Making of British History* (London: Routledge Press, 1995), 147–50.

Scottish reforming decisions peculiarly important to one another. The urgent need to consider the Anglo-Scottish implications of official religious policies was not instantly apparent to the statesmen of both countries after 1534. An awareness of this perspective, and the formulation of effective British policies, would be largely a process of trial and error, learned over time and with varying degrees of success by different politicians. The force of circumstance, however, ensured that the active European interests of both governments could not outweigh the fundamental importance of their relations with one another.

As they came to terms with the demands of coexistence with a regime of another religious complexion, English and Scottish officials were ambivalent in their attitude to the close conjunction of the realms. Their communications in the period after Henry's challenge to Rome were permeated with references to the geographical factor. These frequently took the form of reminders and warnings, with both countries preparing to resist 'the contagious influences of neighbours'.[10] From other quarters, however, there would in time develop more providential readings of the favoured positioning of the realms, being 'so nere neighbors, dwellyng with in one land, compassed within one sea, alied in bloude, and knitte in Christes faithe'.[11] Ambitious schemes were devised for the augmentation of the natural bonds between the English and Scots by the establishment of religious harmony. Whichever of these interpretations was followed, it was evident that the reformation changes inspired concentrated consideration of the physical relationship between England and Scotland. This led inevitably to the reinterpretation of religious and political links between the realms.

The exact nature of the relationship between the two kingdoms was problematic. Their history was indelibly marked by England's medieval assertion of suzerainty over the vassal kingdom of Scotland, and although the claim had been relinquished in 1328, it had not been forgotten. Indeed, Henry VIII would revive it in 1542 as a central feature of his declaration of war against Scotland. Its use to England lay in the fact that it could be invoked to support military aggression against the king's rebellious 'subjects' in the north, effectively denying Scottish claims to independent sovereign status. The Scots themselves for the most part vehemently

---

[10] *Letters of James V*, ed. R. K. Hannay (Edinburgh: HMSO, 1954), 362.
[11] *The Complaynt of Scotlande vyth ane Exhortatione to the thre Estaits to be vigilante in the Deffens of their Public Veil*, ed. J. A. H. Murray (Early English Text Soc., extra ser. 17; 1872), 208.

opposed English pretensions, arguing 'that Scotland is nocht nor neuir was ane part of Ingland'.[12] The inherited antagonisms and xenophobia proceeding from these disputes were compounded by the addition of the religious difference between the realms from 1534. Further complications arose from England's evocation of its imperial standing in relation to the break with Rome.[13] This could be used in an exclusive sense, with no intended reference to Scotland, but it could equally reinforce England's claims to superiority over the northern kingdom by portraying Scotland as a lesser component of the putative English empire.

The delicate diplomatic circumstances of the Henrician reformation meant that the English had to consider their use of such contentious theories very carefully. The forceful pursuit of their medieval or imperial ambitions might prove successful in subduing Scottish opposition to reform. Alternatively, the resort to coercion might prove disastrous, merely confirming England's diplomatic isolation. Another possibility was to allow all disputed claims to fall into disuse, in the hope that such a show of magnanimity might be the means of winning the Scots to the cause of reform. The reformation raised the stakes dramatically in relations between England and Scotland, leading contemporaries to re-examine their troubled history, and to reassess the present relationship between the realms. In their diplomatic as well as their religious relations, this was a defining period. The English found themselves grappling with their customary assumptions and certainties in the altered circumstances created by the reformation. For Scotland, meanwhile, there arose an opportunity to participate in a redefinition of the bond between the kingdoms.

The result of these discourses was that a number of alternatives to the traditional English ambition of union through conquest began to present themselves. Thinking on the various possibilities for co-operation between the kingdoms was diverse, and included proposals for dynastic union, political alliance, and loose religious confederation. Significantly, these contributions came from both countries. The age-old hostilities between English and Scots were certainly not eliminated by their espousal of reformed opinions. Mutual suspicions remained in some cases stronger than ever and there was no direct correlation between Protestant sympathies and support for a closer amity between the realms. The intrusion of

[12] William Lamb, *Ane Resonyng of ane Scottis and Inglis Merchand betuix Rowand and Lionis*, ed. R. J. Lyall (Aberdeen: Aberdeen University Press, 1985), fo. 362ʳ.

[13] John Guy, 'Thomas Cromwell and the Intellectual Origins of the Henrician Revolution', in Alistair Fox and John Guy (eds.), *Reassessing the Henrician Age: Humanism, Politics and Reform, 1500–1550* (Oxford: Blackwell Publishers, 1986), 158–63.

reforming considerations into Anglo-Scottish affairs did, however, force the English to re-evaluate their unthinking rehearsal of anachronistic claims to superiority. The medieval arguments might still emerge with monotonous regularity, but they no longer offered the only means of defining the relationship between the realms. The types of alliance being suggested on the part of both English and Scots were not entirely new. The idea of a dynastic union, for instance, had very recently been put into practice through the marriage of James IV to Margaret Tudor. What was novel after 1534 was the additional requirement of religious agreement between the realms, and the urgency of the English wish for such an accord. Having set themselves against the combined weight of the Catholic forces of Europe, the English were keenly aware of the dangers of close-range enmity with their Scottish neighbours. Scotland had once been a distinctly secondary foreign policy consideration as far as England was concerned. Proverbs testified to an order of priorities which saw action in the north as a mere prelude to continental campaigning, with one advising 'who that entendyth Fraunce to wyn, with Skotland let hym begyn'.[14] The Scots were now an important consideration in their own right, however, and the signs were that they intended to make some capital from their new found influence. They would certainly not be passive bystanders as the English sought to impose their reforming agenda throughout Britain.

In the course of these deliberations on reform and amity, the crucial importance of the European setting remained apparent to all. The English were especially sensitive to the knowledge that foreign alliances might offer an attractive alternative to Anglo-Scottish collaboration, recognizing that Scotland might seek to explore the possibilities of bolstering its orthodox religious stand with the backing of powerful Catholic princes. England could likewise cultivate Protestant alliances with Lutheran powers in the attempt to gain a measure of diplomatic security. Either country might choose to value such European connections above the amity with the neighbouring realm, but the price of such a decision was the maintenance of the problematic Anglo-Scottish religious frontier. The essential question at issue was whether the two realms were prepared to live with their confessional difference, and all its associated difficulties. These, it rapidly emerged, included the cross-border encouragement of religious dissent, subversive fugitive activity by rebel subjects, and the constant threat of intervention by the European allies of the neighbouring realm. Even if the

---

[14] R. B. Merriman, *Life and Letters of Thomas Cromwell* (Oxford: Clarendon Press, 1902), i. 43.

government of one country might seem ready to tackle these problems as they arose for the sake of upholding their existing religious loyalties, the other might count these dangers unacceptable, and so persist in their efforts to eliminate the religious divide.

Their positions on this dilemma were, it seems, very much a matter of personal inclination. While James V played up the threat posed by English heresies for all he was worth in his appeals to the papacy for grants and preferments, he appeared ultimately resigned to the Protestant inclinations of the English Church. Henry VIII, by contrast, was unable to contemplate a peaceful coexistence with Catholic Scotland. Henry's paranoia concerning the dangers from England's Catholic enemies demonstrated how assessments of the threat posed by foreign affiliations remained a critical element in the calculations of both governments. Anglo–Scottish considerations could not be separated from the wider European environment in which the realms existed. The friction between the two countries during the reign of Mary Tudor also showed that religious agreement could not in itself create political harmony, or override antagonistic diplomatic ties. Within this larger context, however, the English and Scottish governments had to take account of one another in all their decisions. Their religious and diplomatic courses would have an immediate impact upon each other. They had the potential either to smooth relations between the realms, or they could offer gains at the other's expense, though only at the risk of incurring future trouble.

The years between 1534 and 1561 therefore saw the introduction of significant additional considerations into an already unsettled Anglo–Scottish relationship. The common cross-border associations and interactions continued as they always had, but with a new set of religiously motivated concerns, which added to the frictions between the realms. The tensions arising from the demands of the English reformation forced both countries to look at one another anew, and not always with greater cordiality than in previous years. There was no smooth advance towards an effective Protestant bond in 1560, just as there would be no complete reformed understanding thereafter. There were, though, signs of a new intensity in the desire from various quarters to achieve a mutually satisfactory accord between the realms.

The greater self-awareness which the combined processes of state formation and religious alteration tended to encourage led naturally to this rethinking of relations between England and Scotland. At the same time, the peoples of the two countries re-examined their perceptions of one another. For many, the old prejudices remained unchanged in their

descriptions of ancient enemies and 'aliene straungers'.[15] The prospect of a
Protestant amity encouraged others to advance far more optimistic views
on the natural friendship and understanding between the countrymen of
two allied realms. In their understanding the English and Scots, far from
being implacable foes, were partners in the godly cause, 'like cuntreymen
and cuntreymen, like frend and frend, nay like broother and broother'.[16] In
the sixteenth century, as in the present day, there was no consensus on the
appropriate relationship between the realms. There was, though, a fundamental re-evaluation of the whole question, and an acceleration of thought
on numerous different forms of alliance. The religious changes which were
initiated by England's break with Rome showed ever more clearly how the
dealings of one country impinged directly upon the affairs of the other. The
following years would see both countries attempting to assess and deal with
the implications of their confessional difference.

[15] *HP*, vol. i, no. 101.
[16] William Patten, 'The expedicion into Scotlande of the most woorthely fortunate prince,
Edward, Duke of Somerset', in John Dalyell (ed.), *Fragments of Scottish History* (Edinburgh,
1798), p. xiii.

I

England's Break with Rome and the Scottish Dimension

Henry VIII's Act of Supremacy, passed by parliament in 1534, marked the beginning of an uncharted phase in the complex history of Anglo-Scottish relations. It soon became clear that England's break with Rome and the religious alteration now in progress could not leave Scotland unaffected. As the English king attempted to enforce his settlement in every corner of the realm, the impact of his actions would reverberate throughout the British Isles. Five years of fruitless negotiations with Rome had denied Henry official sanction for his second marriage, and his eventual, momentous decision to defy papal authority created a host of security concerns. The 1533 Act in Restraint of Appeals may have asserted confidently that the spiritual authorities of the 'empire' of England would act 'without the intermeddling of any exterior person or persons';[1] but in fact the realm was by no means isolated from potentially hostile adherents of Rome. The Henrician settlement would need to extend beyond centralized lowland England to the traditionally turbulent frontier regions of the north, the west, and the Irish lordship. More troubling still was the menacing presence of the independent Catholic kingdom of Scotland. The new regime could be threatened from both within and without.

While Henry and his ministers grappled with the implications of the royal supremacy, the orthodox Scottish government began to sense the difficulties that it, too, would face as a result of England's defiance of Rome. The new reforming sympathies of the English Church set in place a confessional divide between the kingdoms of England and Scotland, and this would create enduring tensions. Henry, it seemed certain, would not be content to live with the threat of Catholic hostility from the north; and so James V faced the possibility of pressure from England either to imitate Henry's defiance of the pope, or at the very least offer a guarantee of neutrality. Furthermore, Henry's reformation brought the Protestant doctrines already beginning to reach Scotland formally onto the British mainland. The danger for the Scottish king was that their increasing penetration of the northern kingdom would become inevitable.

[1] M. D. Palmer, *Henry VIII*, 2nd edn. (Longman, 1983), 100.

The introduction of the new doctrines even to England would be a controversial process, and among Henry's subjects the potential for disaffection was alarming. Popular opinion was likely to be stirred by any dramatic modifications to traditional customs and observances. At best, a weight of conservative resistance could do much to impede the enforcement of change; while the more radical of the king's subjects might take the Henrician measures as a licence to reform, promoting extreme views and raising the threat of anarchy. These dangers, compelling enough in settled southern England, were even more disquieting in the distant borderlands. Henry was also acutely conscious of the fact that his actions would have immediate implications for England's place in a whole network of European alliances. The dealings of Francis I and Charles V were of supreme importance to the king, and such powerful Catholic princes could do much to intimidate the new head of the Church in England.

The two distinct threats to the Henrician regime—domestic and international—were formidable. Critically in terms of Anglo-Scottish relations, they also shared the common element of potential Scottish involvement. During the 1530s it became apparent that Scotland was uniquely placed to play a dangerous dual role in exacerbating orthodox opposition to England's reformation. The population of northern England, not known for its compliance with royal dictates, could look to Scotland as a powerful ally in resisting change. So, too, could supporters of orthodoxy in Ireland, particularly given the strength of long-established cultural and familial bonds between the Gaelic peoples of Ulster and the Scottish Highlands. On the wider European stage the Scots could offer a gateway for Catholic powers to intimidate the schismatic English king at close quarters. It would be difficult, in fact, for James V to avoid some form of engagement with Henry's religious endeavours, whether collaborative or obstructive. The geographical advantage that made Scotland so inviting as far as Catholic Europe was concerned created its own problems for the orthodox-minded Scottish king. The period therefore saw both kings struggling with the complications arising from the new confessional distinction between their countries. The English reformation introduced a volatile religious dynamic into Anglo-Scottish relations.

I. HENRICIAN REFORM AND THE GOVERNMENT OF THE NORTH

The borderlands, as Henry and his chief minister Thomas Cromwell recognized, were in a position to offer serious opposition to central government if anti-reforming opinion coalesced under any notable leader. On the northern frontier this danger carried with it the additional, fearsome prospect of intervention from Scottish sympathizers. In the north, as in Wales and the Irish lordship, a well-established pattern of local government saw crown authority exercised by prominent nobles, who derived strength from their powerful affinities and regional standing. The service of magnates such as the Dacres, the earls of Kildare, and the Gruffydd connection in Wales offered a proven and usually effective means of extending royal authority to remote, geographically inhospitable, and historically independent regions.[2] In the atmosphere of heightened vulnerability occasioned by the king's divorce, however, the independence of such nobles took on a sinister aspect. Long-standing, but unorthodox practices for maintaining order came under critical government scrutiny, and local feuds were seen in terms of the potential they offered for damaging, religious-coloured unrest.

The king's particular fears regarding the Scottish frontier were not eased by the conduct of certain royal deputies in the north. William, Lord Dacre became warden of the west marches in 1527, taking over the post from his father Thomas, who had been lord warden of all the marches.[3] These were admittedly demanding positions, owing to the lawlessness of notorious areas such as the English liberties of Tynedale and Redesdale, and the Scottish district of Liddesdale. Among the Armstrongs, Grahams, and other border 'surnames' or clans, local and personal allegiances were more affecting than any national loyalties. Matters were complicated by disputes over the borderline itself, with whole areas along the 110-mile frontier officially acknowledged as 'Debatable'.[4] The Dacres had only recently displaced the Nevilles and Percys as the dominant force in local affairs. Though not entirely without regional back-up, having benefited from a large section of the Percy lands, they did lack substantial financial and

[2] Steven G. Ellis, *Tudor Frontiers and Noble Power: The Making of the British State* (Oxford: Clarendon Press, 1995), 5–8, 20; Glanmor Williams, *Recovery, Reorientation and Reformation: Wales c.1415–1642* (Oxford: Clarendon Press, 1987), 248, 253.

[3] *SP*, vol. iv, no. 161; *LP*, vol. iv/2, no. 3022; Rachel R. Reid, *The King's Council in the North* (Wakefield: EP Publishing, 1975), 92–3; M. L. Bush, 'The Problem of the Far North: A Study of the Crisis of 1537 and its Consequences', *Northern History*, 4 (1971), 42–3.

[4] *SP*, vol. iv, nos. 174, 179; W. Mackay Mackenzie, 'The Debateable Land', *SHR* 30 (1951), 117–20, 110.

military support from the government. In an attempt to maintain control they were forced to improvise, and although their unorthodox measures brought a degree of stability to the region, collaboration and protection deals with Scottish officials and borderers were a dangerous means of exercising royal authority.[5]

This became apparent in the new circumstances of independence from Rome, when the king's sharpened suspicions led him to strike out at his prominent regional governors in turn, as Steven Ellis and others have demonstrated.[6] Dacre, a prime target, was heavily fined and dismissed from office in 1534 on the grounds of collaboration with the Scots. The rumours that he was a supporter of Queen Catherine had done nothing to help his cause, and, although spared from execution, he was effectively disabled as an independent governing force in the north.[7] The potential for Scottish involvement in opposition was also highlighted in Wales, where the influential Rhys ap Gruffydd found himself accused of planning to join with James V and raise forces from the Isle of Man, Ireland, and Scotland, to invade England and depose Henry. It was claimed that Gruffydd had spoken disparagingly of Anne Boleyn, providing further ammunition for the treason charges that led to his execution in 1531.[8] In Ireland, meanwhile, the royal deputy Gerald Fitzgerald, ninth earl of Kildare, was summoned to answer accusations of treasonable activity in the lordship, and eventually died while imprisoned in the Tower.[9]

There was a complex relationship between the demands of Henrician reform and these dramatic interventions in local government. The aim of extending unchallenged royal authority was clearly desirable in itself, and Cromwell's ambitions in this area were more than a mere feature of the crown's religious policies. Equally, though, it seems unlikely that the actions of either Henry or Cromwell in this period arose purely from a disinterested commitment to royal centralization and the standardization of regional administration, as some historians have argued.[10] The government's apprehensions as to whether the borderlands would acquiesce

---

[5] Ellis, *Tudor Frontiers*, 157–9, 169; *LP*, vol. iv/2, nos. 4420, 4421.

[6] Ellis, *Tudor Frontiers*, 174–8; Hiram Morgan, 'British Policies before the British State', in Bradshaw and Morrill (eds.), *British Problem*, 70.

[7] *LP*, vol. vii, nos. 676, 679, 727; Rae, *Scottish Frontier*, 171.

[8] Williams, *Recovery, Reorientation*, 255–6; *LP*, vol. v, nos. 563, 683, 720(14); *CSP Span.*, vol. iv/2, no. 853.

[9] *LP*, vol. vii, nos. 530, 614, 957.

[10] Brendan Bradshaw, 'Cromwellian Reform and the Origins of the Kildare Rebellion, 1533–1534', *TRHS*, 5th ser. 27 (1977), 77; Steven G. Ellis, 'Thomas Cromwell and Ireland, 1532–1540', *HJ* 23 (1980), 500; G. R. Elton, *England under the Tudors* (Methuen, 1965), 175–9, 184.

in the religious alteration, and whether Scotland might exploit opportunities to intervene, brought a new urgency to their task. The push for increased central control over outlying areas was energized by the security crisis that the reformation threatened to create if local governors proved unreliable.[11] Although the king's strategy achieved limited success with the appointment in Wales of the loyal Rowland Lee to head the reinvigorated Council of the Marches,[12] the implications of the change for the northern border were far more troubling. An unsuccessful experiment with Northumberland and Cumberland as wardens of the east, middle, and west marches led Henry to assume the wardenship in person. His deputies were Sir William Eure and Sir Thomas Wharton, but their own optimistic assessments notwithstanding, the two proved ineffectual in their efforts to maintain stable and effective royal government.[13] The newly appointed governors were weakened by their inability to draw directly on existing military strength and sheer manpower through connections with established affinities. In Ireland, too, a rebellion by supporters of Kildare, who presented their actions as a Catholic crusade, meant that the government of the Pale of the new lord deputy, Skeffington, relied increasingly on expensive imported military strength, and yet proved incapable of resolving the tensions surrounding the government's reforming measures.[14] Here and in the north, royal interference with existing power structures created more difficulties than it solved, and intensified pre-existing tendencies to resist reform.

On the northern marches the emasculation of the wardens left them virtually helpless in the facing of increasing border tensions during the 1530s. The poorly policed frontier itself was a nagging worry to the government in the altered religious climate. Even at the best of times there were constant currents of unrest associated with the 'reset' in one kingdom of rebels from the other, despite formal arrangements for days of truce, redress of complaints, and exchange of offenders.[15] The reorganization of government and subsequent attempts to introduce fundamental changes to religious practices and traditions were significant destabilizing factors in an already unsettled region. The habitual collaboration, or 'intercommuning',

[11] John Morrill, 'The British Problem, c.1534–1707', in Bradshaw and Morrill (eds.), *British Problem*, 20–1.
[12] *LP*, vol. x, nos. 129, 130, 453; Williams, *Recovery, Reorientation*, 259–63.
[13] Bush, 'Problem of the Far North', 45–6, 53–6.
[14] *SP*, vol. iii, nos. 81, 82, 86, 87, 92; Ellis, *Tudor Frontiers*, 225–9.
[15] Robert Pitcairn (ed.), *Ancient Criminal Trials in Scotland* (Edinburgh: Bannatyne Society, 1833), i. 144–6.

between subjects of the two countries carried ominous overtones, given the new religious distinction between the realms.[16] Difficulties surrounding the enforcement of Henrician reform revealed how Henry's fear of dissent in the extremities of the realm became a self-fulfilling prophecy.

II. JAMES GRUFFYDD AP HYWEL AND THE SCOTTISH THREAT

The activities of one particularly energetic opponent of the king's religious reforms demonstrated the dangers of Scottish involvement in borderland disaffection. In Wales the implementation of religious and governmental reform had apparently been straightforward, following the removal from power of Rhys ap Gruffydd, whose loose talk concerning the king's divorce sealed his fate. The new president of the Council of the Marches, Lee, proved to be an utterly reliable royal servant, under whom the work of incorporating Wales fully into the kingdom of England proceeded at a great rate, with the statutory measures comprising the Act of Union, 1536–43.[17] If Gruffydd himself had been dealt with, however, Henry had not destroyed his entire family connection. It was based in the strategically significant region of south-west Wales, readily accessible from the continent, and offering an entry point to both England and Ireland.

During the complicated proceedings that eventually led to Gruffydd's execution in 1531, he was for a time joined in the Tower by his uncle, James Gruffydd ap Hywel, also implicated in the alleged conspiracy against Henry. Although subsequent events are somewhat obscure, Hywel apparently confirmed the charges that led to his nephew's death. Whether Hywel acted out of revenge for Gruffydd's part in thwarting a land deal (as a descendant of Gruffydd later claimed), or whether questioning or torture wore him down, he certainly provided the damning evidence.[18] In anticipation of the reworded Treason Act of 1534 the tempting offer was made to him, 'that in layinge treason to the sayd Rees Griffyth, the sayd James should have his pardone', as would an accomplice, Edward Lloyd. In fact, by the time the enterprising Hywel was acquitted he had already managed to escape from the Tower, seeking sanctuary in Westminster, but with the formal grant of pardon on 20 June 1532 he was free to return to Wales.[19]

[16] Ibid. 126, 133, 145, 160.

[17] Williams, *Recovery, Reorientation*, 262–9.

[18] W. Llewelyn Williams, 'A Welsh Insurrection', *Y Cymmrodor*, 16 (1903), 29–30, 46–8.

[19] Ralph A. Griffiths, *Sir Rhys ap Thomas and his Family: A Study in the Wars of the Roses and Early Tudor Politics* (Cardiff: University of Wales Press, 1993), 291–2, 107; *LP*, vol. v, no. 1139(18).

The authorities had cause to regret striking this deal for Gruffydd's conviction. The charges alleging his intention of raising forces in the Isle of Man, Ireland, and Scotland under the command of James V were almost certainly groundless, but ironically his accuser Hywel, now at liberty, went on to form extensive seditious contacts in both Scotland and Ireland. The allegations against Gruffydd were highly significant: even though they targeted the wrong man, they gave expression to the king's fear that the borderlands would recognize and exploit a shared hostility to Henrician reform. Hywel's subsequent career of opposition to the king, pursued throughout the British Isles, demonstrated the reality of a three-sided threat to the English reformation, with Scotland playing a critical role in the co-ordination of opposition. Hywel, motivated by grandiose personal ambitions, his professed allegiance to the old religion, and attachment to the cause of Princess Mary (also Princess of Wales),[20] exploited to the full the Scottish regime's aversion to Henrician reform

Less than one year after securing his freedom, Hywel took his wife Alice, daughter Sage, and a retinue of around ten men to Ireland, where, he claimed, he would buy horses for the king and queen, Cromwell, and Sir Edward Baynton (vice-chamberlain to Anne Boleyn). This curious boast aside, he actually spent his time canvassing opinion in Drogheda as to Henry's reforms. His next move, as a servant-turned-informer later claimed, was to coerce the crew that took them to Ireland to sail on to Whithorn in Scotland.[21] Here Hywel managed to make the acquaintance of Lord Fleming, and so began to multiply his contacts in the Scottish government, claiming that he had come to them for 'socor and refuge'. During a month in Edinburgh in July 1533 he spoke several times with the chancellor, Dunbar; William Stewart, lord treasurer; and Thomas Erskine, the king's secretary, spending time in Dunbar's house, and receiving from him 160 crowns. Supplications to the council also secured Hywel a number of meetings with the king himself. Royal favour was reflected in James's decision to appoint to Hywel and his family a castle south-west of Edinburgh.[22] It was thought that James was more interested in Hywel's beautiful 15-year-old daughter than anything else, but these impressive connections nonetheless made Hywel a more serious opponent than he might initially have appeared.

From Edinburgh he moved on to Dalkeith and then to Leith, altogether

---

[20] *LP*, vol. xii/1, no. 845.
[21] BL Cotton Calig. Biii, fos. 30–1 (*LP*, vol. vi, no. 876); *LP*, vol. vi, nos. 1547–8.
[22] BL Cotton Calig. Bvii, fo. 176; PRO SP 1/81, fos. 63–4 (*LP*, vol. vi, no. 1591); BL Cotton Calig. Biii, fo. 258 (*LP*, vol. vi, no. 803).

spending around nine months in Scotland.[23] In the time since he had left England, Hywel's resourceful courting of possible allies in all three kingdoms, his local power base, and his contacts at the highest levels aroused fears that his far-fetched plans might actually have some substance. He was unabashed in his assessments of his own influence, 'alledging himself to be the gretest man in Wales, and rightfully discended of bloode to be prynce of Wales And that he with the Lyon of Scotlande should subdue all England', while in the company of the Scottish statesmen. During his further travels on the continent from 1534, Hywel repeated these claims, telling the Duke of Holst that he was 'a greate man of Englande and banished for the princes dowager's sake', and informing Melanchthon, whom he met in 1537, that 'he held land of his own in which he could raise 12,000 soldiers, and was moreover governor of Wales, but spoke rather freely against the divorce'.[24]

Not surprisingly, these inflated claims and dangerous associations, which began to filter through to the English government from 1533, caused great consternation. The identity of the mysterious Welsh rebel plotting against the king was unclear until Hywel's arrival in Edinburgh, but on realizing his illustrious background and connections, the government began to make strenuous efforts to apprehend him.[25] During negotiations for an Anglo-Scottish peace, Magnus and his colleagues told the Scottish commissioners that Henry 'dothe not a litle marveile whye that the king thair master intending to enter Amytie and peas woll receive, mainteyne, or suppoorte w[ith]ynne his Realme any youre Rebelles as of liklihoode this Welshe man is'.[26] The Scots would only answer that their king had not spoken to him, but within days Wharton received sure knowledge of Hywel's meetings with James. The secrecy surrounding the affair did nothing to lessen English fears. While Cromwell's informants followed Hywel's progress through Flanders and Germany later in 1534, investigations into his associates in all corners of Britain continued. One of his servants, apprehended in December 1533, was questioned as to Hywel's boasts of Irish support, and the identities of his friends and helpers in Wales, Scotland, and Ireland. In January 1534 Cromwell noted his intention to look further into Hywel's Welsh allies, and as late as 1536 the pursuit of a former servant, now in England, continued. The meeting that Hywel somehow

[23] PRO SP 1/81, fos. 63–4 (*LP*, vol. vi, no. 1591).
[24] Ibid., fo. 63ᵛ; BL Cotton Vit. Bxxi, fo. 99ᵛ (*LP*, vol. vii, no. 710); *LP*, vol. xii/1, no. 845.
[25] *SP*, vol. iv, nos. 245, 247; BL Cotton Calig. Biii, fos. 30–1 (*LP*, vol. vi, no. 876).
[26] BL Cotton Calig. Biii, fo. 164ᵛ (*LP*, vol. vi, no. 802); BL Cotton Calig. Biii, fo. 258 (*LP*, vol. vi, no. 803).

procured with Melanchthon in the following year must have been particularly galling to Henry, who was still trying unsuccessfully to persuade the reformer to come to England.[27] The fact that Hywel also became embroiled in the Kildare rebellion in Ireland created more dangerous links between disaffected subjects in the borderland regions. Furthermore, the rebellion drew attention once again to Scotland's ability to aggravate the English government, as Scottish soldiers were known to be lending their assistance to the Irish rebels. The rising appears to have been motivated initially by resentment at Henry's treatment of Gerald Fitzgerald, the ninth earl. It soon took on a religious colour, however, as support for the earl's son, Thomas lord Offaly, and his adherents multiplied. In September 1534, according to a report of the imperial ambassador Chapuys, Hywel left Germany to join the Irish insurgents. This, the ambassador thought, 'will not diminish the troubles of those here, for he is a man of courage and good sense, and of the principal lineage of Wales, who could put the king to terrible confusion by his partisans if the affairs of Kildare continue to prosper'.[28] Hywel had presumably encountered the unrest in the Kildare connection during his previous visit to Ireland, and may have sensed an opportunity to fulfil at least the first stage of his plan to raise the British Isles in an uprising against Henry. In the event, however, he was back in the Low Countries before the end of the year.

The immediate threat posed by the Kildare revolt subsided after the government's capture of Offaly, the newly created earl of Kildare, in August 1535. His submission, however, did not bring an end to the simmering unrest in the lordship, and there were sporadic flare-ups throughout the rest of the decade. Accumulating evidence of Scottish collaboration with the rebels, and indications, too, of some Welsh involvement made the troubles both financially exhausting and worrying for the English government. James, when tackled by the council, denied all knowledge of participation by his subjects in the rebellion, allowing only that some of the poorer inhabitants of the Isles might have sailed to Scotland.[29] The commanders of the English armies, however, were all too aware that Scottish troops were in Ireland. There were also suspicions that English

---

[27] PRO SP 1/81, fos. 63–4 (*LP*, vol. vi, no. 1591); BL Cotton Titus Bi, fos. 459–60 (*LP*, vol. vii, no. 108); *LP*, vol. x, no. 254; John Strype, *Ecclesiastical Memorials; relating chiefly to Religion, and the Reformation of it . . . under King Henry VIII . . .* (Oxford: Clarendon Press, 1822), i/1., 359.

[28] *LP*, vol. vii, no. 1193.

[29] *SP*, vol. iv, no. 281; vol. iii, nos. 92, 96, 124, 178; *LP*, vol. viii, no. 448; *CSP Span.*, vol. v/1, no. 84.

Observant friars, expelled from their houses in 1534, were encouraging the unrest.[30] In the course of a serious uprising Scotland appeared to have been encouraging Irish, Welsh, and English opponents of the king to join together in challenging his religious and governmental measures. The disquiet that this knowledge caused the English government was considerable. Fear of Scotland's possible role in concerted and multi-sided borderland resistance was reflected in the prolonged interrogation faced by the young earl of Kildare following his capture: he was quizzed as to the extent and identities of his allies in England, Ireland, Scotland, and Wales; the promises of support he had received; and his associations with both James V and Charles V.[31] For a brief but frightening moment, the extensive contacts which the Irish rebels were known to have had with Scotland and Wales threatened to make a reality of James Gruffydd ap Haywel's wild schemes for a British uprising against the king. Even after the initial scare, continuing reports of the presence of Scottish soldiers in Ireland reminded Henry of the danger of the frontier regions, and the particular threat posed by the Catholic kingdom to the north. Events of these early years of the establishment of Henrician reform gave an emphatic demonstration of Scotland's capacity to unsettle the regime.

III. CROMWELL AND AN EVOLVING BRITISH POLICY

As his investigations into James Gruffydd ap Hywel and the earl of Kildare revealed, Cromwell was directly involved in uncovering dissent. He was obliged to devote much time to the matter owing to the king's paranoid fear of sedition, but this was, for Cromwell, more than a mere duty. His own reformed convictions and acute recognition of the strategic threats to England's reformation made him relentless in pursuit of its critics. Cromwell displayed consistency and pragmatism in his defensive priorities, and from as early as 1523, when he was a mere member of Wolsey's household, his advice to the king was to secure the northern border. In a speech prepared for the parliament of that year, Cromwell set out the tactical advantages of eliminating the threat from Scotland before turning to the continent. The preferred means of accomplishing this, he believed, would be through a union that none of Henry's predecessors had been able to effect. Suggesting that the king 'Joyne the same Realme unto his' Cromwell detailed his ambition of conquest, a theme that he would tone down considerably in later years.[32] If the speech was ever given it did not have the desired result, but Cromwell's reasoning expressed his clear conception of England's defence and security needs, however unglamorous in the king's eyes. His contacts with members of the Irish administration, such as John Alen, also informed his plans to strengthen the position of the crown in the lordship.[33] Well before the religious instabilities and tensions of the 1530s, therefore, Cromwell planned the consolidation of authority in the borderlands.

In the wake of the religious schism Cromwell's lofty plans for conquest in the north were remodelled as he intensified his efforts to safeguard England's frontiers. This was not the time to attempt to subdue Scotland completely, as the extension of the Henrician reformation to northern England, Wales, and Ireland was raising formidable problems of implementation and potential for popular disturbance. Cromwell's council memoranda spelled out time and again the need to look to the country's defences, while investigating every manifestation of dissent. The danger from the northern border was uppermost in his mind, as he made a note 'to sende explorateurs and espies into Scotlande, and to see and perceyve their practises, and what they intende there', and to improve defences and fortifications. The consideration of this particular threat from the north, together with the aims of establishing a settled polity in Wales, and subduing the Irish rebels, reveal Cromwell's developing consciousness of the inhabitants of all three kingdoms.[34] The security crisis brought about by the king's divorce highlighted the significance of associations between them in their various reactions to reform: by force of circumstance, therefore, Cromwell thought in British terms, as he attempted to enforce the changes within the king's dominions, while averting the possibility of outside interference.

Henry's militaristic ambitions ensured that Cromwell was not exclusively occupied with events at home; and the continental outpost of Calais, where the conservative deputy Lisle was troubled by a sect of radical sacramentaries, also demanded attention.[35] A defensive operation focusing on the British Isles, however, was a central aim for Cromwell during the 1530s. A similar motivation would later inform the actions of William Cecil, as Elizabeth I's principal secretary from 1558. Cecil would be an ardent advocate of a united Protestant British Isles, within which Ireland would be fully conquered, and Scotland bound to England by a firm alliance.[36] Jane

[33] Bradshaw, 'Cromwellian Reform', 74–5; Ellis, 'Thomas Cromwell', 500.

[34] *SP*, vol. ii, no. 20; BL Cotton Titus Bi, fo. 419 (*LP*, vol. vii, no. 48); *LP*, vol. vii, nos. 49, 50, 108.

[35] MacCulloch, *Cranmer*, 111–12.

[36] Stephen Alford, *The Early Elizabethan Polity: William Cecil and the British Succession Crisis, 1558–1569* (Cambridge: Cambridge University Press, 1998), 8, 52–3.

Dawson has argued that 'the British context of early Elizabethan foreign policy was a necessity, not a choice',[37] and the same can equally be said of Henrician foreign policy from 1534: the very foundations of the Elizabethan insecurity lay in the circumstances created by England's break with Rome. Cromwell's realization of the unsettling force of religious tensions led him to consider the likely benefits offered by a common religious bond with Scotland, and successive English embassies urged this upon James. The desirability of a Protestant amity between the countries would later become an article of faith for Cecil.

The circumstances facing the two ministers were far from identical. While Cromwell's priority was the safeguarding of the realm during the introduction of controversial religious changes, Cecil's main concern was the resistance of the Stuart claim to the throne. They shared, however, a keen sense of geography, and a perception that the defence of the kingdoms should be treated as a single problem. This led both to recognize the importance of securing and maintaining Scottish amity. In 1523 Cromwell wrote of the folly of thinking to keep possessions in France, 'seuowryd from us by the ocean see', advocating instead an alliance with Scotland, joined to England 'as a membre by nature dyscendyng apon the hole'.[38] In 1559 Cecil's imagery was much the same in his argument that Scotland should be at peace with England, 'as they both make but one isle divided from the rest of the world'.[39] By the beginning of Elizabeth I's reign Cecil was able to draw on a generation's worth of thinking on the advisability or otherwise of some form of Anglo–Scottish alliance. The final loss of England's continental possessions and the encircling threat from the Guises sharpened and refined his British defence policies, but there were fundamental similarities between his thinking and that of Cromwell in the 1530s. Both were painfully aware of the vulnerability of England's frontiers, and convinced of the need to secure these first.

In general, Cromwell's concern was with all manifestations of hostility to the religious changes, whether real, suspected, or anticipated, and he personally supervised the investigation of suspicious individuals and incidents. There were numerous straightforward cases of openly expressed disapproval for the king's divorce, sympathy for Catherine of Aragon, and contempt for reform. Certain episodes, however, hinted at more disruptive currents of thought by raising the possibility of a Scottish-aided reaction to Henry's measures. Depositions from Leicestershire brought to light a

[37] Dawson, 'William Cecil', 202.
[38] Merriman, *Life and Letters*, i. 43–4.
[39] *SSP*, i. 375.

rumour that 'if the king of Scots came to England he would bring 40,000 with him, and by the time he came to Leicester the king of England would have little power', while an Oxfordshire man was accused of saying that 'he trustyd to see the king of Scottes were the fflower of England'.[40] Such far-fetched claims rarely posed any genuine risk, but Cromwell's policy was to assume that they might contain the seeds of an uprising, and act accordingly.

In addition to the time-consuming inquiries into native unrest, there was the further problem of Scottish criticisms of Henry voiced within the king's own realm. In 1531 one John Scot, a Scotsman who had been travelling in Italy and the Holy Land, came to Paul's Cross in London to launch a vicious attack on the king's divorce and separation from Rome. With his 50-day imprisonment Scot escaped very lightly, though Buchanan believed that 'if he had been found possessed of the smallest common sense he would have been in danger of his neck'.[41] Subsequent offenders, however, were taken more seriously. Word reached the council in February 1534 of a Scottish friar preaching in Newark that the king's reforms were heresies, as was his defiance of the pope. Despite extensive investigations the authorities could not lay their hands on him, but another fellow-countryman was less fortunate. In July 1534 the suspect was sent to Cromwell by Sir William Fitzwilliam with the message 'I thinke verrely that he is, or wold bee, of the same soort and facion the Mayde of Kent was Or elles surely he is a glorioux and a subtell false knave'.[42] His fate is not known, but punishment, if the comparison was just, would have been extreme. The government was in no mood to deal with another, Scottish-supported, Elizabeth Barton. Cromwell's measured consideration of this threat and others like it, and his particular attention to the northern border, was highly necessary in the uncertain religious and diplomatic climate from 1534. Events had shown that the fear of a three-sided reaction to Henry's reforms, in which Scotland would play a prominent part, was not altogether groundless.

IV. THE FUGITIVE PROBLEM

The cases of vocal Scottish opposition brought onto English soil indicated what Cromwell had already suspected; that the northern border would be a particular point of weakness for the Henrician regime. As long as Scotland

[40] *LP*, vol. vii, no. 847; PRO SP 1/104, fo. 225ᵛ (*LP*, vol. x, no. 1205).
[41] George Buchanan, *The History of Scotland*, trans. with notes and continuation by James Aikman, 2 vols. (Edinburgh: Blackie, Fullarton & Co., 1827), ii. 305.
[42] PRO SP 1/82, fos. 235–6 (*LP*, vol. vii, no. 261); PRO SP 1/85, fo. 41 (*LP*, vol. vii, no. 930).

remained committed to the old faith, critics of Henry could make their presence felt within, or very close to, his lands. Even more worryingly, opponents of the English alteration could consider flight across the border as an alternative to compliance. For James V, too, the frontier with England was a powerful focus of concern, the integrity of the orthodox Scottish Kirk apparently being threatened by the spread of the new doctrines. Not only could Protestant sympathizers within Scotland find encouragement from allies south of the border, but critics of the Kirk could flee to England and beyond. The passage of religious exiles across the border in both directions was a striking development of the 1530s, the refugees including friars, clergy, reformers, and laypeople, some wishing for a simple place of refuge, others making a more public statement of defiance by their actions. Whether they were evangelists for the new faith or defenders of the old, the exiles caused great anxiety to their respective governments.

Predictably, Cromwell was quick to appreciate the dangers of the fugitive problem, whose first real manifestation followed the suppression of the Observants and Carthusians in 1534–5. The government targeted these religious orders at an early stage, thanks to their outspoken and unapologetic defence of Catherine of Aragon, and obvious disdain for the Henrician settlement. Two of the most conspicuous Observant opponents of the king, friars William Peto and Henry Elston, fled to Antwerp in 1533 after delivering hostile sermons in Henry's presence at Greenwich.[43] Scotland was the place of exile chosen by still more Observants following a general visitation of the order by royal commissioners in 1534. Their escape was apparently made with the aid of the religious conservative Sir Thomas Wriothesley. Either the king's intense suspicion of the whole order had not yet matured, or he was simply unaware of the assistance offered by his minister to these opponents of reform. Whichever was the case, the exiles were fortunate to escape the fate of their defiant brethren in England, taken to the Tower by the cartload in June 1534.[44] Many of those who fled northwards remained in Scotland for some years. According to a list drawn up by Cromwell, eighteen Observants were thought to be still in Scotland early in 1538.[45]

Their opposition to their schismatic king was applauded by Adam Abell, a fellow Observant of the Scottish house of Jedburgh, who, in 1537, expanded the chronicle of world history that he had completed in 1533 to include the events of the past four years, and England's rebellion against

---

[43] *Collectanea Anglo-Minoritica, or, A Collection of the Antiquities of the English Franciscans, or Friers Minors . . .* (Thomas Smith, 1726), 231–2.
[44] Ibid., 233; NLS MS 1746, fo. 123ʳ; *LP*, vol. vii, no. 856.
[45] PRO E36/153, fos. 1–2 (*LP*, vol. vii, no. 1607).

Rome. According to Abell's account, which was very probably first-hand, 'Many bred[ren] of obs[er]uance of or religioun fled ye p[er]secutioun of ye said king hare fra ingland and came in scotland and wes graciuslie resauit be our brethir as we wer oblist baith in ye rewll and law of natur'.[46] The comment gives a valuable insight into the exiles' reception: sympathetic Scottish friars were evidently fully aware of events in England, and willing to shelter their suffering co-religionists, through a combined sense of duty and compassion.

Among members of the Carthusian order in England resistance to the royal supremacy was equally entrenched. John Houghton, Robert Laurence, and Augustine Webster, priors of the houses of London, Beauvale, and Axholme, were famous early victims of the revised treason law of 1534, their executions in May 1535 earning Henry condemnation throughout Europe.[47] Despite the death of their prior, members of the London Charterhouse continued to defy the king's efforts to bring them to acknowledge his headship of the Church for some years, though continued pressure finally brought them to submit in May 1537.[48] The Carthusian house of Mountgrace in Yorkshire was also notable for its refusal to concede the royal supremacy, at least two of its members attempting to flee north of the border rather than accept the religious settlement. The prior refused to grant official permission to Richard Marshal and James Neweye to leave the house for Scotland, but they attempted the journey regardless, making their escape in July 1535. Their exile was a brief one, however, as they were tracked down after a matter of days, the Council of the North reporting their capture to Cromwell.[49]

The Mountgrace house, whose intransigence before the royal commissioners persisted to the end of the decade, was an inspiration to neighbouring friaries. The Cistercians of Jervaulx proved unreceptive to a crown-sponsored preacher, Thomas Garrard, who was sent in July 1535 to preach the royal supremacy to the brethren. His sermon was interrupted by one George Lazenby, who, according to the dark hints of royal agents, had been consorting with the Mountgrace Carthusians.[50] Lazenby was executed for his bravado, but a fellow friar, Thomas Madde, made his own stand by retrieving Lazenby's head for a decent burial, and then fleeing to St Andrews.[51] Another who found his way to St Andrews was the Dominican

[46] NLS MS 1746, fos. 120ʳ, 122ᵛ-123ʳ.

[47] *LP*, vol. viii, nos. 666, 726.

[48] E. M. Thompson, *The Carthusian Order in England* (SPCK, Macmillan, 1930), 476.

[49] *LP*, vol. viii, no. 1038.   [50] Ibid., nos. 1025, 1033.

[51] Henry Foley (ed.), *Records of the English Province of the Society of Jesus . . . in the Sixteenth and Seventeenth Centuries*, 7 vols. (Burns and Oates: 1875–83), iii. 239.

prior of Newcastle, Richard Marshall, one of a number of Blackfriars to cross the border. Marshall suffered a crisis of conscience when called upon to pray for Henry as supreme head of the Church, explaining to the brethren he left behind that 'I cowde not abyde in englande w[ith]owt fawlyng in ye kynges indignation', and although he remained resolute in his opinions, his human weakness compelled him to flee rather than 'tary and suffer deth as others has don'.[52] His feelings seem to have been shared by friar Henry Maxton, who accompanied him to Scotland, and joined him in securing a transfer to the Scottish province of the Dominican order.[53] The prior of the Cambridge Blackfriars, Robert Buckenham, also left for Scotland in 1534, although he stayed only temporarily before moving on to Louvain.[54]

On hearing that his subjects were evading compliance with the supremacy by fleeing to Scotland Henry was furious, finding the further knowledge that some were publicly condemning royal policy intolerable. Though little is known of the conduct of many of the refugee friars, whose names disappear from view after their flight, a number were actively critical of the king. Henry was incensed at the audacity of 'some English Observants who go about preaching there that this king is schismatic',[55] ordering that steps be taken to stem the flow of religious rebels across the border. He was determined that the 'foxes and wulfis present at large and let lows oute of Cloysters' should 'fere tapproche nere unto those partes and tabstayne themselfes frome ronyng into Scotland'.[56] In the course of several official embassies to Scotland from 1535 formal requests were made to James V to assist in the apprehension of offenders.[57]

James himself had to contend with the same problem in reverse, since England, now apparently following the path of continental reform, was an attractive prospect for some of his subjects. Lutheranism had as yet made limited progress in Scotland, the interest in the new doctrines being concentrated in Ayrshire and the coastal towns of the south-east.[58] There were, however, some Scottish Protestants who saw much to be gained by crossing the border southwards. The public execution of Patrick Hamilton for his Lutheran opinions in 1528 gave the impetus to a number of early

---

[52] BL Cotton Cleo. Eiv, fo. 128a (*LP*, vol. x, no. 594).
[53] John Durkan, 'The Cultural Background in Sixteenth Century Scotland', in McRoberts (ed.), *Essays*, 328.
[54] George B. Parks, 'The Reformation and the Hospice, 1514–1559', *Venerabile*, 21 (1962), 205–6.
[55] *LP*, vol. viii, no. 48.
[56] PRO SP 1/155, fo. 181ᵛ (*LP*, vol. xiv/2, no. 748).
[57] Ch. 2, Secs. II and VIII.
[58] Donaldson, *Scottish Reformation*, 29–30; Sanderson, *Ayrshire*, 41–6.

exiles, and in the course of the 1530s their numbers increased considerably. As might have been expected, it was outspoken friars who took the lead, and in 1534 John Grierson, provincial of the Scottish Dominicans, and John Bothwell, warden of the Franciscans, appealed to the lords of the council for their help in preventing the tide of 'freris at are tholit pas furth of the realme in apostasy'.[59] By 1539 Norfolk was reporting the 'dayly' arrival in England of refugees seeking his assistance.[60] In Knox's view, the Scottish exiles found England to be an acceptable place of refuge which, if not as advanced in the true faith as they would have liked, at least ensured that they 'eschaped the tyranny of merciles men, and war reserved to better tymes'.[61]

As Knox's account indicates, the known reforming sympathies of many of the Scottish exiles made it difficult or impossible for them to remain at home. One of these was Alexander Alane, or Alesius, an Augustinian canon from St Andrews, who had been converted to Lutheranism after witnessing the trial and execution of Patrick Hamilton. A violent clash with his prior, Patrick Hepburn, led to a spell of imprisonment, before Alesius managed to escape first to Dundee, and then Sweden and Wittenberg. He travelled to England on a brief mission from Melanchthon to the king in 1535, and returned in 1536 to spend four years in the company of Cromwell, Cranmer, and other influential English reformers.[62] Among the other exiles was James V's confessor and Dominican prior of St Andrews, Alexander Seton. After preaching on justification by faith and pointedly failing to make any reference to pardons, purgatory, pilgrimages, or prayer to the saints in his sermons, Seton was denounced for his heretical opinions. He fled to Berwick, and when a letter to James offering a justification of his views received no reply, he travelled to London to make his stay in England a permanent one.[63] Two more Dominican priors, John MacDowell of Wigtown and John MacAlpine of Perth, journeyed to England in the mid-1530s, as did the Dominican friar John Willock from Ayr.[64] The depletion of the Scottish province can have been only partially offset by its reception of the various Blackfriars from England.

[59] James Kirk, 'The Religion of Early Scottish Protestants', in id. (ed.), *Humanism and Reform: The Church in Europe, England and Scotland, 1400–1643* (Studies in Church History, subsidia 8; Oxford: Blackwell Publishers, 1991), 379.

[60] BL Cotton Calig. Bvii, fo. 228 (*SP*, vol. iv, no. 358).

[61] Knox, i. 54.

[62] J. H. Baxter, 'Alesius and Other Reformed Refugees in Germany', *RSCHS* 5 (1933–5), 93–5.

[63] Knox, i. 48–52.

[64] Anthony Ross, 'Some Notes on the Religious Orders in Pre-Reformation Scotland', in McRoberts (ed.), *Essays*, 200, 227.

Representatives of other religious orders who travelled to England in this period included John Lyne, a Franciscan, and Andrew Charteris, a Carthusian from Perth, who fled in 1538, before moving on to Germany and the Low Countries. Apostate friars formed a large proportion of the Scottish exiles, but members of the regular clergy and laypeople whose attachment to reformed tenets was equally firm joined them. The parish priest of Tillbodie, Thomas Cocklaw, left Scotland in 1538 rather than obey a summons from the bishop of Dunblane relating to his recent marriage. He was later to be found preaching in London, along with an Augustinian canon from Cambuskenneth, Robert Logie.[65] Henry Henderson, an Edinburgh schoolmaster, was another who travelled south in order to evade a summons for heresy in 1534.[66] With the departure of these and other Scottish Protestants, James faced an exile problem as intractable as Henry's own.

The issue pinpointed the difficulty that both kings would experience in trying to maintain the integrity of distinct religious regimes, while their efforts were constantly undermined by a land border, shared language, and the familiarity between borderers. Associations between countrymen were inescapable, and in the circumstances of the 1530s it was only to be expected that religious rebels of both nationalities would see the frontier as an escape route. Henry made strenuous efforts to lay his hands on his exiles in Scotland, his attitude being that 'it cannot be holsom for our comen wealthe to permyt them to wander abrode'.[67] There is little direct evidence of James's opinions on the matter, although Marillac, the French ambassador in London, commented that, 'many Scots have passed into England who follow the same errors, and [that] the Scotch king and the Cardinal of Mirapoix have enough to do to remedy it'.[68] In general, however, James's natural exasperation and alarm seem to have been overshadowed by his still more pressing worry that Lutheran opinions would infiltrate his realm. His priority, as stated in sanctimonious letters to popes Clement VII and Paul III, was to preserve the purity of the Kirk from the 'plague' of English heresies.[69] This concern with rooting out Protestant opinions meant that James did not appear enormously troubled by the flight of his religious rebels. The same could not be said of Henry, however, and this was to have important implications for later negotiations on the exchange of fugitives.

[65] Calderwood, i. 123–4, 113–14.   [66] Knox, i. 57–8.
[67] *SP*, vol. ii, no. 82.   [68] *LP*, vol. xiv/1, no. 585.
[69] *Letters of James V*, 276, 327.

V. 'AN OBEDIENT SON OF THE CHURCH'

The Scottish king's public pronouncements on the insidious threat posed by the new doctrines made clear that he wished to be seen, by the papal curia above all, as a staunch defender of orthodoxy. There were sound fiscal reasons for doing so, and in the circumstances of the 1530s James showed himself fully aware of the leverage that the English schism gave him. His letters to Clement VII and Paul III dramatized the 'contamination' with which England threatened Scotland, 'separated as they are by no sea, river or Alpine heights, speaking the same language, practising the same customs'. He related how he had valiantly resisted the enticements of his powerful neighbour, asserting 'that he would rather look for favours meted out by the hand of constituted authority than unlimited profit from a less reputable source'.[70] James thus made clear that his continued loyalty came at a price, and he juxtaposed declarations of support for the Catholic religion with requests for grants, appointments, and an extension of royal authority over presentments. His public show of orthodoxy was seen in assurances to Rome that 'neither Lutheranism nor any other heresy will be suffered to invade Scotland'. A parliamentary act of 1535, following on from an earlier measure in 1525, further signalled a determination to prevent Protestant doctrines from penetrating the realm. James's expressions of fervency earned him the praise of Clement VII for preserving the kingdom 'without injury from the perfidious Lutheran heresy, although it is flourishing in the next country'.[71] More importantly, the Scottish king was duly rewarded with the grant of five of Scotland's wealthiest benefices to his illegitimate, under-age sons between 1534 and 1541, and with the confirmation by Paul III of the royal right of nomination in 1535.[72]

It would be easy to draw the conclusion that this depiction of 'an obedient son of the Church'[73] was little more than a shrewdly judged financial move. To the extent that James's personal beliefs can be uncovered, however, it is possible to detect signs of a genuine concern for the health of the Kirk. He made the state of the religious orders his business, urging the

---

[70] Ibid., 424, 327.

[71] Maurice Taylor, 'The Conflicting Doctrines of the Scottish Reformation', in McRoberts (ed.), *Essays*, 245; *APS* ii, 295, 341; Kirk, 'Religion of Early Scottish Protestants', 369.

[72] R. K. Hannay, *The Scottish Crown and the Papacy, 1424–1560* (Edinburgh: Historical Association of Scotland, 1931), 11; Jamie Cameron, *James V: The Personal Rule, 1528–1542*, ed. Norman Macdougall (East Linton: Tuckwell Press, 1998), 290–1.

[73] *LP*, vol. vii, no. 1000.

eradication of abuses among the Carmelites, and writing of his wish for the good rule of the Observants, with the repression of 'ye insolence of yame that would eschew the yoke of God and folow thair sensualitie'.[74] He was also patron to a number of evangelical-minded courtiers, including James Kirkcaldy of Grange, James Learmonth, Henry Balnaves, and John Bellenden; and the poet Sir David Lindsay, whose works in these years unapologetically set out an Erasmian-inspired reforming agenda, was held in high royal esteem as Lyon King.[75] The king's associations with supporters of ecclesiastical reform suggest an interest in their views on the regeneration of the Kirk, these occasionally straying closer towards the new learning than official pronouncements to Rome might suggest. James's correspondence with Erasmus gave additional proof of his regard for humanist ideas, and a parliamentary act of 1541 'for the reforming of kirks and kirkmen' indicated that the king was prepared to give his full backing to a programme of ecclesiastical renewal. This would tackle, among other things, the problem of 'the unhonestie and misreule of kirkmen baith in witt knawlege and maneris'.[76]

There is undoubtedly some difficulty in reconciling the king's professed devotion to the Roman Church and his obvious interest in internal reform, with his eager willingness to deplete the Kirk of its material strength through the acquisition of Church revenues and appropriation of papal authority. Such practices were, however, of long standing, and James was merely one in a long line of Scottish monarchs eager to shore up the wealth of the crown through papal grants and favours.[77] In the circumstances of the 1530s he was able to derive all manner of concessions, financial and political, from Rome, and, like his forebears, James would certainly not have hesitated to enhance his own hold over the Kirk at the expense of papal influence. He could thus consolidate his royal authority in all areas of government, while also taking advantage of a degree of latitude to pursue humanist reform. From this perspective it could be argued that James's expressions of piety were not merely calculated, and his concern for the Kirk and the eradication of the abuses within it was genuine, even if his attitude towards its finances was short-sighted. His interventions in the affairs of the Observants and Carmelites were entirely consistent with his

[74] *Letters of James V*, 339; W. M. Bryce, *The Scottish Grey Friars* (Edinburgh: W. Green, 1909), i. 105.
[75] Carol Edington, *Court and Culture in Renaissance Scotland: Sir David Lindsay of the Mount 1486–1555* (Amherst, Mass.: University of Massachusetts Press, 1994), 46–9, 26.
[76] *APS* ii. 370.
[77] Marcus Merriman, *The Rough Wooings: Mary Queen of Scots 1542–1551* (East Linton: Tuckwell Press, 2000), 168–171.

professed interest in humanist reforms, and this, in turn, was compatible with an essential orthodoxy of belief. The king's official commitment to those aspects of the faith most vulnerable to challenge by the reformers was seen in the series of acts passed by parliament in 1541, upholding the sacraments, worship of the Virgin, papal authority, and images as an aid to devotion.[78]

For a variety of reasons, therefore, James resisted the persuasions of English ambassadors during the 1530s as to the advisability of Protestant reform. He was doing well out of his professed attachment to Rome, and had no wish to engage in religious deliberations with the English king or his ministers, whose proposals were consistently more radical than his own humanistic concerns.[79] Although Henry's royally led state Church may in fact have held some appeal for James, who was himself attracted to an ideal of imperial kingship, the Scottish king found himself able to gain the substance of control over his Church through concessions from Rome. His disinclination to follow the English lead in religious affairs was reinforced by the influence of clerical advisers who strongly opposed English reform and supported the auld alliance with France. Archbishop David Beaton of St Andrews, who received the grant of a cardinalate in December 1538, held resolutely pro-French, anti-reforming opinions, as did Gavin Dunbar, James's chancellor and archbishop of Glasgow.[80]

In refusing to give any ground during his discussions with the numerous English embassies that would be sent by Henry, James was by no means taking the easy course of action. There may have been compelling personal, financial, and political reasons for maintaining loyalty to Rome, but James was also uncomfortably aware that his opposition to England's religious proposals would make cross-border relations extremely tense. Like Henry, he was learning the dangerous implications of sharing a border with a regime of a differing confession. It was a measure of his fundamental aversion to Lutheran teachings that James was prepared to hold out against the mounting pressure from England to imitate its reformation. At the same time, though, he took care to minimize friction between the countries by avoiding militant declarations of Catholic ideology, and fostering amicable personal relations with the English king. James therefore found himself treading a delicate diplomatic path, and giving little indication to England of the real range of his reforming interests.

[78] *APS* ii. 370–1.
[79] Ch. 2, Sect. II.
[80] Margaret H. B. Sanderson, *Cardinal of Scotland: David Beaton, c.1494–1546* (Edinburgh: John Donald, 1986), 67–8; D. E. Easson, *Gavin Dunbar, Chancellor of Scotland, Archbishop of Glasgow* (Edinburgh: Oliver & Boyd, 1947), 55–7.

It was ironic that Henry, who had a deep-rooted aversion to religious debate and controversy, found himself presiding over far-reaching evangelical discussions and advances as a result of the circumstances of his divorce, while James seemed to be keeping quiet his genuine enthusiasm for the regeneration of religion in Scotland. The reversals and inconsistencies in English religious policy in the later 1530s revealed the extent of Henry's unease with Lutheran reforms though, like James, he maintained a more resolute public stance. In reality the two kings were probably closer than they would have cared to admit in their distaste for the extremes of Protestant opinion, and views on the merits of internal reform in an orthodox context. The governments kept up their antagonistic positions, however, and the Scottish disapproval of English-style reform was made plain in a series of heresy prosecutions in 1538–9. Proceedings were directed by Beaton in the diocese of St Andrews and by Dunbar in Glasgow, with trials taking place in Edinburgh, Leith, Stirling, Perth, Dundee, and Ayr.[81]

Among the charges against individual heretics were some specific accusations of adherence to English heresies, and the reading of works originating in England. In Perth it was noted that several suspects were in possession of English bibles, and one Martyne Balkesky was convicted in 1539 on the charge that he owned 'certane Inglis [heretical] bukis'. In 1538 the Franciscan friar Jerome Russell was executed in Glasgow for his espousal of 'Inglishe menes opynyons'.[82] England was thus singled out as a dangerous threat to the purity of the Scottish Kirk, this allegation coming through with particular force in the articles brought against Sir John Borthwick in Edinburgh in 1540. The most damning charge against him was that he had 'persuaded people that the heresies of England, or most of them, are good and just', and had 'prayed the Church of Scotland might be brought to like ruin as that of England'.[83] Henrician reform had certainly made a favourable impression on Borthwick, who escaped by fleeing to England, where he embarked on a career in diplomatic service to the king. Such episodes demonstrated the cross-border appeal of reform, but did nothing to lessen the increasing religious tensions between the realms.

---

[81] *A Diurnal of Remarkable Occurrents that have passed within the country of Scotland, since the death of King James the Fourth, till the year 1575*, ed. T. Thomson (Edinburgh: Bannatyne Society, 1833), 23; Knox, i. 61–5; Kirk, *Patterns*, 4–8.

[82] Pitcairn, *Ancient Criminal Trials*, i. 252; BL Cotton Calig. Bvii, fo. 233 (*SP*, vol. iv, no. 351).

[83] *LP*, vol. xv, no. 714; John Spottiswoode, *History of the Church of Scotland*, ed. M. Russell (Edinburgh: Spottiswoode Society, 1847), i. 138.

VI. SCOTLAND AND THE PILGRIMAGE OF GRACE

As a corollary of the anti-reform stance of its government, Scotland had already shown its willingness to receive English Catholic fugitives. The exiles' lengthy stays in Scotland, and the fact that the authorities could not or would not silence their criticisms of Henry, support the idea that they were both welcomed and protected. There is no sign that the Scottish government made real efforts to apprehend the Observants sought by Henry in 1535, whatever might have been said to English ambassadors. The problem, already a nagging concern to Henry, became of far more importance in the wake of the risings known collectively as the Pilgrimage of Grace in 1536–7. Now English suspicions that Scotland was harbouring religious rebels were even more insistent. The revolt itself was the most serious domestic uprising faced by any Tudor regime, and was the result of a multiplicity of grievances that came to a head in the autumn of 1536. The relative importance of these complaints is a subject of ongoing historiographical debate: agricultural and economic grievances were certainly in evidence, as was the issue of tenant rights, and resentment of the invasion of traditional inheritance practices represented by the Statute of Uses. It seems certain though, as Geoffrey Moorhouse has most recently argued, that the fundamental unifying factor in this 'pilgrimage' was religious discontent relating to the rapid Henrician innovations, and especially the recent onslaught on religious houses.[84]

Whatever the concerns of the mass of insurgents, their proximity to the northern border both alarmed and activated the government, with Darcy warning that even 'a small bussyness of Insurreccones w[ith]in yt yor shir of northumb[er]land is mor sla[n]derus being so ny to the scottes, and by them mor sett furth'.[85] The rising began in Lincolnshire, and although this region was pacified relatively quickly, unrest rapidly spread to Yorkshire, Northumberland, Cumberland, Westmoreland, and Durham, as well as parts of Lancashire and Cheshire. By the start of 1537 England's entire border region was in a state of open rebellion. Armies were swiftly mobilized to suppress the rising, while royal proclamations alerted the commons to the danger of leaving their lands prey to Scottish assaults. Some of the

---

[84] Michael Bush, *The Pilgrimage of Grace: A Study of the Rebel Armies of October 1536* (Manchester: Manchester University Press, 1996), 1–3, 409–10; C. S. L. Davies, 'The Pilgrimage of Grace Reconsidered', *Past and Present*, 41 (1968), 54–5, 62–9, 72–4; Moorhouse, *The Pilgrimage of Grace* (Weidenfeld & Nicolson, 2002), 28–30, 37, 191–4.

[85] PRO SP 1/106, fo. 291ʳ (*LP*, vol. xi, no. 563).

rebels took seriously the warning that the Scots would exploit England's weakness in order to launch an invasion, and one of the articles of the Cumberland rebels specifically charged the government with failing to protect the borderlands from hostile incursions.[86] Aside from these traditional expressions of Anglo-Scottish hostility, however, was another strand of opinion that saw in Scotland a potential ally in defence of the old religion.

The most immediate assistance Scotland could offer was to provide sanctuary for defeated insurgents trying to evade capture; and the perception among Scottish observers such as Adam Abell that the revolt was a purely religious affair heightened their readiness to receive English exiles.[87] Among those who took advantage of this were rebel Observants who had illegally re-entered their house in Newcastle in December 1536. They were promptly expelled by Norfolk, but managed to make their escape before he received orders from the king to keep a strict hold on these 'sowers of sedition'.[88] Following the second wave of rebellion in early 1537, the government embarked on severe retribution against the rebel leaders and their adherents, while Cromwell directed investigations into 'such ringleaders as cannot yet be gotten, but as we think be fled out of these parts'. They included a number of figures who later surfaced in Scotland, such as William Leche (who was to play a part in the infamous murder of Somerset Herald on the borders in 1542), William Woodmansey, Edward Middleton, and Edward Asche or Ashton, the so-called 'friar of Knaresborough'. Some of the insurgents questioned by the Council of the North in 1537 confessed to knowledge of the flight of fellow rebels to Scotland, and their information was seized on by the government.[89]

Armed with the proof that Scotland was playing host to fugitive rebels, Henry and his officers made numerous requests to the Scottish council for the return of Englishmen known to be sheltering in Jedburgh Abbey and elsewhere. Jedburgh, home of the sympathetic Abell and his Scottish Observant brethren, was evidently a sure refuge for English dissidents, and so a particular trouble spot. With James in France, immersed in the business of negotiating his marriage, it was Dunbar who responded to Henry, telling him that all steps would be taken to ensure that 'faveure, ayde and recueille nane salbe patent nor be coloure in ony sorte gevin unto youre rebellis and brokin man at this tyme within this realme'. In February 1537 a messenger was indeed paid to tell the border wardens 'nocht to ressatt Inglismen fleing

[86] *LP*, vol. xi, no. 826; Moorhouse, *Pilgrimage*, 161, 213; Ellis, *Tudor Frontiers*, 240.

[87] NLS MS 1746, fo. 125ʳ.

[88] K. Brown, 'The Franciscan Observants in England, 1482–1559', D.Phil. thesis (Oxford, 1987), 207–9; PRO SP 1/117, fos. 17–20 (*LP*, vol. xii/1, no. 666).

[89] *LP*, vol. xii/1, nos. 416, 1012.

fra justice to be done be the duke of Norphok',[90] and James, on his return from France, reiterated Dunbar's assurances. Both the king and his chancellor, however, had already offered generous assistance and financial support to the rebel Hywel, and there was, it seemed, little effective will within the Scottish government to take positive action on Henry's behalf. When the English government did manage to detain two of the Observant exiles, Thomas Danyell and Henry Bukkery, this was only because they had returned voluntarily to England, offering to refuse 'their old cankered opinions', and to 'submytt them holly to yor highnes'. The treatment they received illustrated Henry's anger at the whole affair: despite Tunstall's pleas for clemency they were searched and interrogated before being convicted of high treason and sentenced to execution in October 1538.[91]

Henry's suspicion that the Scots were abetting his rebels was exacerbated by a series of wild rumours uncovered in England during and after the risings. A Berwick merchant claimed at the height of the troubles that James had a force of 20,000 ready on the border,[92] and in Edinburgh Scots were heard to boast that 'their kyng shulde be kynge of Ingland and Scotland yn London byfore mydsom[mer] day'. This information was provided by Robert Dalyvell, a saddler who had spent two years in Scotland, and who claimed to have had a vision in which an angel appeared to him, 'sayeng to hym aryse and showe yor prynce that the Skottes wolde not be trewe to hym'.[93] Further rumours in Leicester said that James had declared himself Duke of York and Prince of Wales, and was planning to lead an invasion from Scotland, which would be headed by 15,000 dispossessed English churchmen.[94] Estimates of the numbers of James's English adherents increased, and in Suffolk the claim was heard that, with the spoliation of the abbeys, 'Many men lost there lyvynges, and they be fledde into Skotland, and that the Skottyssche kynge hadd three score thowsand of good Inglyssche men owte of the same abbeys'.[95] Popular imagination was evidently stirred by the combination of religious discontents and the recent unrest, together with the perception that Scotland might be called on to intervene.

Some of the rumours which spread in the aftermath of the Pilgrimage were rather more convincing, their detail even hinting at the real danger of a second rising. The Council of the North heard the confession of John

[90] *HP*, vol. i, p. xviii, no. 38.
[91] PRO SP 1/126, fo. 148; *LP*, vol. xii/2, no. 1045; vol. xiii/2, no. 516.
[92] *LP*, vol. xi, no. 1044.
[93] BL Cotton Calig. Bi, fos. 122–3 (*LP*, vol. xii/2, no. 80).
[94] *LP*, vol. xii/2, no. 6.
[95] PRO SP 1/138, fo. 179 (*LP*, vol. xiii/2, no. 776).

Patenson, who asserted that 'many of them that were fled to Scotland had returned and lay about Hull and Alnwick', and some of the commons in Beverley had asked that the banished men return to England 'with as great a company of Scots as they might bring'.[96] In another episode, some townsmen from Scarborough boarded the ship of James V as it returned to Scotland from France, kneeling before him and telling him that they 'thanked god of his sound repayre saynge that thay had long loked for hym and how thay weyr slayn and opressed desyering hyme for godes sak come in and he showd have all'; while in Whitbarn, further along the coast, James was told that if he had invaded five months before, his English supporters would have taken him to London.[97] Though the information on the latter events was well substantiated, most of the claims and prophecies in circulation at this time were a combination of speculation and invention. Their wide currency, however, showed that Henry's subjects appreciated Scotland's power to disturb the religious settlement and the kingdom itself. While the king and his advisers were unsettled by this knowledge, there were signs that some of the population saw the potential for Scottish assistance in the fight to resist religious innovation.

VII. SCOTTISH PROTESTANTS AND ENGLISH REFORM

The frustration felt within English governing circles at Scotland's lack of co-operation over the delivery of rebels may have been partly mitigated by the knowledge that some of James's own rebels were now playing a useful part in the propagation of evangelical reform in England. Although James apparently showed little interest in his fugitive subjects, he would hardly have been pleased to hear that his one-time confessor and other leading churchmen were prospering in the English Church. Alexander Seton became established with the help of Charles Brandon, Duke of Suffolk, who assisted him in gaining denization in 1539, and presented him to the rectory of Fulbeck in the same year. Eventually Seton entered Brandon's household as one of his chaplains, and it was here that he died in 1542.[98] The Dominican John Craig also benefited from an influential patron, becoming a tutor in the family of Lord Dacre during the early 1530s.[99] George Buchanan was in England only briefly in 1538 before he travelled on to

---

[96] *LP*, vol. xii/2, no. 918.

[97] BL Cotton Calig. Bvii, fo. 216; *LP*, vol. xii/2, no. 422.

[98] S. J. Gunn, *Charles Brandon, Duke of Suffolk* (Oxford: Blackwell Publishers, 1988), 161.

[99] Kirkwood Hewat, *Makers of the Scottish Church at the Reformation* (Edinburgh: MacNiven & Wallace, 1920), 351.

France, but in this time he joined the employ of Sir John Rainsford of Essex.[100]

The security which attachment to prominent noblemen and politicians offered was well appreciated, and for their part the patrons put the reforming commitment of the exiles to good use. By far the most ubiquitous and influential patron of the Scottish refugees in this period was Cromwell. It was at his instigation that the Dominicans John MacAlpine and John MacDowell gained preferment under Bishop Nicholas Shaxton of Salisbury, and he was also behind the nomination of Alesius as king's scholar at Cambridge University, of which he was chancellor.[101] Cromwell later engineered the appointment of William Learmonth as one of Anne of Cleves's chaplains, so bringing Scottish exiles into the heart of the court, if only for a brief time.[102] Cromwell's interventions on behalf of the Scottish exiles was not always successful: he was unable, for example, to persuade his contacts in the Scottish government to reverse the heresy charge against Sir James Hamilton of Linlithgow, the brother of Patrick Hamilton.[103] In general, though, he was a powerful ally to those Scots in England for reasons of faith.

Cromwell's solicitude for the exiles was not a disinterested one. Where he could, he took advantage of their zeal to reinforce the government's efforts to promote reform throughout the realm. In Cambridge Alesius gave a decidedly Lutheran tone to his lectures on the Psalms, this according fully with Cromwell's injunctions for the universities set out in October 1535.[104] Meanwhile John MacDowell was drafted in to the London Charterhouse to lend weight to the campaign to bring the friars to submit to the royal supremacy. He was there for several days, examining suspicious books, organizing attendance at the Paul's Cross sermons, and making personal efforts to win over the recalcitrant friar John Rochester, though without success.[105] MacDowell's next mission, along with MacAlpine, was to further the Protestant cause in Salisbury, where Henrician reform had given fresh ammunition to a long-running jurisdictional dispute between the bishop and the mayor. The Scots became chaplains to Shaxton, who was himself a confirmed radical, and they were among the first to preach the

---

[100] John Durkan, 'Scottish "Evangelicals" in the Patronage of Thomas Cromwell', *RSCHS* 21 (1982), 134.

[101] Gotthelf Wiedermann, 'Alexander Alesius' Lectures on the Psalms at Cambridge', *JEH* 37 (1986), 16–17.

[102] Durkan, 'Scottish "Evangelicals"', 146.

[103] *LP*, vol. viii, no. 734.

[104] Wiedermann, 'Alesius' Lectures', 17.

[105] BL Cotton Cleo. Eiv, fo. 35ᵛ (*LP*, vol. ix, no. 283).

royal supremacy in the city. MacDowell's time there was particularly stormy, as he became involved in a controversy with a popular Franciscan, Friar Watts, and was imprisoned by the city authorities in 1537 after preaching against papal authority.[106] Nevertheless, he and MacAlpine, who was related by marriage to Miles Coverdale, were leading figures in the introduction of the reformed religion and vernacular Bible to Salisbury.

Alesius played an especially important role at a formative stage in the English reformation, over and above the impact made by his teaching in Cambridge. Disputes over his lecturing there, together with his personal objections to the Ten Articles of 1536, caused him to leave his position as king's scholar, and he moved on to London, where he made a living as a physician. It was here in February 1537 that he attended, apparently by chance, a vice-gerential synod of bishops under Cromwell's direction. The meeting was convened to discuss the doctrinal formulary which would become known as the 'Bishops' Book', and Alesius's contribution to the debate was a controversial one. His advocation of a scripturally based faith recognizing only two sacraments, and his belief in justification by faith alone, earned the approval of Cranmer, Latimer, Shaxton, and Edward Foxe of Hereford, among others. The bishops were divided, however, and conservatives including Lee of York, Longland of Lincoln, and Sampson of Chichester supported Stokesley's vehement criticisms of Alesius.[107]

It is striking that Alesius's exhortations to the bishops were made in uncompromising apocalyptic terms. In the speech he composed for the second day of the disputation he warned, 'ye must knowe that in the latter dayes there shal come mockers', urging that the bishops should distinguish between the true and false churches. They must, he said, beware of those who would defend pernicious and damnable doctrines under the pretence of holiness.[108] This resonant and powerful language would later become a pervading characteristic of the writings of the Marian exiles of the 1550s, both English and Scottish. Alesius, who had suffered his own experience of persecution and exile, and had witnessed martyrdom in the death of Patrick Hamilton, anticipated the apocalyptic ideas that held such relevance for these later exiles. He was thus at the forefront of the developing apocalypticism seen in contemporary writings on reform, his own use of this imagery predating the better known works of John Bale by some years.

Alesius was not given the chance to elaborate on his arguments before the bishops, however. His own account of his arrival on day two relates how a

---

[106] *LP*, vol. viii, no. 767; vol. xii/1, nos. 746, 755, 756, 824.
[107] Alexander Alesius, *Of the Auctorite of the Word of God agaynst the bisshop of London . . .* (?Leipzig, ?1537; *RSTC* 292), sigs. Aiv[r], Av[r], Avii[r], Biii[r].   [108] Ibid., sigs. Cii[v], Eiii[r].

messenger was sent to inform him 'that the other bishops were grevosly offended with me, that I being a stranger shulde be admitted unto their disputacio[n]'.[109] The publication of his prepared speech in Germany, probably before the year was out, may have afforded Alesius some consolation, but he was not the only exile to meet with xenophobia in England. Its intrusion into religious affairs demonstrated that the prospect of Anglo-Scottish co-operation in reform was always in danger of being tinged with traditional hostilities. These might be used as a cover for religious antagonisms, or they might genuinely obstruct cross-border reforming initiatives. In the course of the Salisbury altercations, the mayor complained to Cromwell that 'Madowell is a Skott borne and hath usyd hym selfe very uncheritably ayenste us the kynges true subiectes', leaving unclear which of these he believed to be the greater sin.[110] The exiled Scottish preacher George Wishart, in Bristol during 1539, became involved in local religious disputes and was subsequently condemned as a 'stiffnecked Skott' who was setting forth 'the moost blasphemous heresy that ever was herd'.[111] Anti-Scottish feeling was not always so explicit, but in many cases undercurrents of conventional animosity towards Scotland must have affected English reception of the zealous Protestant exiles, especially in areas hostile to reform.

Such sentiments cannot have been universal, as Scottish priests and apostate friars formed a notable presence in the English Church during the 1530s, receiving hospitality and preferment at many levels. They were thus able to exercise some influence over the pace and direction of reform, a fact recognized even by their enemies. The charges against Wishart in 1539 acknowledged that his sermons 'brought many of the Comons of this Towne into a greate errour, and dyuers of theym were persuaded by that hereticall lecture to heresy'.[112] The success of John Willock's preaching in England was later the subject of a poem by John Johnston (professor of theology at St Andrews, 1612):

> With glad, light heart I southwards turned my helm,
> To enrich with Gospel truth the neighbour realm.
> I sowed the seed divine on English soil,
> And many a soul upraised repaid my toil.[113]

[109] Ibid., sig. Bviiᵛ.

[110] PRO SP 1/117, fo. 272 (*LP*, vol. xii/1, no. 838).

[111] BL Cotton Cleo. Ev, fo. 361; Robert Ricart, *The Maire of Bristow is Kalendar*, ed. L. Toulmin Smith (Camden Society, NS 5; 1872), 55.

[112] Ricart, *Maire of Bristow*, 55.

[113] NLS Adv. MS 19.-3.-24, fo. 32. This 20th-cent. English trans. of Johnston's Latin verse can be found in Hewat, *Makers of the Scottish Church*, 164–5.

While the reliability of this romanticized account might be questionable, there was a noticeable growth in Protestant adherence in the areas surrounding the house of Willock's patron, the marquis of Dorset, at Bradgate in Leicestershire. In the later sixteenth century the bishop of Lincoln attributed this to the influence of John Aylmer, another of Dorset's chaplains, but his Scottish colleague might have been equally responsible.[114]

In some cases the exiles themselves made favourable assessments of the benefits they brought to English religion. Robert Richardson, a former Augustinian from Cambuskenneth, who came to England in the mid-1530s, reported to Cromwell in January 1537 that he had been preaching in York, Guisborough, Kendall, and Penrith, 'to such effect that much people here do bow their hearts to obey God's word and the Prince's laws'. From the time of his arrival in England Richardson had sought Cromwell's patronage, and during the first wave of the Pilgrimage uprisings had offered the minister unsolicited advice on the necessity of sending wise preachers into the north of England. It seems likely that Cromwell finally gave in to Richardson's petitions, employing him to preach in those areas affected by the revolt. Whether Richardson was as successful as he claimed is open to question, especially as the region was again engulfed by rebellion in March and April of that year. Despite this setback he went on to obtain a place in the king's service, and by the early 1550s was an established minister in London merchant circles.[115]

Richardson managed to avoid the problems faced by several of his compatriots from the later 1530s, as Protestant reform in England was slowed and all but halted, and their patron Cromwell fell from grace. The conservatism of the religious measures of these years, seen in the Act of Six Articles, 1539, and the 'King's Book' of 1543, was a distinctly unwelcome development for the exiles who had come to England in expectation of greater freedom to propagate the gospel. MacAlpine and Alesius made plain their opinion of the new turn in English reform by leaving the country for Germany.[116] Others were caught out by the renewed traditionalism, clashing with the ecclesiastical authorities when they refused to comply with Henrician reform. Seton was denounced by Bishop Bonner of London for his preaching on the subject of justification by faith, and his denial of the efficacy of masses and prayers for the dead. In December 1541 he was

[114] Claire Cross, *The Puritan Earl: The Life of Henry Hastings, Third Earl of Huntingdon, 1536–1595* (Macmillan, 1966), 131, 138.

[115] *LP*, vol. xii/1, nos. 305, 5; *The Diary of Henry Machyn*, ed. John Gough Nichols (Camden Society, 1st ser. 42; 1848), 91, 218, 262, 269, 290.

[116] Kirk, *Patterns*, 4; MacCulloch, *Cranmer*, 251.

forced to make a humiliating recantation at Paul's Cross.[117] Another victim of Bonner's was Willock, then parson of the parish of St Katherine Coleman in London. After defying an injunction in which he was specifically prohibited from preaching in any church except his own, Willock was imprisoned in the Fleet for 'preaching against confession, holy water, against praying to saints, and for souls departed; against purgatory, and holding that priests might have wives'.[118] George Wishart, meanwhile, was convicted of heresy following the disturbances in Bristol, and over the course of two weeks in July 1539, carried a faggot on his back through two different parishes. Cromwell, though still in government at this time, was effectively powerless to intervene on Wishart's behalf.[119]

Despite the difficulties of these later years of Henry's reign, the exiles continued, where they could, to pursue diverse and influential careers within the English Church. From the early 1530s onwards several had established themselves as substantial figures in the promotion of the evangelical cause, while others showed themselves to be able and committed preachers at a more humble level. Their presence gave testimony to the futility of attempts to maintain a rigid separation between members of the Churches of England and Scotland.

VIII. THE CONTINUING ENGLISH CATHOLIC PRESENCE IN SCOTLAND

In comparison with the well-documented activities of Scottish Protestant exiles in England, the continuing presence of English Catholic priests and friars in Scotland throughout the 1530s and 1540s is a phenomenon that has largely escaped the notice of historians.[120] The fate of many of the Catholic rebels who left England after 1534 is not known, but the government was still doggedly pursuing certain high-profile individuals in 1541. Of the eighteen Observants thought by Cromwell to be exiled in Scotland, only two, Peter of Mainz and John Jobbe, are known to have returned to England

---

[117] Calderwood, i. 92–3; Charles Wriothesley, *A Chronicle of England during the Reigns of the Tudors from AD 1485 to 1559*, ed. W. D. Hamilton (Camden Society, 2nd ser. 11; 1875), i. 132.

[118] Foxe, v. 448.

[119] Martha C. Skeeters, *Community and Clergy: Bristol and the Reformation c.1530–c.1570* (Oxford: Clarendon Press, 1993), 54–5.

[120] The small number of works that note the significance of these fugitives include John Durkan, 'The Cultural Background', in McRoberts (ed.), *Essays*; Brown, 'Franciscan Observants'; and Bryce, *Scottish Grey Friars*.

by 1539.[121] Their brethren appear to have made Scotland a permanent place of refuge, realizing that, whatever the inconsistencies of Henrician religion, the break with Rome was not about to be reversed. Though some years had passed since their initial escape, the king was relentless in his efforts to track down the friars and any other English Catholic fugitives reportedly in Scotland. Cromwell drew up numerous lists of names to be passed on to the Scottish council, with the request that the rebels be detained. It was a constant worry to the English government that its exiles could apparently voice criticisms of the king at will, out of his reach in Scotland.

In fact, the majority of the friars faded into the background once safely settled across the border, content to practise their faith free from the threat of persecution. Though some spoke out publicly against the king, overt criticisms subsided relatively quickly. A number of prominent Englishmen would attract controversy during their time in Scotland, but for different reasons. Richard Marshall, the Newcastle Dominican, was admitted to the University of St Andrews in 1547, where his views on the subject of intercessory prayer sparked off a heated and long-running debate between scholastic and humanist theologians. His opinion that prayers should be directed to God alone met concerted opposition from those who insisted on the efficacy of prayer to the Virgin and saints. The dispute provided ammunition for Lindsay in his criticisms of aspects of the traditional religion, and even gave rise to a popular saying, 'To whome say you your Paternoster?'[122] Marshall was therefore at the forefront of theological discussions concerning humanist-inspired notions of a Christocentric religion and spiritual regeneration. He attended the provincial council of the Scottish Kirk in 1549, and his assistance was sought by Archbishop John Hamilton in the compilation of a new catechism in 1552, intended as an official formulary of faith.[123] Marshall's role in its authorship was an English contribution to Scottish reform at the highest levels. Another English exile at the university, Richard Smith, was also approached by Hamilton to assist in the work. Though he turned down the offer, Smith, the former principal of Alban Hall in Oxford, was evidently well respected in Scotland.[124]

The Scottish careers of these two well-placed English Catholics in the later years of Henry's reign and beyond reveal a Kirk which was both

[121] *SP*, vol. iv, no. 378; Brown, 'Franciscan Observants', 210–11.

[122] *The Works of Sir David Lindsay of the Mount 1490–1555*, ed. Douglas Hamer, 2 vols. (Edinburgh: STS, 3rd ser. 1; 1931), ii, 403; Calderwood, i, 273–5.

[123] *Statutes of the Scottish Church*, ed. David Patrick (Edinburgh: SHS, 1st ser. 54; 1907), p. 86; Durkan, 'Cultural Background', 301–2.

[124] John Gau, *The Richt Vay to the Kingdom of Heuine*, ed. A. F. Mitchell (Edinburgh: STS, 1888), pp. xlvii–xlix.

welcoming towards the exiles, and receptive to their differing theological viewpoints, Smith's beliefs being more orthodox than those of Marshall.[125] The academic community in St Andrews had active connections with the reformed churches on the continent, and the admittance of non-Scottish clerics gave no particular cause for comment. In political terms, however, the arrival of Catholic scholars from England had a far greater import. This was made plain in 1540, when the Englishmen Richard Hilliard and Henry Bretton were accorded full fellowship of the university. They were described as fugitives from England, who had come 'for the protection of the Christian faith',[126] and so their presence was seen from the start as a gesture of defiance against English reform.

Bretton had been preaching in Scotland since 1538, and travelled on to Rome later in 1540.[127] Hilliard was a more recent arrival, and he remained until 1543, his associations in that time raising very real fears in England. Before coming to Scotland he had been chaplain to the conservative Bishop Tunstall of Durham, and in the later 1530s had done his best to obstruct the government's plans for the dissolution of the greater religious houses. In particular he had counselled the prior of Mountgrace, John Wilson, to refuse all demands to surrender the house.[128] Not surprisingly, Hilliard became a prime target of government inquiries following his arrival in Scotland in December 1539. He had left Tunstall's palace in London in November, and for the next four weeks travelled northwards, staying with members of his own and Tunstall's families, and preaching in Stockton, Gateshead, Morpeth, and Alnwick, doubtless on the theme of resistance to the king's commissioners. Exhaustive investigations by the government uncovered his damning criticisms of the evil of Henry's reforms.[129]

The decision by Beaton to make elaborate provisions for both Hilliard and Bretton's welfare in Scotland was charged with political significance, given their seditious activities. Hilliard had initially approached Dunbar on his arrival in Scotland, and the chancellor received him favourably, promising him assistance if he proved himself a good man and holding out the offer that he might preach in Scotland.[130] It was Beaton who took care of Hilliard's immediate needs, however, arranging his lodging and paying for

[125] Strype, *Ecclesiastical Memorials*, ii/1. 62–7.

[126] J. H. Baxter, 'Dr Richard Hildyard in St Andrews, 1540–1543', *St Andrews Alumnus Chronicle* (June 1955), 2.

[127] *Letters of James V*, 366.

[128] *LP*, vol. xv, nos. 125, 747.

[129] *SP*, vol. iv, no. 363; BL Cotton Calig. Bvii, fo. 251 (*LP*, vol. xiv/2, no. 724); *LP*, vol. xiv/2, no. 750.

[130] *Rentale Sancti Andree 1538–1546*, ed. R. K. Hannay (Edinburgh: SHS, 2nd ser. 4, 1913), 93, 95, 107, 121, 137; BL Cotton Calig. Bvii, fo. 243 (*LP*, vol. xv, no. 32).

his day-to-day expenses in St Andrews. Hilliard therefore enjoyed the backing of the most eminent figures within the Scottish government, and in 1540 was even accorded an audience with the king at Linlithgow. It seems likely that Beaton sought and gained royal sanction for his patronage of Hilliard, a sensible precaution, as English demands for his return became more insistent. It was probably for Hilliard's protection that he was moved to the cardinal's house at Monymele in 1543.[131]

The favour shown to Hilliard, who was after all an English rebel of merely middling rank, can only be explained in terms of the tensions arising from the religious division between the countries. Leaders of the Scottish Kirk seem to have been more militant than their king in opposing English reform, seeing their protection of Henry's rebels both as a demonstration of their opposition to English heresies, and a means of striking a blow at the completeness of the Henrician reformation. Bishop John Hepburn of Brechin was one of the influential Scottish churchmen who extended his protection to English refugees, taking both Richard Marshall and Henry Maxton into his household in 1547.[132] It also seemed that laymen and women were prepared to welcome the religious exiles: Adam Abell noted that English Observants were graciously received 'be ye seculair stait' as well as by members of their own order.[133] James V himself lent his support to Henry Bretton, Hilliard's companion, as he left Scotland for Rome, telling the pope that Bretton was 'a learned Englishman', who had escaped to Scotland 'after encountering many dangers for his constancy to the Faith'.[134] The complicity of the Scottish king and government in what Henry regarded as the treasonous behaviour of his subjects gave a dangerous dimension to England's fugitive problem. Hilliard, like James Gruffydd ap Hywel, the Observant friars, and the Pilgrimage rebels before him, found refuge and ready assistance in Scotland.

Events from 1534 showed the English government very clearly how affairs in the borderlands and on the Scottish frontier could disrupt the smooth progress of reform. For James V English developments gave an unwelcome indication of the way in the newly Protestant regime could threaten the peace of the orthodox Scottish establishment, which was beginning to make progress in exploring the possibilities for humanist reform. The tensions in England's border regions resulted from Henry's invasive reorganization of

---

[131] BL Cotton Calig. Bvii, fo. 243 (*LP*, vol. xv, no. 32); Sanderson, *Cardinal of Scotland*, 123.

[132] Bede Jarrett OP, *The English Dominicans* (Burns, Oates & Washbourne, 1937), 169.

[133] NLS MS 1746, fo. 120ʳ.

[134] *LP*, vol. xiv/1, no. 439.

local governing patterns, and they were an inevitable consequence of his creation of a formal religious differentiation between England and Scotland. The northern border was a distinctly inadequate dividing line between the peoples of two theoretically antagonistic Churches. In practice, Scottish evangelicals were able to play an active part in the English reformation, while at the same time, English Catholic theologians helped to shape religious debate within the Kirk. The crossover of personnel ensured there was no rigid separation of the Churches, as did the fact that currents of opinion were not as diametrically opposed as their official positions suggested. While English reformers were divided on the question of advancing the Protestant reformation, members of the Kirk were engaging in lively discussions on internal reform and the removal of abuses.

The customary hostility between the countries complicated their religious exchanges. English exiles to Scotland were fortunate to receive a warm welcome from the cosmopolitan university society of St Andrews, and from statesmen who had vested interests in befriending them. From the population at large, too, there was a surprising absence of xenophobia, though this impression may simply be due to a scarcity of records. In England many exiled Scots clearly earned the enmity of their audiences for their nationality as well as their radical doctrines. The reformation changes therefore introduced new complexities into Anglo-Scottish relations. More than anything, they underlined the fact that alterations within one country had an immediate relevance for the other, and indeed all of the British Isles, whether or not this was welcomed. The cross-border debate persisted, and the regimes were affected both by direct contributions from reformers, and reactions to religious developments elsewhere. Henry suspected that his efforts to extend reforms universally through his realms were being undermined by Scotland; and for his part, James was conscious of the attraction which English reform held for some of his subjects. The mutual distrust between the monarchs was an underlying theme of protracted official negotiations between the countries from the time of England's declaration of the royal supremacy, until relations broke down altogether in 1542.

Anglo-Scottish Diplomacy and Europe, 1534–1542

As the English government realized uncomfortably in the years after 1534, Scotland's continuing orthodoxy had implications for the foreign alliances of both countries. The difficulties in relations between Henry and James naturally affected their European partners, all of whom were forced to reconsider their position with regard to England following the religious schism. The king's defiance of the pope offered a cast-iron justification for aggression and even invasion, should any excuse be needed. Knowing this, Henry could not rest while his nephew in Scotland retained his apparently unswerving attachment to Rome. James's own attitude towards alliances with the leading Catholic powers was more ambiguous. On one hand his religious differences with his powerful neighbour indicated that their support could offer much-needed military back-up in the event of hostilities. Such a damaging and unlooked-for conflict was, however, something that he was very keen to avoid. Throughout his dealings with Henry and the English ambassadors sent during the course of the 1530s, James would remain distinctly reluctant to invite any open breach between the countries. While not allowing himself to be swayed by the various English arguments in favour of defying the papacy, he would make none of the vigorous declarations against Lutheranism that characterized his letters to Rome during this period.

Both kings showed themselves anxious to circumvent the open religious antagonism that could spark Anglo-Scottish enmity and possibly escalate to wider European conflict. Their strategies, however, were very different. James favoured a delicate balancing act of assuring the pope of his Catholic credentials, while attempting to maintain amicable relations with Henry in spite of their religious disagreements. Henry, however, could see no solution other than a religious understanding between England and Scotland, based on his own reforming principles. The resulting prospects for a diplomatic understanding were weak. The English government nevertheless began to devote much energy to its relations with Scotland, formerly a far lower priority for a king who always preferred the excitement of continental campaigning. Until this point Henry's foreign policy was shaped primarily by the dominating Habsburg–Valois rivalry, with England tending from 1526 towards alliance with France. After the break with Rome, however, Henry became increasingly preoccupied with Scotland, and in particular with the nature of James's religious policy.

Ideally, then, Henry aimed to persuade James to follow his example in casting off allegiance to Rome, but at the very least he hoped to induce the Scottish king to desist from aiding his own rebellious subjects. Henry had a host of additional schemes designed to guard against diplomatic isolation, but the maintenance of good Anglo–Scottish relations was seen as a vital first step for two nations sharing a single island form. James, though, was not about to join England in a reformed alliance, and his resistance to persuasion gave a revealing indication of his fundamental aversion to Protestant doctrines. He was as conscious as Henry, however, of the dangers of hostility at such close quarters, and no doubt welcomed the advantage that the altered diplomatic situation gave him. The resulting ambivalence in his attitude towards England served both to complicate and protract negotiations between the countries.

I. THE REGROUPING OF ALLIES

In December 1533 Henry set out his new intentions in foreign policy in a letter to his ambassador in France, Sir John Wallop. It was, he believed, essential, 'not only to experiment with our olde auncient freendes and confederates, to knowe and to be assured, howe they woll concurre with Us, and what aide and socours We shall receave of them in this case, but also by all good means to acquire and geete oother new freendes, and so to conjoyne Ourself in amitie with them'.[1] He would cast a wide net in his search for allies, but Scotland was a consistently high priority. England's only international land frontier was its northern border, and it was particularly vulnerable at the end of 1533 due to an ongoing territory dispute. This was a minor contention, and peace negotiations were underway by the beginning of 1534. Henry, however, was noticeably anxious to speed on the talks, and agitated by the delays of Scottish ambassadors.[2] His new-found interest in securing James's friendship led to a series of diplomatic overtures in the following years. Conscious that this attention was uncharacteristic, Henry assured Sir Adam Otterburn in 1534 that he had 'frequently

---

[1] *SP*, vol. v, no. 389.
[2] *LP*, vol. vii, nos. 114, 530.

shown regret at his not having sooner recognized the virtues and goodwill of his nephew of Scotland'.[3] Henry was also careful to cultivate his existing allies, eager for powerful European backing. He hoped to reinforce his friendship with Francis I through the proposal of marriage settlements between his daughter Mary and the dauphin, and between Princess Elizabeth and the duke of Angoulême. After 1535 he also embarked on discussions over a possible marriage between himself and the duchess of Milan, while furthering negotiations for a formal amity with Charles V.[4] In addition, Henry's diplomatic initiatives included discussions with the Lutheran princes and cities of Germany, who were fast establishing themselves as a major political force.[5] This indiscriminate courting of European powers reflected the vulnerability which defiance of the papacy had brought on England.

By contrast, James's status within the complex network of foreign alliances was visibly enhanced from the early 1530s. Until this point Scotland was a minor player in European affairs, traditionally allied with France, and usually involved in international conflicts in this capacity. England's self-imposed religious isolation, however, gave Scotland a strategic significance that James was quick to realize. While labouring the threat from English heresies in order to extract financial gains from the pope, he continued to pursue his own goal of reinforcing his amity with France. The Franco-imperial enmity in this period meant that Charles V was also keen to establish friendly relations with Scotland, seizing on any indication that the auld alliance was faltering. James therefore found himself courted by all sides. He received the imperial Order of the Golden Fleece from Charles in 1532, and the Order of the Garter from England three years later, with Charles and Henry both directing embassies to Scotland to learn more of his intentions.[6] James himself took the opportunity to encourage good relations with Christian of Denmark, and with Ferdinand, King of the Romans; all the while continuing negotiations for his own marriage to Madeleine, daughter of the king of France.[7]

The reversal in the normal balance of power between England and Scotland was significant. Henry found himself in the unattractive position of being one of many suitors for James's amity, though he arguably needed Scottish friendship far more than any of his rivals. The potential for foreign

---

[3] The king's comment was relayed to Charles V by the imperial ambassador Chapuys in a letter of 28 Jan. 1534: *CSP Span.*, vol. v/1, no. 7.

[4] *LP*, vol. viii, nos. 380, 399, 537; *SP*, vol. v, no. 417; *LP*, vol. viii, no. 433.

[5] *SP*, vol. ii, no. 20; vol. v, no. 389.

[6] *Letters of James V*, 222, 297, 264.

[7] Ibid., 206, 271, 255.

intervention through Scotland, the basis of England's weakness, was apparent to all. Catholic princes were actively encouraged by the papacy to take action, and lost no time in assessing the benefits and risks this might entail. With the tense relations between Henry and Charles V, imperial consideration of Scotland's strategic usefulness was especially deliberate. Chapuys advised Charles V as early as May 1533 that 'the king of Scots might be the true instrument to redress matters here', believing that popular opinion in England was so hostile to Henry's religious settlement that any outside invasion would be widely supported. His assessments were perhaps over-optimistic, but he continually counselled Charles to launch an attack in conjunction with Scotland, assuring him that 'at the least disturbance your majesty could make this kingdom would be found in estimable confusion'. England's other borderlands were also the subject of his interest, as he judged that there was sufficient unrest in Wales to lead to rebellion, while informing Charles that 'Ireland is of no little importance, especially considering its vicinity to Wales'.[8]

Chapuys would have been encouraged to hear that the imperial admiral, Andrea Doria, received Welsh and Scottish offers of support for an attack upon England in the summer of 1533, beginning with the invasion of Calais. The origin of these offers is not clear, but through discussions with the dissident lords Darcy, Hussey, and Sandys, Chapuys believed that an imperial campaign would be welcomed, and that Charles would have 'the hearts of all this kingdom'.[9] Chapuys was not alone in considering the possibility of acting through England's borderlands and frontiers. The papal nuncio in France, Rodolfo Pio, bishop of Faenza, was another fervent advocate of intervention, agreeing with the French Cardinal du Bellay that Paul III should do all he could to advance James's interests in France, 'as he might be able to use the king of Scotland in avenging the Church against the king of England'.[10] This kind of speculation naturally led to rumours of imminent threats to English security. Before the peace with Scotland was concluded, a report was heard that 'the Emperor intends to banish a great number of Spaniards and send them to Scotland to assist James in his war against England, saying that the Englishmen shall be well beaten next summer'; and another story from the imperial court claimed Charles would 'set the Scots against the Irish and the Irish against England, with a great number of Spaniards'.[11]

[8] *LP*, vol. vi, no. 541; vol. viii, no. 48; *CSP Span.*, vol. v/1, no. 109; *LP*, vol. vii, no. 957.

[9] *LP*, vol. vi, no. 902; *CSP Span.*, vol. v/1, no. 257; *LP*, vol. viii, no. 48.

[10] Faenza to Mons. Girolamo Dandino, 23 Oct. 1536: *LP*, vol. xi, no. 848.

[11] *LP*, vol. vi, nos. 138, 821.

The wide-ranging conjecture over Scotland's possible position in a league against Henry tended to assume that James would automatically launch an attack on England given the right opportunity and sufficient backing. His co-operation, however, could not be taken for granted, as it was far from certain that he would readily take offensive action. The Scottish king appreciated the breathing space that Henry's pursuit of an alliance brought him, and would be reluctant to forgo this for English hostility, and perhaps that of other Lutheran powers. This did not mean that he would be induced to imitate England's reformation, as Henry and Cromwell hoped. By contrast James could also see that the advantage of orthodoxy lay in the assurance of papal support, and the backing of at least one of Charles V and Francis I, if not both. James's personal preference and the influence of his councillors led him to maintain a lively interest in strengthening the auld alliance with France. He wrote to Montmorency in 1535 that 'it should not only in these days be preserved but also strengthened', and his determination to secure a marriage settlement gave proof of his firm commitment to it.[12]

At the same time, however, James took care not to antagonize England needlessly. Like Henry, he faced the problem of sharing an island with a potentially hostile power and its allies. The same geographical factors which made Scotland such an attractive prospect for the pope, Charles V, and others, made James himself wary of ill-considered aggression towards his powerful neighbour. In their formal correspondence, then, both kings continued to make fulsome declarations of familial affection and admiration, and James received the Order of the Garter with an assurance of his appreciation of 'the interteniment of lufe, frendschip and kyndnes . . . and weill of pece contractit betwix us'.[13] English ambassadors to Scotland were favourably received, however unwelcome their commissions, and James even made excuses to the pope for continuing his talks with Henry, telling Paul III that he was 'impelled by ties of blood to leave nothing undone to save the situation'.[14] The result of James's cordiality was to raise unrealistic expectations in Henry and Cromwell as to their chances of converting the Scottish king. These misguided hopes, fed by the continuing quest for allies, meant that English efforts in Scotland were doggedly pursued throughout the decade.

---

[12] *Letters of James V*, 289, 255, 257; SRO MS GD 149/264, fo. 18.
[13] SRO MS GD 149/264, fo. 63 (*Letters of James V*, 297).
[14] *Letters of James V*, 311.

II. EARLY DIPLOMATIC INITIATIVES

The Anglo-Scottish peace agreed in May 1534 was the foundation for a concerted English campaign, masterminded by Cromwell, to establish a religious amity with Scotland. Henry's impatience to conclude the treaty, and his unusual willingness to back down over the disputed territory of Cawe Mylles, signalled the seriousness of his desire to bring James onto the same side of a widening confessional divide.[15] So, too, did the absence throughout the decade of any reference to England's customary assertions to suzerainty over Scotland. The English by no means abandoned the disputed title, but for the time being at least, the bid to make an ally of the Scottish king took precedence over the pursuit of their antiquated claim.

Henry would no doubt have been unsettled to learn of the dissembling of the Scottish ambassadors in London to negotiate the peace. With the Franco-Scottish alliance undergoing some strain, as discussions over James's marriage to Madeleine faltered, Otterburn was doing his best to foster friendly relations with Charles V, telling Chapuys that James was not genuinely interested in his negotiations with England and their schismatic king. It was necessary for now to 'amuse them with the prospect of peace', but 'whatever the terms of the peace they were about to conclude, that would not prevent the king, their master, from seizing the very first opportunity of waging war on the English'.[16] His attempt to ensure imperial support for Scotland in the event of any real threat to the auld alliance made Otterburn play down the negotiations. At the same time, however, he was assuring Henry, 'quhow beit we can nocht agre in ye opinionis concerning ye auctorite of ye Paipe and kirkmen, zeit nochttheles I knaw perfytle yat ye Kingis Hienes my Soverane will keip his kyndnes and trety of peax'.[17]

Superficially Otterburn's message was positive, but the comment gave a telling insight into the Scottish government's interpretation of the amity: they prized the security that the agreement offered, but maintained their general distaste for English reform. There are hints that some popular sentiment in Scotland was similarly disapproving, with the evidence that unidentified writings spread in England before the conclusion of the war accused Henry of 'tyranny, infidelity and schism'.[18] All in all, the basis for a lasting religious alliance appeared very shaky. This did not stop Cromwell

[15] *LP*, vol. vii, no. 214; Morrill, 'British Problem', 15.
[16] Chapuys to Charles V, 14 May 1534: *CSP Span.*, vol. v/1, no. 57.
[17] *SP*, vol. iv, no. 274.
[18] *LP*, vol. vi, no. 975.

from directing a charm offensive at the Scottish ambassadors, perhaps suspecting that their loyalties were wavering. Both Otterburn and Bishop William Stewart were visited constantly by English ministers, and invited to splendid banquets. When asked for his opinion on propaganda justifying the divorce and religious reforms, however, Otterburn was unable to conceal his distaste, later telling Chapuys that anyone in Scotland who had dared to challenge apostolic authority thus would have been burned without mercy.[19]

Despite this notable failure, the English campaign to build support in Scotland proceeded with Lord William Howard's diplomatic mission of 1535. He was to foster good relations between the countries with the presentation of the Order of the Garter to James, along with a gift of geldings and rich garments. He was also to encourage the idea of a meeting between the kings, while secretly assessing the impact of the recently concluded mission of the imperial ambassador, Eriksson.[20] Another important aim of his visit would be to secure the return of the fugitive English Observants known to be in Scotland: they had recently come to Henry's attention, and he was determined to induce James to send them to England. According to the account of the Scottish Franciscan Abell, it was a principal objective of the mission to require that James 'send agane to Ingland or forsaid bredr[en] at fled his p[er]secutioun to keip yare obs[er]wans amang ws'.[21] Both James and the queen dowager, Henry's sister Margaret, received Howard warmly, but the concrete results of his mission were few. His proposal for an interview brought no immediate answer, and his requests for the extradition of the rebel Observants and the restitution of the Douglases were likewise ignored. After only a short time James hastened Howard back to England, so Chapuys heard, 'for fear he should contaminate anyone at his court with his heretical doctrines'.[22]

It was no surprise, then, that Henry's next ambassadors to Scotland, William Barlow, prior of Bisham, and Thomas Holcroft, met with even less success. Since Howard's statesmanlike approach had achieved so little, the new tactic from England was to focus less on diplomatic honours and niceties, and more on the menace posed by the papacy to all Christian kings.

[19] *CSP Span.*, vol. v / 1, nos. 7, 45; *LP*, vol. vii, no. 14.

[20] *SP*, vol. iv, no. 266; *LP*, vol. viii, no. 48.

[21] NLS MS 1746, fo. 123ᵛ. In fact Abell indicates that it was an apostate friar sent by Henry who made this demand—he was perhaps referring to William Barlow, prior of the Augustinian house at Bisham, who would travel to Scotland in late 1535–6 as one of Henry's ambassadors. A detailed account of this earlier embassy recorded by Chapuys (*LP*, vol. viii, no. 48) suggests that it was actually Howard who first made the request in January 1535, although it may of course have been repeated in Barlow's later mission.

[22] *HP*, vol. i, nos. 14, 15; *CSP Span.*, vol. v / 1, no. 142; *LP*, vol. viii, no. 333.

Set against this was the example of the English king, who 'valiauntly hath vanquished the Popishe puissant power', to the immense benefit of his realm and subjects. Barlow and Holcroft arrived in Scotland in November 1535. There was a delay of some weeks before they finally met James, who had been in the north of the country, but they proceeded to carry out their instructions as soon as opportunity arose. Accordingly, they warned the Scottish king of 'the damnable delusion, the deadly deceyte and pestilent perversitie of them whiche have envegled the eyes of kinges, enchaunted the heringes of princes, and charmyd soo the wittes of rulers, that neyther might they see, here, ne descerne what their office was to doo'.[23] Barlow eloquently described Henry's long endeavour to search out the truth in Christ's doctrine, and his wish to share with James his realization of 'the thral captivity under the usurped power of the Bishop of Rome and his ungodly laws'. This knowledge, together with James's 'probable experience within your dominions' should be enough to lead him to embrace God's word.[24]

James's reaction, however, left much to be desired. The English gift of certain religious writings did not go down well, and he wrote reproachfully to Henry that 'we may nocht of our consciens bot first kep our part towart God and our obediens till Haly kyrk, as all our forbearis hes done'. Buchanan related how the king passed the 'pestiferous writings' to his councillors without even looking at them, and an account written by Cardinal Reginald Pole in the preface to his *De Unitate Ecclesiae* lent added drama to the scene, praising the king's 'glorious deed in casting into the fire the books that were sent to him'.[25] A subsequent incident in the course of the mission revealed the depth of misunderstanding between the two parties. As the ambassadors began one of their orations a violent thunderstorm arose, leading James to make the sign of the cross, 'not so much for the horror of the thunder, as he said, as of what the same ambassadors suggested'.[26] The message of the apocryphal story was clear: the embassy had brought no harmony of purpose, but rather undisguised horror from James at the thought of making a common religious cause. Before the year was out the two ambassadors returned with no progress to report. Chapuys

[23] *HP*, vol. i, no. 22.
[24] Strype, *Ecclesiastical Memorials*, i/2. 231.
[25] *HP*, vol. i, no. 23; Buchanan, *History*, ii. 312; *LP*, vol. xvi, no. 404.
[26] Chapuys's account of the thunderstorm in a letter to Charles V, *LP*, vol. x, no. 141, is in effect inverted in the translation which appears in *CSP Span.*, vol. v/2, no. 9: here it appears that the 'terrific words' uttered by Scottish ambassadors in London caused Henry VIII to cross himself for fear. This seems to be an error in translation rather than a parallel incident, and the theme of mutual religious remains absolutely clear.

took some pleasure in passing the news on to Charles V, telling him, 'they have lost their labour for they got nothing but ridicule'.[27]

This was only the first stage of the mission, however, and Barlow returned to Scotland with Howard early in 1536, aiming 'dulcely to inculce in to the said King of Scottes hed' the arguments in favour of reformation. Their tactics were carefully planned, so Barlow was to concentrate on the religious aspects, while Howard would 'inculce and harpe uppon the string of honour and proffit' that royal supremacy would bring. With the queen dowager they would use more forceful persuasion, to 'bete in to her hed' the advantages of an interview between the kings. Finally, they would ascertain which of the king's advisers would support them.[28] This time the ambassadors were the object of suspicion even before their arrival, and the safe-conducts which they received from James ordered them not to 'promote any strange opynyons', and to 'derogat noo thing in word nor dede agaynst the authoryte of Sacred holly Churche'. James had evidently been alarmed at the forceful tone of the previous embassy, but his precautions aroused indignant protests from Barlow and Howard, who declared that this treatment was 'not usuall befor tymes betwene fryndes nor seldome co[n]dicionede among enimyes'. It was an inauspicious start to the mission, and matters did not improve on their arrival in Edinburgh, where, Barlow complained, James's 'lyenge freers' preached blasphemously against the truth in their presence, while his 'spyrytuall ungostely Counselloures' spread vicious rumours against them.[29]

A third visit to Scotland, again by Barlow and Howard, in April 1536, did little to improve the situation. The question of a meeting between the kings remained problematic, with James and his councillors seemingly unable to commit themselves to any definite arrangement.[30] For three years, then, determined efforts to gain James's allegiance through a variety of religious, political, and financial arguments had failed. The English ambassadors repeatedly met with disappointment in their official aims, though they may have exploited limited opportunities to preach and proselytize during their time in Scotland. In the two to three weeks spent by Barlow and Howard waiting for James in Edinburgh in November 1535 they, together with Robert Ferrar who accompanied them, would have had some opportunity

[27] *LP*, vol. x, no. 141.

[28] *HP*, vol. i, no. 26.

[29] BL Cotton Vesp. Cxiii, fos. 249–50 (*LP*, vol. x, no. 287); BL Cotton Calig. Biii, fos. 195ᵛ, 194ᵛ (*SP*, vol. iv, no. 288).

[30] Robert Keith, *History of the Affairs of Church and State in Scotland, from the Beginning of the Reformation to the Year 1568*, ed. J. P. Lawson and C. J. Lyon, 3 vols. (Edinburgh: Spottiswoode Society, 1844), i. 41; *SP*, vol. iv, nos. 295, 296; *Letters of James V*, 318–21.

to gauge popular opinion.[31] A fragmentary account suggests that Barlow indulged in some unlicensed preaching during December, attracting a 'gret audiens' as word spread.[32] He affirmed on his next visit that he would apply for a preaching licence 'to publysshe the trewth of Goddes worde amonge theym', believing that 'though the Clergy shall repyne, yet many of the laye peple wyll gladly gyve herynge'. There may have been cause for optimism, then, in the evidence of growing interest in some quarters in the reformed doctrines. Where the government was concerned, however, the lasting impression left with the ambassadors was of resolute hostility to reform and 'Scotysshe dissemblinge mutabilyte'.[33] Their assessment was harsh, but their judgement of official Scottish animosity towards Henry's religious settlement was all too accurate.

III. THE CATHOLIC INTERNATIONAL REACTION

In the light of these failed diplomatic advances, the problems that were complicating Anglo-Scottish relations acquired a European dimension. James was making very pointed references in his correspondence with the papacy to the difficult task of resisting English reform and keeping the Kirk free of Protestant heresies. Although his comments were thinly disguised bids for financial backing from Rome, James's advertisement of his predicament might also inspire European intervention on his behalf, either through papal instigation, or through independent action by Catholic powers. The Scottish king was undoubtedly facing twin threats from spreading heretical doctrines and the possibility of religiously motivated aggression from England, but his willingness to become a focus of opposition to Henry was highly questionable. This did not stop widespread speculation over his possible role in challenging the English schism. Neither did it ease varied suspicions within the English government: of foreign encouragement of Scottish orthodoxy, offers of assistance in the harbouring of English fugitives and of aid to borderland rebels, not to mention proposals for direct invasion.

The contentious issue of the cross-border rebels of the 1530s was one of the earliest to be affected by European involvement. The problem, as James

---

[31] Andrew J. Brown, *Robert Ferrar: Yorkshire Monk, Reformation Bishop and Martyr in Wales, c.1500–1555* (Inscriptor Imprints, 1997), 29–30.

[32] BL Cotton Vit. Bxiv, fo. 161 (*LP*, vol. ix, no. 1021).

[33] BL Cotton Calig. Biii, fo. 194ʳ (*SP*, vol. iv, no. 288); *SP*, vol. iv, no. 296; C. Patrick Hotle, *Thorns and Thistles: Diplomacy between Henry VIII and James V, 1528–1542* (Lanham: University Press of America, 1996), 95–6.

saw it, was that his exiled subjects might decide to return from their places of refuge in England and throughout Europe, and attempt to spread reformed doctrines among their countrymen. The number of Scottish religious refugees was considerable, partly due to the absence of any large-scale persecution in Scotland.[34] Most did not yet seek to go back to Scotland, but the number of exiles who did attempt the return journey caused James serious anxiety. One James Melville, an apostate Observant friar, came to the king's attention in September 1534 when he returned from Germany, allegedly 'infected' with Lutheran doctrines that he intended to spread among the population. James wrote to Clement VII that he had imposed a restraint on Melville in the effort to check the 'plague' of Lutheranism, 'which has spread beyond all expectation and is no longer confined within the borders of Germany'; and he kept a close watch on the friar for some years.[35]

Scottish Protestants did not have to return to their country in person in order to try to influence the development of the Kirk. In June 1533 James received a letter from the Catholic controversialist John Cochlaeus, claiming that Alexander Alesius, the Scottish reformer, was concealed in Wittenberg, and was translating Luther's books to send them into Scotland.[36] James knew only too well that reformed literature and propaganda was continuing to find its way to Scotland, despite the parliamentary prohibitions of 1525 and 1535, and so he was harsh in his reaction to additional threats of Protestant infiltration. When Henry appealed to him in 1535 to restore the religious exile James Hamilton of Linlithgow to his position and lands in Scotland, the king replied that he would do so only if 'the said James wer reconsalit to the bosum of Halykirk, quhilk is ay oppin to thame that ar penitent'.[37] In 1536 James communicated to Paul III his fear of Hamilton's malign influence, and of the possibility that he would 'obtain the pope's pardon and return to Scotland to enjoy his former position, and to corrupt the people by disseminating heresy'.[38] Loyalty to the Roman religion was made a prerequisite of his return to Scotland.

Henry was less shy of executing religious dissidents when he could lay his hands on them. When Francis I apparently attempted to advise greater leniency, Henry rounded on him sharply, as Cromwell reported to ambas-

---

[34] Michael Lynch, *Scotland: A New History*, 2nd edn. (Pimlico, 1992), 187; Jane E. A. Dawson, 'The Scottish Reformation and the Theatre of Martyrdom', in Diana Wood (ed.), *Martyrs and Martyrology* (Studies in Church History, 30; Oxford: Blackwell Publishers, 1993), 259–61.

[35] *Letters of James V*, 275–6, 287, 315.

[36] Ibid. 241, 260.

[37] *HP*, vol. i, no. 16; *LP*, vol. viii, no. 734.

[38] The quote comes from a summary of James's letter to Pope Paul III, 7 Jan. 1536: *Letters of James V*, 307.

sador Sir John Wallop, delivering the message that he considered it 'neyther thoffice of a frende nor of a brother' that Francis should 'counsaile the kynges hyghnes to banysshe his traytours into straunge p[ar]tes where they myght have good occassion tyme place and oportunyte to worke their feates of treason and conspiracie the better agaynst the kinges highnes and this his realme'.[39] Nevertheless, religious critics of the king managed to escape to a number of European countries, as well as to Scotland, and Cromwell's policing of dissent and sedition therefore had to take in a continental dimension. Henry's difficulties with his exiles were not helped by the fact that James appeared to be encouraging his fellow Catholic princes to collaborate in the sheltering of religious refugees. While extending his own protection to Henry's rebels, James wrote to Ferdinand I in 1534, 'this partnership of kings, especially in the matter of the faith, is particularly gratifying as offering a place of refuge from the Lutheran madness to learned and loyal men'.[40]

Members of the Observant order were prominent among the English refugees on the continent. In addition to the eighteen friars noted by Cromwell as being in Scotland by 1538, twelve more were thought to have gone 'overseas'.[41] The minister was particularly worried by the activities of William Peto who fled to Antwerp, a notable centre of opposition to English reform. Here Peto joined a number of other Observants in devising and disseminating propaganda against the king, while communicating with famously outspoken critics of Henry including both Thomas More and John Fisher.[42] They also had disturbing connections with Reginald Pole, whose noble birth and repute for learning made him one of the most formidable of Henry's exiles. Since leaving England in 1532 Pole had been subjected to continual pressure to retract his opinions against the king's proceedings, and declare his support for Henry. He chose instead to write his definitive work against the divorce, *De Unitate Ecclesiae*, in 1536, and was constantly pursued by English assassins thereafter.[43] Peto's association with Pole lay in a mission to Scotland that he undertook at the instigation of the newly elevated cardinal in 1537. This information came from Cromwell's agent in Brussels, John Hutton,[44] and although the exact purpose of the visit remained a mystery, the news was enough to cause Henry great alarm.

[39] PRO SP 1/95, fo. 159ᵛ (*LP*, vol. ix, no. 157).
[40] *Letters of James V*, 271.
[41] PRO E36/153, fos. 1–2 (*LP*, vol. vii, no. 1607).
[42] *LP*, vol. vi, nos. 726, 899, 900, 1369; *SP*, vol. v, nos. 372, 383.
[43] Merriman, *Life and Letters*, i. 202–4.
[44] *LP*, vol. xii/2, no. 635.

Pole's menace lay in his connections with disaffected exiles on the one hand, and powerful foreign princes on the other. His expanding associations with opponents of the king could be seen in the composition of his household at the English hospice in Rome in the early 1540s. Pole was made superintendent of the hospice, originally a refuge for English pilgrims by Paul III in 1538, and it became the centre for a network of contacts stretching from Rome to Antwerp, England, and Scotland.[45] Pole's entourage included figures with potentially valuable English and Scottish links, such as Robert Buckenham, the Dominican prior who had fled to Scotland from Cambridge in 1534. Richard Hilliard, notorious for his flight to Scotland and close links with Beaton, Dunbar, and other leading Scottish churchmen, came to the hospice directly from St Andrews in 1543, and was made auditor of its accounts. Another member of Pole's circle was James Gruffydd ap Hywel, the well-placed Welsh rebel who had raised such anxieties in England by his scheming in Ireland and Scotland.[46] Hywel came to the hospice by way of the Low Countries and Germany, where he had been soliciting the support of princes and city authorities, though he was continually forced to move on as Cromwell's agents caught up with him.[47] The varied acquaintances and contacts which Pole and his company had with Scotland, and indeed all areas of the British Isles, formed a threatening bond between Rome and Henry's own domestic critics. How Pole might choose to utilize such connections was not clear, but he was evidently a dangerous enemy.

Henry's fear that foreign powers would exploit unrest among his own subjects was realized even before Pole began to develop his network, with signs of European interest in the Kildare rebellion. This was another essentially internal security crisis that was given an added edge by foreign intervention. Henry was already aware of illicit Scottish collaboration with the Irish rebels, and their plight now attracted the attentions of Charles V and the papacy. Chapuys kept a careful watch on events in Ireland and urged Charles to intervene, telling him, 'every day I am importuned to write to you about it from innumerable quarters, and am assured that on the least rising got up by your majesty the whole realm would declare in your favour'. He praised the strength and bravery of the forces of Desmond and other rebel captains, claiming that they expressed the fervent wish for aid

[45] Brian Newns, 'The Hospice of St Thomas and the English Crown 1474–1538', *Venerabile*, 21 (1962), 145, 175.

[46] Ibid. 185–7; Parks, 'The Reformation and the Hospice', 203–8.

[47] BL Cotton Galba Bx, fo. 72; *LP*, vol. vi, nos. 1547–8; vol. vii, nos. 710, 1567; vol. x, nos. 529, 530, 535.

from Spain.[48] Though Chapuys may have been overstating the case, the rebel leader O'Brien did write to Charles, setting out his own Spanish ancestry, and appealing for military backing. There is no evidence that substantial aid was forthcoming, but reports reached England that Charles had sent ambassadors into Ireland and Scotland to excite the rebels further.[49] The insurgents also secured the verbal backing of the pope, after sending a messenger to Rome in May 1535 to rebuke him for allowing so many souls to perish.[50] With such high-level sympathy for Henry's rebels, it became clear to the king that his domestic troubles, especially the unrest in the borderlands, would leave him vulnerable to the threat not just of Scottish but of heavyweight European interference.

IV. THE PILGRIMAGE OF GRACE AND A EUROPEAN CHALLENGE

It was an ardent hope of the papacy from an early stage that foreign interest in Henry's problems might lead to the formation of a league against England.[51] James V's resistance to English diplomacy meant that he was seen by Rome as a key player in any attempt on England, and, as ever, it was the geographical factor that gave Scotland its disproportionate significance. The necessary impetus for the co-ordination of opposition to Henry came from European-wide repugnance at the executions in England of Thomas More, John Fisher, and the Carthusian priors,[52] and from the outset the pope took pains to include Scotland in his plans. James received a letter setting out Paul III's intention of depriving Henry of his throne, and urging him to act with his fellow princes for the execution of justice and defence of the faith. Francis I and Charles V were also called on to support the publication of the bill of excommunication and deprivation against Henry. The agent for this purpose would be Pole, who resisted all English arguments against taking on himself 'the vainglory of a red hat', and accepted his appointment as cardinal and legate *a latere* in preparation for the campaign.[53]

Papal ambitions for the legation were transformed, however, with news of the outbreak of the Pilgrimage of Grace in England in the autumn of 1536. On hearing of the English rebellion, the pope's advisers seized on the

---

[48] *LP*, vol. vii, no. 1095; *CSP Span.*, vol. v/1, no. 9.
[49] *LP*, vol. vii, no. 999; *CSP Span.*, vol. v/1, no. 102.
[50] *CSP Span.*, vol. v/1, no. 164.
[51] *LP*, vol. vi, no. 774.
[52] *LP*, vol. viii, nos. 666, 948, 985.
[53] *Letters of James V*, 293; *LP*, vol. xi, nos. 1354, 1353.

opportunity to extend the range of Pole's mission. Far-reaching plans, largely dreamt up by the nuncio Faenza in France, directed that Pole should go to England, with full Scottish backing, to become a figurehead for the insurgents. The success of the rebels would be further assured by the financial and military backing of France and Spain. Faenza's enthusiasm for the idea was fired by his meetings with Beaton at the French court, and with James who arrived in October 1536 for the conclusion of his marriage. The nuncio was favourably impressed with both, considering that James was 'of the best disposition, well inclined to religion, and conscious of the king of England's errors'. His judgement that the king was 'ruled' by Beaton, probably arising from Beaton's eagerness to convince him of the king's orthodoxy and pliancy, was misguided; but the important point was that James seemed willing to take his place in the papal league.[54] In fact James was initially reluctant, his apprehension at the prospect of inviting English aggression outweighing any desire to comply with the papal campaign. By the beginning of 1537, however, his alliance with France being assured, he became altogether more co-operative and told the pope that 'the cause of true religion would, as it did with his ancestors, count for more than any human bond of relationship'.[55] By this late stage James may also have judged that the plans for the legation were beginning to run out of steam, meaning that he would not be called on to make good his promises.

Faenza eagerly relayed to Rome James's declaration that 'he will always act with the assistance of France to bring England to reason, having 40,000 men of war in that kingdom, being much loved of the people and utterly opposed to Henry's methods'. Sensing that Francis was not enthusiastic over the plans to act against England, Faenza also did his best to encourage him, telling him 'that Scotland appeared to me the true bridle of England'.[56] Chapuys, meanwhile, was pushing Charles V to play his own part in this God-given opportunity to strike at England,[57] and for a short period the threat of foreign interference with Scottish assistance seemed real. The pope sent money to the pilgrims in November 1536, and in January 1537 Pole began his mission to the Habsburg and Valois courts. From here he would travel to England, it was reported to Charles V, to 'admonish the king in public to return to the obedience of the Church, and secretly to favour as much as he can the cause of the rebels'.[58] To encourage James V to

[54] *LP*, vol. xi, nos. 848, 1194.

[55] James V to Paul III, 5 Jan. 1537: summarized in *Letters of James V*, 327.

[56] *LP*, vol. xi, nos. 1173, 1250.   [57] *CSP Span.*, vol. v/2, nos. 104, 114, 121.

[58] Ibid., nos. 122, 128, 134; C. Höllger, 'Reginald Pole and the Legations of 1537 and 1539: Diplomatic and Polemical Responses to the Break with Rome', D.Phil. thesis (Oxford, 1989), 21–5.

play his part in supporting the mission, Paul III sent Campeggio to Scotland to present him with a sword and cap consecrated on Christmas Eve, praying that James, 'so often vainly solicited to defile his realm with heresies from across the border, may have blessing from on high, God strengthening his right hand with the sword and covering his head with the cap whereon the Holy Spirit is figured as a dove'.[59] James responded positively to the pope's persuasion, professing undying loyalty to Rome, and telling Faenza that if he had a brother who only thought of opposing the Apostolic See he would have him hanged. These sentiments were fully supported by Beaton, to whom the promise of a cardinalate was being held out.[60]

The stage seemed set for a forceful challenge to England as the government struggled to cope with debilitating internal unrest; but in fact the papal campaign suffered from two fundamental flaws. The first was the fragility of the Franco-imperial alliance, with the two powers still at odds over the disputed duchy of Milan. Unwilling to come to terms, they were reluctant in the extreme to combine on behalf of the papacy, whatever they may have told Paul III. Henry took the opportunity to reinforce his own alliance with France, and so Pole's mission was seriously compromised, as Francis tried to conciliate the English king by secretly sending him details of the legation.[61] The second problem was of poor planning by the papal curia, the whole enterprise being launched several months too late to have any chance of coinciding with the English uprisings. After almost two years of preparation, the legation was only beginning to gather pace in March 1537, by which time the disturbances had largely subsided.[62] This meant that James was never called on to give his promised assistance in the offensive against England.

In the event, therefore, James could persist in his protestations of allegiance to Rome, and willingness to contribute his aid, without ever being put to the test. If Charles and Francis had been able to put aside their differences, the danger to England could have been immense, but whether James would actually have been ready to participate in an onslaught on England was not clear. He was prepared to overlook a considerable degree of unofficial cross-border collaboration between Henry's rebels and his own subjects, but at the same time he took great pains to avoid causing overt offence to Henry during their negotiations. The reaffirmation of the auld alliance through James's marriage to Madeleine made him more willing to

[59] *LP*, vol. xii/1, no. 414; *Letters of James V*, 328.
[60] *LP*, vol. xi, no. 1250; vol. xii/1, no. 931.
[61] Höllger, 'Reginald Pole', 28, 36, 42; *SP*, vol. iv, no. 314; vol. v, nos. 463–8.
[62] *LP*, vol. xii/1, no. 779; Bush, *Pilgrimage of Grace*, 407.

take the risk of opposing England, but still, in April 1537 when Pole was expelled from France, James refused Faenza's request that he receive the cardinal in Scotland.[63] Even with the assurance of French friendship, James preferred to preserve amicable Anglo–Scottish relations. The danger to Henry, however, was that James might yet be induced to fulfil his promises to Rome. Although the legation had stood little chance of success, it was now widely recognized that Scotland was vitally important to any Catholic league, 'because of its proximity and hostile neutrality to England, and the piety and ardour of the king'.[64]

V. THE SCOTTISH AND EUROPEAN DANGER IN 1539

In 1537 Henry was saved by the absence of consensus between the powers called on by the papacy to unite against England. In 1539, however, the out-look was very different, and for a time the realm seemed in genuine peril. A second papal initiative to publish the bills against England, again with Pole as its figurehead, had as its sound basis the ten-year Franco-imperial Truce of Nice, agreed in June 1538. The Treaty of Toledo, concluded in the fol-lowing January, included the further resolution that neither Francis nor Charles should have any secret dealings or alliances with Henry.[65] The might of these two powers made this a fearful combination, and full note was taken of their partnership with Scotland, which appeared to offer them ready access to England. Henry was mindful of the renewed danger to the realm, and Chapuys noted that, on the news of the grand and sophisticated enterprise being prepared against him, the king was 'surprised, bewildered and perplexed at what has happened, and that he has evidently lost a good deal of his former bravery and buoyancy of spirits'. Wriothesley summed up the problem more succinctly, writing to Cromwell that 'Englande is made but a morsel amonge these choppers'.[66]

With the strategic value of Scottish participation now evident, James was called on once again to play a pivotal role in events. This time the legation, beginning on 2 January, would involve a delegation to the Scottish as well as the imperial and French courts: the aim would be to secure agreement on a co-ordinated trade embargo against England, and the publication of the papal censures throughout Europe. Pole undertook to gain the backing of

---

[63] Höllger, 'Reginald Pole', 32.
[64] *LP*, vol. xii/1, no. 923.
[65] *SP*, vol. v, nos. 496, 498; *LP*, vol. xiv/1, no. 62.
[66] *CSP Span.*, vol. vi/1, no. 7; PRO SP 1/144, fo. 27^r (*LP*, vol. xiv/1, no. 433).

Charles V in Toledo, while the papal commissary Latino Giovenale would go first to Paris with Giberti, Bishop of Verona, and then on to Edinburgh. Giovenale's commission in Scotland was to make absolutely clear papal outrage at the recent events in England.[67] The venture was an ambitious one, and in order to exercise his authority more effectively in distant Scotland, Paul III assented to James's appeals that Beaton be raised to the status of cardinal. The formal grant was made in December 1538, and part of Giovenale's mission would be to deliver the red biretta to Beaton, who would then take responsibility for publishing the bills.[68]

Henry's troubles with Pole, not to mention his earlier dealings with Thomas Wolsey, had aroused in him an intense suspicion of high-ranking Roman clergy. The news that a cardinal would be residing permanently on his northern border was very unwelcome, particularly as Beaton seemed to share none of James's reluctance to make an open stand against the schismatic English Church. As Henry feared, Pole saw in Beaton a powerful ally for the defence of the faith, and immediately wrote to congratulate him on being chosen for the cardinalate at a time of such danger for his kingdom. Pole warned that they should both, as cardinals, be prepared to shed their blood for faith, but expressed his hope that Beaton's work in keeping Scotland free from 'the contagious influences of neighbours' might influence his own country to seek reconciliation with Rome.[69] This, of course, was exactly what Henry wished to avoid. From the start, though, there was some doubt over whether Giovenale would actually reach Scotland. In March 1539 it was decided that Beaton should travel to France for the ceremony, an indication that the legation was not running smoothly. Once again, it seemed, Henry's salvation would lie in the vested interests that continued to prevent Charles and Francis from uniting against England. Each made their commitment to the suspension of trade dependent on the actions of the other, and the resulting lack of progress meant that, as in 1537, Scotland was left on the sidelines. The stalemate was reached as early as March, but only in August did the pope admit defeat, and recall Pole to Rome.[70]

The abandonment of both papal initiatives before the point where James would be required to take concrete action against Henry left unanswered the question of whether he was really prepared to declare his formal opposition to England. James had no scruples, however, about giving tacit

---

[67] Höllger, 'Reginald Pole', 127–33; *Letters of James V*, 361.
[68] *Letters of James V*, 349–51, 358; Höllger, 'Reginald Pole', 132.
[69] *Letters of James V*, 362.
[70] Höllger, 'Reginald Pole', 157, 171–5; *LP*, vol. xiv/2, no. 52.

support to other critics of Henry, as his treatment of English religious exiles illustrated. His entanglement in the affairs of the Irish Geraldine League during the later 1530s gave additional proof of a willingness to deepen Henry's governmental problems. The league was formed by the coming together of the rebel leaders O'Donnell and O'Neill, who had gained possession of the Kildare heir, Gerald Fitzgerald, with the aim of reinstating the house of Kildare and affirming their commitment to papal supremacy. To this end, they stated their willingness to take James V for 'thayre Kynge and Lorde',[71] and sent a delegation to Edinburgh in July 1538 'to praye ayde of the Scottishe King'. James would not make any public proclamation of support for the rebels, but evidence of a Scottish presence within the forces of the Geraldine League was overwhelming. English agents learnt that the Irish had the backing of more than 2,000 Scots 'now dwellyng in Ireland', and that O'Donnell was petitioning James for 6,000 redshanks as reinforcements.[72]

The rebels also went to Rome with their complaints against Henry, sending a messenger to describe to Paul III his usurpation of papal authority, and to promise that most of Ireland was 'ready to rise against England at the bidding of the Apostolic See, because they will not be governed after the order of the Church of England'.[73] The English government gained some impression of the diversity of the rebels' contacts on their investigation of a French ship driven onto the coast of South Shields by a storm in March 1539. The 'nyst of traytours' on board included an English priest, Robert More, who had recently fled to Scotland where he had 'railed and spoken rebellious words against the king', and an Irish friar carrying various writings and letters. These were directed to the pope, and Cardinal Pole, and to Dieppe and Paris, one of them being written by Gerald Fitzgerald himself, and they laid out the grievances of the Irish rebels. Cromwell set about the interrogation of the suspects, declaring it 'a myracle that god drave them hither to be disclosed and punyshed'.[74] The more he heard of the rebels' activities, the more it became clear that their supporters, both in Scotland and on the continent, were numerous and powerful.

Continuing reports of the communications between the Irish rebels and Scotland made the government certain that James was a 'speciall cumforter and abetter' of their enterprise, and fears grew that such outside assistance

---

[71] Morgan, 'British Policies', 72–3; *SP*, vol. iv, no. 372; vol. iii, no. 242.
[72] *SP*, vol. iii, no. 270; *LP*, vol. xiv/1, no. 1027.
[73] *LP*, vol. xiii/1, no. 77.
[74] BL Cotton Titus Bi, fos. 263–4 (*SP*, vol. ii, no. 120).

would spur on Geraldines and Catholics from within the Pale. By September 1539 the council in Ireland judged that the danger was greater than ever, and 'that there was never seen in Irland so great an hoost of Irishmen, and Scottes, bothe of the oute Yles, and of the mayne land of Scotland'.[75] The rebels were also doing all they could 'to excite the Emperor, the Frenche King, and other forreyn Princes, to take their partes',[76] and so the danger from the second papal legation had barely passed before Henry was faced with another potentially European-wide assault. English worries were fuelled by the knowledge that, in April 1540, 'certain gentlemen of English Ireland' had been with James, who was supposedly preparing to go 'to Ireland and make himself lord of those who refuse obedience to this King'. In fact, when O'Neill did appeal directly to Scotland for aid, James was non-committal, and unwilling to make a decision on such a 'weighty' subject.[77] James was consistent in his disapproval of English reform, and fully prepared, by roundabout means, to assist Henry's critics and generally make life difficult for the English king. What he would not do, however, was endanger the security of his own realm by making his opposition to England a matter of public policy.

VI. ENGLISH RESPONSES TO THE SCOTTISH AND INTERNATIONAL THREAT

The defeat of the Geraldine rebels at Bellahoe in 1539,[78] coming after the collapse of the second legation, led to some relaxation of the English security alert of that year. The failure of these challenges to the government was never a foregone conclusion, however, and for several months tensions had run high. Henry responded to the crisis in various ways, some more constructive than others. His chances of shaking the alliance between Francis and Charles were reduced by the recall of their ambassadors from England, and by the cool reception that his own ambassadors to their courts received. One means of striking at the effectiveness of the legation was seen in Henry's attempt to deflect Pole's purpose through the intimidation of his family. The trial and execution of numerous associates and relatives of the cardinal may have done something to satisfy a desire for revenge, but if the king sought to interrupt Pole's diplomatic mission he was disappointed.[79]

[75] *SP*, vol. iii, nos. 272, 275.
[76] Ibid., no. 287.
[77] *LP*, vol. xv, nos. 570, 697, 710; *SP*, vol. iv, no. 372; *Letters of James V*, 400.
[78] Morgan, 'British Policies', 73.
[79] Höllger, 'Reginald Pole', 83–90; Merriman, *Life and Letters*, i. 207–8.

Neither did the naming of Pole and a number of other individuals in a parliamentary act of attainder in June 1539 have any discernible affect. The varying Scottish connections of Henry's religious opponents were evident in a list that included Robert Buckenham, James Gruffydd ap Hywel, William Leche, a number of other exiles and leaders of the Pilgrimage of Grace, together with still more 'who have adhered to the bishop of Rome, the King's enemy, and stirred seditions in the realm'.[80]

Many of these rebels remained at large, some of them actively involved in the papal campaign, and England responded by intensifying defensive preparations and security arrangements on the borders and coasts. Though the south coast was an obvious focus of concern, detailed attention was also paid to the northern border, and particularly the fortresses of Berwick and Carlisle.[81] James's conduct of his diplomacy in the preceding years had in no way encouraged the English to believe that the frontier was safe from Scottish or foreign aggression. Suspicions were heightened by Francis I's despatch of his minister Lassigny to Scotland at the beginning of 1539, and by regular reports that the duke of Guise was planning to lead French forces to Scotland.[82] On first being told of the 'secret machinations' of the Scots, French, and others, Henry had bluffed that he 'should not sleep at all the worse for it', but would 'promote the Word of God more than he had ever done before'.[83] The frantic musters, repair of fortifications, and provision of munitions belied his words, however, and Castillon wrote to Montmorency before leaving the English court, 'it is easy to see they are afraid of something here'.[84]

Henry's retaliatory and defensive measures dealt with the immediate danger to the realm, but improvements to its long-term security and diplomatic standing required more positive action. Renewed efforts to ally England with the Schmalkaldic League appeared to founder on essential theological differences, however, hardly surprising given the increasingly conservative tone and general uncertainty of English religious debate in the later 1530s.[85] Such problems led Henry to recognize that he could not risk alienating himself completely from his former Catholic allies. Previous embassies to Scotland had yielded no tangible benefits, but both Henry and

[80] *LP*, vol. xiv/1, no. 867.
[81] Ibid., nos. 400, 655, 670, 770.
[82] Hotle, *Thorns and Thistles*, 121–5, 129.
[83] *LP*, vol. xiv/1, no. 466.
[84] Ibid., no. 144.
[85] MacCulloch, *Cranmer*, 137–8, 213–21, 245; J. J. Scarisbrick, *Henry VIII* (Harmondsworth: Penguin, 1972), 474–5; Strype, *Ecclesiastical Memorials*, i/1. 346, 355, 508, 525, 548.

Cromwell were loath to admit defeat in the crusade to win James to the cause of reform. In 1539, then, at the height of England's security scare, preparations were made for another diplomatic mission to Scotland.[86] It was to be conducted by Sir Ralph Sadler, who was less of a fiery propagandist than Barlow, but an able diplomat and convinced Protestant nonetheless. His principal objective would be to detach James from his allegiance to the Catholic league, and convince him of the evils of the Roman religion. In the event the mission did not take place until the following year, probably delayed when the immediacy of the European threat had passed. The instructions prepared for Sadler in 1539, however, revealed the extent of English anxieties aroused by the papal schemes against Henry.

Sadler's commission directed him to begin by reassuring James that England's defence preparations, which had been starting to attract attention, were intended only for the safeguard and surety of the kingdom. He was to assert that these were necessary precautions against the pope and his adherents, whose conspiracies tended to the subversion of the whole commonwealth. As Barlow, Holcroft, and Howard had done in 1535–6, Sadler was to make dire warnings against the enticements of the bishop of Rome, and the 'fayer paynted wordes' of the clergy. Direct reference to Pole's legation came in the allegation that the pope was sending some of his principal ministers 'to evill reaporte backbyte and sklaundre his majestie to the princes of Christendom', and to defame the king only for his abolition of Roman superstitions. Sadler would acknowledge the difficulties of trying to 'dissuade a thing alredy so persuaded and beaten into his sayd nephew's heed', but persist in his description of the craft, illusion, and deceitful practices of Rome. The commission contained a far from complementary assessment of James's susceptibility to the influence of his churchmen, in its advice that he use prudence with his 'simplicitie', and ignore the opinion of the clergy that he was 'as brute as a stocke'.[87]

Together with these seemingly unintentional insults, Sadler's exhortation contained certain arguments that demonstrated Henry's misjudgement of the nature of James's relationship with Rome. The pope and his collaborators, it was alleged, were targeting James only 'bicause his realm adjoyneth unto England, and as a prince and a king, on whose perill and daunger they have not moch regard, but only for thair own purposes, to be

---

[86] BL Cotton Calig. Bi, fos. 52–69. The year of this commission is variously put at 1541, in *SSP* i. 50–6; and at 1537 in *LP*, vol. xii/1, no. 1313 and *SP*, vol. iv, no. 320. Its references to the papal legation, and to the dangers posed by cardinals make 1539, taking into account Beaton's recent elevation, a more plausible date.

[87] BL Cotton Calig. Bi, fos. 53^v, 58^r, 59^r, 56^r, 57^r.

a ringleader and chief setter-forth of hostilitie against his uncle, not carying whither both uncle and nephew shuld consume ech other'.[88] James knew full well that his importance to the legations lay in his unique opportunity to intimidate Henry from the north, and so this would have been no startling revelation to him. The allegation that the pope cared nothing for his survival, however, was not altogether fair. Both Clement VII and Paul III prized James's fidelity to Rome at a time when such constancy could not be counted upon, and the financial concessions that he managed to wring from them in return were a small price to pay. Paul III hoped that the schemes against England, with James's vital contribution, might induce Henry to see the error of his ways, but even if they did not, the loyalty of Scotland was some consolation. Henry's aim of creating a breach between the Scottish king and the papacy, even if the mission had gone ahead, would have stood little chance of success.

VII. SADLER'S EMBASSY AND THE NORTHERN CONSPIRACY

Though the threatened attempt through Scotland did not materialize in 1539, the danger of a religiously inspired invasion from the north remained. In his own dealings with Scotland, therefore, Henry was sensitive to any indication that opinion there was hostile to his reforms, either among politicians or the population at large. For this reason he reacted violently on hearing, in December 1538, that certain seditious ballads originating in Scotland and reportedly devised by James's churchmen, were circulating on the borders.[89] The bishop of Llandaff, president of the Council of the North, complained to the Scottish king that the writings railed against Henry, upheld the wrongfully usurped authority of the pope, and aimed to foster mortal hatred between the realms. Sir William Eure also wrote to James to reiterate the charge that the authors, who he believed to be Scottish men 'of evil disposition, yea, and of cankered malice', intended to create a grudge between the two kings, and to dissolve the amity they had established. Eure had discovered 'an other mischevous and vilanous ryme' containing 'devilishe and fantasticall prophesis' against Henry, which he immediately sent to James in order to substantiate the English complaints.[90]

Confronted with heated English demands that the books be suppressed and their authors punished, James was conciliatory, still wishing to avoid

---

[88] Ibid., fo. 66.
[89] *SP*, vol. iv, no. 353.
[90] *LP*, vol. xiv/1, nos. 147, 178; *SP*, vol. iv, no. 356.

any rupture in Anglo–Scottish relations. As soon as he became aware of the English grievances he ordered that the borders be searched for defamatory ballads and songs, though he added that the story had probably been 'imaginate and devisit' by Englishmen, since this was the first he had heard of it.[91] When the complaints became more insistent, however, he renewed his charge for the suppression of the ballads, offering a reward for the detection of their authors. James promised Eure that he would make stricter inquiry than he had already done, and a royal proclamation ordered that none should publish or read the works, but instead destroy them on pain of their lives. James was evidently taking care to calm the incipient tensions of the affair, although his speculation that the writings may have been the work of Scottish rebels 'resident and interteneyt' in England allowed him to remind Henry that he had certain complaints of his own.[92] This aside, Henry was gratified by James's prompt action, thanking him for his handsome respect to the proximity of blood between them, the reverence shown by a dutiful nephew to his uncle, and his consideration for their sincere love and alliance.[93]

The swift resolution of what had threatened to become a divisive issue may have raised in Henry over-optimistic expectations of James's amenity to English direction in other matters. The urgent need to hinder Scotland's involvement with the Catholic league had passed, but Henry lived in hoped that he might yet form a Protestant partnership with James. He was encouraged by the news from Eure that James's councillor, Thomas Bellenden, whom he described as 'a man inclyned to the soorte used in our Soverains Realme of England', had asked him for 'an abstracte of all suche actes constitutions and proclamations as ar passed within this the King our Soverains Realme, touching the suppression of religion'. Bellenden believed that James might 'studie the same', and an account of the Epiphany play performed before the royal court in 1540 seemed to offer proof that the king was open to 'the reformation of the mysdemeanours of Busshops, religious personnes, and preistes, within the realme'. The drama, almost certainly the work of Sir David Lindsay, was vehemently anticlerical, and when it was concluded, James was said to have summoned Dunbar and various other bishops, to warn them that unless they took steps to reform their abuses, he 'wold sende sex of the proudeste of thaym unto his uncle of

---

[91] BL Cotton Calig. Biii, fo. 181 (*LP*, vol. xiv/1, no. 170); BL Cotton Calig. Biii, fo. 191 (*LP*, vol. xiv/1, no. 176).

[92] *SP*, vol. iv, no. 355; *LP*, vol. xiv/1, no. 241; BL Cotton Calig. Bvii, fo. 238; BL Cotton Calig. Bi, fo. 295 (*LP*, vol. xiv/1, no. 232).

[93] *LP*, vol. xiv/1, no. 406.

England, and, as those were ordoured, soe He wolde ordour all the reste that wolde not amende'.[94]

These tantalizing signs of the Scottish king's eagerness to embark upon reform were all that was required, and in January 1540 plans for Sadler's embassy to Scotland were resurrected. If Henry thought he detected in James an inclination towards Protestant reform, however, he was mistaken. The Scottish king's chief interest was in tackling the abuses within the Kirk in order to fortify it against English heresies, and his reforming ambitions apparently did not extend as far as those of courtiers such as Bellenden and Lindsay. Nevertheless, Sadler was sent to Edinburgh with instructions to recommend once more that Scotland follow the example of England in casting off the pope's usurped power. The centrepiece of his mission was a collection of letters retrieved from a ship that had been wrecked in Bamborough. They included a communication from the cardinal to his agent in Rome, Andrew Oliphant, which, the English alleged, gave indisputable proof that Beaton sought to take over spiritual jurisdiction in Scotland. After offering James the traditional sweetener of a gift of geldings, Sadler launched into his arguments, elaborating on the tyrannous ambitions of churchmen, and offering to pass on the intercepted letters. He did his best to convince James of the financial benefits of taking religious properties into his own hands, and urged him to reinforce the amity with England, so much safer than any pact with France or the emperor.[95]

It seemed unlikely, however, that rehearsal of these by now familiar arguments would have the desired effect. James initially kept Sadler waiting while he attended mass in the chapel of Holyroodhouse, and after hearing the ambassador out, revealed that he already knew of Beaton's letters to Rome, and even had his own copies of them. Sadler was forced to admit to Henry that James 'excused the cardinal in every thing, and seemed wondrous loath to hear of any thing, that should sound as an untruth in him'. Sadler's condemnation of papal authority was no more effective, with James asserting that, while he might exercise authority in temporal matters, he committed charge of spiritual affairs solely to the pope.[96] The king's vindication of his minister and his policies was complete, and in answer to Sadler's arguments against foreign alliances, James gave the provocative reply, 'there is a good old man in France, my good-father the king of France, that will not see me want anything'.[97] Sadler did not even raise the

---

[94] BL Royal MS 7C xvi, fo. 137 (*SP*, vol. iv, no. 366).
[95] BL Cotton Calig. Bvii, fo. 245 (*SP*, vol. iv, no. 365); BL Cotton Calig. Bvii, fo. 247; *SSP* i. 3–13.
[96] *SSP* i. 17–45.
[97] Ibid. 30.

next subject on his agenda, Henry's demand for delivery of the religious rebel Richard Hilliard. Instead he sent Cromwell a depressing account of the lack of wise and learned advisers disposed to God's word, along with complaints that he and his men were being subjected to taunts and animosity from James's churchmen.[98]

The message of antipathy to English reform could not have been clearer, and so England's security concerns in the north remained alive. Henry was increasingly wary of Scottish ties with France, believing that 'the Scots are wont to dance to French music', as Marillac reported to Francis I.[99] His suspicions of Scottish bad faith were only intensified by the rumours of their interest in the Northern Conspiracy, the plan by a number of gentlemen and priests for a religious uprising in Pontefract, uncovered in April 1541. Estimates as to the numbers involved in the plot varied between 50 and 100, and its focus upon an area of previous insurrection evoked worrying parallels with the Pilgrimage of Grace.[100] In other respects, the intended rising was very different in character, with an aristocratic flavour and almost exclusively religious grievances. As in 1536, however, it was thought that the plotters were 'perhaps emboldened and encouraged in their undertaking by the fact that for some time past there has been a rumour that the Scotch were stirring on the border', and they 'were not without hope of being aided by the king of Scotland'.[101] On detection of the conspiracy, a number of those who were not apprehended 'fled, some to Scotland, and others to mountain and desert places', in the words of Marillac.[102] The mention of Scotland in connection with the plot did nothing to calm Henry's anxieties, and informed his decision to travel to the north of his realm later that year. Rather than securing the amity that he had so consistently worked for, he had simply received a reaffirmation of Scotland's ties with France, and of James's propensity to aid his seditious subjects.

VIII. DIPLOMATIC STALEMATE AND THE ROAD TO WAR

It was on the issue of religious fugitives that Anglo-Scottish negotiations eventually reached deadlock. With the collapse of the latest English deputation, and accumulating evidence that James was deliberately protecting

---

[98] Ibid. 46–8.

[99] *LP*, vol. xvi, no. 650.

[100] Ibid., nos. 449, 763, 769.

[101] Chapuys to Charles V, 17 Apr. 1541, and Chapuys to the Queen of Hungary, 1 May 1541: *CSP Span.*, vol. vi/1, nos. 156, 158.

[102] *LP*, vol. xvi, no. 763.

English rebels, Henry rapidly began to lose patience. The illusion of a sincere alliance between the two kings, sustained by ties of blood and affection, was becoming hard to sustain. The exile issue came to dominate cross-border discussions largely at Henry's instigation, but James, too, was exasperated by English efforts to make what capital they could from Scottish exiles in England. In December 1539 he complained directly to Henry that 'all maner of fugitives, malefactourris, our evill subjectis fleing of our Realme, ar indifferentlie recept and kepit in zour Realme';[103] but no redress was forthcoming. Indeed, when Sir James Colville arrived in Carlisle from Scotland in September 1540, Henry summoned him to London, and gave him generous financial rewards in return for information. James reacted by ordering Colville and the earl of Angus, George Douglas, and James Douglas of Parkhede, to appear and answer treason charges.[104] As all four were known to be in England it was not likely that they would comply, but the proclamation was an official censure of their actions.

James was naturally bothered by the escape of his subjects, but for Henry the rebel issue became a fixation. Since 1535 he had been seeking Scottish co-operation in the return of his religious critics, but polite repetition of the message that 'the delyv[er]e of them myght be hyghe plesur to ye kinges highnes' had brought no result. Henry therefore ordered his wardens to keep a tight hold on two rebels specifically sought by James: Andrew Bell and George Rutherford, or 'Cokbanke'.[105] He also began investigations into the identities and whereabouts of 'Scots men rebels reset within England', and 'English rebels reset within Scotland', with a view to striking a bargain with James. Henry's list of his rebels gave their names in no apparent order, evidently intending to give the impression that all were similarly insignificant border thieves, whom James should have no qualms about returning. Tacked onto the end of the Charltons, Robsons, and Hunters, however, was a more noteworthy group, comprising Pilgrimage insurgents and religious exiles known to be still in Scotland.[106] Religious offenders such as the Observant friars Barton and Simpson, the rebel leader Edward Asche or Ashton, and Richard Hilliard, were the troublemakers in whom the king had most interest. To add to the catalogue of Hilliard's crimes, word had come to England that he was being protected by Beaton, 'who enterteyned hym in moste gentil maner', while the exiles William Leche

[103] *SP*, vol. iv, no. 361.
[104] *LP*, vol. xvi, nos. 2, 380; *HP*, vol. i, no. 57.
[105] PRO SP 1/155, fo. 167ᵛ (*LP*, vol. xiv/2, no. 730); *LP*, vol. xv, nos. 85, 131.
[106] BL Royal MS 7C xvi, fos. 140–2 (*LP*, vol. xv, no. 96).

and Nicholas Musgrave were being looked after by James' V's surgeon. One Arkryges, a friar from Cartmell, was now 'a broder in the Abbay of Holy Rudus', and John Priestman had found shelter in Newbattle Abbey.[107]

Outrage at this Scottish complicity with English fugitives was in no way lessened by James's contention that he could not authorize their return. He argued that 'we tak na grete regard of sic personis, and quhat falt ony freir relligiouse or uthir kirkmen within oure Realme committis, in ony maner of sort', leaving the handling of such persons to 'yair Ordinaris, Archibisschoppis or Biscoppis, or sic other yair prelattis as ar yame immediate superiouris be law of Halikirk'. This pronouncement was first made early in 1540, and it was one to which James would return frequently during the debate between the governments.[108] His disingenuous assertion that he would not encroach on papal authority within his realm was scarcely credible, since he could certainly have returned Henry's rebels had he wished. He had noticed and intended to expose, however, Henry's efforts to class all rebels alike as habitual border offenders. There was, in Scottish eyes, 'a greate difference between thoffenders desired by the partye of Scotland, and those which were requyred by the sayd Wharton', and no amount of arguments that English religious rebels were also unrepentant traitors who deserved extradition could convince James otherwise.[109] Henry challenged James head-on, telling him that his ideas seemed 'of such sorte as is neyther maynteynable by Goddes lawe, ne yet by the saide treatye of peax passed betwixt us'. He professed himself willing to believe that the Scottish king had simply been led astray by 'sinistre meane and counsaill', but James remained unmoved, alleging that Henry's innovations since the time of their treaty in 1534 released him from his requirement to honour it.[110]

English frustrations finally came into the open after the fiasco of the proposed meeting between the kings at York, planned for September 1541. The English had sought an interview between Henry and James, and perhaps also Francis I, since 1534, and the matter was brought up time and again by Henry's ambassadors. The endless Scottish prevarications and disputation of the terms supposedly agreed for the meeting, however, was indicative of their half-heartedness in the project. Though James was not wholly averse to the idea, a number of his councillors, led by Beaton, certainly were. Until 1541 their counsels prevailed, but during Beaton's absence in France that year, James was worn down by English persuasions,

---

[107] *LP*, vol. xv, no. 160; *HP*, vol. i, no. 106.
[108] *SP*, vol. iv, nos. 368, 379; *HP*, vol. i, no. 65.
[109] *HP*, vol. i, nos. 75–6.
[110] *SP*, vol. iv, no. 381; *HP*, vol. i, no. 66.

and Henry travelled to York in August to await his arrival.[111] The lavish preparations to receive the Scottish king continued well into September, though many seemed to doubt that he would keep his appointment with Henry. Marillac told Francis I that he found it difficult to believe that James would venture so far into England against the advice of his prelates, and Beaton also gave the French king confident assurances that James 'wald in na way meit wyt him howbeit yair wes grete wayis soucht be ye king of ingland to yat effect'.[112] Even Henry's own councillors were pessimistic, Wharton telling the council that James's advisers were utterly divided, and that James himself was waiting on the advice of Beaton.[113]

James's failure to come to York, despite his recent change of heart, can probably be explained by fears in Scotland for his safety, following rumours that a kidnap attempt was planned. Amazingly, this desperate proposal, devised by Wharton, was at one stage considered seriously by the English council.[114] It was swiftly dismissed, but the possibility that news of it had been leaked to Scotland would explain James's controversial decision to avoid the meeting. The snub to Henry was significant, and there is no doubt that this was instrumental in pushing him towards war with Scotland. In the king's *Declaration of the just causes of the warre with the Scottes*, published at the end of the year and best known for its revival of English claims to suzerainty over Scotland, it was a central theme. The charge was levelled that James 'speaketh an other langage to all the worlde in deeds, and therby so toucheth us in honour and denegration of iustyce, as we be inforced and compelled to use the sworde'.[115]

The problem, however, was more than one of wounded pride. In his dealings with Scotland, Henry had pinned all his hopes on a personal meeting, convinced that the force of his own persuasion could win James to his way of thinking. The meeting would, moreover, be the means of resolving once and for all England's exile problem, the centrality of which has not been recognized in accounts of the deteriorating relationship between the countries. One of the principal points of the *Declaration*, therefore, was the charge that James 'receyued and entretiegned suche rebelles, as were of the chief and principle, in sterringe the insurrection in the North agaynst us'.[116] Scottish perceptions of the causes of the war highlighted the same issue.

[111] *LP*, vol. xvi, nos. 941, 1115; *HP*, vol. i, nos. 83–4.
[112] *LP*, vol. xvi, no. 1130; A. Lang (ed.) 'Letters of Cardinal Beaton', *SHR* 6 (1909), 154; *LP*, vol. xvi, no. 1182.
[113] *HP*, vol. i, no. 85.
[114] Hotle, *Thorns and Thistles*, 171; *SP*, vol. iv, no. 390.
[115] *Complaynt of Scotlande*, 193, 197.
[116] Ibid., 193.

A tract by one of James's own councillors, William Lamb, both defended James's conduct over the York affair, and justified Scotland's reception of 'auld mendicant freris, prestis, prechouris, and techeraris of spirituale jurisdictioun, seikand saffete of yair lyfe', with the accusation that Henry 'wes nocht saciate in vij or viij zeris of persecutioun and scheddin of his awin subdittis bluid'.[117] Adam Abell was also forthright in his vindication of Scotland's reception of English friars who, he said, left England to 'come in Scotland fra ye ewill and p[er]uersit religious men (allan[er]lie of name) quhair yai myt not keip yare obs[er]uance'.[118]

Their differences over the intractable rebel problem were a key factor in souring relations between the kings, and a measure of the unresolved religious tensions between the realms. Henry was infuriated by James's insistence that he knew of no English exiles in Edinburgh, save the merchants who were there on legitimate business. This was hardly consistent with the information from English spies that a number of rebels 'hayth beyn sens in the town of Edynborgh, and in the company of the Lord Maxwell'.[119] Henry railed at 'the untrouth and incertainty whiche hathe ever appered in that nation, what a nombre of our rebelles be their entreteyened by the king himself and other his nobles, contrary to the treaties of peax betwene us, what preparations they have made and [do] daily make in Scotlande . . . and also howe they depende holly uppon Fraunce'.[120] Henry's growing conviction that the French were the dominant force in Scottish government meant that he saw sinister undertones to any new developments. A meeting with James would have allowed him to make a last-ditch effort to allure Scotland away from the auld alliance, but instead French forces seemed to be closing in from the north and south. This was the more galling given that Henry's other main preoccupation at this time, and one for which he showed true enthusiasm, was his planned campaign in France. Through the summer of 1542, however, English efforts were concentrated on preparing for hostilities with Scotland.

Attempts by James to repair the damage done by his failure to appear at York, through embassies to England in December 1541 and continuing into 1542, had little effect.[121] It was now only a matter of time before the retaliatory raids and rising tensions on the border would lead to an open

---

[117] BL Cotton Calig. Bvii, fo. 348ᵛ, (fo. 359ᵛ according to alternative folio nos).

[118] NLS MS 1746, fos. 122ᵛ–123ʳ.

[119] *SP*, vol. iv, nos. 379, 362.

[120] Henry VIII to the earls of Westmoreland and Cumberland, 20 May 1541: *HP*, vol. i, no. 69.

[121] *HP*, vol. i, nos. 106, 76, 112; *SP*, vol. iv, no. 386; Keith, *History*, i. 46; SRO MS GD 249/2/2, fo. 83.

breach. James had consistently shied away from the prospect of military confrontation, but his conciliatory attitude towards England overlay a stubborn resistance to the idea of religious collaboration. Henry could not shake the Scottish king's commitment to orthodox Catholicism, and so resorted to force to achieve his ends. The events of the short-lived Anglo-Scottish war of 1542 are well known: the Scots scored a notable success at Haddon Rigg in August, where they captured Sir Robert Bowes and other leading members of the English army. In November, however, a poorly executed advance on English forces at Solway Moss led to the decisive defeat of the much larger Scottish army. This disaster was followed two weeks later by the death of James V.

England's success was more complete than any could have expected, but a minor episode occurring simultaneously gave a bitter reminder of the vexing exile question. Shortly before James's death, an English messenger to Scotland, Somerset Herald, was murdered as he began his return journey. The incident was taken seriously, as the personal safety of such officials was by custom universally respected, and Henry immediately sent stinging letters of rebuke to James.[122] Though the Scottish king was sympathetic, he lost no time in pointing out that the culprits were in fact the Englishmen William Leche and John Priestman.[123] Both had been in Scotland since the Pilgrimage of Grace, and had been named in Henry's demands for the delivery of his rebels, so the question of who should bear responsibility for their crime was far from clear.[124] Henry had no doubts, however, that the murder was one more demonstration of Scottish duplicity. The fact that the incident arose from James's protection of his rebels gave, in the words of Henry's councillors, direct evidence of 'what compasinge hath ben and ys in Skotland ymagyned agaynst your majestie'.[125]

The mutual grievances of Henry and James over the issue of religious fugitives were never satisfactorily resolved, and this factor was critical in bringing the countries to the point of open war. James had tried hard to avoid this outcome, realizing the particular damage which conflict at such close quarters could bring. For this reason he resisted the persuasions of English ambassadors, as his Catholic convictions dictated, but continued to receive English embassies more or less courteously throughout the 1530s. When he informed Norfolk that he 'wold never breke with the King his uncle during

---

[122] *SP*, vol. iv, no. 407.
[123] Ibid., no. 406.
[124] Ibid., nos. 405, 404.
[125] *LP*, vol. xvii, no. 1166; *HP*, vol. i, no. 246.

his life',[126] James's sentiment was probably genuine. He had not counted, however, on Henry's unrelenting determination to force his hand on the religious issue.

The Scottish king, hardly comfortable to find that he now shared a land border with a regime of a differing confession, seems to have been prepared to maintain an amicable relationship with England. Henry, however, would not countenance such an amity, remaining too fearful of the wider opportunities for concerted European threats to England to leave the religious divide unaddressed. This factor was far more than merely 'an element in the diplomacy leading up to the war':[127] it was the root cause of England's insecurities in 1542. Having failed to convince James by conventional diplomatic tactics, Henry abandoned such niceties and fell back on the timeworn English claim to superiority over Scotland as his justification for war. Events took a dramatic turn, however, when news of the Scottish king's death reached England in December 1542. The beginning of a royal minority under an infant queen, barely two weeks old, seemed to offer Henry an unrivalled opportunity to achieve the religious and defensive objectives which his persistent diplomatic advances had failed to accomplish.

[126] Cameron, *James V*, 288.
[127] Ibid. 292.

3

The Pursuit of a Godly Conjunction

James V's unexpected death in December 1542 opened an entirely new phase in Henry VIII's policy towards Scotland. The previous decade had seen the English king doing his utmost to move James towards an English-style reformation against papal authority, then resorting to violence when his approaches failed. The sudden removal of the king who had so consistently opposed Henrician reforms altered the picture completely. The infant Mary's accession to the Scottish throne seemed to Henry an unmissable occasion to resolve England's diplomatic problems and religious insecurities at a stroke, through the marriage of the Scottish queen to Prince Edward, now 5 years old. Rather than attempting vainly to coax Scotland into adopting a friendly, pro-reform stance, Henry could assure himself of the country's allegiance with a Protestant dynastic alliance. The opportunity was presented to Scotland as a providential moment: the godly union would create a strong, defensible island, united under the banner of the reformed religion, and able to withstand all the dangers Catholic Europe could present.

The fortuitous events of December 1542 gave Henry's Scottish policy a momentum of its own, but its fundamental aims were unchanged. The opportunistic marriage scheme, pursued determinedly in the wake of the diplomatic defeats of the 1530s, appeared to offer a simple, all-embracing solution to Henry's Scottish problem, promising to resolve security concerns relating to Catholic agitation on the northern border, and Scottish collaboration with English rebels in Ireland. The king would hardly pass over any opportunity to raise the profile of the Tudor dynasty, moreover, and the union would undoubtedly strengthen his hand in Europe. A minority government would give Henry scope to accomplish his ends by exerting his considerable influence upon the governor, or better still, taking on the position himself. In the event, two weeks of undignified power wrangling ended with the appointment of James Hamilton, Earl of Arran, as regent.[1] Though in many respects ill fitted for the post, Arran was demonstrating an attachment to reform that suggested he might prove susceptible to English direction.

---

[1] *HP*, vol. i, no. 273.

The transformation of the political scene had not, however, eliminated certain intractable complications in recent Anglo-Scottish dealings. There remained a powerful, orthodox, pro-French party headed by Cardinal Beaton, whose obstructive potential had already been seen in its protection of Henry's religious rebels. Beaton would not take kindly to an aggressive English hand in the direction of policy. It was also apparent that, while Arran and his close supporters might approve of the Protestant tone of the union proposal, its acceptability to the government as a whole and the population at large could not be taken for granted. At this stage the progress of Protestant opinion in Scotland was patchy, and it was far from clear that reforming enthusiasms would extend to support for a vision of godly union which seemed so closely tied to notions of English superiority. Scotland's vulnerability following the death of its king was patently obvious, and English proposals to exert a guiding hand in government would need to be carefully handled. For all the favourable rhetoric surrounding the marriage scheme, there were constant undercurrents of xenophobia from both sides during the years of the Rough Wooing. The two countries, it seemed, found it difficult to abandon their traditional antagonism in favour of a surely based alliance.

I. THE POTENTIAL FOR SCOTTISH REFORM

Proposals for the godly union would test Scottish attitudes to England, and to an alliance whose implications for Scotland were as yet unknown. Speculation over the future of the kingdom's freedoms and liberties revealed a mixture of opinion, ranging from cautious optimism to wariness, and downright antagonism. The Protestant framework within which English terms were offered only compounded these differences. The Scottish establishment remained avowedly loyal to Rome in 1543, but there were unmistakable signs within the Kirk and literate lay circles of an eagerness for the removal of abuses and purification of religion.[2] Indeed, the late king had presided over varied religious discussion within his own court. This interest was often entirely orthodox, concentrating on the eradication of the worst excesses and failings of the Church. In some instances, however, it could offer encouragement for the spread of Protestant opinion. This would by no means translate directly into support for English aims, but it might conceivably offer a platform on which Henry could build a party to resist Beaton and his adherents.

[2] Edington, *Court and Culture*, 46–52.

The new humanist learning centred on the universities, encouraged by Hector Boece in Aberdeen, and John Hepburn in the newly founded college of St Leonard's at St Andrews. Scottish scholars also travelled readily to Paris, Padua, Rome, Louvain, Cologne, and other continental university cities.[3] The Kirk was noticeably receptive to European reforming influences, and churchmen such as Alexander Myln, prior of the Cambuskenneth Augustinians, and Thomas Crystall and Robert Reid, successive abbots at Kinloss, became distinguished promoters of orthodox renewal.[4] The resulting climate of questioning and reflection produced a number of writings expressing deep dissatisfaction with the country's spiritual health. George Buchanan's *Franciscanus* was a savage satire on the 'mystereis and abuses of the friers', and Robert Richardson's commentary on the Augustinian order highlighted its weaknesses in 'these wretched days'.[5] Alongside these largely orthodox criticisms were signs, too, of more heterodox views. The early history of heresy in the country was sparse, with groups such as the Kyle Lollards remarkable for their novelty.[6] James V's parliamentary measures against Lutheran literature, however, attest to the arrival of English bibles and other reforming works in Scotland from the mid-1520s, and in 1534 the king noted that 'divers tractatis and bukis translatit out of Latin in our Scottish toung be heretikis, favoraris, and of the sect of Luther' were circulating in Leith, Edinburgh, Dundee, and other east coast ports.[7] Simple possession of such works was treated as evidence of heresy, and though trials were infrequent, the controversy they provoked suggested that victims' opinions were attracting some support. The burning of Patrick Hamilton in 1528 was a landmark in the history of Protestantism in the realm, both as a sign of the penetration of Protestant doctrines and as an incentive to some of his contemporaries, including Alexander Alesius, to adopt the reformed religion.[8]

The boundaries between orthodox complaints, anticlericalism, and definite adherence to Lutheran doctrines were inexact, however, and the

[3] Kirk, 'Religion of Early Scottish Protestants', 362; John Durkan, 'Education: The Laying of Fresh Foundations', in John MacQueen (ed.), *Humanism in Renaissance Scotland* (Edinburgh: Edinburgh University Press, 1990), 150–1; Durkan, 'Cultural Background', 278–80.

[4] Mark Dilworth, *Scottish Monasteries in the Late Middle Ages* (Edinburgh: Edinburgh University Press, 1995), 22, 28; John Durkan, 'Giovanni Ferrerio, Humanist: His Influence in Sixteenth-Century Scotland', in Keith Robbins (ed.), *Religion and Humanism* (Studies in Church History, 17; Oxford: Blackwell Publishers, 1981), 183–4.

[5] Calderwood, i. 129; Robertus Richardinus, *Commentary on the Rule of St Augustine*, ed. G. Coulton (Edinburgh: SHS, 3rd ser. 26; 1935), 27.

[6] Sanderson, *Ayrshire*, 41–2.

[7] Kirk, 'Religion of Early Scottish Protestants', 376.

[8] Ibid. 369, 372.

degree of potential support for any wholesale Protestant reformation was unclear. Some notable anticlerical reforming works of the 1530s and 1540s pushed the bounds of orthodoxy to the limits and beyond. *The Richt Vay to the Kingdom of Heuine*, a translation of a Danish work by John Gau, a Scottish exile in Sweden, contained humanist-inspired pleas for better preaching, use of the vernacular, and development of inward spirituality, alongside decidedly Lutheran views on justification by faith and the inefficacy of good works.[9] Gau had links to a number of other advocates of reform, having been a contemporary of Sir John Borthwick and Sir David Lindsay at St Andrews. James Wedderburn enrolled at the university some years later, as did his brother John, at a time when George Buchanan and Henry Balnaves were studying there.[10] John was assisted by his brother in the production of the famous *Gude and Godlie Ballatis*, a vehemently anti-clerical collection of satirical verses based largely on German originals, rejecting aspects of the Roman religion such as purgatory and merit through good works in favour of reforming opinion.[11] The plays of Sir David Lindsay were also fiercely critical of 'the proudest Prelatis of the kirk', attachment to 'superstitious pylgramagis', 'grawin Ymagis', and other features of traditional religion.[12] Lindsay himself, however, remained essentially orthodox in his commitment to the Church, though uncompromising in his criticism of its failings. Lindsay's one-time fellow students and now colleagues in government, Sir John Borthwick and Henry Balnaves, took their own views a stage further: Borthwick fled the country in 1540 following his explicit endorsement of Cromwellian-influenced Protestantism, and Balnaves produced a tract in 1548 on the doctrine of justification by faith.[13] Individual theological opinions evidently varied considerably within this prominent group, but a readiness to countenance some degree of reform was widely shared.[14]

Opportunities to promote reform appeared transformed with the changed complexion of Scottish politics from 1543. Under an authoritative and respected Catholic king persuasion had been the only means of obtaining official sanction for religious change. Lindsay's had therefore been an important voice at James's court, with his exposure of the most glaring

[9] Gau, *Richt Vay*, 104, 99, 5, 83, 4–5, 25.
[10] Ibid., p. ix; *A Compendious Book of Godly and Spiritual Songs, commonly known as 'The Gude and Godlie Ballatis'*, ed. A. F. Mitchell (Edinburgh: STS 39; 1897), p. xx.
[11] Calderwood, i. 142–3; '*Gude and Godlie Ballatis*', 1–230.
[12] Lindsay, *Works*, i. 48, 51; Edington, *Court and Culture*, 7.
[13] Knox, i. 61, 226.
[14] Carol Edington, 'John Knox and the Castilians: A Crucible of Reforming Opinion?', in Mason (ed.), *John Knox and the British Reformations*, 30–3.

abuses of the Kirk and attempts to encourage magisterial reform. The alternatives were to act in defiance of the establishment and risk the harsh penalties meted out to Patrick Hamilton and others, or to seek sanctuary outside the country, like the many religious exiles in England and on the continent. The institution of a minority government, however, offered a more direct means of implementing reform, with the possibility that a Protestant reformation might come from the very top through direct political and parliamentary intervention in religious affairs. Attempts to influence opinion through satire and drama did not disappear: Lindsay's *The Monarche* (1548–53), for example, was directed to governor Arran and his brother John Hamilton, abbot of Paisley.[15] Efforts to mould opinion in this way, however, were superseded by the quest to exert a direct influence on government policy. This was a struggle fought out between Henry and his Scottish allies on one side, and Beaton's church party on the other.

Henry could derive encouragement from signs that certain Scottish reformers approved of his magisterial reformation. Lindsay, whose diplomatic contacts with England during the 1530s gave him first-hand experience of reform there, made much of the king's duty to deal with clerical abuses in *The Complaynt* (1529–30) and *The Testament* (1530):[16] he had clearly hoped that James V would follow Henry's example in taking order with the Church, even if he did not advocate thoroughgoing Protestant reformation (this version of reform would actually have suited Henry very well). Gilbert Kennedy, 3rd Earl of Cassillis, was already a reforming enthusiast when he arrived in England as one of the Solway Moss prisoners in 1542; and his association with Cranmer during his short stay in the household of the archbishop seems to have confirmed his support for English plans in Scotland.[17] The contacts of English border officials also told them that Balnaves and Sir Thomas Bellenden were important potential allies. English efforts from 1543 therefore concentrated on the cultivation of a party around governor Arran. By this means Henry hoped finally to oversee the anti-papal reformation that Cromwell's diplomatic efforts had consistently failed to achieve. The new approach was one with which the king felt far more comfortable, and only days after the Scottish king's death Henry's agents were taking steps 'to have perfyte intelligence of the state of Scotland', and assessing the Scottish nobles, 'to fele theyre myndes towardes your highnes'.[18] Whether Henry would prove able to manipulate

---

[15] Greg Walker, 'Sir David Lindsay's *Ane Satire of the Thrie Estaitis* and the Politics of Reformation', *Scottish Literary Journal*, 16 (1989), 6: Lindsay, *Works*, i. 199.

[16] Lindsay, *Works*, i. 51, 65, 86.

[17] MacCulloch, *Cranmer*, 295–6.

[18] *HP*, vol. i, no. 262.

Arran and his supporters sufficiently to secure both the marriage and a Protestant reformation, however, seemed questionable. In men such as Angus and Douglas, Cassillis, and Glencairn, Henry had the beginnings of a Protestant Anglophile party, but its ascendancy was not unchallenged and neither was its loyalty unquestioning. More importantly, its combination of pro-English and pro-reforming sentiments did not seem guaranteed to win widespread popular support.

II. A PREMATURE REFORMATION, 1543

Plans for the advancement of the English godly purpose rapidly took shape at the beginning of 1543. The Solway Moss prisoners were summoned to court, where the king extracted from them a promise to further the marriage plans, and have Mary delivered into his keeping. A select group thought to be bound by Protestant sympathies, including Cassillis, Glencairn, Fleming, and Maxwell, was also required to pledge the transfer of the kingdom to Henry in the event of Mary's death. Pensions secured their support, and it was hoped that they, along with Angus and Douglas who now ended their fourteen-year exile in England, would provide the nucleus for a notable pro-English party in government.[19] Even at this moment of strength and opportunity, however, there were barely hidden undercurrents of suspicion in England's dealings with Scotland. As Henry saw it, he was prepared of his beneficence to suspend hostilities and offer to the Scots the magnificent prize of union with his own kingdom. If they rejected his proposals out of ungodliness and sheer foolishness, he would simply use military might to achieve the same ends. He warned the Scottish council, 'thinke not that we woll wast tyme in communicacion of wordes, ne upon trust of fayre langage, pretermit thopportunitie offered of God to unite thiese two realmes': they were to be sure that 'we will prosecute you and use you in your deserts as the case will require'.[20]

Arran, it seems, was not averse to the reforming tone of the English proposals, and in his delicate early months as governor saw the advantages of going along with Henry's dynastic ambitions. The first step was to put secure distance between himself and his formidable rival, Beaton, and so at the end of January the cardinal was arrested and imprisoned.[21] Arran then wrote to Henry, 'we ar myndit with the grace and help of God, to put som

[19] Ibid., no. 276 (ii and iii); *LP*, vol. xviii/1, no. 22.
[20] *HP*, vol. i, no. 269.
[21] Ibid., no. 289; Keith, *History*, vol. i, p. 68; Merriman, *Rough Wooings*, 115.

reformatioun in the stait of the kirk of this realme', also confiding to Sadler that for five years he had never taken the bishop of Rome to be more than a bishop, 'and that a very evil bishop'.[22] His next move was to appoint two apostate friars, Thomas Guilliame and John Rough, to preach Protestant reform at court, and English agents noted that their sermons were markedly anti-papal.[23] Henry was delighted at the appearance that detaching Scotland from its troublesome allegiance to Rome might be so straightforward. The favourable signs continued as other burghs including Aberdeen appointed their own Protestant preachers, and news reached the English council that the Bible and other English reforming works were 'mervelously desyred now of the people in Scotlande' and 'if there were a carte lode sent hither they wolde be bought every one'.[24]

Such works were, of course, forbidden by statute, but March 1543 saw a milestone in the history of Protestantism in the realm, when the Scottish parliament passed an act sanctioning the reading of the Scriptures in the vernacular. The session dealt with some momentous business, as the main item on the agenda was the discussion of the marriage and union proposal. This resulted in the despatch of ambassadors to England to consult on the matter with the king and his commissioners. A bill proposed by Lord Maxwell and sponsored by Balnaves, among others, then allowed that all persons might have and read the Old and New Testaments, provided they were of good and true translation, and that there was no disputation upon them. Although this recognized a practice that was already widespread, the measure did not pass without protests from Dunbar and other spiritual lords.[25] Opposition was further signalled in petitions to Arran for the release of Beaton, and for the governor's assurance that their estate might stand and continue in its present condition, 'and not followe the cast of England'.[26] The division within the parliament gave an indication of the uncertainties that would be apparent in the population at large. At this time, though, the English and reforming interest prevailed and so the churchmen were left unsatisfied.

Henry was evidently eager to make the most of signs of reforming enthusiasm, recognizing that in this fervour lay his best hope of wielding any measurable influence in Scotland. His support for the act making the scriptures readily available there, however, was followed just two months

---

[22] *HP*, vol. i, nos. 282, 289; *LP*, vol. xviii/1, no. 324.

[23] *HP*, vol. i, nos. 298, 301; Knox, i. 95–6; Spottiswoode, *History*, i. 143.

[24] Ian B. Cowan, *The Scottish Reformation: Church and Society in Sixteenth Century Scotland* (Weidenfeld & Nicolson, 1982), 100; BL Add. MS 32649, fo. 196ᵛ (*HP*, vol. i, no. 316).

[25] *APS*, ii. 415; *LP*, vol. xviii/1, nos. 273, 281; Edington, *Court and Culture*, 170.

[26] *HP*, vol. i, nos. 332, 365.

later, in May 1543, by an act in England prohibiting Bible-reading to all householders below the level of yeomen, and to all women except those of gentle and noble status.[27] This inconsistency indicates that the promotion of reformed doctrines north of the border was in fact a matter of some ambivalence for the king, at a time when he appeared to be moving back to a more conservative religious position. Arran's willingness to sponsor reform was gratifying, but Henry was anxious that it should be both moderate, and firmly guided by secular authority. The crucial factor was the rejection of papal authority, and anything more should be strictly supervised. Henry did not want to see unchecked reforming activity in Scotland any more than he did in England, where, for much of the 1540s, the Catholic conservatism of Norfolk, Wriothesley, Bonner, and others, held sway over the evangelical sympathies of Cranmer, his clerical colleagues, and Hertford.[28] Plans for distributing the Scriptures in Scotland, though they were central to the drive to encourage pro-English sentiment, and specifically support for a Henrician-style rejection of Rome, sat uneasily with the state of reform within the English Church.

Henry's instructions to Arran betrayed a degree of anxiety. Even before the arrival of ambassador Sadler in Scotland, Suffolk was counselling Arran on how carefully controlled reform could bring the people to 'knowe the better howe to eschue sedicion'.[29] The initial response was heartening: on meeting Sadler, Arran reiterated his earnest desire for reformation, and asked not only for more English bibles, but also for copies of the English reformation statutes and injunctions.[30] Henry, encouraged to hope that he might export his own brand of reformation across the border, devised a systematic scheme covering the supervision of Scripture-reading, suppression of the monasteries, and consolidation of the religious union through the marriage of Arran's son to Elizabeth Tudor. In fact, the primary aim of this second godly marriage would be to keep Arran from any thoughts of marrying his son to the Scottish queen; but the first two aspects of the reforming agenda set out Henry's genuine hopes for Scotland. The king stressed that the Scriptures should be received 'reverently and humbly', and his order that 'politique handelyng' be used in the suppression of religious houses reflected an overriding concern that reform should be closely controlled.[31] The key was to avoid all 'diversitie in opinions' according to

[27] MacCulloch, *Cranmer*, 310–11.

[28] Ibid. 289–94, 308–11, 351–4.

[29] *HP*, vol. i, no. 299.

[30] *SSP* i. 108.

[31] Merriman, *Rough Wooings*, 116; BL Add. MS 32650, fos. 123–30, 124ʳ, 125ʳ (*HP*, vol. i, no. 348).

the 'King's Book', which Henry and his bishops were in the process of completing.[32] Arran assured Henry that he would 'not fail to publish it here, desiring with all his heart that these two realms may concur, not only in unity of the true understanding of God's word, but also, by all other good means, to be knit and assured one to another in perfect amity'.[33]

Henry was unquestionably cautious in his approach to this Protestant enterprise in Scotland, but at the same time was delightedly aware that Arran's willingness to contemplate a carbon copy of the Henrician alteration in Scotland offered a tantalizing opportunity to mastermind reformations in both realms. The king's authoritative direction would bring about religious harmony, and a peaceful extension of his royal authority through the projected marriage of Prince Edward to the Scottish queen. His Scottish allies seemed to share his vision, and Douglas painted a harmonious picture of the union, with 'subjects of both the realms having liberty to have intercourse, and to resort one with another without safe conduct, which shall engender a love and familiarity betwixt them'.[34] By synchronizing religious changes, Henry could, furthermore, silence the damaging cross-border debate, which was a continual source of tension when the regimes were of differing confessions. The problem of religious exiles could be all but eliminated, allowing the realms to present a united front against external aggression. The earl of Moray's assertion that 'if all were oone we shulde be strong ynoughe to plucke the Great Turke oute of his denne'[35] would have held great appeal for Henry. The king may not have been primarily interested in the Ottoman threat, but would have found this image of Anglo-Scottish muscle highly seductive.

Henry's exact intentions in adopting this policy towards Scotland in the later years of his reign are a contentious issue. According to one interpretation, his vision of the dynastic alliance was informed by grandiose imperial ambitions, while another suggestion is that the main focus of his interest was always France, and 'Scotland was a comparatively remote and secondary theatre of war'. More recently, David Head has demonstrated the importance to Henry of creating an Anglo-Scottish axis to undermine the potency of the auld alliance, arguing that France remained the object of his military ambitions.[36] The king undoubtedly remained eager to launch a

---

[32] *A Necessary Doctrine and Erudition for any Christen Man* (T. Berthelet, 1543; *RSTC* 5168), sig. Aii^v ('King's Book' hereafter).

[33] *SSP*, i. 128.

[34] Ibid. 70.

[35] *HP*, vol. i, no. 298.

[36] Head, 'Henry VIII's Scottish Policy: A Reassessment', *SHR* 61 (1982), 1–2, 22–4; Scarisbrick, *Henry VIII*, 550, 563.

major French campaign, his goal of leading his armies there in person being perhaps more important in the 1540s than ever. Scotland was, however, far more than a mere distraction in 1543. Ever since the break with Rome it had occupied a central position in Henry's considerations, by reason of its strategic significance for Catholic Europe. His ambitions there related less to the creation of an empire than to the resolution of pressing security issues, arising from the confessional divide. The marriage, rather than being a long-standing policy aim, offered a neat opportunity to secure England's frontiers.

This was part of a three-sided policy in the early 1540s, aiming to find lasting solutions to the security concerns that the Henrician reformation had created. In Wales the completion of the Acts of Union represented, in theory at least, an extension of centralized administrative control throughout the principality and marcher lordships. In Ireland, meanwhile, the king's assertion of sovereignty in 1541 was an attempt to make crown authority uniformly effective across the whole island, abolishing the distinction between the Gaelic lordships, and the areas already under English control.[37] Henry's Scottish policy, too, was shaped by the unchanging objective of establishing the dominance of royal government in order to eliminate the particularly acute borderland and frontier dangers in the north. The proposed dynastic union of the kingdoms of England and Scotland was seized on as offering a convenient means to this end.

III. THE FAILURE OF THE PROTESTANT INITIATIVE

Though developments of the first months of 1543 seemed to promise much as far as this aim was concerned, the king and his agents were beset by nagging suspicions of their 'friends' in Scotland. Henry feared that Angus, Douglas, Glencairn, and the others would not live up to their fair words, nor would they prove capable of holding in check the powerful opposition of the cardinal. On both counts his apprehensions were realized well before the year was out. From the first, Arran's malleability had threatened to be as much of a hindrance to England as an advantage: while Sadler heard that he was 'a very gentle creature, and a symple man easie to be ruled', Douglas thought him 'the most wavering person in the world'.[38] Arran's commitment to English interests began to be seriously doubted after the return to Scotland of his brother, John Hamilton, abbot of Paisley in April.

---

[37] Williams, *Recovery, Reorientation*, 267; Morgan, 'British Policies', 73.

[38] *HP*, vol. i, no. 337, *LP*, vol. xviii/1, no. 338.

Optimism within the English government as to Hamilton's Protestant inclinations proved unfounded,[39] and despite determined efforts by Sadler over the following months, Arran was drawn closer towards the Catholic, pro-French camp.

Arran's change of heart was also hastened by the return to the political scene of Beaton, whose period of strict captivity lasted less than four months. English agitations over the surety of the cardinal's keeping were continually expressed, and although he was successfully excluded from the March parliament, he was subsequently transferred from Blackness to his own castle of St Andrews. Sadler's prediction that this move would be 'the readiest way to lose both the castle and him' appeared to be borne out, when Beaton got the better of his guard, Seton, and returned to play a full part in government by the middle of the year.[40] When Sadler asked that Beaton be apprehended once more and sent to England, Arran merely 'laughed and said, the Cardinal had liever go into Hell'.[41] By July Beaton's position was sufficiently secure that he could mount a challenge to Arran's government, leading armed supporters to Linlithgow to try to gain custody of the young queen. Though their attempt was unsuccessful, they made a mutual bond to defend the queen against England, 'for the defence of the Faith and the Holy Church, and preservation of the liberty of the realm'.[42]

Beaton headed a body of opinion that opposed the Greenwich Treaties for the marriage and union, even as they were concluded in July 1543. Scottish unease had been evident in the parliamentary directions for the ambassadors sent to England in March. Mary's delivery to England, Henry was to be told, would be 'ane ryt he and ryt grete Incovenient to the realme of scotland'. The envoys were also to insist that their realm 'stand in the awin libertie and fredomes as It Is now and hes bene In all tymes', retaining its name, its privileges, and significantly the control of its own strongholds. Some popular comment surrounding the discussions was openly hostile, leading Sadler to conclude, 'they would rather suffer extremity than be subject to England'.[43] In May Beaton drew together the opposition of the kirkmen in a convention of the clergy in St Andrews.[44] This did not succeed in blocking official agreement, but the treaties in their final form were clearly designed to safeguard Scottish sovereignty, through their recognition of the liberties and freedoms of the realm, and acknowledgement of the

[39] *SSP* i. 145; Merriman, *Rough Wooings*, 122.
[40] *LP*, vol. xviii/1, nos. 124, 157, 318, 324, 391.
[41] Ibid., no. 348.
[42] *SSP* i. 233–4; Sanderson, *Cardinal of Scotland*, 167.
[43] *APS* ii. 411–13; *LP*, vol. xviii/1, no. 325.
[44] *SSP*, i. 187–9.

auld alliance with France.[45] Henry's demand for the immediate delivery of Queen Mary to England had caused 'great sticking' until he finally agreed that she should remain in Scotland until the age of 10.[46] He had evidently been unwilling to leave her to the mercies of the factious Scottish nobles, but his insistence on her removal to England, despite heartfelt objections from the Scottish parliament and the ambassadors James Learmonth and Henry Balnaves, demonstrated an overbearing refusal to compromise.[47] Henry abandoned entirely the more reasoned and subtle approach taken by Cromwell during the 1530s, when English embassies to Scotland held out the implicit suggestion (whatever the English opinion on Scotland's status might really have been), that the alliance they sought would be one of Protestant equals. Under James V the initiatives had come to nothing, but in 1543 a more conciliatory bearing might have made some headway with the wary Scots. Instead, Henry's impatience at their objections to things 'that be faisible ynough!' merely added to fears that his true intention was conquest and subjugation.[48]

The short-lived official Protestant reformation was brought to an abrupt end with Arran's defection to the cardinal's party in September 1543. Only days after the final ratification of the Greenwich Treaties, Arran received absolution at the cardinal's hands in the house of the Stirling Greyfriars. He admitted that 'by his consente the Freres of Dundee was sakked', and gave his assurance that he would henceforth support the profession of monks and friars.[49] This was a triumph for Beaton and his orthodox supporters, but in truth Henry's project for a Scottish reformation had been limping along for some time. Arran's early enthusiasm for English-style reform was probably genuine, but he seems to have been swayed both by the powerful presence in government of Beaton and Hamilton, and by a persistent hope that his son rather than Henry's might marry the Scottish queen.[50] Though saying the right things to English ambassadors, he was noticeably reluctant to proceed with the dissolution of the religious houses, a measure guaranteed to arouse the wrath of the churchmen. Neither did Henry's 'King's Book' achieve the hoped-for impact in Scotland, Sadler admitting to the council, 'I see not that the same is liked much of any party here'.[51] Arran's Protestant preachers disappeared from court, and, more worryingly for

[45] *LP*, vol. xviii/1, no. 804; Sanderson, *Cardinal of Scotland*, 166.

[46] *LP*, vol. xviii/1, no. 664; *SSP* i. 212.

[47] *LP*, vol. xviii/1, no. 402; Jenny Wormald, *Mary Queen of Scots: A Study in Failure* (George Philip, 1988), 57–8.

[48] *HP*, vol. ii, no. 60.

[49] Ibid., no. 30.

[50] Merriman, *Rough Wooings*, 135.   [51] *SSP* i. 129, 264.

England, so too did leading Anglophiles such as Maxwell, Somerville, Rothes, Gray, and Balnaves, all of them imprisoned by the cardinal.[52] All this posed a serious question mark over the implementation of the treaties.

The reversal in Henry's fortunes was indicative of the turbulent atmosphere in government and wider Edinburgh society. Expressions of fierce anti-English feeling in the city combined patriotic resentment and opposition to England's version of reform. Ill feeling was immeasurably worsened by Henry's command in September for the seizure of Scottish merchant ships allegedly trespassing in English waters, an ill-disguised measure of retaliation for Arran's betrayal.[53] Even before this Sadler feared for his personal safety, writing to Henry in July, 'such malicious and dispiteful people, I think, live not in the world, as is the common people of this realm'. Only days later he was shot at while walking outside his Edinburgh lodging, and he was specifically blamed for incidents of mob violence at religious houses in Dundee and Edinburgh itself, the charge being levelled 'that the onely cause of my lyeng here is to put downe the Kyrke'.[54] The iconoclastic episodes themselves indicated that distaste for reforming ideas was by no means universal, but at the end of 1543 the climate in Edinburgh was vehemently xenophobic, and was inflamed further by England's warlike preparations. The hostility to England therefore owed as much to Henry's governmental ambitions in Scotland and his assault on mercantile interests as to distaste for English reforming intentions. Although pockets of support for reform had come to light in Edinburgh, Dundee, Perth, and other parts of the country, suspicion of Henry's intentions was a more widely shared sentiment. The very term 'English' became an insult, and Angus, Maxwell, and Glencairn lost no time in pointing out how they were exposed to ridicule and resentment for their loyalties.[55] English efforts could not dent Beaton's large popular following in St Andrews and beyond, whose Catholic and French sympathies were in direct competition with Henry's aims. The dowager and cardinal together encouraged this opposition, using the language of the halykirk, commonwealth, and liberties of the realm, and warning that to ally with England would be 'to precipitate themselves voluntarily into everlasting slavery'.[56]

By the end of the year Beaton appeared firmly in the ascendant, as the

[52] Ibid. 158; Knox, i. 105–6; Edington, *Court and Culture*, 60.

[53] *HP*, vol. ii, no. 10; Lynch, *Edinburgh*, 68.

[54] *SSP*, i. 235, 237; *HP*, vol. ii, no. 14.

[55] *HP*, vol. ii, no. 11; Kirk, 'Religion of Early Scottish Protestants', 391–2; *LP*, vol. xviii/1, no. 374; *SSP* i. 165–6.

[56] *The Scottish Correspondence of Mary of Lorraine, 1543–1560*, ed. Annie I. Cameron (Edinburgh: SHS, 3rd ser. 10; 1927), no. 32; Buchanan, *History*, ii. 330–1.

December parliament repudiated the Greenwich Treaties, reaffirmed the auld alliance, and appointed the cardinal to be chancellor of the realm.[57] On paper, all English progress was overturned, although the popular reforming activity in Edinburgh and a number of other towns hinted at currents of opinion which did not fit neatly into the anti-English and pro-Catholic mould encouraged by the cardinal's supporters. Parliament took the opportunity, however, to reinstate acts 'aganis heretikis and thar dampnable opinionis incontrar the fayth and lawis of halykirk', and early in the new year, Beaton presided over heresy trials in Perth which led to a number of executions.[58] Shortly afterwards, Henry's leading noble allies, Angus, Douglas, Glencairn, Cassillis, and Lennox, were reconciled with the Scottish government, offering to contribute to its 'trew and manlie resistence of our auld innemes of Ingland'.[59] Though Douglas assured the king that their hearts were still with England, there was little cause for English optimism at the start of 1544.

IV. THE RENEWAL OF CAMPAIGNING

Henry's fury at the duplicity of his so-called 'friends' was predictable. They had mishandled the exceptional opportunity offered to him at the start of 1543 to solve his security concerns and religious isolation at almost no cost, and he intended that they would suffer for it. Revenge raids on the lands of Douglas and others were followed in the spring by a major assault on Edinburgh and the lowlands. The notorious instructions given to the earl of Hertford on 10 April 1544 were that he should 'put all to fyre and swoorde, burne Edinborough towne, so rased and defaced when you have sacked and gotten what ye can of it, as there may remayn forever a perpetual memory of the vengeance of God lightened upon [them] for their faulse-hode and disloyailtye'.[60] The campaign marked a qualitative change in official English policy in Scotland. Henry now, as he had done briefly in 1542, abandoned all pretence of a will for amicable union. The price in protracted negotiations, complex conditions, and the pacification of hostile elements in the Scottish government was far too high. He would attempt to secure fulfilment of the treaties by beating the Scots into submission, and if they remained stubborn they would at least be in no state to contemplate further opposition.

[57] *APS* ii. 429–31, 442.
[58] Ibid. 443; Knox, i. 117–18.
[59] *LP*, vol. xix/1, nos. 24, 33.
[60] *HP*, vol. ii, no. 154; BL Add. MS 32654, fo. 81ʳ (*HP*, vol. ii, no. 207).

The warfare, continuing for the rest of Henry's reign and into that of Edward VI, was thus a punitive and practical exercise. Its primary object was to lay to waste as much land as possible, destroying towns and supplies, and leaving the Scots subdued and chastened. Amid this broad devastation Henry ensured that the real targets of his wrath, the churchmen, were clearly marked out. There was a conspicuous religious dimension to the campaigning, as the king wished to leave the Scots in no doubt as to the folly of their persistence in the doctrines of Rome and loyalty to the cardinal. The religious houses of the borders and lowlands were principal targets for English armies; partly for their wealth and importance as focal points for communities, but also for their symbolism of Scotland's stubborn adherence to the old religion. Having been unable to convince Arran to suppress them by the authority of government, Henry ordered his armies to level their buildings to the ground. The abbeys of Holyrood, Newbattle, Coldingham, Jedburgh, Kelso, Melrose, and Dryburgh were assaulted in 1544–5, along with churches and religious houses in Haddington, Eccles, and Roxburgh, and the popular Loretto shrine near Musselburgh.[61] Many of the same buildings suffered again in 1547, when Somerset's raids extended as far north as Balmerino and Dundee.[62]

English captains took some grim satisfaction in reporting to Henry, and later the protector, Somerset, their exploits in this regard. In September 1544 Sir Brian Layton captured 'many monkes and chanons' on the borders, and in October 1547 Lord Wharton told Somerset that the submission of a number of Dumfries Greyfriars, was 'no litle comfort for the ynglyshmen to see'.[63] In a notable incident of 1547 Sir John Luttrell, a commander of the English forces, was 'elect abbot' of the abbey of Inch Colm, being 'stalled in his see thear accordyngly' with his 'coovent' of hackbutters and other soldiers.[64] For their part, some of the Scottish armies fought under Catholic standards and in defence of orthodoxy against English heresies. William Patten, a member of Somerset's armies at Pinkie, described 'a banner of whyte sarcenet' on which was painted a woman representing the Roman Church, 'makynge her peticion unto Christ her husbond, that he woold not now forget her, his spouse, beyng skourged and

---

[61] 'The late expedicion into Scotlande . . . 1544', in Dalyell (ed.), *Fragments*, 9, 11–12, 14–15; David McRoberts, 'Material Destruction caused by the Scottish Reformation', in McRoberts (ed.), *Essays*, 421–3; *Diurnal*, 32, 40.

[62] McRoberts, 'Material Destruction', 424; Ian B. Cowan and David E. Easson, *Medieval Religious Houses: Scotland . . .*, 2nd edn. (Longman, 1976), 27.

[63] *HP*, vol. ii, no. 318; *CSP Dom. Add.*, pp. 336–7; PRO SP 15/1, fo. 122ᵛ (*CSP Dom. Add.*, p. 345).

[64] Patten, 'Expedicion into Scotlande', 81.

persecuted, meanynge at this tyme by us'.[65] Conversely, the English presented their efforts as the execution of a righteous punishment upon the ungodly Scots. This interpretation was elaborated by later Protestant historians who saw the whole episode as a sorry precursor of the Protestant victory of 1559.[66]

The targeting of religious buildings and property could not be expected to advance English reforming interests north of the border, except in the purely practical sense of demolishing the material possessions of churchmen, and interrupting their religious devotions. In 1544, however, it apparently did something to satisfy Henry's desire for revenge on Beaton, whom he singled out as the block to all his endeavours in Scotland. Proclamations issued at the height of the war impressed upon the Scots that 'the very grounde and occasion of this your trouble and calamities, which now God by his mighty hande, sendeth uppon youe, is the Cardynal', whose corrupt influence upon Arran had brought the realm 'to the imminent ruyne and miserye wherin youe nowe see it'.[67] English armies were instructed to do particular hurt to Beaton, and 'so to spoyle and turne upset downe the Cardinalles town of St Andrews, as thupper stone may be the nether, and not one stick stande by an other'. Lord Seton was punished with particular severity, a report of Hertford's raids of 1544 recording, 'We dyd hym ye more despyt, because he was the cheife laborer to helpe theyr cardynall out of pryson, the onely auctour of theyr calamytie.'[68]

Henry's animosity towards Beaton related not just to the cardinal's ingratitude towards offers of advancement if he would only leave his red hat and support the English alliance. Beaton's unshakeable adherence to Rome was a constant reminder to the king of the European dimension to his security fears. During the 1540s the prospect of another Catholic league against England seemed remote, and events of 1539 had demonstrated to Henry that, even under optimum conditions, the Catholic princes of Europe were singularly unwilling to combine against him. He could not, however, ignore the possibility that one or more might heed the calls of the pope for action against his schismatic realm. Beaton had not been slow to inform Rome of the renewed danger from 'the contagion of English impiety', and, remarkably, Arran himself was begging Paul III to commit the kingdom to his protection, even as he was simultaneously assuring Henry of his forwardness for reform.[69] Beaton was also in contact with Pole, Henry's

[65] Ibid. 72–3.
[66] Ibid. 11, 75; Knox, i. 122; Calderwood, i. 178.
[67] *HP*, vol. ii, no. 222.
[68] Ibid., no. 207; Patten, 'Expedicion into Scotlande', 9.
[69] *LP*, vol. xviii/1, nos. 494, 542, 543.

implacable opponent, still at large in Rome during the 1540s. The Scottish cardinal had secret correspondence with Pole and received his servants in Scotland on at least one occasion.[70] Sadler's comparison of the traitorous Beaton with 'our cardinal Poole' was intended as a warning to Arran, but was a telling comment on Henry's own suspicion of their associations.[71]

Papal involvement in the Anglo-Scottish conflict from 1543–4, and the reappearance of the troublesome Pole brought unwelcome echoes of the legations of the 1530s, when orthodox European powers had taken note of Scotland's strategic potential. In October 1543 another papal legate, Marco Grimani, was sent to Scotland, where he was well received by Beaton and his fellow churchmen. He was sympathetic to their plight, and he dramatized their misfortunes for the sake of securing further aid from Rome, writing to Cardinal Farnese that the realm was divided and full of heresy, and 'unless God provide for it, they shall shortly hear of Scotland what they hear of England'.[72] Although he 'maid greit promisse to the Governour and estaittis of the realme, of support for thair defence aganis Ingland' his actual contribution to the government's war effort was minimal, as he himself recognized in a letter of apology to Mary of Guise.[73] His presence did, however, help to foster Scottish contacts with Catholic Europe, which were, in any case, in a healthy state due to the Guise interest in Scotland.

The Franco-Scottish connection that the Scots had refused to relinquish during the negotiations of 1543 was intensely frustrating to Henry, as it ran so immediately counter to his own interests in Scotland. England's ferocious campaigning in the mid-1540s brought in numerous French advisers and troops on the side of the government party headed by Mary of Guise and Beaton. The two had formed a somewhat uneasy alliance following a failed bid by the dowager to establish her own party during 1544, but their attachment to France provided a common bond.[74] The revolt of Arran and later Angus to their camp, together with Lennox's flight to England in the summer of 1544, further strengthened their hand against England.[75] Henry's fortunes in France, meanwhile, suffered when Charles V abandoned a joint Anglo-imperial campaign to sue for a separate peace with

[70] *LP*, vol. xx/1, nos. 30, 508, 696.

[71] *LP*, vol. xviii/1, no. 572.

[72] Merriman, *Rough Wooings*, 166–7; *Scottish Correspondence*, no. 27; *LP*, vol. xviii/2, no. 299.

[73] John Leslie, *History of Scotland from the Death of James I, in the Year 1436, to 1561* (Edinburgh: Bannatyne Society, 1830), 179–80; *Foreign Correspondence with Marie de Lorraine from the Originals in the Balcarres Papers, i. 1537–1548*, ed. Marguerite Wood, 2 vols. (Edinburgh: SHS, 3rd ser. 4, 1923), no. 71.

[74] *Scottish Correspondence*, nos. 84, 86, 90.

[75] Calderwood, i. 178.

Francis I at Crépy. Against this background of tense wars on two fronts, rumours that the French were also planning to invade Ireland, and set up the exiled Kildare figurehead Gerald Fitzgerald, were an unwelcome complication. Henry had been aware for some time of the French claim that Fitzgerald was 'King off Yrland, and that the King our master hathe disheretyd him of hys ryght'.[76] Their plans for action in both Ireland and Scotland revived all Henry's concerns over the vulnerability of his borderlands.

V. PROTESTANT PROGRESS AND THE ASSURING PHENOMENON

The rallying of Catholic powers around Scotland in the face of English assaults in the 1540s reinforced the impression created by Beaton and his allies of an aggressively Protestant English regime bringing its full force to bear on the embattled Catholics of Scotland. Scottish resistance to the godly union intended by the Greenwich Treaties continued to be expressed in terms that identified the defence of the commonwealth and liberties of the realm with traditional religious loyalties. This equation, however, was not a universal one. The background of humanist and reforming debate in the country, and the instances of group activity by Protestant sympathisers in 1543–4 indicated that a significant body of opinion might be prepared to challenge the orthodox patriotic line. In their conduct of the war in these years, English armies focused on taking advantage of reforming sentiment where it existed, and attempting to foster it in areas where it was absent, in the hope that this would bolster support for the marriage scheme. Their interventions in Scotland evidently aroused very mixed feelings from the native population, but the various signs of reforming zeal from the Scots offered the English their best hope of finding allies in their 'godly purpose'.

The principal English weapon in securing a firm Protestant commitment from the Scots was that of assurance. This was a conventional tactic of war, whereby individuals would effectively become collaborators with the opposing army, offering pledges and receiving protection and sometimes payment as reward. Both Henry and Somerset used the system systematically, and on an unprecedented scale during the 1540s.[77] On one level it referred to the high-ranking Scottish 'friends' who pledged themselves to further English interests in return for pensions, but it was increasingly used

---

[76] Palmer, *Henry VIII*, 74–5; Morgan, 'British Policies', 74; *SP* vol. iii, no. 306.
[77] M. H. Merriman, 'The Assured Scots: Scottish Collaborators with England during the Rough Wooing', *SHR* 47 (1968), 12–13; Lynch, *Scotland*, 206.

to bind non-noble individuals and groups to the English cause. The total number of assured Scots can only be guessed at, but according to this wider definition, there were several thousand at the height of the English efforts.[78] The place of religious motivation in the decision to assure is a problematic issue. As Marcus Merriman has demonstrated, a multitude of secular reasons could play their part, with many committing themselves to England through the hope of financial gain, obligation to social superiors, or simple fear. In the face of the invading armies, there were compelling reasons to consider assuring 'for safty of tham, thar wyf barnis and gudis'.[79] On the border, kin groups often assured en masse: 56 Crosiers, 32 Nixsons, and 24 Ollyvers took assurance in Teviotdale in June 1544.[80] From the English point of view, the usefulness of assuring lay in the potential which it offered for a relatively cheap and simple extension of royal authority, as with the concurrent surrender and regrant scheme launched by the government in Ireland.[81]

The evangelical dynamic behind the assuring phenomenon, however, should not be underestimated. In the first instance, the opportunity to secure English protection under the banner of reform offered to some Scots in occupied areas the option of remaining in their native country, and yet practising their reformed beliefs. The steady stream of religious exiles to England slowed considerably after 1543 as more and more took advantage of this. By remaining in Scotland, Protestant enthusiasts were, in fact, rather better off than their countrymen in England, who found the religious regime of Henry's later years less godly than they would have liked. Seton, Willock, and Wishart were among a number of Scots who attracted adverse attention from English authorities for their Protestant proselytizing during the 1540s.[82] A handful of exiles did still make their way to England on the grounds of the danger they were in for their faith. David Maitland arrived in 1544, having been 'trublit for the useng off the New Testament'. He was received into English pay and became a spy for Lord Wharton under the alias 'Ze wait quha'. James Skea, a chaplain from Orkney, left Scotland during the reign of Edward, 'for fear of burnyng for the word of God', and was also granted a pension by the government.[83] Increasing numbers, however, became staunch supporters of Protestantism within Scotland.

The religious overtones to the practice of assuring could be marked. The

[78] *CSP Dom. Add.*, pp. 331, 346.
[79] Merriman, 'Assured Scots', 18–21.
[80] *LP*, vol. xix/1, nos. 641, 692.
[81] Morgan, 'British Policies', 73.
[82] Ch. 1, Sect. VII.
[83] *LP*, vol. xix/1, no. 1021; vol. xxi/1, no. 958; *CSP Scot.*, vol. i, no. 206.

circumstances of the English reformation lent new weight to the notion of making a covenant with the godly king Henry, and later Edward. The taking of an oath on the New Testament, and conclusion of the ceremony with the 'kissing of the buik with all the solempnities of the said assurance'[84] were acts redolent with the symbolism of acceptance of the evangel. Oaths frequently contained religious clauses, with Lennox, Angus, Cassillis, and Glencairn being required in March 1544 to 'cause the worde of God to be truely taught and preched among them, and in their countreys, as the mere and only fundation from whens procedeth all truth and honour'.[85] The wearing of the red cross of the English army by the assured was another rite infused with meaning. It was on one level an emblem of English patriotism, but it had potent religious significance as a reminder of the cross that appeared in a vision to the Emperor Constantine before he went into battle. Aside from the contentious claims to imperial hegemony associated with Tudor references to Constantine, contemporaries were well aware of the evangelical significance of 'the English badge, the reid crosse'.[86] As far as some Scots were concerned, it was a repellent image, and in retaliation to England's appropriation of this symbol, Scottish churchmen used their own version of the cross to rally opposition to the invading troops. Ormiston informed Somerset that 'ane certan of schurll preistis' had 'dewyset the fyer crois to pais throwcht the realme, als sowine as yowr graice army taikis Scots grownd'.[87]

As the taking of assurances developed into a large-scale phenomenon during the course of the wars, instances of insincere religious conversions, betrayals, and general duplicity among England's supposed adherents inevitably multiplied. Henry had long complained of the 'crafty jugglings' of his noble friends, and the defeat inflicted on the English at Ancrum Moor in February 1545 gave an even more spectacular demonstration of the dangers of blanket assuring. Here, the high-level defection of Angus was mirrored on the battleground by the desertion of the assured Scots of Teviotdale and the Merse. The reliability of the surnames in these areas had long been suspected, and they were universally blamed by the English for the overthrow.[88] Such incidents give ammunition to the argument that the religious impact of assuring was fatally diluted when applied across entire regions. Clearly this could occasionally be the case. The Scottish informer Ninian Cockburn told Wharton in October 1547 that he was

[84] *CSP Scot.*, vol. i, no. 63; Merriman, 'Assured Scots', 15.
[85] *CSP Dom. Add.*, p. 341; *LP*, vol. xix/1, no. 522; *SP*, vol. iv, no. 492.
[86] *Complaynt of Scotlande*, 218–19.   [87] *TA* viii, 408; *CSP Scot.*, vol. i, no. 40.
[88] *LP*, vol. xix/1, no. 297; vol. xx/1, nos. 253, 285, 301.

grieved to see his countrymen feigning support for reform, 'more for your pleasour then for Goddes sake!'.[89]

For at least some of the assured Scots, however, the aim of godly reform was paramount. Among England's genuine supporters were men such as Sir John Borthwick, and Dr Michael Durham, a former physician of James V, who entered English service along with his brother, Henry Durham. They, and a number of their fellow countrymen, put themselves entirely at the disposal of the Henrician and Edwardian regimes, travelling between the countries on intelligence-gathering missions, and offering opinions on the union.[90] Advice on the best means of making it a reality came from many quarters. One John Elder, who described himself as a Highland redshank, sent the king a topographical description of the Scottish realm. An accompanying letter played heavily on Henry's distrust of 'the Dewils convocacion, and the father of mischeif, Dauid Beton ther cardinall, with beelzebubs flesmongers, the abbotes and their adherentes'; but offered the more uplifting hope that 'boithe the realmes of England and of Scotland may be joynede in one; and so our noble Maiestie for to be superiour and kynge'.[91] Henry and Somerset also received enthusiastic recommendations on the godly conjunction from James Henrisoun, an Edinburgh merchant, who espoused the cause with true evangelical fervour. His writings on the subject commended him to Henry, and he was taken into English pay.[92] The efforts of Henrisoun and others assisted the English in their acquisition of information, dissemination of propaganda, and extension of their power base in lowland Scotland.

Only a minority of the assured Scots were so explicit about their attachment to reform, but the overall significance of the evangelical dimension of assuring seems to be greater than has sometimes been suggested. It was an adaptable practice and might be framed entirely in secular terms, for short-term military purposes; but its ritual, ceremonial, badge of uniform, and godly rhetoric could give it an unmistakably Protestant flavour. That this was sometimes lost amid the confusion and disruption of war was not surprising, and the evangelical impulse gave no guarantee that assurances would be taken in the same spirit by the Scots. The English hoped, however, to use assuring as a means of bringing order and justice to areas traditionally considered both lawless and godless; their intentions towards

---

[89] *CSP Scot.*, vol. i, no. 73.

[90] *APC*, i, 450; ii. 114, 157, 172, 227, 242; *LP*, vol. xix/1, nos. 234, 589.

[91] BL Harleian MS 289, fos. 4–5; BL Royal MS 18A xxxviii, fos. 1–17; *Miscellany of the Bannatyne Society*, ed. D. Laing (Edinburgh: Bannatyne Society, 1827), i. 7–8.

[92] *LP*, vol. xxi/1, nos. 462, 979.

the savage Irishry being much the same.[93] As Shrewsbury wrote to Henry, the borders had long lived without justice, 'yet in tyme, after they have felt the swetnes, wealthe and quyetnes, that maye growe of the same, we doubte not but it shalbe very acceptable to them'. Somerset, too, believed that 'when they see the effect and commodity of it, they will embrace it'.[94]

Where contracts were entered into for resolutely secular reasons, the prolonged contact of the assured Scots with English armies and literature, sometimes over periods of years, could create a reforming interest where none had previously existed. Henry sent Lennox to the borders in 1545, the Scottish government suspected, 'in the intent to lawbour and solist the bordoraris of this part and utheris gentill men of thir countreis that he may mak be his lawbour and the king of Ingland monye to tak the faith of Ingland'; and Somerset aimed to make use of captive Scottish friars, 'if any of them be hable to preche to doo so, and expose thabuses heretofore crept in amonges them'.[95] Scottish castigation of those who betrayed their country by assuring also recognized its religious significance. A government letter to the sheriff of Roxburgh in 1544 called for urgent preparations on the borders to resist the English, who 'will nocht faill to draw the inabytouris thairof to thair faytht and opunyoun of Ingland'. Lord Methven, summarizing for the dowager 'quhat is the caus that Inglis men is fawvorit and the auttorite nocht obeyit nor servit', decided that the primary reason was that 'part of the legis has tayn new apoynzionis of the scriptour'.[96] Some opponents of England even entered into competing Catholic assurances. Walter Ker of Cesford and Walter Scot of Branxholme ended their feud in 1546 to bind themselves 'be the faith and treuthis in thair bodyis, the haly Evangellis tuichet, under the pane of perjure and infamete', to resist the English.[97]

The religious dynamic of the practice of assuring could therefore be a powerful weapon for either side in the conduct of the war. The English particularly welcomed the evangelical commitment of men such as Alexander Crichton of Brunstone and John Cockburn of Ormiston, whose regional standing in the Lothians made them useful allies.[98] They aligned themselves with England in the early stages of the Rough Wooing, and when they were penalized by their own government for their 'diverse and enorme

---

[93] Brendan Bradshaw, 'The Tudor Reformation and Revolution in Wales and Ireland: The Origins of the British Problem', in Bradshaw and Morrill (eds.), *British Problem*, 54–5.

[94] *HP*, vol. ii, no. 386; *CSP Dom. Add.*, p. 340.

[95] *Scottish Correspondence*, no. 94; PRO SP 15/1, fo. 107ʳ (*CSP Dom. Add.*, pp. 340–1).

[96] *HP*, vol. ii, no. 364; *Scottish Correspondence*, no. 172.

[97] *RPC* i. 22–3.

[98] Merriman, 'Assured Scots', 23–4.

crymes' in this regard, the English made sure they were well rewarded.[99]
The extent of Ormiston and Brunstone's Protestant fervour could be seen
in their protection of the reformer George Wishart, who returned from
England to embark on an eighteen-month preaching tour of the Lothians,
the east coast, and Ayrshire in 1544–5. Along with several other local lairds,
including John Lockhart of Bar, they risked their safety to accommodate
and provide for Wishart, whose Zwinglian-influenced sermons attracted
large audiences in Montrose, Dundee, Ayr, Leith, and a number of other
towns. Ultimately, Wishart could not escape the agents of Beaton, sent to
track him down early in 1546.[100] The trial and execution of the reformer,
however, only strengthened the resolve of the most passionate Scottish
adherents of Protestantism; and they looked to England to support their
hopes for reform.

VI. THE CASTILIAN ENTERPRISE, 1546–1547

The zeal of a core group of assured Scots gave a timely boost to English
endeavours in Scotland. Through their actions and writings they brought
to life the ideal of a Protestant partnership, helping to sustain the hopes of
other Anglophiles north of the border. Naturally enough, Henry did what
he could to maintain this enthusiasm, offering pensions and promises to
bind them to the English cause. The force of their fervent reforming interest, however, was not easily controlled. The king's encouragement of his
Scottish allies bred in a small minority an expectation of imminent and
revolutionary change, to be achieved with the full backing of the reformed
English regime. They would only later discover that Henry was not
prepared to play the part of their Protestant saviour. The hardening of the
English Church towards its evangelical wing was at this time claiming some
prominent victims, among them not only figures such as Anne Askew, but
also a number of exiled Scots. One 'Dodd, a Scotchman', was burned in
Calais, having been apprehended in possession of certain German books,
and in 1546 an anonymous Scottish friar, judged 'more mete for Dunbar,
then for London' through his lack of learning, was committed to the Tower
for his associations with the convicted heretic Dr Edward Crome.[101]
Henry's concern over the unleashing of religious radicals by the introduction of reform to Scotland had been signalled in his advice to Arran in 1543.

[99] *RPC* i. 82; *APC* ii. 178–9, 318, 365.
[100] Lynch, *Scotland*, 187; Edington, *Court and Culture*, 172–3; Knox, i. 125–37.
[101] Foxe, v. 523; *SP*, vol. ii, nos. 243, 244, 246; *APC* i. 418–19.

His difficulty, however, was that in loyal and willing activists such as Ormiston, Brunstone, and Rothes lay his best hope of effecting the marriage and union scheme. Whether the king liked it or not, the Protestant rallying cry was invaluable in casting English campaigning as a godly crusade against the popish oppressions of the kirkmen who fronted Scottish opposition.

Henry was drawn into the role of liberator of the troubled Scottish Protestants through his ill-judged involvement in the plotting behind the assassination of Beaton in 1546. A conspiracy against the cardinal had been brewing for some years, but the deciding factor for those involved was his responsibility for the execution of Wishart, their spokesman in the cause of reform.[102] Beaton's murder, as the event that precipitated a full-blown rebellion against the government, was a crisis point for its perpetrators and their Protestant supporters in Scotland. The fact that it took place with the backing of Henry and his council, perhaps even at the king's instigation, brought England directly into the governmental confusion that followed. Henry, it was clear, had never intended to plunge so far into the turbulent affairs of the Scottish rebels. He had been seduced by the scheme against Beaton, first brought to his attention in 1544, thanks to its promise to remove from the Scottish political scene his most persistent and worrisome opponent, and the author of the reversals of 1543. The king had been reminded all too recently of Beaton's dangerous connections with Pole, Rome, and English Catholic exiles on the continent. When Brunstone, Norman Leslie of Rothes, and their fellow conspirators approached him with a proposal to remove permanently the 'worker of all your mischief', therefore, Henry seized at the chance. Sadler informed Brunstone that, although the king would not become involved, 'it were an acceptable service to God to take him out of the way'.[103]

The deed was eventually carried out on 29 May 1546, the cardinal being surprised in his own castle of St Andrews by a group which included Norman Leslie, William Kirkcaldy, and John Leslie of Parkhill.[104] With the murder accomplished, events moved on with a startling momentum. The perpetrators took possession of the castle, where supporters from the town and surrounding area swiftly joined them.[105] All demands from Arran's government for their surrender were refused, and they awaited the English aid that would transform their coup into nothing less than the overthrow of the established religion, and the government with it, should there be any

---

[102] Knox, i. 169–72.
[103] *HP*, vol. ii, nos. 218, 223; *LP*, vol. xx/1, nos. 1106, 1178.
[104] Sanderson, *Cardinal of Scotland*, 225–7; Knox, i. 174–7.
[105] Keith, *History*, i. 124.

attempt to impede them. From Henry's perspective, such a sequel was entirely unexpected, and even more unwelcome. With the successful removal of Beaton, an act applauded by his ministers, the king's purposes were fulfilled. Henry did not wish to risk further action on behalf of the rebels, which would leave him open to the charge of contravening the recent peace with France, in which Scotland was comprehended. For the Castilians, however, this was simply the start of their ambitions.

The Scottish government was aware of the religious challenge it faced, and parliament responded to the dishonouring of the clerical estate with an act of 1546 against the damaging and spoiling of religious buildings. Arran informed the pope that Beaton had been 'treacherously slain', and an envoy was sent to Rome to appeal for assistance against the English-aided rebels.[106] Nevertheless, as the months passed and the Castilians remained at large in St Andrews, their Protestant following grew. While they fortified themselves within the castle and prepared to withstand the hostile forces sent by the governor to besiege them, they made full use of this opportunity to set out their reforming agenda. Among the new arrivals was John Rough, one-time chaplain to Arran, who took on the role of preacher to the brethren in the castle. Early in 1547 Rough was instrumental in launching the preaching career of John Knox, previously a member of Wishart's retinue, and now in the castle as tutor to the sons of Ormiston and Sir Hugh Douglas of Longniddry. According to Knox's own account, nothing had been further from his mind than to lead the Protestant campaign, but the persuasions of Rough and the godly inhabitants of St Andrews brought him to a realization of his vocation.[107] Both Knox and Rough preached in the parish church of the Holy Trinity and engaged in public disputations with their orthodox critics, having considerable contact with the inhabitants of Fife, and sympathetic members of the government, such as Lindsay.[108]

The Castilians eagerly exploited their chance to embark on an unofficial reformation in St Andrews during their fourteen months in the town. They were unable to extend their efforts beyond this corner of Fife, however, because their dynamic action in the weeks immediately following the murder was not matched on the part of the English government. The plan to take over the cardinal's castle, making it the base for a challenge to the governor, had formed no part of the plotters' negotiations with England. Henry wished to keep his part in the murder entirely covert, and his think-ing on official religious change continued to require first and foremost that

[106] *APS* ii. 470; *LP*, vol. xxi/2, nos. 6, 277.

[107] Spottiswoode, *History*, i. 168; Knox, i. 184–9.

[108] Knox, i. 193, 201–2; Calderwood, i. 229–30; Edington, *Court and Culture*, 62–4.

it be 'semely and in order'.[109] His encouragement of the subversive scheme to kill the cardinal had led Rothes and his accomplices to expect more intervention than Henry was ready to countenance. In consequence, the Castilians spent an uncomfortable few months receiving the minimum of military supplies and victuals needed to defend themselves against besieging government forces, but deprived of the major expeditionary force for which they had hoped.[110] They managed to despatch envoys to England, who were favourably received to the disgust of the official ambassador, Otterburn, but Henry would not take any drastic steps on their behalf. Eventually the Castilians themselves arranged an appointment with the governor for a cessation of hostilities until absolution for their crime arrived from Rome.[111]

It was while Otterburn was still in London, in January 1547, that Henry died. As far as the Castilians were concerned, the accession of the young Edward VI and swift installation of Somerset as protector held out some faint hope that they might receive more assertive English backing. Somerset's confirmation of his intention to assist them as the late king had wished was reassuring, as was the careful continuation of the wages of those inside the castle, and pensions to England's leading supporters.[112] Over the months, however, the Castilians had lost the advantage of their surprise action, and in June 1547 a French expeditionary force arrived in Scotland ahead of the English navy. The result was the submission of the castle to the French, and the removal of the Castilians to various places of imprisonment in France, or, as in Knox's case, to the galleys.[113] Knox would later see England's effective desertion of the Castilians as part of God's punishment for their reported licentiousness and high living in the castle;[114] but the more prosaic explanation lay in both Henry's and Somerset's reluctance to underwrite such a risky enterprise in a climate of diplomatic uncertainty.

VII. SOMERSET AND THE REVIVAL OF THE GODLY UNION

The ambitions of a radical minority thus ended in defeat and imprisonment. Henry's own plans for godly union had been wholly different, and at the king's death, Somerset was unable to devise a satisfactory solution to the

---

[109] 'King's Book', sig. Aiii^r.
[110] *SP*, vol. ii, nos. 252, 254; *TA* ix. 29.
[111] Knox, i. 182; *LP*, vol. xxi/2, nos. 455, 461, 524, 580, 611; *RPC* i. 58.
[112] *APC* ii. 12–13.
[113] *Diurnal*, p. 44; Keith, *History*, i. 128–30.
[114] Knox, i. 204–5.

Castilian episode. The incompatibility of the aims of the Scottish rebels and the English king had reflected the gulf between their interpretations of the purpose of their alliance: while Henry was always interested primarily in neutralizing any potential threat from Scotland, the party he had cultivated in Scotland was developing a more visionary view of their co-operation. The new protector was, by inclination, far readier to countenance the idea of radical reforming activity, whether north or south of the border. He was, however, held back by his need to maintain the friendship of Charles V, particularly following recent French intervention in Scotland.[115] The atmosphere in court and government at the start of the new reign was there-fore one of more convinced, but decidedly cautious, Protestantism. Otterburn deduced that there would be no substantive change in English policy towards Scotland, and gloomily told the dowager and council, 'I see na thing bot as the ald kyng wer levyng and ilk day I heir of our infelicite'.[116] This impression, however, was not entirely accurate. Somerset pledged himself to revive the flagging marriage and union project; but he did so in the firm belief that the Protestant conjunction was both right and necessary for the welfare of both kingdoms. While sharing the defensive concerns that had motivated Henry, he displayed a stronger ideological commitment to the plan, and genuine desire to become the liberator of Scottish Protestants.

Somerset's credentials for the role were dubious: his personal Protestant convictions were undoubted, but his bloody campaigning record in Scotland made him an unlikely figurehead for the Scots. Nevertheless, the protector made an appeal to the inhabitants of Scotland, in his *Epistle or Exhortacion to Unitie and Peace*, to forget former differences and look to the innumerable benefits that would ensue from a peaceful conjunction. James Henrisoun, Somerset's close associate and adviser, took up the same theme in his *Exhortacion to the Scottes to conform themselfes to the honorable, Expedient & godly Union* and *Godly and Golden Book*. Just as Henrisoun's works were 'corrected and defended' by the protector, so Henrisoun almost certainly had some input into Somerset's writings. Their tracts made vivid use of a number of central images, notably that of an island severed from the rest of the world, and the complete body or family, perfect in all its constituent parts. On these grounds they urged the wisdom and value of an alliance based on a common faith.[117] In Henrisoun's *Exhortacion*, the figure of Britain made a stirring plea for a union founded on the truth of God's

[115] M. L. Bush, *The Government Policy of Protector Somerset* (E. Arnold, 1975), 2–3.

[116] *Scottish Correspondence*, no. 130.

[117] *Complaynt of Scotlande*, 238–46, 208–36; *CSP Scot.*, vol. i, no. 285; Mason, 'Anglo-British Imperialism', 170–5.

word, asking 'hath not the almighty prouidence severed me from the reste of the worlde, with a large sea, to make me one Islande? hath not natures ordinaunce furnished me with asmany thinges necessary, as any one grounde bringeth furth . . . And hath not the grace of Christ illumined me over all, with one faith?'[118] In Somerset's *Epistle* it was God himself who addressed the realms, telling them, 'I of my infinite mercie & love to your nacion, had prouided a Prince to the one, and a Princesse to the other, to be ioyned in my holy Lawes, and by the Lawe of nature, and the worlde, to have made an unitie, concorde, and peace, in the whole Isle of bothe realmes.'[119] The appeals to geographical fortune and dynastic opportunity would resurface regularly in Anglo-Scottish deliberations over the coming years.

Henrisoun was seemingly untroubled by the assumption of English superiority so unacceptable to many Scots. His *Exhortacion* faithfully recounted the ancient 'Brutus myth' of the original division of the island in England's favour, along with the other arguments of Henry VIII's *Declaration of the just causes of the warre with the Scottes* of 1542. English hegemony was also explicit in Somerset's *Epistle*, which reminded the Scots that the English were 'superiors in the field and masters of a great part of your realm', though still trying to claim that they came as 'rather Countreymenne, then Conquerours'.[120] Immediately on his assumption of power, Somerset had made overtures to the Scottish government indicating his willingness to mitigate the strict terms of the Greenwich Treaties by allowing Mary to remain in Scotland until the time of her marriage. He took pains to make his approach appear more even-handed than that of the late king, attempting to forestall further fighting in 1547, with a proclamation enumerating the same unionist arguments that would later appear in the *Epistle*. The underlying threat of brute force, always present in Henry's dealings with the Scots, however, remained. When the Scottish government blocked publication of Somerset's proclamation, the protector led his troops to victory at Pinkie in September 1547.[121]

The battle was celebrated in the singing of the Te Deum throughout the churches of England,[122] and it inspired a number of works of triumphalist propaganda. William Patten, an official of the Marshalsea court, produced a diary of the campaign, and the reformer John Hooper, then in Zurich,

---

[118] *Complaynt of Scotlande*, 232.
[119] Ibid. 240.
[120] Ibid. 213–15, 238–9.
[121] *Scottish Correspondence*, nos. 126, 141; Keith, *History*, i. 130; *TA* ix, 110; Knox, i. 212–13.
[122] *APC* ii. 517.

dedicated a work to Somerset. Their writings repeated the standard arguments in favour of union, based on their island shape and common customs, conditions, and language, but in unattractively exultant terms that held the slaughter of the Scots by a smaller English force to be the work of God.[123] Patten, in particular, gave graphic descriptions of dead bodies 'as thik as a man may note cattell', and rivers which 'ran al red with blood'. This was not guaranteed to win Scottish support, and neither were Patten's hackneyed rants against Rome, no more successful in 1547 than they had been when delivered by Barlow in 1535–6.[124] Patten's arguments against the insidious Roman threat, juxtaposed with the depiction of the close-knit island form of the realms, testified to England's continuing insecurities. Scottish fears that the English were in fact intent on imperialist aggression, however, were fed by works such as Nicholas Bodrugan's *Epitome of the title that the Kynges Maiestie of Englande hath to the souereigntie of Scotlande* in 1548, and by Somerset's efforts to persuade the French king of England's just grounds for intervention in Scotland.[125] English agents in Scotland struggled valiantly to distribute and promote Somerset's *Epistle* there in 1548, sending word that it had been favourably received, but official plans for a union were no further advanced.[126]

The Scots did not receive these proud English assertions of the divine justice of their cause in silence. James's councillor William Lamb, also a judge of the College of Justice, was sharply critical of England's reasons for entering into war in his 'Ane Resonyng of ane Scottish and Inglis Merchand betuix Rowand and Lionis' (*c*.1547). Lamb took the justifications of Henry VIII's *Declaration* and systematically demolished them, while making clear his distaste for the king's treatment of his Catholic subjects.[127] This serious and reasoned rebuttal of English claims was followed in 1549 by an impassioned plea for Scottish unity. Robert Wedderburn, whose brothers had compiled the *Gude and Godlie Ballatis*, sent out a more religiously orthodox appeal to his fellow Scots in *The Complaynt of Scotlande vyth ane Exhortatione to the thre Estaits to be vigilante in the Deffens of their Public Veil*, urging them to look to the well-being and protection of the commonwealth, whose weakened state had prepared the ground for England's assaults. Wedderburn made a bold stand against customary arguments for union,

---

[123] Patten, 'Expedicion into Scotlande', in Dalyell (ed.), *Fragments*; Strype, *Ecclesiastical Memorials*, ii/1. 26–7.

[124] Patten, 'Expedicion into Scotlande', pp. 67–8, xvii–xx.

[125] *Complaynt of Scotlande*, 248–56; BL Cotton Calig. Bvii, fos. 335–8 (*CSP For. 1547–1553*, no. 112).

[126] *CSP Scot.*, vol. i, nos. 156, 168; *CSP Dom. Add.*, p. 360.

[127] BL Cotton Calig Bvii, fos. 343–64 (alternatively fos. 354–75).

asserting that 'there is nocht tua nations undir the firmament that ar mair contrar and different fra uthirs as inglis men and scottis men, quhoubeit that thei be vitht in ane ile, and nychtbours, and of ane langage'. The natures of the two peoples, he thought, were 'as indifferent as is the nature of scheip and voluis'.[128]

Somerset followed up his victory at Pinkie with the erection of English garrisons along the border and south-east coast of Scotland. This was his preferred means for pressurizing the government into renewed consideration of the 1543 treaties, while extending English influence in lowland Scotland. The fortification of Broughty Craig was followed by the installation of garrisons at Roxburgh, Lauder, Haddington, and Dundee, and a string of other forts.[129] This hugely expensive policy failed to achieve its ultimate goal, but was not completely fruitless between 1548 and 1551. It was intended that these powerful establishments should be instruments for the advancement of reform, and so the pace of assuring was stepped up, and Protestant preachers sent to accompany the armies. Dundee, where 'most of the honest and substantial men favour the Word of God and would be glad to become English' according to Sir Andrew Dudley, was notably forward in responding to this military evangelization, and formed a base for efforts throughout Angus and Fife.[130] Interestingly, Somerset appointed two Scots, both of them cross-border exiles, to preach in occupied areas: John Rough, who had left St Andrews for England in 1547, was sent to Dumfries in 1548. John Willock, meanwhile, accompanied the troops under the command of the marquis of Dorset, 'preaching the word of God with much labour on the borders of Scotland' in 1550–1.[131] The intention, perhaps, was to try to break away from the association between reformed views and long-standing English hostilities; and John Knox's ministry in Berwick and Newcastle from 1549 may also have played some part in this.[132]

In these areas of direct English occupation and influence, some increase in Protestant adherence was undoubtedly achieved, but elsewhere, England's military aggression could just as easily hinder the advance of reform. Many were alienated by the enervating warfare, together with the

---

[128] *Complaynt of Scotlande*, 1–186, 106–7.

[129] M. H. Merriman, 'The Forts of Eyemouth: Anvils of British Union?', *SHR* 67 (1988), 146–7.

[130] Bush, *Protector Somerset*, 13–15; PRO SP 50/4, fos. 65–7; SP 50/2, fos. 10–11, 148–9, 159–60 (*CSP Scot.*, vol. i, nos. 228, 56, 107, 114); *CSP Scot.*, vol. i, nos. 71, 74, 129.

[131] John Rough left the Castle of St Andrews for England before the French assault in the summer of 1547. *CSP Dom. Add.*, p. 354; *Original Letters relative to the English Reformation*, ed. Hastings Robinson, 2 vols. (Cambridge: Parker Society, 1846–8), vol. i, no. 147; vol. ii, nos. 202, 203.

[132] *APC* ii. 274; Knox, i. 231.

English government's blinkered insistence on making the Greenwich Treaties their starting point for discussions on union. Sir David Lindsay, who had shown himself so open to the idea of Henrician reform in the earlier 1540s, could find nothing favourable to say about England's policy towards Scotland after the death of James V. Instead, he expressed the views of many when he mourned the destruction and confusion brought about by the Anglo-Scottish hostilities.[133] Somerset's failings in Scotland were brought home with even greater force when his loyal supporter Henrisoun finally lost patience in 1549. Henrisoun's counsel concerning English policies in Scotland fell on deaf ears once too often, and he set out a list of rebukes and criticisms in letters to Somerset and his advisers. He informed them that he, who had 'served your grace more faithfully than is known', would no longer be a spokesman for England's cause in Scotland, warning that God would 'pwnysche unthankfulnes'.[134] His reconciliation with the Scottish government in 1551 showed the strengthening support for the pro-French policies of the dowager.

VIII. THE ASCENDANCY OF THE FRENCH INTEREST

Henrisoun's defection from the English cause was symptomatic of the flaws in England's strategy in Scotland. Despite its limited evangelical successes, Somerset's garrison policy was increasingly oppressive. English commanders, seemingly frustrated by their lack of concrete advances in Scotland after 1547, became brutal and uncompromising towards the subdued Scots. Somerset's border officials told him in January 1548 that the unassured on the borders 'shal feele of the whypp', and Wharton was of the opinion that 'to be won of theyme must bee with fyer and sworde'. The protector himself asserted 'thatt after so moche loseness ther must some severite bee used towardes such as shall break good order'.[135] Terms of assurance became stricter and their benefits fewer, while those who were suspected of reneging on their agreements were dealt with ever more severely. In March 1548 Lord Wharton ordered the hanging in Carlisle of six assured Scots who had broken their pledges to England. Their offences were declared at the time of execution, 'that the people of the countrie may fully understand the same'. When the Scottish government declared that

---

[133] Lindsay, *Works*, i. 255, 359.
[134] BL Cotton Calig. Bvii, fos. 482–4; *CSP Scot.*, vol. i, nos. 352, 357.
[135] *CSP Scot.*, vol. i, no. 140; PRO SP 15/2, fo. 27ᵛ, 15/3, f. 59ᵛ (*CSP Dom. Add.*, pp. 366, 396).

any assurers taken prisoner would be put to death as rebels, Somerset reacted with a proclamation stating that 'henceforth no Scotsman taken in arms against England shall be used as a prisoner, but immediately slain'.[136]

Under these circumstances, it was difficult to sustain Somerset's contention that the English came as allies and equals in the godly cause. Whether or not the protector and his governmental colleagues truly subscribed to this notion, their actions in Scotland betrayed their words; and in the later 1540s even their words were failing to live up to earlier promises. Wharton could barely speak of the Scots under his charge without decrying their falsity, ignorance, and general worthlessness. In a typical comment he told Somerset 'they have always been ancient enemies with a continual use of untruth to this realm'. He added, 'I knowe my selfe to be the worst beloved with them ... whereof I am glad'.[137] This antipathy was extreme, but the same quality of xenophobia constantly surfaced in English dealings with Scotland. The English admiral Lord Clinton, recommending John Melville to Sir John Luttrell, took care to add, 'I wold not wyshe that ye shoulde put any gret confydence to hym nor other', and Luttrell himself told Somerset that he had declined the suits of certain Scots for assurance, as he did not think 'thatt my dutye was to stuffe thes placys with Scottyshemenn'.[138]

The incongruous association of this hostility with the evangelical message of reform threatened to render the godly offensive counterproductive. The Scottish council made its distaste for English heresies plain in its response to a supplication from the kirkmen of the realm shortly after Beaton's murder. The petition expressed the fear that 'pestilencious hereseis aganis the blissit Sacrament of the Altar' would 'spred, increse and ryse dalie mair and mair', and the government promised that the laws of the realm would be executed against all named heretics.[139] The dowager and her orthodox advisers therefore took what steps they could to minimize the effects of England's design to spread godly reform. The fact that the evangelical impulse behind the English push in Scotland came from a regime that was now secure in its own Protestant convictions meant little. An unshakeable connection had been forged between Somerset's stated reforming intentions and his apparent ambition for the conquest and subjugation of Scotland.

In their extremity the Scots turned to France to assist them in repelling

---

[136] *APC* ii. 546–7; *CSP Dom. Add.*, pp. 371–3; *CSP Scot.*, vol. i, no. 348.
[137] *CSP Dom. Add.*, pp. 325, 347, 366, 387; PRO SP 15/2, fo. 65ʳ (*CSP Dom. Add.*, p. 384).
[138] *Scottish Correspondence*, nos. 180, 191.
[139] *RPC* i. 61–5.

the English advance. Henry II seemed only too willing to step in since, like Henry VIII before him and Arran even now, he was keen to advance his own son as a potential suitor to the Scottish queen.[140] Since 1545 French military commanders and advisers had been a permanent presence in Scotland, their forces intervening at crucial moments to obstruct English tactics. After their decisive action at St Andrews in July 1547, French troops returned to Scotland late in the year and combined with the dowager's forces to assault English fortifications. They won Dundee and Dumfries back from the protector's armies, and kept up constant pressure on the garrisons.[141] In June 1548 an expeditionary force of around 8,000 arrived on the east coast of Scotland, and at once laid siege to Haddington, the heart of England's network of communications and supplies. The dominant French presence from then onwards induced many of the assured to forsake the English, while also giving the government the opportunity to proceed with severity against confirmed collaborators. The English were finally forced to leave Haddington in September 1549, and their departure signified the failure of Somerset's military objectives.[142]

The price of French aid was the promise from the Scots that their queen would be sent to France for betrothal to the dauphin. In the parliament of July 1548 the estates agreed to the ambassador d'Essé's terms in return for the promise that France would safeguard the 'fredome liberteis & Lawis' of their kingdom.[143] As an alternative to the dynastic union offered by England, the French marriage had distinct advantages: it could claim to draw on the ancient friendship between the kingdoms of Scotland and France, rather than selling itself as a means of ending deeply entrenched hostilities; it contained the pledge that France would defend Scotland's status as an autonomous kingdom, rather than holding out the prospect of an ill-defined and probably disadvantageous union; and finally, it was predicated on the traditional religious loyalties which still held sway in government, instead of the new reforming sentiments which as yet had more limited appeal in Scotland. Parliament records stated that support for the French marriage was unanimous: the dowager, governor, and estates assented to it 'all in one voice'.[144] In fact there appears to have been considerable apprehension before the matter was agreed. Even the Catholic historian Leslie noted that one body of opinion within the parliament,

[140] Merriman, *Rough Wooings*, 296.
[141] NLS Adv. MS 29. 2. 5, fos. 63, 68, 70, 71; *CSP Scot.*, vol. i, nos 117, 134; *CSP Dom. Add.*, pp. 352, 360; Merriman, 'Assured Scots', 27.
[142] PRO SP 50/4, fos. 137–9 (*CSP Scot.*, vol. i, no. 247); *CSP Scot.*, vol. i, no. 356; Calderwood, i. 261.
[143] *APS* ii. 481.
[144] Ibid.

despite French assurances, feared that the amity might make Scotland 'moir subject and bound unto thame, yea, as a province joynit unto France be mariage, as Britangze and Normoundie ar subject at this present'.[145] These misgivings appear to have been overcome, however, and in July 1548 Mary set sail from Dumbarton to France.

The French alliance performed an important short-term service for the Scottish government, driving English troops out of their fortified bases, and finally ending the long-drawn-out Rough Wooing. With the English government simultaneously making peace with France on the continent in the 1550 Treaty of Boulogne, agreement was reached that all forces, French and English, should withdraw from Scotland. A formal Anglo-Scottish peace in 1551, and the division of the Debatable lands of the west marches a year later officially ended disputes between the two countries.[146] The English, like the Scots, welcomed the return of more settled conditions, but there was no disguising the fact of their comprehensive failure in Scotland. The marriage between Mary and Edward had finally eluded them and, worse than this, the prize of dynastic alliance had gone to France. In April 1550 the dowager, governor, and council of Scotland gave thanks to the French king, as 'the sure and onlie defendar and relieff, under God, of all this realme', who had 'deliverit the samyn forth of the thraldome in the quhilk it wes for the tyme, and saifit it fra the apperand perpetuale subjectioun it wes hable to have fallin in'.[147] With French encouragement, Scotland seemed bent on distancing itself from England and maintaining its Catholic loyalties.

As far as England's hopes of a godly union were concerned, the picture certainly looked bleak in 1551. English ministers made feeble efforts to keep the marriage project alive even at this late stage, but Edward VI's own appeal to Mary of Guise to 'persuade the King of France to leave the mariage of the Quene of Scotlande with his eldest sone', and 'aggre that he mycht marie hir' smacked of desperation.[148] Finally it became clear that England's marriage plan must be written off; but there were hints that the cause of reform in Scotland was not entirely overthrown. From 1543 onwards, the periodic signs of Protestant reforming energy in various

---

[145] Leslie, *History*, 234; Robert Lindsay of Pitscottie, *The History and Chronicles of Scotland*, ed. A. E. J. G. Mackay, 3 vols. (Edinburgh: STS, 42, 43, 60; 1899–1911), ii. 106; Calderwood, i. 256.

[146] *APC* ii. 430, iii. 29; *CSP Scot.*, vol. i, no. 374; BL Harleian MS 289, fos. 36–9; *APC* iii. 491–2.

[147] *RPC* i. 86–8.

[148] *CSP For. 1547–1553*, nos. 351, 387; Leslie, *History*, 240.

Scottish burghs and districts indicated that orthodox and pro-French opinion was not all-encompassing. The later military activity under Somerset, brutal though it was, did much to disseminate reforming propaganda, bibles, and other literature in the borders and lowlands.

There was also some comfort for England in the various signs that the Franco-Scottish alliance was not as surely founded as it might first have appeared. On top of the hesitations expressed by the Scottish estates before Mary was sent to France, there were differences between French and Scottish commanders during the wars, and another source of contention was the strong French presence in the administration of Mary of Guise.[149] The sum of English efforts since 1543, however, was disappointing. The rigidity of their approach, and savageness when it failed, won them few friends in Scotland. Alexander Gordon, brother of the earl of Huntly, assessed the problem in simple terms: 'thocht the wysdome off Ingland be extemit greitt, thay gane nocht the rycht way to mak unuon off thyr twa realmis'.[150]

---

[149] *CSP Scot.*, vol. i, no. 336; *Scottish Correspondence*, no. 201.
[150] *Scottish Correspondence*, no. 151.

4

Humanism and Reform

The ignominious conclusion to England's Rough Wooing of Scotland left relations between the two countries bruised, and their religious differences no nearer to resolution. The Treaty of Norham, drawn up in June 1551, brought both nations some respite from the bitter campaigning of recent years; but with the avoidance of the religious question by commissioners for the peace[1] the English government in effect acknowledged its failure to secure the proposed godly alliance. There followed a relaxation of the relentless pressure which the governments of Henry and Somerset had exerted upon Scotland in their quest for a Protestant understanding to eradicate dangerous cross-border associations. With the conclusion of the peace, the subversive potential of such activity seemed rather less disturbing, and neither country was in the mood to revive a prolonged and fruitless conflict for this cause alone.

The end to England's aggressive evangelization in Scotland made for a distinct change in the religious climates of both countries during the 1550s. The Scottish Kirk, having suffered extensively through the damage to border and lowland religious buildings, and not least the murder of its primate, Beaton, was afforded some space to regroup and prepare for the challenge from the reformers. English churchmen, meanwhile, were embarking upon a course that would take their establishment in a decidedly Protestant direction. A growing enthusiasm for European reformed theologies superseded the Henrician preoccupation with the confessional stance of Scotland, taking the focus of England's religious interests away from the northern border. In the wake of the intensive, frequently hostile, religious contacts between the governments, a new distance was established between the Protestant reformation planned by Cranmer in England, and the orthodox reforms outlined for Scotland by Archbishop John Hamilton, Beaton's successor in St Andrews.

The differing religious loyalties of the two archbishops were evident. Cranmer had, since the early 1530s, been a convinced Protestant, and his priority after 1547 was to bring about a significant advance from the religious conservatism of the Henrician Church. Hamilton's reforming

---

[1] *CSP Scot.*, vol. i, nos. 371, 374; Mackenzie, 'Debateable Land', 124.

efforts, by contrast, were designed to shore up the orthodox Scottish establishment against the encroaching Protestant threat. It is nevertheless possible to detect a surprising degree of correspondence between their Erasmian-influenced approaches to the task of reform. Both hoped to unite the disparate elements in their respective Churches through the eradication of abuses and improvement of educational standards. In their shared belief in the possibility of inclusive and all-embracing reform, Cranmer and Hamilton had more in common than might be supposed, though the parallels between their methods could not disguise their variance on fundamental questions of faith.

After the accession of Mary Tudor, however, reforming endeavours in both England and Scotland had a mutual goal: to establish universal adherence to Catholic doctrine and practice. The more positive dimension of English Catholic renewal, for a long time unrecognized in traditional accounts of the reign, took account of the same humanist priorities which characterized Hamilton's plans for the Kirk. The two countries were closer in religious terms than at any time since 1534, if on rather different grounds than those aspired to by Henry VIII. Their churchmen, however, were indifferent if not oblivious to the potential for an Anglo-Scottish Catholic combination. The diplomatic antagonism between the Tudor and Guise governments both ruled out any such possibility and threatened to provide Protestant dissenters with a potent common cause in resisting popish doctrines and foreign oppression.

I. SCOTTISH EXILES AND THE EDWARDIAN CHURCH

A tradition of historiography based on Foxe makes much of the idea that Edward VI's accession marked a decided break with the past, setting English reform on an entirely new course, which would be disastrously interrupted by the king's early death and Mary's accession. From the moment of his coronation, it was true, the king was greeted as a godly young Josiah, who would preside over a model Protestant Church, leaving behind popish abuses for good. English Protestants and foreign observers clearly expected great things of Edward. In May 1549 the Strasbourg reformer Paul Fagius wrote to Conrad Hubert, 'Though he is still very young, and very handsome, he gives for his age such wonderful proofs of his piety, as that the whole kingdom and all godly persons entertain the greatest hopes of him'.[2] The myth-building, which intensified after the king's death, carries some danger of masking the strong elements of continuity and

---

[2] Foxe, v. 697; Knox, iii. 266, v. 475; *Original Letters*, vol. i, no. 160.

moderation in Edwardian reform and the extent to which it deliberately attempted to build on Henrician precedent. It cannot be denied, however, that the personal inclinations of the protector, Archbishop Cranmer, and other leading figures in church and state brought a significant advance from the equivocation of Henry's later religious policies towards a more surely founded commitment to reform.

The reforming complexion of the new regime was manifest, even if the necessity of conciliating Charles V in the interests of war constrained Somerset's official expressions of Protestantism in 1547. Somerset himself was a convinced Protestant, and a patron of English and foreign divines, including John Hooper, Thomas Becon, William Turner, and Valérand Poullain. He was in contact with Martyr and Calvin, and showed a genuine desire to strengthen the reforming resolve of the regime.[3] His chief political rival, the religious conservative Wriothesley, was removed from power shortly after Somerset took office, leaving the way clear for a programme of Protestant reform to take shape. The protector's disgrace and downfall in 1551 would bring no interruption to the evangelical advance, moreover, as the duke of Northumberland was also regarded as an ally of the reformers, acquiring a reputation among them as 'a diligent promoter of the glory of God'.[4] Throughout the reign the agenda for reform was mapped out by Cranmer, himself a supporter of leading foreign divines such as Peter Martyr and John à Lasco. The archbishop took careful steps to implement measured change that would embrace the reformed religion, while satisfying a range of Protestant views.[5]

One of the distinguishing features of reform under Cranmer's direction was the high regard in which it was held by European theologians. Large numbers of foreign Protestant exiles were driven to seek refuge in England from 1548, following the imposition of the Augsburg Interim, Charles V's conservative religious settlement, on imperial dominions. The protector's government warmly welcomed them, and in 1550 a Strangers' Church was established in London to accommodate the sizeable Dutch, German, Italian, and French populations in the city. Under its superintendent, à Lasco, the congregation was allowed a remarkable degree of latitude to practise its own form of worship, free from the threat of intervention or persecution.[6] Another strangers' community was established in Glastonbury under the

---

[3] Bush, *Protector Somerset*, 68–70, 109–11; *CSP Dom. Edw. VI*, no. 419.

[4] MacCulloch, *Cranmer*, 365–6; *Original Letters*, vol. i, no. 43; vol. ii, no. 192.

[5] Strype, *Ecclesiastical Memorials*, ii/1. 321; John Strype, *Memorials of the Most Reverend Father in God Thomas Cranmer* (Oxford: Clarendon Press, 1812), ii. 279.

[6] G. J. Cuming, *A History of the Anglican Liturgy* (Macmillan, 1969), 43; *Original Letters*, vol. ii, nos. 260, 263; *CSP Dom. Edw. VI*, no. 448.

French minister Poullain, and it too enjoyed extensive religious freedom.[7] The new prominence of the English Church in international circles was diligently fostered by Cranmer, and by lay patrons of foreign divines, such as Henry Grey, Marquis of Dorset. In private households and the universities, concentrations of European and particularly Swiss churchmen and students, testified to English enthusiasm for developing Protestant theologies.

Cranmer believed that this internationalist approach could enable him to bring the English Church to play a leading role in European reform. His abiding hope was to call a reformed general council to displace the mistaken authority of Trent, and restore the practices and principles of the primitive church throughout Europe. Cranmer set out his ambition in a letter to Calvin, asking, 'shall we neglect to call together a godly synod, for the refutation of error, and for restoring and propagating the truth?' With this vision in mind Cranmer extended invitations to Bullinger, Melanchthon, and other prominent foreign divines, informing them, 'we have thought it necessary to have the assistance of learned men, who, having compared their opinions together with us, may do away with all doctrinal controversies, and build up an entire system of true doctrine'.[8] These two reformers, though sympathetic, were not persuaded to come to England. Martin Bucer was successfully installed at Cambridge University, however, while Martyr took up a post at Oxford where he became the focus for a circle of Zurich-inspired reformers, such as John ab Ulmis and John Rodolph Stumphius.[9]

Cranmer's foreign connections were diverse, but there was apparently no place for Scotland in his schemes. This was hardly surprising, given the state of official relations between the countries from 1547. The first years of Edward's reign had seen the conclusion of their protracted military struggle, during which the Scots had stubbornly refused to be drawn away from Rome. In reality, popular opinion north of the border was in no way unanimous in its attachment to Catholicism, and reforming opinion had begun to win adherents in many larger burghs and some militarized areas. In the immediate aftermath of the Rough Wooing, however, there would be little mileage for any English-led reforming initiative. European divines following England's fortunes in Scotland had at one stage been optimistic: ab Ulmis wrote to Bullinger in June 1550, 'we have full confidence too

---

[7] *CSP Dom. Edw. VI*, no. 577; *APC* iv. 180.

[8] MacCulloch, *Cranmer*, 394; *Original Letters*, vol. i, nos. 9–14.

[9] Strype, *Ecclesiastical Memorials*, ii/1. 189; Jane E. A. Dawson, 'The Early Career of Christopher Goodman and his Place in the Development of English Protestant Thought', Ph.D. thesis (Durham, 1978), 64.

respecting Scotland, that when she has been thoroughly subdued, she will embrace the true and wholesome doctrine of Christ with her whole heart'.[10] From 1551, however, their interest in events in the north faded, as the campaign of persuasion and coercion initiated in Scotland by Henry VIII finally came to an end.

Unofficial cross-border contacts, though, remained as vigorous as ever. Associations between religious sympathisers in the two countries, whatever their inclination or purpose, were an enduring irritant to official ecclesiastical policies, and the Kirk's rejection of English Protestant advances did not prevent Scottish evangelicals from embracing Edwardian reform. A number of the exiles who had gone to England during the 1530s and 1540s welcomed the opportunity to play a part in a more avowedly Protestant Church. John Willock, leaving his ministry in London, was appointed to the benefice of Loughborough, which he held until his death in 1585. He also retained his position as a household chaplain to the marquis of Dorset, and so developed close personal ties with a circle of European reformers. Bullinger made 'affectionate mention' of the Scot in the preface to the fifth volume of his *Decades*, causing Willock to thank him for 'your exceeding kindness and incredible regard to myself'.[11] John Rough, after a stint as preacher with the armies of the Protector, practised his ministry in Carlisle, Berwick, and Newcastle, before finally settling in Hull.[12]

The long-established Scottish exiles were joined in England during the 1550s by more of their countrymen, attracted to the new reforming enthusiasm of the Church. Scottish evangelicals formed a notable presence in the London merchant community, as the diary of Henry Machyn reveals. Robert Richardson and John MacDowell, two more Scots who had been in England since the 1530s, were regular preachers in the city, as was John Mackbrair, a former Cistercian of Glenluce, who fled Scotland in March 1550. Their doctrines evidently found favour within this traditionally forward Protestant group.[13] Some of the other exiles of earlier years had stayed in England only briefly before moving on to various parts of Europe, but the invigoration of religious policy from 1547 reawakened an interest in English religious affairs. Alexander Alesius, now in Leipzig, had remained in contact with Cranmer since his hasty departure from England following the passage of the Act of Six Articles. In 1549 he provided the archbishop with a Latin translation of the Book of Common Prayer produced by the

[10] *Original Letters*, vol. ii, no. 196.

[11] Hewat, *Makers of the Scottish Church*, 133–4; *Original Letters*, vol. i, no. 147.

[12] Foxe, viii. 444.

[13] Machyn, *Diary*, 3, 6, 13, 24, 91, 218, 262, 269, 290; Kirk, 'Religion of Early Scottish Protestants', 381.

English Church, signalling his approval of recent religious developments in England.[14]

The most prominent of the newly arrived Scottish refugees in Edwardian England was undoubtedly John Knox, released from the French galleys in 1549. His decision to settle in England rather than Scotland gives an indication of his differing assessments of the hopes for godly reform in the two countries. The English government, for its part, seemed happy to receive Knox. He was granted a £5 reward by the Privy Council and appointed minister of Berwick, where he took over from his St Andrews colleague, John Rough. It seems likely that this was a deliberate move on the part of the government to fortify reforming opinion in a traditionally conservative region.[15] For the next three years Knox exercised public ministry for the first time in his career, and his preaching in both Berwick and Newcastle attracted support and criticism seemingly in equal measure. The appeal of his doctrines was such that a sizeable immigrant Scottish population settled in Newcastle, to the consternation of the English government. Knox's forthright sermons denouncing the idolatry of the mass brought him into conflict with his superior, Bishop Tunstall of Durham, leading to a summons to appear before the Council of the North in April 1550. Knox found several aspects of the 1549 Prayer Book unacceptable, particularly the retention of traditional practices such as kneeling to receive communion. His solution was to omit this from his own services, a measure for which he was unapologetically defiant.[16]

Having begun his career in the dangerous siege conditions of St Andrews, Knox's methods were distinctly confrontational. His approach evidently found favour within the border community, among English and Scots alike. Furthermore, Knox received a measure of protection from the favour shown to him by Northumberland, who gave his English career a boost by appointing him one of six royal chaplains in 1551. Northumberland's own beliefs were not extreme, but he was courting the support of religious radicals in government following his coup against Somerset, and he therefore came to Knox's defence in a dispute with the mayor of Newcastle over his radical preaching. It was Northumberland's intention to use Knox as a 'whetstone' to sharpen Cranmer's attitude to reform, planning to have him preferred to the bishopric of Rochester or, failing that, to the lucrative benefice of All Hallows, Bread Street.[17] Knox

---

[14] Baxter, 'Alesius', 97–8; Strype, *Cranmer*, ii. 300.

[15] *APC* ii. 274; Jasper Ridley, *John Knox* (Oxford: Clarendon Press, 1968), 84.

[16] *APC* iv. 238; 'A vindication of the doctrine that the sacrifice of the mass is idolatry', in Knox, iii. 33–70.

[17] Knox, iii. 297; *CSP Dom. Edw. VI*, nos. 803, 747; *APC* iv. 190.

proved reluctant to accept high office and desert his congregations in the north, but in London during the autumn of 1552, he made an impressively bold impact on religious debate at court. On being invited to preach before the king at Windsor, he inveighed against the inadequacies of English reform, and the personal failings of some of the king's closest advisers. It was Knox's interventions in the revision of the Book of Common Prayer which really enraged Cranmer, however, as the result was the interruption of the new Prayer Book's print run in order to make last-minute adjustments, spelling out that kneeling at communion was not intended to imply adoration.[18]

Knox's controversial contribution to religious debate through this Black Rubric, and his subsequent involvement in the preparation of the Forty-Two Articles, brought him to sudden prominence in England. His views, not moderated by an appearance before the Privy Council in April 1553, placed him in the extreme wing of the Edwardian Church, alongside reformers such as à Lasco and Hooper, newly returned from Zurich.[19] This group wished for a definitive adherence to Swiss doctrines, leaving behind man-made ceremonies and remnants of the traditional religion. Although Cranmer seems personally to have shared their enthusiasm for the teachings of Zurich and Geneva, their radicalism posed a threat to his dearly held vision of a universal Protestant communion. He did what he could to neutralize this challenge: in February 1550, for example, another fervent Scottish preacher and one of Cromwell's protégés, William Learmonth, was brought before the archbishop to answer for his seditious preaching against secular authorities and the Prayer Book.[20] There was a distinct Scottish presence, then, among the radical voices that sought immediate change in preference to a more gradualist approach. The state of religion in England clearly took precedence over the affairs of the Kirk for Knox, Willock, and their fellow exiles in the latter years of Edward's reign. Their Scottish background made them well accustomed to European influences, and they focused on the English Church, with its continental allies, as offering the best opportunities for godly reform.

---

[18] Calderwood, i. 280–1; Ridley, *Knox*, 107; Knox, iii. 175–6; *CSP Dom. Edw. VI*, no. 725; *TRP* i. 538–9.

[19] *APC* iv 148; *Original Letters*, vol. i, nos. 36, 38–40.

[20] *APC* ii. 379–80.

II. REFORMING ARCHBISHOPS: CRANMER AND HAMILTON

If reformers in England were looking to Zurich and other continental cities for inspiration from 1547, Scottish churchmen too were engaging eagerly with European religious debate. The Kirk's official position of loyalty to the Roman Church proved no obstacle to the reforming enthusiasms which increasing numbers of clerics and literate laypeople had been displaying in recent years. The lively interest in humanist-inspired initiatives for renewal and regeneration, evident for some decades, continued to inform religious deliberations in Scotland. Indeed, the welcome return of peace conditions after the debilitating warfare of the 1540s allowed for more conscious consideration of possibilities for reform, freed from the stifling English military presence that had continually pressed for the repudiation of Rome. Religious debate in these years was wide ranging and far from wholly orthodox, though it was a Catholic undertaking directed by Archbishop Hamilton that harnessed much of the Scottish reforming zeal.

Hamilton's personal convictions are not easy to pinpoint. In 1543 he had come to Scotland from France with the reputation of a moderate reformer, raising hopes among Anglophiles that he might co-operate with the English-led Protestant drive. These were disappointed when he allied himself with Beaton's Catholic party, thereby associating himself with Roman resistance to the new learning.[21] In 1549 Hamilton was elevated by his half-brother, Arran, to the see of St Andrews, in a move calculated to consolidate the Hamilton connection in the key government positions. If the appointment was motivated by dynastic ambition, Hamilton nevertheless seemed to take seriously the challenge of reforming the orthodox establishment. His plans for the Kirk indicated that he was not a diehard supporter of the old religion; and he would later prove equivocal in his attitude to the full-blown Protestantism of the religious revolution of 1559–60.[22] His intention on becoming archbishop, however, was to introduce thoroughgoing reform in an orthodox framework, and to this end he presided over three provincial councils, in 1549, 1552, and 1559. These important sessions set out an ambitious reforming agenda, which took detailed account of the decrees being produced by the Church's General Council in Trent. A series of statutes addressed every aspect of religious life in Scotland, pointing to the need to raise moral and educational standards among the clergy, provide for

---

[21] Knox, i. 105; Buchanan, *History*, ii. 329; Ch. 3, Sect. III.

[22] Merriman, *Rough Wooings*, 122, 213; James K. Cameron, '"Catholic Reform" in Germany and in the Pre-1560 Church in Scotland', *RSCHS* 20 (1979), 116; Gordon Donaldson, 'The Scottish Episcopate at the Reformation', *EHR* 60 (1945), 353.

the instruction of the laity, and generally tackle the catalogue of abuses which detracted from the spiritual integrity of the Kirk.[23]

In his apparently strong personal commitment to the task of internal reformation, Hamilton had much in common with Cranmer: both arch-bishops considered it their duty to devise comprehensive schemes for church reform, focusing on unity and inclusiveness, and avoiding conten-tious extremes of opinion. Although they were acting entirely independ-ently of each other, Hamilton and Cranmer each modelled their efforts on the example of another reforming archbishop, elector Hermann von Wied of Cologne. Von Wied had embarked on a programme of orthodox yet conciliatory reform in the diocese of Cologne during the 1530s, producing a set of canons in 1536, which, together with the Catechism or *Enchiridion* of John Gropper, set a contemporary standard for humanist-inspired Catholic reform. These proved unacceptable to his orthodox flock, however, and so the archbishop commissioned Bucer and Melanchthon to devise a compromise document which would attempt to satisfy both Catholic and Lutheran shades of opinion. In 1543 they produced the *Simplex et Pia Deliberatio*, but this too was unsuccessful in pacifying the local population. In 1546 von Wied, by now a Lutheran convert, was forced to retire from office.[24]

The Cologne documents failed in their primary purpose, but there was inspiration for both Cranmer and Hamilton in the robust recognition by an energetic archbishop of the need to tackle the moral and intellectual deficiencies of an ecclesiastical establishment.[25] Copies of von Wied's canons, published together with Gropper's *Enchiridion* in 1538, were imported into both Scotland and England, while an English translation of the tract of 1543 was also published in London in 1547 and 1548. Cranmer himself owned at least one edition of the work in the original Latin.[26] Hamilton appears to have been primarily interested in the canons of 1536 as

[23] *Statutes*, ed. Patrick, pp. 84–190.

[24] G. J. Cuming, *The Godly Order: Texts and Studies relating to the Book of Common Prayer* (Alcuin Club Collections 65; SPCK, 1983), 68–72; Franz Lau and Ernst Bizer, *A History of the Reformation in Germany to 1555* (A. & C. Black, 1969), 115.

[25] MacCulloch, *Cranmer*, 393, 'It would be entirely in character if Cranmer saw the failure of one reforming metropolitan of the Universal Church as a call to action for himself, who held the equivalent office in England'; Cameron, '"Catholic Reform"', 117, 'It is perhaps not altogether fanciful to suggest that the archbishop [Hamilton] saw himself cast in a role similar to that of a German prince bishop such as the Archbishop of Cologne'.

[26] James K. Cameron, 'The Cologne Reformation and the Church of Scotland', *JEH* 30 (1979), 41; Hamilton, *The Catechism set forth by Archbishop Hamilton, together with the Twopenny Faith*, ed. A. F. Mitchell (Edinburgh, 1882), p. xi; Cuming, *Godly Order*, 69; Von Wied, *A Simple and Religious consultation of vs Herman by the grace of God Archbishop of Colone, and prince Electoure* (J. Daye and W. Seres, 1548; *RSTC* 13214); MacCulloch, *Cranmer*, 393.

source material for the provincial councils, and the same decrees were drawn on by English churchmen in the later part of Henry's reign.[27] Cranmer, meanwhile, made use of the later *Deliberatio*, with its more definitively Protestant bias in his religious formulations. In this way the Catholic Church of Scotland and reformed establishment of England could both take inspiration from the example of Cologne's reform at different points in its evolution. The English and Scottish reforming programmes also shared a number of other common sources, such as the *Paraphrases* of Erasmus, and the 'King's Book' of 1543.[28] The result was that, in their origins, humanist spirit, and intentions, if not in the most basic questions of faith, there were some unexpected similarities between the reforms outlined by Hamilton in Scotland and Cranmer in England.

Edwardian and Scottish Reform and the Example of Cologne

An examination of the Edwardian religious injunctions of 1547 and the statutes of the Scottish provincial councils, two officially antagonistic reform programmes, illustrates some of these parallels. The English measures, to be enforced by a visitation of the Church, were derived largely from Cromwell's injunctions of 1536 and 1538.[29] The Scottish statutes were more closely based on the Cologne provisions, which were well known to the members of the provincial council.[30] Their common purpose though was to tackle the most glaring deficiencies in the Churches, while providing frameworks for thorough and long-term renewal. In the areas of clerical lifestyle, morality, and education, then, there were conspicuous similarities between the programmes. Like the Cologne canons, they aimed to ensure that priests were responsibly carrying out their duties, and duly ministering the sacraments without attempting to charge for their services.[31] Both schemes also recognized that preaching was a primary responsibility of priests. The English and Scottish provisions alike ordained that it should take place four times each year, with the reading of the epistles accompanied by instruction of laypeople in the basic articles of the faith. The Edwardian injunctions stated that parishioners should learn the Pater

---

[27] Cuming, *Godly Order*, 69.

[28] Strype, *Ecclesiastical Memorials*, ii/1, 45; Edward Cardwell (ed.), *Documentary Annals of the Reformed Church of England, 1546–1716*, 2 vols. (Oxford: Oxford University Press, 1839–44), vol. i, p. 9; *TA* x. 50.

[29] Foxe, v. 165–71.

[30] Cameron, '"Catholic Reform"', 113.

[31] Ibid. 106–8, sects. 2, 5, 8; Cardwell, *Annals*, vol. i, pp. 8–10, nos. 6, 8; *Statutes*, ed. Patrick, pp. 89–94, 109–10, 124, nos. 171, 173, 175–8, 180–1, 202, 222.

Noster, Creed, and Ten Commandments, being examined on their knowledge of them at Easter. The Scottish canons added to the list the Hail
Mary, seven sacraments, and seven deadly sins.[32]

Where the Cologne measures promised the publication of a handbook,
Gropper's *Enchiridion*, to assist priests in this task, the Edwardian injunctions ordained the publication of a collection of homilies by the king's
authority, and the Scottish statutes promised a catechism to offer guidance
to the clergy.[33] The idea of creating scholarships for the training of candi-
dates for the priesthood was also present in the English and Scottish
programmes, and again a precedent had been set by Cologne, where plans
were made to award stipends to poor students, and to send canons of the
diocese to university. The Edwardian injunctions, like those of 1536,
ordered that beneficed clergy award exhibitions to scholars at Oxford or
Cambridge, 'to the intent that learned men may hereafter spring the more'
for the edification of the Church. A Scottish statute providing university scholarships for monks sounded a similar note, expressing the hope,
that 'there may go forth from them and flourish anew men of letters and
preachers eminent in sacred eloquence'.[34] On a variety of secondary matters, such as the observance of the Sabbath, distribution of alms, and repair
of church buildings, there were more correspondences between the
Edwardian injunctions and the Scottish statutes.[35]

There were also, of course, obvious differences of theological emphasis
between English injunctions whose purpose was to initiate a decisive shift
from the conservative religious tendencies of Henry VIII's final years, and
Scottish statutes embodying an essentially orthodox Catholic viewpoint.
The English measures began by reinforcing all laws and statutes against the
authority of Rome, and went on to order an end to religious processions
and devotion to images. Their implementation in 1547–8 gave scope for a
violent rejection of the traditional religion in many instances.[36] This
distanced the English reforming effort from that in Scotland, where one
of the provincial council's statutes explicitly defended fasts, feasts, and
images, saintly intercession, and other contentious Catholic doctrines.[37]

---

[32] Cardwell, *Annals*, vol. i, pp. 6–7, 10, 13–14, nos. 2, 4, 9, 21; *Statutes*, ed. Patrick,
pp. 101–4, 108, 124–5, nos. 192, 195, 199, 223.
[33] Cameron, '"Catholic Reform"', 107 (sect. 6); Cardwell, *Annals*, vol. i, p. 19, no. 32;
Statutes, ed. Patrick, pp. 143–7, no. 253.
[34] Cameron, '"Catholic Reform"', pp. 109–10, sect. 12; Cardwell, *Annals*, vol. i, p. 12, no.
15; *Statutes*, ed. Patrick, p. 106, no. 198.
[35] Cardwell, *Annals*, vol. i, pp. 15–16, 11–12, 17–19, nos. 24, 14, 29, 16; *Statutes*, ed.
Patrick, pp. 138–9, 103, 119, 114, nos. 245, 194, 217, 210.
[36] Cardwell, Annals, vol. i, pp. 5, 7, 14, nos. 1, 3, 23; Foxe, v. 717–18.
[37] *Statutes*, ed. Patrick, pp. 126–7, no. 225.

The overriding concern of the Scottish statues, however, was to reform immorality among the clergy while improving educational standards. Although limited mention was made of more controversial aspects of the old religion, the decrees preferred to focus on the training and behaviour of churchmen. In this respect they had much in common with the English injunctions, which, though inevitably preoccupied with superstitious Catholic hangovers, displayed the same primary concern with clerical standards. In their humanist tone and broad range of interests the programmes closely resembled each other.

Henrician Reforming Precedent in England and Scotland

Cranmer and Hamilton shared a wish to see reform accomplished in an orderly and measured manner, retaining traditional practices where permissible, and making changes that would be widely acceptable. In this, both were influenced by Henrician precedent; Cranmer in his desire to guide more conservative opinion in England towards his reforming agenda, and Hamilton through his recognition that an English-influenced view of reform had gained some ground in Scotland during the 1540s. Henry VIII's 'King's Book' was published in England in the first year of Edward's reign, and had a measurable influence on certain of Cranmer's religious compositions. It also provided the inspiration for large sections of the *Catechisme* produced at the request of the Scottish provincial council of 1552, so finally having the impact on Scottish religious opinion that Henry VIII had sought in 1543. Once again, English and Scottish use of the same source material produced similarities in their reforming proposals, this time in the doctrinal formulas set out under Hamilton's direction in Scotland, and Cranmer's in England.

In devising their schemes for reform the archbishops shared a basic | goal, drawing on a sentiment set out in Henry VIII's preface to the 'King's Book'. This announced the late king's intention to remove 'diuersitie in opinions', so that 'al thinges shuld be done semely and in order'. Cranmer was a firm supporter of this vision of religious change, and the stated aim of the Order of Communion laid out for the English Church in 1548 was to avoid the danger of 'unseemly and ungodly diversity'. The 1549 Prayer Book reiterated Henry's quotation from Paul, with the exhortation, 'Let all things be done among you . . . in a seemly and due order'. Hamilton's hopes for the reform of the Kirk showed a similar preoccupation with the divisions caused by 'sa mony sectis of doctrine, sa gret diversitie of opiniouns, sa mekil contentioun and sa detestabil heresis'.[38] He, like Cranmer, urged that people eschew and put away their variance and dissension in matters of faith.

In addition to their agreement on the purpose of reform the archbishops both hoped to emphasize the doctrinal common ground among members of their respective Churches. Their statements of faith aimed to draw in as wide a spectrum of opinion as was deemed acceptable within each Church. Obviously the parameters of this 'acceptable' opinion would be different in each case, but still the similarities between the pronouncements of the Protestant and Catholic establishments could be startling. This can be seen in the almost identical definitions of faith in Cranmer's homily on the subject, and in the Hamilton *Catechisme*, both drawing on the exposition in the 'King's Book'. Cranmer wrote, 'there is one faith, which in scripture is called a dead faith, which bringeth forth no good works, but is idle barren, and unfruitful . . . Another faith there is in scripture, which is not, as the forsaid faith, idle, unfruitful, and dead, but worketh by charity . . . so this may be called a quick or lively faith'[39] while the *Catechisme* asserted, 'thair is ane fayth, quhilk is general, deade and ydil. Also yair is ane fayth, quhilk is special, leiffand and wyrkand . . . This faith is alwayis ionit with hoip and cheritie, and werkis throw lufe'.[40] It is notable that Cranmer's description included a reference to the bringing forth of good works through faith: his firm conviction was that good works were always the result rather than the cause of justification, a view that moved resolutely away from traditional Catholic teaching.[41] Although this particular extract from the Hamilton *Catechisme* makes no mention of good works, the matter is addressed shortly afterwards; and again, the similarities between the English and Scottish interpretations are striking. According to the Scottish document, 'Quhair this faith is nocht present, gud werkis can nocht help to salvatioun', and, it concluded, faith 'is nevir with out gud werkis'. In a lengthy homily focusing entirely on good works, Cranmer asserted that, although no deeds could bring justification, 'faith is no true faith without works'.[42]

When addressing the controversial issue of justification by faith directly, the reformers again drew on common sources and so offered surprisingly similar pronouncements; so where the 'King's Book' spoke of the need for

---

[38] 'King's Book', sig. Aiii; Joseph Ketley (ed.), *The Two Liturgies AD 1549 and AD 1552 of the Reign of Edward VI* (Cambridge: Parker Society, 1844), 1, 155; John Hamilton, *The Catechisme* (St Andrews: J. Scot, 1552; *RSTC* 12731), pref.

[39] *Miscellaneous Writings and Letters of Thomas Cranmer*, ed. J. E. Cox (Cambridge: Parker Society, 1846), 135.

[40] Hamilton, *Catechisme*, fo. lxxxii.

[41] MacCulloch, *Cranmer*, 210.

[42] Hamilton, *Catechisme*, fo. xciv; Cranmer, *Misc. Writings*, 141–3.

an inward faith to be adjoined to hope and charity for a man's justification, Cranmer's homily stated that the faith required for righteousness did not exclude repentance, hope, love, and fear of God. The archbishop's essential belief in the perfect sufficiency of Christ's mercy for salvation was here expressed in a way that offered no contradiction to the Scottish position on the same issue. The Hamilton *Catechisme* asserted that faith, meaning belief, fear, and hope, was what justified a man.[43] The apparent consensus between the Catholic Scottish Kirk and the reformed English Church on these central tenets, superficial though it may have been, was a remarkable demonstration of the search within each establishment for common ground as the basis for unity.

On another sensitive issue, the mediation of Christ and the place of the saints, the reformers again avoided extreme interpretations. All laid a notable emphasis on Christ's perfect sacrifice through his Passion, and all could agree that Christ alone was the mediator of mankind's redemption.[44] Concerning the subject of the communion of the saints, the 'King's Book' had been equivocal, asserting that although their intercession was good and profitable, it was only made effective through the mediation and intercession of Christ. Cranmer made no mention of the saints in his homilies, this in itself demonstrating his rejection of the notion of saintly intercession, but a catechism produced for the Edwardian Church by John Ponet, Bishop of Winchester in 1553, was more outspoken on the invocation of saints as 'a fond thing, vainly feigned and grounded upon no warrant of scripture'. The Hamilton *Catechisme*, though, took a moderate viewpoint, stating that the saints were able to aid mankind with their prayers even more in heaven than they had done while alive, but that Christ was the only true mediator, and prayers should be directed to God alone.[45]

The Scottish position on this latter point was a departure from strict Catholic teachings, and reflected the impact of the recent lively controversy at St Andrews, in which the English exile Richard Marshall had played such a prominent role. The dispute, centring on the question of whether the Pater Noster should be directed to God alone or to the Virgin and saints, remained unresolved, but the *Catechisme* came down firmly on the side of Marshall and other humanist scholars, in its focus on God alone. Marshall was in fact one of the principal authors of the *Catechisme*, and Hamilton's

---

[43] 'King's Book', sig. Aii; Cranmer, *Misc. Writings*, 129; Hamilton, *Catechisme*, fos. xciii–xciv.

[44] 'King's Book', sigs. Bii, Ciii; Cranmer, *Misc. Writings*, 128–9; Ketley (ed.), *Two Liturgies*, 504; Hamilton, *Catechisme*, fo. clxxxxvii.

[45] 'King's Book', sig. Ciii; Ketley (ed.), *Two Liturgies*, 532; Hamilton, *Catechisme*, fos. clxxxxvi–clxxxxviii.

choice of this Englishman to devise an official statement of doctrine for the Kirk indicates the extent to which he hoped to appease humanist and reforming opinion, while remaining in communion with the Catholic Church.[46] So, too, did the provincial council's consideration of English editions of the New Testament, and Hooper's *Declaration of the ten holy commandements*.[47] Although Marshall's views on intercessory prayer were not strictly orthodox, he remained loyal in his commitment to Rome, having fled to Scotland in 1536 as a result of his refusal to acknowledge the royal supremacy. Consequently, the *Catechisme*, though forward-thinking in many respects, was in no sense anti-papal or hostile to Rome. Its famous absence of specific references to the papacy reflected the year of its production, 1552, before the Council of Trent had produced its definitive backing for the spiritual authority of Rome. It may also have been considered prudent to avoid areas likely to arouse controversy in contemporary Scotland: the usurped authority of Rome had by this time been a target of Protestant dissenters for some years. The acknowledgement of the authority of general councils, and the provincial council's wholesale incorporation of decrees from Trent, however, demonstrated a fundamental loyalty to Rome.[48]

This is a reminder that the basic theological distinctions between the reforming schemes in England and Scotland remained impossible to ignore. Where the 'King's Book' and the Hamilton *Catechisme* enumerated seven sacraments, Ponet's catechism described only two.[49] The Scottish *Catechisme*, like the 'King's Book', contained a full explication of transubstantiation, but Ponet's work bluntly asserted that this could not be proved by scripture; and the Hamilton *Catechisme* was alone in its defence of the doctrine of purgatory.[50] Cranmer's homilies and other works, although they sought to encompass a range of reformed opinion, nevertheless gave strong testimony to the archbishop's committed belief in such Protestant fundamentals as predestination, justification by faith alone, and the spiritual rather than bodily presence of Christ in the Eucharist. Later documents of the Edwardian reformation, such as the revised Prayer Book of 1552, emphasized the theological differences between the Churches still

[46] Ch. 1, sect. VIII; *Statutes*, ed. Patrick, p. 86; Hamilton, *Catechisme*, fos. clxxxxv–clxxxxviii.

[47] *TA* x. 50; John Hooper, *A declaration of the ten holy commandements* (Zurich, 1548, 1550; *RSTC* 13746–50).

[48] Donaldson, *Scottish Reformation*, 35; *Statutes*, ed. Patrick, pp. 126, 98–103, 112–14, 118.

[49] 'King's Book', sigs. Eiv–Mi; Hamilton, *Catechisme*, fos. cxxii–clxv; Ketley (ed.), *Two Liturgies*, 532–4.

[50] Hamilton, *Catechisme*, fos. cxlii–cxliii; 'King's Book', sigs. Gii–Giv; Ketley (ed.), *Two Liturgies*, 534; Hamilton, *Catechisme*, fo. cci.

further.[51] In their approaches to the task of reform, however, the two Churches were not as distant as these distinctions might imply. The common goal of both Cranmer and Hamilton, expressed in documents as distinct as the English Order of Communion of 1548, and the Kirk's 'Twopenny Faith' of 1559, was to arouse a fervent spirituality in laypeople.[52] The aim of minimizing damaging controversies to produce inclusive settlements made for greater similarities than might be supposed in the tone and conduct of their separate schemes for reform in England and Scotland.

III. CONCURRENT SCHEMES OF CATHOLIC REFORM

The extent to which the Marian Church in England perpetuated this moderating and conciliatory approach to reform after 1553 has not always been recognized. The historiography of the reign, following Foxe and Knox, has traditionally depicted Marian Catholicism as an oppressive return to Roman subjection, leading to the notorious burning of hundreds of Protestant martyrs, and the enforced exile of many more godly subjects. According to Knox, the accession of 'that idolatress Jesabel, mischevous Marie, of the Spaynyardis bloode; a cruel persetrix of Goddis people', was disastrous for the flock of Christ, resulting in 'not only the dispersion and scattering abrode, but also the apperinge destruction of the same, under these cursed, cruel and abhominable idolaters'.[53] It is, admittedly, difficult to reconcile the fearsome Marian anti-heresy drive with the image of a regime seeking to draw subjects of diverse religious opinions into a unified establishment. Nevertheless, a focus on the themes of discontinuity and oppression has obscured much of the diversity of Marian reform. The English Catholic revival featured a number of the humanist tendencies that informed both earlier Edwardian measures, and Hamilton's plans for the Kirk. Marian Catholicism had striking parallels with Scottish reform, although their exact relationship was far from straightforward.

The work of Lucy Wooding offers a persuasive alternative to traditional depictions of Marian religion, demonstrating the versatility of Catholic reformers' approaches in this period. The Council of Trent was yet to conclude the definition and consolidation of the Church's teachings, which

---

[51] MacCulloch, *Cranmer*, 392, 428, 463–4; Ketley (ed.), *Two Liturgies*, 193–358.

[52] Ketley (ed.), *Two Liturgies*, 1–8; Hamilton, *The Catechisme set forth by Archbishop Hamilton, together with the Twopenny Faith*, ed. Mitchell.

[53] Knox, i. 244, iii. 267; Foxe, vi. 350.

would create the basis for a co-ordinated Counter-Reformation offensive. Catholic reformers therefore took advantage of a degree of latitude to experiment with appeals to Henrician tradition, the ideals of the primitive Church, and the authority of Scripture.[54] Their use of the printing press as a vehicle for catechization in England has been significantly underestimated. Primers and other religious writings continued to be produced in substantial numbers, and authors such as Thomas Watson, John Proctor, and John Angel took pains to emphasize continuities with earlier Henrician teachings, while avoiding uncompromising expressions of orthodox tradition.[55] Not all Catholic theologians were so accommodating, and Richard Smith's *Assertion and Defence of the sacramente of the aulter* condemned all preaching and popular religious discussion, with a rigid justification of both the Church's traditions, conveyed by 'continuall vse & receiued custome, during many hundreth yeares', and its right to interpret scripture.[56] Others, however, focused on areas of the faith that held a powerful appeal for Protestant opinion, such as the saving power of Christ's Passion, the need to cultivate inward spirituality, and the supreme authority of scripture. The same themes appeared in the formulations of the Kirk, and in the works of Scottish reforming enthusiasts such as Sir David Lindsay.

The aim of implementing essentially orthodox Catholic measures which would prove acceptable to as much reforming opinion as possible was not therefore an exclusively Scottish endeavour during the 1550s. When it became clear that Mary Tudor's reign would bring the English Church back to Roman obedience, the task of Catholic reform began in earnest. Bonner's visitation of his London diocese, to which he was restored in September 1553, began even before the nation's reconciliation with Rome.[57] Cardinal Reginald Pole arrived in England as papal legate late in 1554, and assumed direction of the enterprise that would bring the country into communion with the Apostolic See once more. The reforming canons produced by his legatine synod in 1556 were intended as the first element of a long-term project for the regeneration of the Catholic faith and

---

[54] Wooding, 'From Humanists to Heretics: English Catholic Theology and Ideology *c.*1530–*c.*1570' D.Phil. thesis (Oxford, 1994), 72–4, 94, 106; ead., *Rethinking Catholicism in Reformation England* (Oxford: Clarendon Press, 2000), 11–14, 121.

[55] Jennifer Loach, 'The Marian Establishment and the Printing Press', *EHR* 101 (1986), 135–48; Wooding, 'From Humanists to Heretics', 108, 77; ead., *Rethinking Catholicism*, 119–21, 143.

[56] Richard Smith, *The Assertion and Defence of the sacramente of the aulter* (J. Herforde, R. Toye, 1546; *RSTC* 22815, sigs. Aiii–Av, fo. 258ʳ.

[57] Gina Alexander, 'Bonner and the Marian Persecutions', in Christopher Haigh (ed.), *The English Reformation Revised* (Cambridge: Cambridge University Press, 1987), 168.

establishment in England.[58] The government's campaign against unrepentant heretics was therefore only one element of the revival, and in fact
existed in some tension with these mediating efforts on the part of English
churchmen and theologians.

The more conciliatory face of the Marian revival was broadly in line with
the plans being devised by the provincial councils of the Scottish Kirk.
Given the similarities of purpose and tone which shaped the Catholic plans
in England and Scotland, it might be thought that there was potential in the
idea of a combined campaign in favour of the traditional religion. Already,
the Hamiltonian measures in Scotland had shown strong similarities with
Cranmer's vision of reform for the English Church. Mary's accession
removed the doctrinal distinctions that had formed the underlying barrier
to an identity of aims between the two countries, with leading figures in
both Churches now motivated by the wish for orthodox Catholic renewal.
For the English Church, an alliance between archbishops Pole and
Hamilton could give a welcome stimulus to orthodox loyalties, as the establishment struggled to win the allegiance of waverers and dissenters. The
Scottish Kirk perhaps stood to gain less through association with the
English persecution from 1555, which was such a source of fear and hostility, both at home and abroad. For churchmen of both countries, however,
there were potential allies across the border for the implementation of
already closely similar, moderate Catholic reform proposals.

The prospect of such a league, however, was ruled out by the political
affiliations of the English and Scottish governments after 1553. It was ironic
that two decades of political tensions based on confessional differences were
not ended by the espousal of the same Catholic faith in England and
Scotland. With their antagonistic Spanish and French alliances bringing
them into the sphere of Habsburg–Valois conflicts, there could be no religious combination between the English and Scottish Churches, however
complementary their reforming intentions.[59] The result was a curious
symmetry between their Catholic reform plans: they showed strikingly
similar Erasmian-inspired aims and conciliatory tones, but were devised
and pursued entirely without reference to one another. Reformers in both
countries drew on Henrician and Edwardian patterns where they could,
emphasizing the same unifying doctrinal themes, and pinpointing the same
educational priorities. In theological terms they spoke precisely the same

---

[58] Rex H. Pogson, 'The Legacy of the Schism: Confusion, Continuity and Change in the
Marian Clergy', in Robert Tittler and Jennifer Loach (eds.), *The Mid-Tudor Polity,
c.1540–1560* (Totowa, NJ: Rowman & Littlefield, 1980), 122–4; Henry Raikes (trans.), *The
Reform of England by the Decrees of Cardinal Pole . . .* (Chester, 1839), pp. 6–62.

[59] Anthony Ross, 'Reformation and Repression', in McRoberts (ed.), *Essays*, pp. 384–5.

language as they upheld sound Roman Catholic doctrine, while seeking to draw out the elements most likely to create a consensus with reformers. They met with differing degrees of success, however, according to the prevailing religious opinion in the two countries, varying levels of state intervention, and contrasting political circumstances.

Episcopal Agendas for Catholic Reform in England and Scotland

The most extensive reforming decrees to be issued by the Marian Church before the arrival of Pole were the visitation articles produced for the diocese of London in 1554. Bonner showed an enthusiastic commitment to the cause of Catholic reform, as witnessed in his detailed inquiries to be directed to the clergy, churchwardens, laity, teachers, and midwives.[60] These were strongly reminiscent of Hamilton's provincial council decrees, and of certain of the Edwardian injunctions of 1547. They investigated the example being set by parish clergy in terms of their appearance, social habits, and the character of their servants and associates; and they aimed to ensure that all priests carried out their sacramental duties without financial irregularities. They showed the same humanist-influenced preoccupation with preaching, ordaining that curates should either preach in person, or procure sufficient replacements to do so, and they were similarly concerned to ensure that parishioners received instruction in the fundamentals of the faith from their priests.[61]

Their adherence to traditional Catholicism was plain in Bonner's specification that this instruction should include the seven sacraments and seven deadly sins: in this they departed from the Edwardian injunctions and took their place alongside the orthodox Scottish statutes. The instruction that archdeacons should 'diligently instruct and teach the priests and curates' moved the emphasis towards a concentration of the tools of learning in the hands of the priesthood, and the same was true in Scotland, where the *Catechisme* was distributed to priests with instructions not to lend it 'to every layman indiscriminately', but only 'to some few laymen worthy, grave, of good faith, and prudent, and chiefly to those who shall seem to desire them for the sake rather of instruction than of any kind of curiosity'.[62] This marked an important shift from the tone of the Cromwellian and Edwardian injunctions, which instructed ministers to 'discourage no man' from reading the scriptures, but 'rather conform and exhort every person to

---

[60] Cardwell, *Annals*, vol. i., pp. 135–67.
[61] Ibid., p. 143, nos. 25, 26; pp. 136–8, nos. 1, 4, 9; 138–9, nos. 10, 13, 14; pp. 141, 144, nos. 18, 30; pp. 140–1, 145, nos. 17, 34.
[62] Ibid., p. 145, no. 34; p. 147, no. 6; Patrick, *Statutes*, pp. 145–6, no. 253.

read the same'.[63] In both Catholic reform schemes, scriptural teaching would be filtered through the clergy. This brought them into line with the Trent decree that the laity be taught only 'the things which it is necessary for all to know unto salvation'.[64] The humanist and educational interests of Catholic reformers, then, operated within certain limits.

The orthodox tone of Bonner's articles was continued in their investigation of the condition of church equipment and ornaments, including the 'high altar of stone', holy water and bread, oil, chrism, and vestments. Mary's repeal of all Edwardian religious legislation meant a return to the ritual and ceremonial of the Church as it was used in the final year of Henry's reign.[65] In practice this was compromised by the fact that much of the necessary church furniture had been removed, sold, or destroyed in the intervening years, but Bonner's interrogations displayed a determination to recover it in his diocese. His references to religious ceremonies revealed, however, a change in emphasis from pre-reformation Catholicism, which again had parallels in Scotland. English churchwardens were asked whether there was holy water at the church entrance for remembrance of 'the shedding and sprinkling of Christ's blood upon the cross', and of the symbolism of the washing and cleansing of the soul; and also whether holy bread and water were provided on Sundays 'to put men in remembrance of unity and concord'. The pax in the church, too, was intended to inspire remembrance of the peace that Christ left his disciples and bequeathed by his death. The descriptions of the inward spiritual meaning of ritual and visual images, together with the stress on Christ's Passion, were also powerful themes of the Scottish *Catechisme*, which offered explanations of the outward signification and inward purpose of each of the seven sacraments, and made constant references to the 'quick remembrance of Christis passioun'.[66]

If Bonner's articles were particularly exercised by the problem of heretics, offenders against the faith, and wilful disturbers of the divine service, this was understandable in the light of the ambitious religious alteration that the Marian regime required. The Scottish councils set forth their own statutes for the extirpation of heresies and, like Bonner's measures, provided an exhaustive list of the offences which should be investigated, including any disparaging of the teaching of the sacraments of the

[63] Cardwell, *Annals*, vol. i, p. 9, no. 7.

[64] *Statutes*, ed. Patrick, p. 101, no. 192.

[65] Cardwell, *Annals*, vol. i, pp. 149–53, nos. 1–16; Strype, *Ecclesiastical Memorials*, iii/1. 83.

[66] Cardwell, *Annals*, vol. i, pp. 149–50, nos. 1–3; Hamilton, *Catechisme*, fos. cxxv–clxv, cxlvii.

Church, or its authority and structure. Both also ordered investigations into the possession by laypeople of books 'containing calumnies and slanders defamatory of churchmen and church institutions, of infamous libels, or any kind of heresy', or, in the English case, 'books of schismatical and slanderous communion, or anything with heretical and damnable opinions'.[67] Additional parliamentary measures in Scotland, and an English proclamation against seditious and heretical books in June 1555, showed the urgent desire of both governments to contain the expression of divisive heresies.[68]

The legatine synod which sat under Pole's authority in 1555–6 produced a further set of Catholic decrees for reform on a national basis. One novel provision was an annual service of thanksgiving for the return of the kingdom to the unity of the Church. Many of the other regulations were by now familiar, concentrating on improving the moral and intellectual quality of the clergy, and reinforcing anti-heresy measures.[69] The decrees concerning preaching and education showed striking similarities with the Scottish statutes of 1549. The synod took care to acknowledge that the pastoral office 'chiefly consists in the preaching of the divine word', where the Scottish statute asserted 'this is the principal duty of bishops'.[70] This was an important acknowledgement of the heightened role of preaching in English and Scottish reformed Catholicism. Pole's plans for the publication of a collection of homilies, 'that the people may not be defrauded of the necessary food of sound doctrine on account of the ignorance of rectors, vicars and others having the cure of souls' echoed the Scottish justification for the 1552 *Catechisme*, which pointed out 'how dangerous it is when the shepherd cannot find the pastures, the leader of the expedition cannot tell the road, and the vicar know not the will of God'.[71] In arrangements for the provision of scholarships in cathedral churches, creating 'a sort of nursery, and, as it were, a seminary of ministers', the Marian measures once more, if unknowingly, imitated Scottish plans for providing education in cathedral churches and monasteries. They also bore a conspicuous resemblance to the subsequent Trent decrees on the subject.[72]

[67] Cardwell, *Annals*, vol. i, pp. 138–9, nos. 8, 10, 13; pp. 156–8, nos. 12–20; *Statutes*, ed. Patrick, pp. 122–4, 126–7, nos. 220, 221, 225; Cardwell, *Annals*, vol. i, p. 161, no. 36.

[68] *APS* ii. 488; *TRP* ii. 57–9.

[69] Raikes, *Reform of England*, pp. 6, 22–8, 33–46, 7–22, nos. 1, 3, 5–9, 2.

[70] Ibid., p. 30, no. 4; *Statutes*, ed. Patrick, p. 101, no. 192.

[71] Raikes, *Reform of England*, p. 32, no. 4; *Statutes*, ed. Patrick, p. 145, no. 253.

[72] Raikes, *Reform of England*, p. 50, no. 11; Duffy, *Stripping of the Altars*, 525.

Doctrinal Formularies of the Marian and Scottish Churches

The correspondences between the articles produced by the Catholic establishments in England and Scotland derived from the fusion of ortho-dox religious loyalties with a humanist-inspired agenda, by churchmen who still hoped to initiate universal, consensual reform. Likewise, the parallels between the doctrinal formularies of the Churches resulted from this conjunction of concerns. The Hamilton *Catechisme* of 1552 and Bonner's influential work of 1555, *A profitable and necessarye doctryne*, to which was adjoined his promised collection of homilies, were entirely separate publications: both, however, were products of this distinct re-ligious climate. Certain specific resemblances between the works derived not from any collaboration between their authors, but from the fact that they made use of a similar collection of orthodox and reformed sources. In England as well as in Scotland, the priorities introduced by the Protestant reforming debate influenced the way in which Catholic reform was conceived and framed, as could be seen in the emphasis upon the inward benefits of ritual and imagery, and the new-found importance attached to preaching and instruction. Bonner and Hamilton each drew on the 'King's Book' and on Cranmer's 1547 collection of homilies, both products of reformed establishments, in their bid to unify Catholic and reforming opinion in their respective Churches.

The 'King's Book', as already demonstrated, provided inspiration for the authors of the Hamilton *Catechisme*, whose discussions of faith and the sacrament of penance were direct borrowings from it.[73] This gave the Scottish work a direct connection with Marian Catholicism, since Bonner's *Profitable and necessarye doctryne* was essentially a revised version of the 'King's Book', with various changes and additions.[74] Bonner's alterations to the Henrician tract, introducing certain central points of Roman Catholic doctrine, were mirrored in the Scottish adaptation of the work, giving an illuminating picture of the manner in which English and Scottish Catholics turned the contents of an anti-Roman though conservative tract to their own, orthodox reforming purposes. Where the 'King's Book' had included tirades against the authority of Rome, for example, Bonner replaced them with references to the 'approued Doctours of the Catholike Churche' and the authority of the four holy councils. The *Catechisme*, too, upheld the determinations and definitions decided by the councils, and both

[73] 'King's Book', sigs. Ai, Fiii–Gi; Hamilton, *Catechisme*, fos. lxxxii, cxlix–clviii.

[74] Edmund Bonner, *A profitable and necessarye doctryne, with certayne homelies adioyned hereunto* (Ihon Cawodde, 1555; *RSTC* 3282); Duffy, *Stripping of the Altars*, 534–6.

works agreed that scripture might be interpreted by the elders of the Church.[75] Though the Scottish *Catechisme* itself contained no specific references to papal authority, Hamilton's address to the 1559 provincial council acknowledged the authority of the Eternal Father and Apostolic See, while Bonner's work upheld the position of Christ's 'chief vycar' and substitute on earth.[76]

Among Bonner's additions to the work were an explication of the seven sins, seven virtues, and eight beatitudes; while he abandoned the Henrician discussions of free will, justification, good works, and prayers for the dead. The Scottish council decrees, too, required that laypeople learn the seven deadly sins, and the Hamilton *Catechisme* also rejected the final sections of the 'King's Book' to set forward its own exposition of merit and intercessory prayer.[77] In their flexible and creative use of this unorthodox Henrician work, English and Scottish Catholics displayed a common desire to assimilate as much reforming precedent as possible, while reworking it for an orthodox setting. The fact that Bonner's accompanying collection of thirteen homilies included two of the compositions from Cranmer's 1547 *Book of Homilies* was again indicative of a desire to appease adherents of reform. Several of the other homilies, such as that 'Of the primacy, or supreme power of the highest gouernor of the militant Churche', adopted a more belligerent tone in their assertion of the authority of the Roman Church and the validity of the papal supremacy.[78] The particular difficulty for English Catholics was to uphold doctrines that had been officially repudiated in the preceding years, and many publications avoided the issue of papal authority altogether: as Wooding has demonstrated, only a tiny minority of Marian Catholic works even addressed the supremacy of Rome.[79] The few that did were forthright in its defence, an approach that was entirely absent in Scotland. The *Catechisme*, for instance, took a more relaxed approach to the primacy of Rome, which, though implicit throughout the work, was never expressly defended.

The differing contexts of the Marian and Scottish reform programmes therefore had some impact upon their content, and upon the problems

---

[75] 'King's Book', sigs. Div–Ei, Kii–Li; Bonner, *Profitable and necessarye doctryne*, sigs. Cii, Pi; Hamilton, *Catechisme*, fos. xv, xix.

[76] *Statutes*, ed. Patrick, p. 150; Bonner, *Profitable and necessarye doctryne*, sig. Iv^r.

[77] Bonner, *Profitable and necessarye doctryne*, sigs. Bbbii–Ccci; *Statutes*, ed. Patrick, p. 108, no. 199; Hamilton, *Catechisme*, fos. clxxxxv–cci.

[78] 'Of the misery of all mankinde, and of hys condempnation to ever lastynge deathe by hys owne synne', 'Of Christian love or Charitye', 'Of the primacye, or supreame power of the highest governor of the militant Churche', in Bonner, *Profitable and necessarye doctryne*, 7–12, 21–6, 42–7.

[79] Wooding, 'From Humanists to Heretics', 84; ead., *Rethinking Catholicism*, 127–35.

anticipated by reformers. The Scottish Kirk hoped to take advantage of much of the manifest reforming enthusiasm of the 1530s and 1540s by drawing it into a broadly orthodox framework. The outspoken Erasmian interests of Lindsay, for example, though they frequently strayed towards heterodox opinion, readily found expression in the Kirk's programme. In *The Monarche* of 1554, he described how,

> Seand the Image of the Rude,
> Men suld remember on the Blude
> Quhilk Christ, in tyll his Passioun,
> Did sched for our Saluatioun.

This focus on images as an aid to remembrance, and on the Passion of Christ, incorporated two central themes of reforming Catholicism. Later in the same work Lindsay's criticism of 'ane Prelat that can nocht preche, | Nor Goddis law to the people teche' further echoed Hamilton's own concerns.[80] The English Church shared the aim of incorporating diverse opinions, but faced the challenge of winning the loyalty of a population which had been subjected to a succession of controversial, often contradictory, religious alterations since the early 1530s. The fierce anti-Roman invective that had accompanied overtly Protestant reforms made the task facing the Marian reformers all the more difficult.

The different problems encountered by the Catholic reform initiatives in England and Scotland reinforced the extent to which these were separate enterprises. The resemblances between their distinctive interpretations of orthodoxy and designs for Catholic renewal were striking, but they arose from a common desire to conciliate moderate reforming opinion, rather than from deliberate collaboration. Cardinal Pole's mission in England was a formidable one, and his difficulties were aggravated from the outset by the delay to his arrival in the country. Earlier in his career, he had been actively interested in the religious climate in Scotland, maintaining close contacts with his fellow cardinal, Beaton.[81] From 1554, however, Pole was fully occupied with the complexities of restoring England to Roman obedience, while at the same time the Scottish Kirk was directing its energies into the task of formulating plans for reform that would negate any Protestant challenge. Knox's assertion that, under Mary Tudor and Mary of Guise 'Sathan intended nothing less then the light of Jesus Christ utterly to have bein extinguissed, within the hole Ile of Britannye'[82] may have implied a concerted British Catholic campaign, but in fact English and Scottish Catholics did not capitalize on their shared concerns during the 1550s.

---

[80] Lindsay, *Works*, i. 268, 358.
[81] *CSP Span.*, vol. xii, p. 62; Ch. 2, sect. V.
[82] Knox, i. 244.

IV. PERSECUTION AND THE POLITICAL CONTEXT

The similarities between the reforming priorities of the Catholic establishments were marked, but not complete. Although the Kirk faced a worsening problem in its attempt to control the spread of heresy during the 1550s, the magnitude of the task confronting the English Church was altogether more daunting. The government's determination to deal with the compelling problem of religious dissent led to its adoption of a policy of rigorous persecution between 1555 and 1558, and this had no parallel in Scotland. Pole's ambitious plans for the improvement of standards in the priesthood focused on the future, and the long-term health of the Church. Meanwhile, Protestant dissenters were daily testing its orthodox position, and the Wyatt rebellion of February 1554 demonstrated the potential gravity of any challenge to the regime.[83] Mary evidently did not object to the anti-heresy policy inspired and controlled by her government, despite the fact that its ruthless implementation seemed distinctly at odds with the more conciliatory reforms being pursued by individual churchmen. The first burning was that of John Rogers on 4 February 1555, and by the time of the queen's death, around 287 Protestants had been executed.[84]

This notorious aspect of the Marian reformation set it apart from the relatively moderate attitude of the Scottish Kirk towards religious dissidents. Despite the comprehensive anti-heresy statutes approved by the provincial council in 1549 there was almost no religious persecution in Scotland during Archbishop Hamilton's period of office, and very little in the whole period down to 1558, as Dawson has noted. In 1550 the layman Adam Wallace was tried in Edinburgh for his repudiation of central Catholic teachings on the sacrifice of the mass, intercessory prayer, the communion of saints, and purgatory. During the proceedings he reportedly drew an English bible from his belt, asking that God's word be his judge, and although Glencairn spoke out in his defence, Wallace was burned at Castle Hill the following day. It would then be eight years, however, before another heresy conviction led to an execution.[85] The lack of anti-heretical zeal in the intervening period was less a conscious policy decision on the part of the Church than an essential concomitant of the governmental aims of the new regent, Mary of Guise, who had persuaded Arran to abdicate in

---

[83] *CSP Span.*, vol. xi, p. 418, vol. xiii, no. 178; *CSP Dom.*, vol. i/2, no. 2; Foxe, vi. 414.

[84] Alexander, 'Bonner', 160–2, 175; Foxe, vi. 591–612; MacCulloch, *Cranmer*, 571–606.

[85] Dawson, 'Theatre of Martyrdom', 260–1; Knox, i. 237–40, 308; Spottiswoode, *History*, i. 178–80.

her favour. As she sought to secure her own position, she aimed as far as she could to placate both orthodox and reformed opinion.[86] A ruthless anti-heresy purge would in no way be compatible with her aims.

The differing concerns of the English and Scottish governments made for a wide divergence between the climates of reform in the two countries. The period of calm experienced in Scotland in one sense suited the temperate spirit of Hamilton's religious policies, and the archbishop's own distaste for persecution.[87] It did, however, leave him bereft of secular backing as he attempted to eradicate the extremes of Protestant dissent from the Kirk. In England the vigorous state intervention in, and direction of, heresy proceedings produced very different problems. Though short-lived, the Marian persecution was intense, and harsh by contemporary standards. Crucially, it also began to prove counterproductive, as it served to publicize the sufferings of Protestants in England. Foxe's catalogue of 'the bloody doings and persecutions of the adversaries, against the faithful and true servants of Christ', was in preparation well before the end of Mary's reign, and contemporaries throughout Europe took note of their plight. Bullinger's fears for bishops Ridley, Latimer, Cranmer, and Hooper led him to write to Calvin, 'I see that we must pray unceasingly for that most afflicted church'. The later execution of these highly regarded divines was universally condemned.[88]

The resentment that the persecution produced did much to negate the reforming work of Pole and other Marian prelates. It compounded suspicions that had from the outset been associated with the return to Roman obedience, particularly the residual uncertainties over the ownership of ex-church property. Pole's arrival in England was delayed until November 1554 while it was established that a papal dispensation would allow laymen to retain former religious lands, and the council were anxious to remind the cardinal that they 'only agree to his interference on the condition of the Pope's dispensing that the holders and possessors of the lands and goods of the late religious houses shall quietly enjoy the same without trouble and scruple'.[89] English distrust of Pole himself ran deep, a legacy of his Roman contacts in the Henrician period. Even after Mary's accession, Lord William Howard could detain Pole's associate Thomas Goldwell in Calais,

[86] *APS* ii. 604; Calderwood, i. 272; Buchanan, *History*, ii. 384.

[87] John Herkless and Robert Kerr Hannay, *The Archbishops of St Andrews*, 5 vols. (Edinburgh, 1907–15), v. 55.

[88] Foxe, vi. 636–76, vii. 406, viii. 3–90, 258; Katharine R. Firth, *The Apocalyptic Tradition in Reformation Britain, 1530–1645* (Oxford: Oxford University Press, 1979), 81–2; *Original Letters*, vol. ii, no. 354.

[89] R. H. Pogson, 'Revival and Reform in Mary Tudor's Church: A Question of Money', in Haigh (ed.), *English Reformation Revised*, 142–3; *CSP For.*, vol. ii, no. 285.

motivated by no other reason than his ingrained distrust of the cardinal.[90] There were also signs of English suspicions that a Spanish influence was behind the repressive policies of Mary's government. A whole series of works produced by Protestant critics and exiles denounced the queen's marriage, and Christopher Goodman's accusation that Mary was ready 'to sell your subjects for slaves to the prowde Spaniards, a people with out a God' was typical.[91] In fact Philip and his imperial advisers were notably cautious in their attitude to the persecution, as they had been over the reconciliation with Rome, but they were castigated nonetheless.[92]

A number of Scottish Protestant exiles in England were affected by the severity of the government's drive against unorthodox opinions. As early as August 1553 the preacher John Melville was committed to Newgate for his seditious teachings. Robert Richardson, whose connections with England dated back to his service for Cromwell in the 1530s, also came to the notice of the authorities for his heretical views. When called on to recant at Aldermary church in July 1555, however, he defiantly maintained his former opinion, and somehow evaded subsequent heresy proceedings.[93] Other exiles took flight once more, and John MacDowell travelled to northern Europe, while John Mackbrair joined the exile congregation in Frankfurt. John Knox also joined the Frankfurt exiles in 1554, before moving on to Geneva.[94] John Willock escaped to Emden after Mary's accession, as did John Rough. Rough, returning to London briefly in 1557, was persuaded to remain as one of the ministers of a large underground congregation in Islington. The story of his trial and execution was immortalized by Foxe, whose account of his betrayal by a false member of the group revealed Rough's firm adherence to the 1552 Prayer Book. It was the custom of the congregation 'to have all the English service without any diminishing, wholly as it was in the time of king Edward the sixth'.[95]

In February 1554 a royal proclamation ordered that all foreign immigrants without the benefit of denization should leave the realm within twenty-four days. This decision was one in which Mary did follow imperial advice, since Charles V had urged it in August 1553, warning that 'the

[90] *CSP For.*, vol. ii, no. 92.

[91] Christopher Goodman, *How Superior Powers oght to be obeyd of their subjects* (Geneva: Iohn Crispin, 1558; *RSTC* 12020; facs. edn., Amsterdam, 1972), 96; Gerry Bowler, 'Marian Protestants and the Idea of Violent Resistance to Tyranny', in Peter Lake and Maria Dowling (eds.), *Protestantism and the National Church in Sixteenth-Century England* (Routledge Press, 1987), 126–32, gives further examples of anti-Spanish propaganda.

[92] *CSP Span.*, vol. xiii, no. 148; vol. xi, p. 161.

[93] *APC* iv. 330; Strype, *Ecclesiastical Memorials*, iii/1. 77, 356.

[94] Durkan, 'Scottish "Evangelicals"', 151; Baxter, 'Alesius', 96; Calderwood, i. 284, 302–3.

[95] Knox, i. 245; Foxe, viii. 443–58.

foreign refugees will oppose her as much as any other class of people, in their fear of a change of religion'.[96] Though large numbers of foreigners obeyed the injunction, others defiantly remained in England, and the Privy Council records repeatedly noted that recalcitrant Scots were refusing to depart.[97] One of these was John Elder, who had formerly offered advice to Henry VIII on a Protestant union of England and Scotland. Following a comprehensive religious conversion, Elder composed a work praising the queen's marriage, and extolling the rare virtues of her new husband. His approval of 'the ceremonies of mariages used in holy catholike churches', and declarations of delight that 'the moste holy Catholike fayth and true relygion of Christ whyche in Englande hath been thys long tyme behynde the post and in Captiuitie is now . . . of all bothe younge and olde, embraced, worshipped and honoured' did not help him, however, and in May 1556 he was given ten days to leave the realm.[98]

The uncompromising tone of the English measures against dissent was far removed from the accommodating atmosphere in Scottish government under Mary of Guise. Her desire to see the marriage between her daughter and the dauphin safely accomplished made her anxious to cultivate the support of influential figures of varying shades of religious opinion, while also avoiding the possibility of patriotic opposition from her Hamilton rivals and their supporters. This was especially true as she advanced her French advisers within the Scottish administration, and set out to persuade the estates to grant the crown matrimonial to the dauphin. The regent's concern was to assure leading figures including Lord James Stewart, Glencairn, and Argyll, that their religious sympathies would not marginalize them.[99] During her administration, therefore, a number of prominent lairds who had been agents of the English government during the 1540s were welcomed back to their former lands and positions. Brunstone, Ormiston, and William Kirkcaldy of Grange were pardoned and restored, as was Henry Balnaves, who expressed his gratitude for 'Your heighnes maist gentill and gracious clemencie schawin to me (undeservit) and to the pure woman my wiff'.[100] James Henrisoun, another one-time collaborator,

[96] *TRP* ii. 31–2; *CSP Span.*, vol. xi, p. 179.

[97] *APC* v. 60–1, 85, 97, 266, 282; vi. 201.

[98] John Elder, *The Copie of a Letter sent in to Scotlande* (J. Waylande, 1555; *RSTC* 7552), sigs. Avii , Fi^v; *APC* v. 266.

[99] Pamela Ritchie, 'The Political Career of Mary of Guise in Scotland, 1548–1560', Ph.D. thesis (St Andrews, 1999), 337–9. On the subject of Mary of Guise's religious policy, and her readiness to encourage leading reformers to play their part in her administration, I would like to thank Dr Ritchie for her valuable additional comments.

[100] Keith, *History*, i. 160; Leslie, *History*, 251; *APS* ii. 520–2; *Scottish Correspondence*, no. 270.

was also formally reconciled to the government, while Michael Durham ended his service for the English government to become a London-based spy for the regent and the French king.[101]

For Hamilton and his allies in the Kirk, the absence of aggressive state-directed persecution ensured that their Catholic reform programme avoided a damaging association with brutal Roman repression. The absence of secular support for the statutes devised by the provincial councils, however, was undoubtedly a weakness in the orthodox campaign. The success with which the catalogue of measures produced between 1549 and 1559 were put into effect is therefore difficult to assess. The ultimate anti-heresy penalties evidently could not be implemented, although milder church censures may have helped in lesser cases.[102] Some of the most debilitating weaknesses in the Kirk, arising from lay appropriation of the system of commendations, were not addressed by the provincial councils, while other proposals, such as the elaborate provisions for the establishment of preachers in every benefice, were too ambitious for the resources and personnel of the Kirk. The statutes relating to the moral and intellectual standards of priests would, like the concurrent measures in England, require some years to bear fruit. When it convened in 1552 the council acknowledged that, 'owing to troublous times and their manifold embarrassments', it was compelled to reissue many of its existing decrees.[103]

The council sounded an apparently contradictory but more positive note, in its confident assertion that the 'frightful heresies' which had run riot in recent years 'have now at last been checked by the providence of All-good and Almighty God, the singular goodwill of princes, and the vigilance and zeal of prelates for the Catholic faith, and seem almost extinguished'.[104] The claim is rather difficult to believe, but the possibility that certain of the improvements outlined for the Kirk were beginning to take effect should not be ruled out. Knox's account, and other Protestant histories of the period, give the impression that the 1550s were essentially years of preparation by godly reformers for their inevitable challenge with the corrupt Catholic establishment. This focus makes no allowance for any progress in Catholic reform. Certain fragments of information, however, offer another perspective, suggesting that orthodox churchmen were taking heed of

---

[101] *Scottish Correspondence*, no. 268; Marcus Merriman, 'James Henrisoun and "Great Britain": British Union and the Scottish Commonweal', in Roger A. Mason (ed.), *Scotland and England, 1286–1815* (Edinburgh: John Donald, 1987), 101–2; *CSP For.*, vol. ii, no. 579.

[102] *Statutes* ed. Patrick, p. 96, no. 185, 'Of crimes which must be punished by appeal to the secular arm'; pp. 122–4, nos. 220, 221.

[103] Donaldson, *Scottish Reformation*, 35, 43; *Statutes*, ed. Patrick, p. 135.

[104] *Statutes*, ed. Patrick, p. 143, no. 253.

the provincial council's decrees. Knox attacked John Sinclair, dean of Restalrig, for his sermon in defence of 'Holy Watter, Pilgramage, Purgatory, and Pardonis' in 1558, but this could alternatively be seen as the recognition by a high-ranking Catholic cleric of his preaching duties.[105] The following year saw Hamilton declare that he and James Beaton, Archbishop of Glasgow, would submit themselves for advice and admonition to certain clerics, another indication of willingness to reform. After the 1559 provincial council session, Lord James Stewart and John Winram 'prechit the word of God' in Fife, seemingly inspired by its Catholic reforming agenda.[106]

These signs suggest that orthodox reforming activity, in line with the council's recommendations, may have been more extensive than Knox-influenced accounts imply. Hamilton's direction of the reforming effort appears to have been resolutely pursued from the time of his appointment as archbishop of St Andrews, and the repetition of certain decrees by the reforming councils signalled a determination to tackle the most serious abuses in the Kirk in the face of serious obstacles. Although Hamilton's familial and material interests were well served by his position, he seems to have been genuinely exercised by the problems facing him as head of the orthodox establishment. The Catholic campaign was undermined, however by the absence of secular support for its anti-heresy penalties, and by the regent's conciliation of leading advocates of Protestant reform. This held out to reforming enthusiasts some hope that they could pursue their interests without reference to the Kirk's national agenda. The ambition of Hamilton and his colleagues for an inclusive scheme to maintain the unity of the Kirk therefore stood little chance of success.

V. EUROPEAN CONFLICT AND THE HARDENING OF BATTLE LINES

The contrasting religious climates of England and Scotland during the 1550s were closely tied to the distance created between them by their conflicting foreign affiliations. Mary Tudor's commitment to Spain and the diplomatic interests of the Habsburgs was firm, while the determination of Mary of Guise to protect the interests of her daughter, who was in France for the entire decade, cemented Scotland's attachment to the auld alliance. Relations between the English and Scottish governments were initially cordial, and a number of commissions for the resolution of long-standing

---

[105] Knox, i. 298–9, 266.
[106] Herkless and Hannay, *Archbishops*, v. 104–5.

grievances on the borders seemed to give substance to the statements of amity between them.[107] In December 1553 the young Scottish queen herself wrote to Mary Tudor of her wish that they might be 'deux Roynes . . . en ceste Isle la ioinctes d'inviolée amitie, aussi bien qu'elles le sont de sang et si prochain lignage'.[108] Their diplomatic alliances, however, were bringing them onto opposite sides of a deepening European conflict.

Tensions between Charles V and Henry II, relating to their habitual differences in Italy and the Low Countries in the mid-1550s, were not lifted by the efforts of Pole, as papal legate, to mediate a truce between them.[109] Consequently, English and Scottish involvement in their dispute seemed inevitable. Imperial interventions in English policy-making consistently warned against the insidious French threat to England. Charles's ambassadors advised Mary 'to keep spies constantly in Scotland to watch what is going on there', since 'that kingdom is at the service of the French, who are nowhere more at liberty'. Renard frequently reminded the queen 'that one object of the alliance between Scotland and France, both of whom are old enemies of England, is to seek an opportunity of usurping this realm'.[110] Scotland's close ties with France were irritatingly illustrated by the incessant passage of Frenchmen through England. More worryingly, it was reported that the French were providing forces for warlike preparations on the border. The French and Scots were also maintaining their involvement in Ireland, an association that had worried the English government since the Kildare rebellion of the 1530s.[111] The suspicions between England and Scotland were mutual, as England's own relationship with Spain and the emperor kept the Scots in fear of possible Anglo-imperial aggression.[112]

These European loyalties may have kept England and Scotland apart in diplomatic terms, but they gave rise to certain common problems. In both countries there developed strong currents of resentment against foreign interference in domestic government during the 1550s. England had shown hesitations over Mary Tudor's proposed marriage to Philip of Spain from the start, and the contract, when it was finally agreed, was hedged around with terms and conditions reminiscent of the safeguards for which the Scots had fought in the negotiations for the Greenwich Treaties in 1543.

---

[107] *RPC* i. 148–50; *CSP Scot.*, vol. i, no. 398; BL Cotton Calig. Bix, fos. 8–13 (*CSP Scot.*, vol. i, no. 401); Leslie, *History*, 253, 256.

[108] PRO SP 51/1, fo. 10 (*CSP Scot.*, vol. i, no. 402).

[109] *CSP Span.*, vol. xiii, nos. 200, 202, 210, 260, 261.

[110] *CSP Span.*, vol. xi, pp. 194–5, 301.

[111] *CSP For.*, vol. ii, nos. 66, 153, 199, 307; *CSP Span*, vol. xii, p. 290, vol. xiii, no. 137; *CSP Scot.*, vol. i, no. 400.

[112] *CSP Span.*, vol. xii, pp. 24–5.

Philip would assist Mary in government, 'saving always the kingdom's laws, privileges and customs', while relinquishing any claim to dispose of the offices of the kingdom, 'which shall be bestowed upon its natives'.[113] These and various other limits imposed on the new king were not enough to lessen English concerns, however, and hostility to the Spanish match was a principal motivation of the Wyatt rebels in February 1554.[114] Philip was warned by Renard that his Spanish retinue should be 'as modest in demeanour as the pride and insolence of the English would have them, for otherwise these people will not be held back from inflicting upon them some irreparable outrage'. Despite the favourable impression made by the king himself, together with public relations exercises such as a genealogy proving Philip's descent from the House of Lancaster, the legendary English xenophobia continued to surface.[115]

Scotland's commitment to amity with France was a far less controversial policy decision. In 1548 the Scottish estates willingly accepted French assistance in their conflict with England. The decision to send their queen to the French court was not made without some reservations, but the auld alliance drew strength from its antiquity, and from a shared resistance to English aggression. Mary of Guise benefited from this foundation of goodwill when she assumed the regency in 1554, and there is considerable evidence, contrary to the impression given by Knox, that her administration was well supported.[116] An undeniable source of tension, however, was her promotion of French advisers such as Roubay and Villemore to the prominent government posts of keeper of the great seal, vice-chancellor, and comptroller of the royal finances.[117] The impression among members of the nobility that French interests were dictating policy was reinforced by novel measures such as the attempt to raise a tax to support a standing army.[118] The presence of French forces in Scotland was another grievance, and resentments came to a head when their commander d'Oysel attempted to launch an invasion of England in 1557, against the combined advice of leading Scottish nobles.[119]

The political communities in England and Scotland therefore faced similar problems in terms of their foreign alliances. There was nothing fundamental or inevitable about their dislike of their European affinities,

---

[113] *CSP Span.*, vol. xi, pp. 265–70, 289–92, 300–1; vol. xii, pp. 2–4.

[114] Ibid., vol. xii, p. 51; Foxe, vi. 414.

[115] *CSP Span.*, vol. xi, pp. 425–6; vol. xiii, no. 5; Foxe, vi. 555.

[116] Keith, *History*, i. 161; Lynch, *Edinburgh*, 72–3; SRO MS GD 1/371/3, fo. 258ʳ.

[117] Leslie, *History*, 251; Calderwood, i. 284.

[118] *CSP Scot.*, vol. i, no. 411; Buchanan, *History*, ii. 381–90.

[119] NLS Adv. MS 29. 2. 5, fo. 70; Knox, i. 255; Calderwood, i. 329; Buchanan, *History*, ii. 390–2.

but there was resentment at the way in which the dominating needs of the Habsburg–Valois conflict in the later 1550s relegated pressing domestic concerns firmly into second place. The bitterness of feeling in both countries made it necessary for the Scottish parliament to legislate against demonstrations of hostility to the French, and for Mary Tudor to issue a proclamation forbidding the mistreatment of Philip's Spanish retinue.[120] Scottish discontents received further expression in the parliament of 1558 when, following the queen's marriage to the dauphin, the estates were persuaded to grant to Francis the crown matrimonial. Arran's public protest against the measure may have been driven by his personal family ambitions, but the unease was widely shared. The existence of a secret clause in the marriage contract, by which Francis would gain the kingdom in the event of Mary's death without heirs, bore out Scottish apprehensions.[121]

In England Philip was not awarded the crown matrimonial, which must have offered some comfort to the government in view of Mary's difficulties in producing an heir. A more immediate concern for the English, however, related to the apparent Spanish direction of foreign policy. In June 1557 Mary proclaimed war against France, officially in response to French provocation through their alleged assistance to the rebels Wyatt and Thomas Stafford. It was no coincidence, however, that Philip was urgently in need of reinforcements against France and the papacy, following the renewal of hostilities in 1556.[122] The mobilization of forces for a conflict centring on the north of France moved the focus of English war preparations away from the northern border where the escalating European tensions brought damaging Scottish and French incursions in the summer of 1557. The communications of border wardens with the government pressed for urgent military assistance, with officials literally 'begging that the ships should sail to Scotland in order to protect England on that side'.[123] The troubles on the Scottish border would only be addressed after the fall of Calais in January 1558 led to a cessation of English military operations on the continent.[124]

England's disastrous losses in 1558 did then have the minor benefit of redirecting military efforts from the European theatre of war towards the realm's other pressing concerns. These related not only to French-led

---

[120] *APS* ii. 499–500; *TRP*, ii. 33–4.

[121] *APS* ii. 506–8, (app. 11) and 605 Keith, *History*, i. 169.

[122] *CSP Span.*, xiii, nos. 297, 306.

[123] *CSP Dom. Add.*, pp. 453–5; *CSP Dom.*, vol. i/11, nos. 22, 24; *CSP Span.*, vol. xiii, no. 338.

[124] *CSP Span.*, vol. xiii, nos. 438, 440, 444.

aggressions in the north, but also to the ongoing involvement of the French and Scots with rebels in Ireland. The government's intensified campaign of conquest and colonization in Ireland from 1556 was being disrupted by agitations in Ulster, and the O'Donnells were notable offenders. Scottish mercenaries were known to be supporting their disturbances, and the earl of Argyll had not only allowed his daughter to marry Calvagh O'Donnell, but had sent his son with men and munitions to assist the rebellion. In February 1556 Sir Thomas Challoner went to Scotland to challenge the regent on the matter, and to make enquiries among other members of the government in the effort 'to boult out the truethe'. He was to 'noate the state of that countrie, the order and manner of there doinges, their inclynacion to peace and quiett with this realme, and what practyses they have with ffraunce . . . what their meaning is in yt matter of Ireland', and 'what preparations have bene made from out of Scottland for the ioyrnie'.[125] England's borders and frontiers therefore continued to create security problems, which the Scots exploited with French backing.

Such activities had, during the reign of Henry VIII, carried threatening religious overtones. Fears of encirclement by powerful Catholic combinations disappeared during Mary's reign, but all this was to change from November 1558. The death of Mary Tudor in this month and the accession of her Protestant half-sister as Elizabeth I, transformed the political and religious complexion of the English regime. As a result the associations between Irish, Scottish, and French opponents of the crown, and indeed all European Catholic powers, once more took on an alarming ideological flavour. Attention focused ever more closely upon the islands of Britain in the wake of the final loss of England's continental possessions, and on the very first day of Elizabeth's reign her new principal secretary, Cecil, made a note to 'consider the safety of all places dangerous to the realm towards France and Scotland, specially in this change'. English ministers negotiating with France reminded the council 'what advantage the French have to annoy them by Scotland', adding ominously, 'What the French pretend by the marriage of the Dauphin with the Queen of Scots is not unknown'.[126] The danger soon became apparent when Henry II chose to advance the Scottish queen's claim to the English throne, challenging Elizabeth's right to succeed on the basis of her illegitimacy in the eyes of the Catholic Church: he proclaimed Mary queen of Scotland, England, and Ireland, and the

---

[125] Jane E. A. Dawson, 'Two Kingdoms or Three?: Ireland in Anglo-Scottish Relations in the Middle of the Sixteenth Century', in Mason (ed.), *Scotland and England*, 115–17; BL Cotton Calig. Bvii, fos. 498–500 (*CSP Scot.*, vol. i, no. 410).

[126] Dawson, 'William Cecil', 200–3; *CSP For.*, vol. iii, nos. 1, 6.

arms of England were blatantly set forth on her household furniture and plate.[127] Given the established French presence in both Scotland and Ireland, England's need to attend to the borders of the realm was urgently reinforced.

At the same time, a legacy of significant religiously and politically motivated disaffection stemming from the difficulties of the 1550s created a climate of ardent expectation of the new queen. The extent of the opposition which Mary Tudor's orthodox policies had inspired can be exaggerated, since it is clear that the return to Roman obedience was not simply the retrograde, oppressive, and universally unpopular move portrayed in older histories of the period. The scale of the government's campaign against heretics was, however, causing widespread alarm by the time of Mary's death, intensifying popular religious anticipations at Elizabeth's accession. The fact that Scottish Protestants, until now left largely undisturbed by Mary of Guise, would also shortly begin to experience a new severity on the part of their Catholic regent would lead them to consider how England's new queen might be induced to advance the Protestant cause north of the border, as well as in her own realm.

Official reforming efforts in the Churches of England and Scotland had, for much of the 1550s, displayed remarkably similar inclusive and conciliatory tendencies, arising from the common humanist impulses of leading reformers. The doctrinal underpinnings of the Edwardian Church were clearly distinct from those of the Scottish Kirk, but the parallels between the establishments in their approaches to reform, and in the tone of official pronouncements, were at times extraordinary. The resemblances became even more meaningful after 1553, with the restoration of English Catholicism under Mary Tudor. The Churches of England and Scotland alike now made it their goal to eradicate the worst and most visible abuses in each establishment, while attempting to cultivate among laypeople an orthodox and reflective inner piety. The religious campaigns were destined, however, to remain entirely independent of one another. After the dogged efforts of Henry VIII to establish some correspondence between England and Scotland's religious regimes, it was ironic that the closest similarities between the reform programmes came under the Catholic administrations of Mary Tudor and Mary of Guise, neither of whom showed any interest in seeking a formal religious alliance.

In the later years of the decade, though, the Catholic stances of the Tudor and Guise governments, together with their powerful and

---

[127] BL Cotton Calig. Bv, fo. 318; Calderwood, i. 437; Leslie, *History*, 269.

unpopular foreign affiliations, began to produce common strands of opposition among distinct groups in the two countries. England's oppressive dynastic commitments, combined with the ever more severe treatment of Protestant dissenters, made for growing unease with the Marian regime. In Scotland the long established French connection was producing new tensions by the end of the 1550s; and while opponents of the orthodox religion were not subjected to the same fierce repression as their English counterparts, the possibilities offered by the accession of a Protestant queen south of the border to some seemed obvious. English and Scottish supporters of the reformed religion would focus on Elizabeth I after 1558 for the realization of their hopes.

5

Protestant Alliances: The Privy Kirks and the Marian Exile

The pursuit of independent Catholic reform initiatives by the Churches of England and Scotland during the 1550s did not preclude continuing associations between Protestant activists in the two countries. The tone of formal ecclesiastical policies, as always, gave only a partial indication of diverse religious sentiments. Supporters of the reformed religion in each country remained diligent in identifying allies in the other, and their shared commitment to furthering the Protestant cause, despite the unfavourable political climate after 1553, was manifested in a variety of ways. One such was their collaboration in the formation of independent congregations in Scotland. The 'privy kirks' found themselves able to exploit the narrow possibilities offered by Mary of Guise's reluctance to persecute on religious grounds. A small number of dissenters, recognizing this limited freedom of action in comparison with the administration of Mary Tudor, left England to join these private congregations. This would foster a significant degree of cross-border Protestant understanding by 1559.

What really gave force and meaning to the common cause espoused by leading English and Scottish Protestant activists at the end of the decade, however, was a set of beliefs formulated within Marian exile communities on the continent during the 1550s. The existence of underground Protestant congregations in Scotland, and indeed in England, in the same period demonstrated that opportunities for reformed worship on the British mainland were not entirely removed; but for many supporters of reform, such covert activity was tantamount to a denial of their faith. For others, the risk of discovery remained a major concern. These considerations, and a variety of others, lay behind the decision of close to 800 men, women, and children to flee to Germany, Switzerland, France, and Italy from January 1554.[1] Though this large-scale exodus of Marian exiles to the continent is a well-studied phenomenon, the presence of substantial Scottish contingents within several of the most prominent 'English' exile congregations

---

[1] Christina Garrett, *The Marian Exiles: A Study in the Origins of Elizabethan Puritanism* (Cambridge: Cambridge University Press, 1966), 32.

has gone largely unnoticed, an oversight on the part of contemporaries and historians alike.

Identifying the Scottish members of these communities, and examining their contribution to the volatile religious and political debate among the exiles, provides an important insight into the development of self-consciously British calls for reformation in 1559–60. By reinterpreting events from the recent past, English and Scottish exiles, principally in Geneva, reached an assurance that their two countries shared a common Protestant destiny. The extension of this vision to include the kingdom of Ireland demonstrated the ambitious range of their thinking. In expressing their beliefs the Genevans exhibited the universal tendency among the exiles to think in apocalyptic terms, offering reproaches, explanations, and exhortations to guide future conduct. Their overtly Anglo-Scottish bias, however, together with their radicalism on the question of obedience to secular authorities, created enduring divisions among the already fractious exiles. While some of the English eagerly adopted their broadened perspective, others reverted to their habitual xenophobia and insularity in their attitude towards Scotland. The British orientation of the Genevan congregation would prove a powerful ideological force behind the movement for further reform in 1559, but the mixed reception it received even from the exiles indicated that it would not be universally adopted.

I. PROTESTANT FORTUNES AND THE PRIVY KIRKS

The Scottish government's reconciliation with prominent Protestant lairds and one-time religious outlaws in the early 1550s was a symbolic step for supporters of reform. It extended the hope that they could continue to practise their worship in private, and perhaps even gain eventual recognition for their beliefs. Mary of Guise herself showed no sympathy with reforming opinion. Sir David Lindsay's plea that she 'mak sum ressonabill reformatioun | On them that dois tramp doun thy gracious word', made in *Ane Satyre of the Thrie Estaitis*, which was performed before her in 1554, struck no chord.[2] The effect of the regent's government policies, though, was to create an environment conducive to private reformed worship in areas of Protestant strength. At a time when the attitude of the English authorities towards dissent was so uncompromising, it was hardly surprising that Protestant sympathizers there began to see the advantages of

---

[2] J. H. Burns, *The True Law of Kingship: Concepts of Monarchy in Early Modern Scotland* (Oxford: Clarendon Press, 1996), 117–18; Lindsay, *Works*, ii. 131.

escaping to Scotland. While many reformers, both English and Scottish, would choose to flee to continental centres of reform from 1554, then, others remained closer to home. The current of Protestant exiles that had flowed between England and Scotland during the 1530s and 1540s was reversed, as a number of reformers travelled north in the bid to escape persecution. Among them were certain Scots who had previously settled in England, such as William Harlaw and John Willock. As Knox noted, 'in that cruell persecutioun, used by that monstour, Marie of England, war godlie men dispersed in diverse nationis, of whom it pleaseth the goodnes of our God to send some unto us, for our conforte and instructioun'.[3] His assessment was melodramatic, but it points to the differing fortunes of Protestant reformers in the two countries.

Knox's account of the expansion of the privy kirks in Scotland, spurred on by the preaching of Harlaw and Willock, gives a picture of resilient bands of godly men and women, gathering their strength and increasing in number for a confrontation with the forces of popery. In this version of events, 'God so blessed the labouris of his weak servandis, that na small parte of the Baronis of this Realme begane to abhorre the tyranny of the Bischoppes', and 'men almost universallie begane to dowbt whetther that thei myght (God not offended) give thare bodelye presence to the Messe'.[4] This interpretation not only detracts from orthodox reforming measures, as already noted, but also threatens to exaggerate the numerical strength of the privy kirks before 1559. The extent of convinced Protestant opinion in these secret gatherings is difficult to assess with any accuracy, though congregations appear to have existed in Edinburgh, Dundee, Perth, Stirling, Ayr, Brechin, and Montrose. In general, however, reforming opinion did not extend far beyond certain distinct areas of the Lothians, Angus and the Mearns, and the south-west.[5] It seems likely that much moderate reforming enthusiasm among the laity was, as Hamilton intended, drawn into the orbit of official plans devised by the Kirk, leaving more extreme Protestant activists clearly in a minority. Paradoxically, the regent's policy of toleration may have actually done something to undermine Protestant resolve by depriving reformers of the sense of fortitude in adversity, which was such a prop to the English in the same period.

The developing network of privy kirks did, however, mark an important advance for the Protestant movement in Scotland. The preaching of Willock, Harlaw, and other reformers such as Paul Methven and John

---

[3] Knox, i. 244–5; Pitscottie, *History and Chronicles*, ii. 136–7.
[4] Knox, i. 298–9.
[5] Kirk, *Patterns*, 13; Donaldson, *Scottish Reformation*, 49.

Douglas was instrumental in sustaining committed pockets of Protestant sympathisers. Knox embarked on his own preaching tour of 1555–6, centring on Edinburgh, Angus and the Mearns, and Ayrshire. This further stimulated reforming enthusiasms as he conducted Protestant services in some areas for the first time. For the most part, however, the areas through which Knox travelled during the course of his nine-month stay had displayed a long-standing interest in reform, as seen in their responses to the English Protestant influence and Wishart's preaching during the 1540s. Knox frequently preached in private houses, and to small, if dedicated groups of supporters, being protected on his travels by loyal Protestant lairds such as John Erskine of Dun and Robert Lockhart of Bar.[6] As a member of Wishart's entourage, Knox had been profoundly affected by the stirring example of the reformer, but the scope of his own activities was initially more limited. The religious atmosphere of the earlier period had been a volatile one, with the aggressive evangelization of the English military effort encouraging outspokenness and risk-taking, building to the Castilian enterprise in 1546. A decade later the latitude of the regent's attitude to reform offered some hope for measured Protestant expansion and consolidation, giving less incentive for an immediate challenge to the regime.

This did not prevent Knox from attracting the suspicion of the authorities, who summoned him to appear in Edinburgh before the archbishop of St Andrews in May 1556. When it seemed that he would arrive flanked by bands of supporters, however, the clergy backed down, and the summons was revoked. The fact that Knox remained in Edinburgh for ten days preaching to his largest audiences yet, demonstrated a growing popular receptivity to Protestant opinion, but Knox's appeal to the regent on the behalf of his fellow preachers was not successful.[7] Knox left the country shortly afterwards, and immediately the bishops repeated their summons, condemning the reformer for heresy and burning him in effigy when he did not comply.[8] He would later compose a fierce protest against the sentence pronounced by the authorities, issuing an impassioned appeal to the nobility 'to bridel and represse theyr folie and blind rage'.[9] For now, however, he was favourably impressed by the fervour that he witnessed in the Scottish privy kirks. Knox had recently been appointed minister to a large exile congregation in Geneva, and had left for Scotland reluctantly, but he found himself rewarded by the godliness of his countrymen. Having previously

[6] Knox, i. 246–51; Cowan, *Scottish Reformation*, 108–10.
[7] Knox, 1. 251–2; iv. 73–84.
[8] Calderwood, i. 318.
[9] Knox, iv. 497.

judged the troubles of the English Church to be 'double more dolorous unto my hert, than ever were the troubles of Scotland', he now wrote to his mother-in-law Elizabeth Bowes from Scotland 'the fervencie heir doith fer exceid all utheris that I have sene'.[10] Before leaving for Geneva Knox prepared an order for reformed worship to be used in his absence.[11] After his years of association with the English Church, under Edward and in exile, he had begun 'to rediscover his Scottish roots' and to formulate hopes for Protestant growth north of the border.[12]

Knox remained in close contact with his godly allies in Scotland. When, in 1557, the Protestant nobles Glencairn, Lorne, Erskine, and Lord James Stewart declared that the cause needed his encouragement, and that they were ready to jeopardize their lives for it, Knox consulted with Calvin, and prepared to join them. On arriving in Dieppe, however, he received further letters indicating that the lords had changed their minds, believing that his arrival would not help their cause. Furious at their prevarication, Knox immediately fired off a letter warning them that their inconstancy brought shame upon them and on himself, and they should consider 'the grevouse plagues and punishmentis of God, which assuredly shall apprehend nott only yow, but everie inhabitant of that miserable Realme and Ile'. Some weeks later, in a rather calmer mood, he wrote to them once more of the duties of those whom God 'hath determinat and apoyntit to be reularis comforteris and manteaneris of uthiris'.[13] Knox believed his arguments led directly to the lords' decision to subscribe a common bond to 'apply our hole power, substance, and our verray lyves, to manteane, sett fordward, and establish the most blessed word of God and his Congregatioun'.[14] Whether or not Knox provided the inspiration for the bond, the action of the lords was hugely significant. Their statement of intention, adopting the form of the traditional and previously secular practice of bonding, articulated their self-imposed responsibilities towards God. Using a mode of expression that their contemporaries would understand very well, the lords thereby made plain their determination to advance the true religion.[15] They may have been few in number, but their bond would be followed by others, and was a momentous step for Scottish Protestantism. With an agreement to use common prayers weekly, and meet in private houses for the

[10] Knox, iii. 133; iv. 217.

[11] Knox, iv. 133–9.

[12] Mason, 'Knox, Resistance, and the Royal Supremacy', 165.

[13] Knox, i. 267–72; iv. 257–86.

[14] Knox, i. 273.

[15] I am grateful to Dr Wormald for her insights into the origins of the 1557 bond, and its importance to the Protestant movement in Scotland.

interpretation of scripture, the movement began to take organizational shape.[16]

The order of common prayer to which the lords referred was almost certainly the English Prayer Book of 1552, which, as Rough's trial revealed, was simultaneously being used by secret Protestant congregations in England. The order may not have completely satisfied more extreme reformers such as Knox, but it was a convenient reformed rite on which the privy kirks could base their services. English religious literature of various sorts played an important part in the development of Protestant opinion in Scotland, as it had done since the early days of England's break with Rome, and private libraries contained works by a range of English Protestant authors. Marjorie Roger, wife of the Edinburgh merchant Adam Fullarton, built up a impressive collection of devotional treatises by means of her husband's trading contacts with England. Her will revealed that she owned copies of Tyndale, Jewel, Becon, Cranmer, Hooper, and 'ane buke of ye lettaris of ye marturis q[uhi]lk wes burnit in Ingland'.[17] An Edinburgh lawyer, Clement Little, also had an extensive library, containing books by Cranmer, Ridley, Becon, Ponet, Jewel, Robert Barnes, and Robert Watson.[18] The proliferation of such works among Scottish reformers before 1559 helped to shape and sustain their Protestant beliefs.

An English influence upon the developing congregations was also apparent in the background of their first leaders. Both Harlaw and Willock had been committed supporters of Edwardian Protestantism as ministers in the Church during the 1540s.[19] Paul Methven, another of the earliest preachers of reform in Scotland, married an Englishwoman, and appears to have had further English connections: in an intriguing comment of 1563, Thomas Randolph wrote to Cecil from Scotland, of 'One Paul Meffane a preacher brought up under Mr Coverdall'. The reference appears to have been to Miles Coverdale, whose Scottish sister-in-law was married to the Scottish reformer and one-time exile to England, John MacAlpine.[20] Such connections reveal an intricate pattern of association and kinship between some of the most prominent Protestant activists in the English and Scottish Churches. Knox's own English background, first in the Edwardian Church, and then in his experiences of the Marian exile, was evident. With the influence of these English associations, and a change in emphasis from

---

[16] Wormald, *Court, Kirk and Community*, 111–12; Knox, i. 273–5.
[17] SRO MS CC 8/8/13, fo. 32; Lynch, *Edinburgh*, 84–5. Professor Lynch kindly supplied me with the full details of the works in Marjorie Roger's library at the time of her death.
[18] Kirk, *Patterns*, 67; EUL MS Dd. 3. 16.
[19] Calderwood, i. 303–4.
[20] Pitscottie, *History and Chronicles*, ii. 136; *CSP Scot.*, vol. i, no. 1163; *DNB*, xii. 366–7.

Lutheran teachings to Swiss doctrines embracing the wholesale reformation of doctrine, worship and morality, Scottish Protestantism began to acquire its distinct character. Its steady, if small-scale, consolidation in the later 1550s was in marked contrast to the oppression being suffered by English reformers. Underground congregations such as the London assembly of John Rough existed in a climate of fear and suspicion, and the fact that even a small number from England sought refuge in the regime of Mary of Guise highlights the varying fortunes of reform in the two countries. The numbers practising covert worship in England are hard to assess, and for many, the best hope appeared to lie either in outward conformity or exile to the continent. As many as 800 chose the latter course.[21]

II. A SHARED EXILE EXPERIENCE

The establishment of exile communities in continental centres of reform continued a tradition of fugitive collaboration in the cause of religion. The Anglo-Scottish border had become a focus for dissenters after the creation of the confessional divide in 1534, but in fact sympathetic cross-border associations persisted whatever the religious complexions of the two Churches. As early as 1511, for instance, a group of Scottish Blackfriars sought sanctuary within the English Dominican province to escape the stern regimen being introduced by a new Scottish provincial.[22] In the later years of the century the two countries would each espouse a Protestant faith, but a number of radical Scottish Protestants would still chose to flee to England following the passage of strict anti-Presbyterian statutes by the Scottish parliament in the early 1580s. Their hope was to 'travail in our vocation as it should please the Lord to give occasion', and an observer at the funeral of one of their number spoke of the 'work of God in bringing him to Londoun', deriving consolation from the thought that 'undoubtedlie his thirty-four dayes teaching wanne some to Christ'.[23]

In the mid-1550s, too, the nominal Catholic consensus between the countries was evidently incapable of deterring cross-border exiles, thanks to the variation in severity between religious regimes. The opportunities afforded by flight within Britain were, however, much reduced.

[21] Garrett, *Marian Exiles*, 30–2.
[22] Ross, 'Some Notes on the Religious Orders', 192.
[23] Gordon Donaldson, 'Scottish Presbyterian Exiles in England, 1584–1588', *RSCHS* 14 (1960–2), 70; *Miscellany of the Wodrow Society*, ed. D. Laing (Edinburgh: Wodrow Society, 1844), i. 450–1.

Although the relatively mild Scottish administration avoided rigorous anti-heresy proceedings, both realms retained their sanctions against religious dissidents, and so the danger of persecution remained. More significant, though, was the way in which the common Catholicism of England and Scotland in the 1550s deprived internal British exile of its ideological symbolism. When their Churches espoused differing faiths, English and Scottish exiles crossing the border could claim to be pursuing the godliness of a purer religious environment and association with devout allies. From 1554 the propagation of the Gospel in Scotland may have offered a worthy objective for a small number of committed preachers; but in general, the exchange of covert religious observance in one country for marginally less covert worship in the other did not have the same idealistic appeal as a complete renunciation of Satan's 'kingdome of darknesse'.[24] The notion that escape could be part of the Lord's plan for the increase of the true religion, though it was a theme of the Scottish exiles of the 1580s, was undoubtedly difficult to sustain when there was no outright confessional gulf between the countries. Under these circumstances it was the reformed cities of the continent that appeared to offer a more rarefied religious atmosphere. John Banks recognized the opportunity the exiles were offered 'to continue our studies; whereby, should it please God to return us to our country, we may be able to refute the doctrines of the papists'.[25]

The practical difficulties of their flight convinced many that they were not seeking mere bodily comfort. Thomas Lever lamented to Bullinger, 'we are deserted by our friends, laughed to scorn by many, spurned by others, assailed by reproaches and revilings', while Knox warned potential exiles of their fate as 'thois that frome realme to realme, and citie to citie, seik rest as pilgremes, and yit sall find none'.[26] The themes of suffering in exile, and parallels with the banishment of the children of Israel, pervaded the thinking of the Marian exiles. In considering the circumstances of their flight they were acutely self-conscious, devoting themselves to the problem of understanding the cause of God's displeasure with his people. Their irresistible tendency in doing so was to focus upon England, since, as they saw it, their country's unique sin was to have received the true religion under the godly king Edward, then rejected it after the accession of Mary. The only way in which they could understand this tragedy was to fix upon their failure to embrace the Gospel wholeheartedly under 'that true Josias'. Their 'listlessness and ingratitude' had brought these plagues upon them,

---

[24] Knox, i. 244.
[25] *Original Letters*, vol. i, no. 142.
[26] Ibid., no. 87; Knox, *Works*, iv. 219–21.

though God had shown his mercy to the remnant of believers now preserved in exile.[27] This interpretation involved a complex fusion of the biblical images of True Church, restored to them under Edward but then rejected; and the 'very electe and chosen people off God' who resisted the return to Rome. Their redemption would lie in earnest repentance and the utter rejection of idolatry. These ideas were expressed endlessly, in apocalyptic terms that presented their struggle as a battle with 'that great Antichrist the man of synne, and chylde of perdicion' in these latter days.[28]

The exiles' obsession with explaining England's decline from the word of God can obscure the fact that their congregations in Frankfurt, Emden, Basle, Geneva, and elsewhere were not exclusively English communities. There was a notable Scottish element to the Marian exile population, not to mention a handful of Welsh refugees, whose existence has been largely overlooked.[29] Contemporaries were sometimes guilty of using the term 'English' as shorthand. The complexities of categorizing large numbers of refugees defeated the notaries of Frankfurt, who classed French, Flemish, and Scottish exiles alike as 'Engländer'.[30] There was similar ambiguity in the letter from the Frankfurt congregation to Knox, inviting him to be their pastor in November 1554. They were, they told him, 'all of one body, and also being of one nation, tongue and country', even though the signatories included their Scottish pastor, John Mackbrair.[31] John Foxe famously referred on the title-page of his *Acts and Monuments* to 'this Realme of England and Scotlande',[32] and further ambivalence could be seen in John Aylmer's *An Harborowe for Faithfull and Trewe Subiectes*, written in Strasbourg in 1559 to distance the exiles from Knox's controversial opinions. Aylmer asserted that Knox felt England's sorrows 'like a good member of that bodie which then suffered', but subsequently described him as a 'stranger' intent on disturbing the English state. Strype noted this inconsistency, but muddied the waters further with the explanation that

---

[27] Jane E. A. Dawson, 'The Apocalyptic Thinking of the Marian Exiles', in Michael Wilks (ed.), *Prophecy and Eschatology*, (Studies in Church History, subsidia 10; Oxford: Blackwell publishers, 1994), 82–4; Thomas Becon, *A Confortable Epistle too Goddes faythfull people in Englande* (Strasbourg, 1554; *RSTC* 1716), sig. Aiii^v; *Original Letters*, vol. i, no. 139.

[28] Dawson, 'Apocalyptic Thinking', 78, 84–9; Becon, *Confortable Epistle*, sig. Aii^v; John Scory, *An epistle written unto all the faythfull that be in pryson in Englande* (Emden, 1555; *RSTC* 21854), sig. Aii^v.

[29] For Welsh exiles see Garrett, *Marian Exiles*, 141, 151, 200–1.

[30] M. A. Simpson, *John Knox and the Troubles begun at Frankfurt* (West Linton: the author, 1975), 138.

[31] *A Brief Discourse of the Troubles at Frankfort, 1554–1558 AD; attributed to William Whittingham, Dean of Durham, 1575 AD*, ed. Edward Arber (1907), 36.

[32] Mason, 'Anglo-British Imperialism', 185.

Knox was virtually English, 'living in England upon Queen Mary's Acces to the Crown, and flying then with the rest of the English in the beginning of her Reign'.[33]

A tendency to disregard the Scottish Marian exiles has persisted among historians. John Eadie's *The English Bible* of 1876 praises the translation of the scriptures produced by the Genevan exiles as 'the self-imposed work of noble-hearted Englishmen', failing to note that the collaborators included the Scotsmen John Knox, William Kethe, and John Baron.[34] Charles Martin's oversight in his 1915 study of the congregation in Geneva is even more glaring: after the departure of the exiles from Geneva, he says, 'a single Englishman was received as a citizen between 1560 and 1570. This was the Scot, Henry Scrimger.'[35] Christina Garrett's *The Marian Exiles* contains frequent references to 'the English communities' and 'John Knox's English congregation at Geneva', despite the fact that her own census recognizes the Scottish identities of at least eighteen individuals. Her list of 'Englishmen at the University of Basle, 1554–59', for example, includes the entry, 'Alexander Cogburnus [Cockburn], Scotus'.[36]

The records kept by the exiles themselves and more detailed registers of the cities in which they took refuge shed more light on the extent of Scottish membership of the 'English' exile congregations. Exact numbers can probably never be arrived at, partly because it may safely be assumed that more Scots are hidden among those listed as English, and also through the concentration of the records upon adult male exiles, with only passing references to wives and children. Some basic information may be ascertained, however. The first minister of the community established at Frankfurt in July 1554 was the Scotsman John Mackbrair, the apostate Cistercian and exile to Edwardian England. His countrymen William Kethe and John Knox were also members of the Frankfurt church, and they were among the number who seceded to form the Geneva congregation in November 1555.[37] Here they were joined by upwards of twenty Scottish exiles, a noteworthy group within a total population that reached around 200.[38] In Basle there was apparently a smaller Scottish presence. John

---

[33] Aylmer, *Harborowe*, sigs. Bi^v, Fii^r; John Strype, *Historical Collections of the Life and Acts of John Aylmer . . .* (1701), 229.

[34] John Eadie, *The English Bible*, 2 vols. (Macmillan, 1876), ii. 30; Charles Martin, *Les Protestants anglais réfugiés à Genève au temps de Calvin, 1555–1560* (Geneva, 1915), 242.

[35] 'Un seul anglais fut reçu bourgeois entre 1560 et 1570. Ce fut l'écossais Henry Scrimger': Martin, *Protestants anglais*, 263.

[36] Garrett, *Marian Exiles*, 23, 25, 42, 51, 57, 357.

[37] *Brief Discourse*, 30–5, 41, 61.

[38] *Livre des Anglois à Genève*, ed. J. S. Burn (1831), 5, 8–11; *Livre des Habitants de Genève*, 1549–1560 ed. P. Geisendorf (Geneva, 1957), i. 91, 138–9, 202, 213; Kirk, *Patterns*, 88.

Baron, presumably accompanied by his wife Anne, had his son baptized there in January 1554, and Alexander Cockburn, son of the Anglophile collaborator, enrolled at the university in 1554.[39]

Within the congregation in Emden was a slightly larger Scottish group, including the former long-term exile to England, John Willock, and John Rough, the Castilian who had gone on to become minister to Hull. Rough was a temporary visitor to Emden before his return to London in 1557, and his famous trial and execution for heresy. Willock was a more permanent member of the church, although he left it to undertake two diplomatic missions to Scotland on behalf of the duchess of East Friesland. There is some question over whether or not Willock was formally appointed as a minister to the congregation, though he did practise for a time as a physician.[40] John MacDowell, the Scottish exile to Salisbury and then London, is also thought to have fled to Emden in 1554, and the Scotsmen David Simson and Laurence Duguid were two more members of the community.[41] This makes a total of at least five in a church whose overall size was not substantial. Local records reveal that thirty-five incomers from Marian England became citizens between 1554 and 1558, and so the Scottish element can hardly have gone unnoticed.[42] There does not seem to be evidence of Scottish membership of the Marian communities at Strasbourg or Zurich, though the deficiencies of the records indicate this cannot be ruled out. The same is true of the smaller congregation at Aarau, although the foundation of this church owed a debt to William Kethe, who assisted with its removal from Wesel in 1556.[43]

The Scottish role in the life and worship of the Marian exile congregations was far from negligible. Many of the Scottish refugees arrived in Europe from England, where they had already experienced religious exile. This suggests a certain degree of identification with English concerns, which may go some way to explaining their apparent invisibility within the Marian exile churches. In Geneva, however, the injection of new blood directly from Scotland reawakened an interest in the state of reform in both countries. The exiles here were seeking sanctuary from both Marian England and Marian Scotland, making it unlikely that the religious and political debate among them would retain its purely English boundaries. It

---

[39] Garrett, *Marian Exiles*, 81, 357.
[40] Foxe, viii. 444; Knox, i. 245, 256; Duncan Shaw, 'John Willock', in id. (ed.), *Reformation and Revolution . . .* (Edinburgh: St Andrew Press, 1967), 51; Pettegree, *Marian Protestantism*, 16–17, 35.
[41] Garrett, *Marian Exiles*, 227, 336, 288, 274; Shaw, 'John Willock', 51.
[42] Pettegree, *Marian Protestantism*, 13.
[43] *Brief Discourse*, 219.

also seemed probable that, in the liberating conditions of their foreign exile, the Scots would be less inclined than some of their English counterparts to hold all aspects of the Edwardian liturgy in static reverence. There was no peculiarly Scottish strand of exile thought, just as there was no unanimity among the English; but the Scottish contribution added a distinct edge to the exile debates.

III. THE PRAYER BOOK CONTROVERSIES

The impact of the Scots upon the Marian exile culture was a varied one. In their capacity as ministers and worshippers, Scottish men, women, and children played an active part in the exile congregations alongside their English brethren. This inevitably involved them in the intense and emotionally charged religious discussions that frequently characterized the exile communities. Differences over the forms of worship to be adopted in exile were more pronounced in some centres than others. Whereas the Marian churches in Strasbourg and Zurich appear to have been relatively calm in this respect, agreeing on their adherence to the second Edwardian Prayer Book,[44] the congregations of Frankfurt and Basle experienced damaging controversies. Essentially, the issue of contention was whether the English order of 1552 should be retained in its entirety, as a mark of fidelity to the Edwardian Church, and the now-imprisoned authors of the liturgy; or whether the opportunity should be taken for further reformation following the example of the 'best reformed churches' in which the exiles were taking refuge.

Their allegiance to leading churchmen, now captive in England and awaiting execution, led many exiles to insist on rigid adherence to the Prayer Book. Such loyalty, they believed, would demonstrate their repentance for their former ungodliness, signifying a first stage in their battle against the forces of Antichrist now raging in England. This opinion was immeasurably reinforced by the publication of writings such as Ridley's *Frendly Farewel*, addressed 'unto all his true Lovers and frendes in God, a little before that he suffred for the testimony of the truthe of Christ his Gospell'. Here the former bishop of London offered his consolation and encouragement to the exiles, together with a lengthy oration on the perfection of the Edwardian Church, which 'had of late the infinite goodnesse and aboundaunte grace of almightye God, greate substaunce, greate ryches, of

[44] W. M. Southgate, 'The Marian Exiles and the Influence of John Calvin', *History*, 27 (1942), 150-1.

heavenlye treasure: greate plentye of Goddes true and sincere worde, the true and wholesome administracion of Christes holye Sacramentes, the hole profession of Christes religion truelye and plainlye sette forth in Baptisme' and numerous other virtues, which Ridley described in full.[45] Similar sentiments pervaded many of the exiles' writings. John Scory praised the example of England's blessed martyrs, whose sacrifice sealed the doctrine of their church 'in the consciences of goddes electe and chosen people', and John Olde's *Acquital or purgation of the moost catholyke Prince Edwarde VI*, was ostentatiously loyal to the Edwardian establishment and its divines.[46]

In fact, Ridley himself showed some flexibility over the adaptation of the English liturgy for use in exile. Writing to Grindal, a member of the refugee church in Strasbourg, he conceded that the circumstances of exile might necessitate the alteration of 'things indifferent, and not commanded or forbidden by God's Word, and wherein the customs of divers countries be diverse'.[47] The assumption was, however, that it should at least form the basis for exile worship, and certain sections of the exile communities raised this idea to an unshakeable principle. The strength of such feeling within a part of the Frankfurt congregation created the grounds for a confrontation with those who preferred to see the exile period as a time for the refinement and purification of their forms of worship beyond anything that England had yet seen.

The Marian settlement in Frankfurt was formally established in July 1554, following the arrival in the city of a small group of exiles led by William Whittingham. According to an agreement with the existing French congregation, whose pastor Poullain had previously ministered to the Edwardian Strangers' Church in Glastonbury, they would share the use of a church in the town, adopting the reformed French order already being observed there. Despite this condition, there appears to have been tacit approval for the use by newcomers of a modified form of the English Prayer Book, Whittingham and his brethren taking the opportunity to discard elements of the order with which they were dissatisfied. In November Knox was invited to be minister to the congregation, replacing his countryman Mackbrair, and the community settled into its round of religious worship. Their adaptation of the 1552 order did not go unchallenged: before the end of the year delegations were sent to Frankfurt from both Strasbourg and Zurich, with heavyweight figures such as Grindal

[45] Nicholas Ridley, *A frendly farewel* ... (I. Day, 1559; *RSTC* 21051), sigs. Avii[v]–Bi[r].

[46] Scory, *Epistle*, sig. Aiii[v]; John Olde, *The acquital or purgation of the moost catholyke Prince Edward VI* (Emden, 1555; *RSTC* 18797), sig. Aii[r].

[47] Knox, iv. 62.

doing their best to convince the congregation to use the unadulterated Prayer Book. A round of discussions within formally appointed committees followed in the first part of 1555, and of two compromise orders that resulted, the second more recognizably English version was finally accepted.[48]

The doctrinal discord among the Frankfurt refugees, however, was only just beginning. Just weeks after the settlement of their liturgy, affairs were thrown into renewed confusion by the arrival of Richard Cox, a prominent Edwardian divine and hard-line defender of the Prayer Book. Although it was at Knox's instigation that Cox and his companions were admitted to the congregation in March 1555, they had no compunction about engineering his removal from office. They made public Knox's assertion, in his *Faithful Admonition*, that Mary Tudor was worse than Jezebel, and Philip of Spain no less an enemy to Christ than was Nero. This forced the hand of the Frankfurt authorities, who were unwilling risk a confrontation with the emperor on the matter, and so agreed to Knox's dismissal as minister.[49] Cox proceeded to reinstate the English order, for which he secured the sanction of the magistrates. His actions were justified with the assertion that 'they would do as they had done in England; and that they would have the face of an English Church'. Knox's retort, 'the Lord grant it to have the face of Christ's Church', encapsulated their differences over the inviolability of the Edwardian order.[50]

The bitter divisions between the Coxian party and Knox's remaining adherents proved impossible to resolve, and in September 1555 a group headed by Whittingham left the city for Geneva. In the course of the Frankfurt contentions, their consultations with Calvin led them to conclude that only by detaching themselves from supporters of the Prayer Book could they attain the purity of worship they sought. Cox and his supporters, denying the charge that they were 'too precise in enforcing English ceremonies, and unreasonably partial to our own country', claimed to be not 'so entirely wedded to our country as not to be able to endure any customs differing from our own'. They were defiant, however, in acknowledging that they retained certain things as a 'concession to the love of our country', and they castigated their opponents, whom they described as 'altogether a disgrace to their country, for whatever has been bestowed from above upon our country in this respect, with exceeding arrogance, not to say impudence, they are treading under foot'.[51] This constant invocation of their

[48] *Brief Discourse*, 23–53; *Original Letters*, vol. i, no. 88.
[49] *Brief Discourse*, 54–70; *Original Letters*, vol. ii, nos. 358, 360; Calderwood, i. 302.
[50] *Brief Discourse*, 54, 62.
[51] *Original Letters*, vol. ii, nos. 361, 358, 357.

country, and veneration for forms of worship simply by virtue of their English heritage, created a gulf between them and the associates of Knox and Whittingham.

The critics of conventional Prayer Book worship who, Cox failed to note, were Scottish as well as English, displayed no lack of regard for the Edwardian establishment, or for its divines and humble professors now suffering persecution. Their ambition, however, was to take their discipline to new heights of godliness, freed from the constraints of parliament and convocation, and the accumulated weight of Henrician and Edwardian tradition. There was a conspicuous Scottish dimension to the group that settled in Geneva to live out these ideals, including Knox, Kethe, and John Baron and his family.[52] It should be noted, however, that theirs was not a specifically 'Scottish' viewpoint. John Mackbrair, for instance, remained in Frankfurt in company with the Prayer Book supporters,[53] and the Genevan community itself was a decidedly mixed Anglo-Scottish group. The divisions between the exiles were very clearly ideological rather than national. The possibility that the Scottish contribution to the exile controversies tended to reinforce attitudes that were less reverential to English forms, however, should not be dismissed. The English and Scottish settlers in Geneva were united by their rejection of an unbending attachment to Prayer Book forms.

As the Genevan community expanded after 1555, there was no recurrence of the divisions that had split the Frankfurt congregation. Elsewhere, however, the disputes continued. John Foxe and John Bale, both of whom supported Prayer Book worship, left Frankfurt for Basle only to find themselves once more surrounded by controversy. Bale wrote to Thomas Ashley in Frankfurt of the acrimonious disagreements created by purists in Basle, who, he said, 'blaspheme our Communion, calling it a popish mas, and say, that it hath a popish face, with other fierce dispisings and cursed speakings'.[54] Bale himself was vehemently opposed to Roman practices, castigating their 'babling prayers, theyr potases, bedes, temples, aulters, songes, houres, belles, Images, organes, ornamentes, Jewels, lyghtes, oylynges, shauinges, religios disgisings, dyuersite of feastes, constrained vowes, fastinges, processyons & pratlinges'.[55] During his time in exile he collaborated with Foxe in the development of an intensely apocalyptic interpretation of the exiles' circumstances, depicting the struggle of the reformers

[52] *Livre des Anglois*, 5–11; Garrett, *Marian Exiles*, 214, 204–5, 81.

[53] Garrett, *Marian Exiles*, 224.

[54] Strype, *Ecclesiastical Memorials*, iii/2, 313–15.

[55] John Bale, *The Image of both Churches after the moste Wonderful and heavenly Reuelacion of Sainct John the Eua[n]gelist* (I. Daye and W. Seres, *c*.1550; *RSTC* 1298), I, sig. Biv˅.

with the forces of Antichrist in precise historical terms. Both reformers, however, combined this imaginative fervour with a conservative attachment to the Prayer Book and its forms. Foxe had numbered himself among Knox's supporters in Frankfurt, and was a lifelong friend of the reformer, but maintained his disapproval of Knox's radicalism in religious affairs.[56]

The English and Scottish exiles in Geneva were distinctive among the exiles for their readiness to experiment with godly discipline. Their idea of the exile period as one of opportunity was not wholeheartedly shared by their counterparts elsewhere. English exiles in cities such as Strasbourg and Zurich undoubtedly appreciated their opportunities to associate with prestigious European reformers. Ponet thanked God 'that he has afforded me for my comforters Bullinger, Melanchthon, Martyr and other most shining lights of his church', and Bullinger himself was impressed by the diligence of the exiles, who 'are so devoted to, and so greatly profit by, their literary and theological studies, that it is impossible not to expect from them the most abundant fruit'.[57] Their consultations and studies, however, do not seem to have led to any significant departure from their devotion to the Edwardian religion. The core group of the Genevan congregation was more receptive to reformed and especially Calvinist influences, having little patience with the half-hearted commitment or dubious motives of some other exiles. Christopher Goodman, who arrived in Geneva from Strasbourg in October 1555, was especially contemptuous of refugees who, 'in fleeing from their Quene, runne to the Pope'.[58] The choice of cities such as Paris, Rome, Venice, and Padua as places of refuge was a sure sign of considerations that were not purely, or even primarily, religious. For the Genevan community, by contrast, the location of their church was intimately related to their godly enterprise.

IV. THE GODLY EXPERIMENT IN GENEVA

In their choice of Geneva for the establishment of their congregation, the English and Scottish exiles affirmed their commitment to the 'simple and pure Order' described by Calvin during the Frankfurt contentions. The setting-up of their new church would allow them to discard the 'things both superstitious, impure, and imperfyte' that survived from the Edwardian

---

[56] R. Bauckham, *Tudor Apocalypse: Sixteenth Century Apocalypticism, Millenarianism and the English Reformation, from John Bale to John Foxe and Thomas Brightman* (Abingdon: Sutton Courtenay Press, 1978), 68–76; Firth, *Apocalyptic Tradition*, 40–6; Knox, v. 5–6.

[57] *Original Letters*, vol. i, no. 55; vol. ii, no. 353.

[58] Goodman, *Superior Powers*, 225.

Church, namely the ritual and ornamentation for which they could find no scriptural warrant.[59] The exiles embarked on their new venture enthusiastically. Goodman had considered it their duty to seek out 'those places where [the Gospel] is set forthe in greateste abundance and perfection, as was after Christes ascension in Jerusalem', and Knox felt that they had found just such a place in Geneva, 'the maist perfyt schoole of Chryst that ever was in the erth since the dayis of the Apostillis'.[60] The Marian church was formally established in the city on 1 November 1555. Knox and Goodman were appointed as its pastors, with Anthony Gilby taking the place of Knox during his initial absence. The selection of elders and deacons completed the congregational structure of the new church.[61]

The exiles based their liturgy upon a settlement that had been agreed in Frankfurt early in 1555, by a committee consisting of Knox, Whittingham, Gilby, Foxe, and Thomas Cole. This drew heavily on Calvin's own *Forme of Prayers* for Strasbourg, and it had been passed over by the Frankfurt congregation in favour of a more English-influenced order. Its reference to the model of the apostolic church, and rejection of the ceremonies associated with the English book, however, recommended it to the Genevan congregation. The *Forme of prayers and ministration of the sacraments*, as it became known, did not turn its back on Edwardian reform altogether: both the exhortation for the Lord's Supper and the marriage service were based on material from the 1552 Prayer Book. It was uncompromising, however, in its rejection of man-made ceremonies, the preface asserting that 'what so ever is added to this Worde by man's device, seme it never so good, holy, or beautifull, yet before our God, whiche is jelous and can not admitt any companyon or counsellor, it is evell, wicked and abominable'.[62] Knox had been arguing for this kind of purity since the time of his interventions in the composition of the second Prayer Book, and in Geneva it seemed he had the chance to achieve it. The influence of the *Forme* would also be felt within both the English and Scottish Churches long after the exile period had ended, since it was adopted, with some modifications, as the *Book of Common Order* for the reformed Scottish Kirk. It was a favoured order among English puritans also, although it never received official sanction south of the border.[63]

[59] *Brief Discourse*, 78–80; Calderwood, i. 297.

[60] Goodman, *Superior Powers*, 228; Knox, iv. 240.

[61] *Livre des Anglois*, 8, 12.

[62] John T. McNeill, *The History and Character of Calvinism* (New York: Oxford University Press, 1967), 150–1; *The Liturgical Portions of the Genevan Service Book . . .*, ed. William D. Maxwell (Faith Press, 1965), 17–32, 51–3; Knox, iv. 160–1.

[63] *Liturgical Portions*, 8; *The Book of Common Order*, ed. G. W. Sprott (Edinburgh: William Blackwood & Sons, 1901), p. xv; Knox, vi. 277–334.

The reformed conviction of their liturgy set the tone for the religious life of the Marian congregation in Geneva, which grew substantially in the years after 1555. English exiles made up the greater part of the newcomers, but they were accompanied by a number of Scottish men, women and children, who came to form a noteworthy component of the total congregation. According to the register kept by the congregation, there were around eleven Scottish exiles within the 187-strong congregation by 1559.[64] This list, however, appears to have been incomplete, and it also focused heavily upon heads of households, being highly inconsistent in its references to the wives, families, and servants of the exiles. The records of the city and of the Geneva Academy established at the end of the decade shed some more light on the Scottish presence in Geneva. The town register records the names of at least four new Scottish citizens received between 1555 and 1559, who are not listed in the records of the congregation itself, despite their evident involvement with the Marian church there. One of the first students to enrol at the academy at its foundation was the Scotsman Peter Young, who is likewise absent from the congregation register.[65] It seems likely, therefore, that there were twenty or more Scottish members of an exile community whose actual size was probably in excess of 200.

The English may have formed the majority of the congregation, but it was a recognizably Anglo-Scottish group. It was also unusual among the exile churches in the attraction it held for Scottish incomers after its initial foundation. There were new Scottish arrivals to the city every year between 1555 and 1559, increasing in numbers in the following decades.[66] Perhaps as a result of its distinctive composition, the English and Scottish brethren in Geneva seemed able to detach themselves successfully from the traditional suspicions that characterized relations between their two countries even at their most cordial moments.[67] During earlier periods of collaboration between reformers, these tensions were never far from the surface, as Scottish preachers in the Henrician and Edwardian Churches had discovered. The disastrous outcome of the Rough Wooing had latterly worsened relations between the countries, and certain sections of the exile congregations shared the habitual xenophobia of the English. The Anglo-Scottish community in Geneva, however, was a thoroughly integrated one, display-

[64] *Livre des Anglois*, 5–11.

[65] *Livre du Recteur de l'Académie de Genève*, ed. S. Stelling-Michaud (Geneva, 1959), vol. i, 9 Nov. 1559; *Livre des Habitants*, 91, 138–9, 202, 213; Dawson, 'Early Career of Christopher Goodman', 162.

[66] Kirk, *Patterns*, 89–90.

[67] Jane E. A. Dawson, 'Trumpeting Resistance: Christopher Goodman and John Knox', in Mason (ed.), *John Knox and the British Reformations*, 132–3.

ing strong cohesion and stability. Goodman, writing to Martyr in Zurich, described 'the happy agreement and solid peace which, by the great blessing of God, we enjoy in this place'.[68]

The congregation's register reveals that there were nineteen baptisms between 1556 and 1558, with Knox and Whittingham each acting as godfather on two occasions, and Goodman on three. One of Whittingham's godsons was Nathaniel, the son of Knox; while the godfather of Knox's younger son, Eleezer, was Miles Coverdale, whose own wife came from Perth. The nine marriages among the exiles reveal their contacts with fellow Protestants of many nationalities. They included that of Whittingham to Katheryne Jaquemayne of Orleans, Sir John Borthwick to the Breton Jane Bonespoir, and Jane Stafford to Maximilian Celsus, 'the Italian precher'.[69] The Genevan exiles were clearly not unique for their formation of ties of acquaintance and kinship within their community and with their European brethren. Rachel, the daughter of John and Anne Hooper, and a member of the Frankfurt church, for instance, had none other than Bullinger for her godfather.[70] The pattern of personal relations in Geneva, however, created a sustaining network of friends and co-religionists, giving the impression of a close-knit but far from insular society, in which distinctions of nationality meant little.

The openness of the Genevan congregation when it came to association with other European refugees in the city left a lasting impression on John Bale, who wrote in 1557, 'Is it not wonderful that Spaniards, Italians, Scots, Englishmen, Frenchmen, Germans, disagreeing in manners, speech and apparel, sheep and wolves, bulls and bears, being coupled with only the yoke of Christ, should live so lovingly and friendly . . .?'[71] The amity between the English and Scots was all the more firmly grounded, since it was far less compromised by the differing 'manners, speech and apparel' which Bale evoked (those Scottish exiles whose backgrounds can be ascertained seem largely to have come from the Lowland regions, rather than the more culturally distinct Highlands).[72] In addition to these Anglo–Scottish bonds, the internationalist perspective of the Genevan exile community marked it out among the Marian congregations. English exiles in cities such as Strasbourg and Zurich, were clearly eager to build on their ties with leading divines such as Martyr and Bullinger, but these were close and well-

---

[68] Knox, iv. 67.
[69] *Livre des Anglois*, 14–16.
[70] *Original Letters*, vol. i, no. 48.
[71] McNeill, *Calvinism*, 178.
[72] Garrett, *Marian Exiles*, 81, 101, 221; Kirk, *Patterns*, 88; Dawson, 'Anglo-Scottish Protestant Culture', 92.

established friendships which had been formed over several decades and, in Martyr's case, during his lengthy stay in Oxford. The general attitude of the English in exile appears to have been noticeably more insular than that of the Genevans.

This inwardness, and the obsessive concern of the Marian exiles to find explanations for their troubles, has led some historians to contend that they focused exclusively on England as the elect nation. William Haller, in his *Foxe's Book of Martyrs and the Elect Nation*, has argued that the writings of the exiles expressed a conviction that the English were a people singled out by God to receive the true faith. In his interpretation, there was a complete identification of Englishness and godliness in the minds of the exiles, as they planned their return to their beloved country to build the new Jerusalem.[73] The publications of the Marian exiles were, it is true, saturated with references to the 'pleasau[n]t & goodly vineyarde' of England, God's special blessings upon 'the Englyshe Jerusalem', and his mercy to the 'true chose[n] children of God in this realm of England', escaping the Marian oppression through their sojourn in exile. The idea that they were concerned with their own country to the exclusion of all others, however, seems misplaced.[74] The cosmopolitan make-up of the exile communities, and their contacts with leading European reformers, were obvious indications of a wider frame of reference than England alone.

The exiles, understandably, were consumed by their need to find the meaning behind the sufferings that they and their close friends had experienced in England. Becon, for one, admitted his 'natural and fervent affection toward this our common country, which as a most tender mother hath tenderly brought me forth, and as a most loving nurse hath hitherto sweetly embraced, kindly fostered and carefully kept me up, whose destruction and utter desolation (if provision betimes be not made) I see unfeignedly to be at hand'.[75] When they exaggerated the great gifts that God had bestowed upon the English, they did so less in self-exaltation than in rebuke to their countrymen for their sinful decline under Mary. Ridley, for instance, spoke of their perilous lack of regard for the Gospel, 'an estimable and a honorable gift of God geven only to the true electes and dearly beloved childre[n] of God', and Becon wrote at length of their need to repent, declaring, 'we feel, yea we Englishmen feel, O Father of mercies

---

[73] *Foxe's Book of Martyrs and the Elect Nation* (Jonathan Cape, 1963), 20, 69–73, 80.

[74] Becon, *Confortable Epistle*, sig. Aiiii^r; Scory, *Epistle*, sig. Bvii^v; Ridley, *Frendly farewel*, sig. Avii^v; Patrick Collinson, *The Birthpangs of Protestant England: Religious and Cultural Change in the Sixteenth and Seventeenth Centuries* (Basingstoke: Macmillan, 1988), 14–16.

[75] *Prayers and Other Pieces of Thomas Becon*, ed. John Ayre (Cambridge: Parker Society, 1844), 253.

and God of all consolation, so great a dung-hill of sin within us, such vileness, such corruptness, such unthankfulness, and such disobedience against thee and thy blessed will'.[76]

The exiles may have been preoccupied with 'this afflicted realme of Englande', but they were concerned, too, to establish their place within a universal church of believers. Foxe's famous work set out to commemorate the sufferings of the godly in both England and Scotland, and he demonstrated the breadth of his thinking when he told Bullinger, 'although I am more immediately concerned with British history, yet I shall not pass over the sacred history of other nations, should it come in my way'. His express opinion was that the true church was 'bound to no one certain nation more than any other'.[77] If the exiles focused upon the example of England in their religious works, this was out of a desire to choose material pertinent to the majority of their readers, a practical choice which Bale explained in his *Image of bothe Churches*. The many Latin publications of the exiles demonstrated their interest in bringing their works into European academic circles, as did their eagerness to attend the lectures and sermons of foreign divines.[78]

These tendencies were a feature of all the Marian congregations, but they were most obviously apparent in Geneva, where their religious aspirations meant that congregation members were ready to see their exile as something more than a short-term expedient. Many English exiles in other communities focused principally upon the time when they might return home. A prayer composed by those in Frankfurt made the fervent appeal, 'restore us, if it be thy will, into our country, with the faithful ministry of thy word . . . in the meantime, whilst we be exiles, give us quiet abiding places'.[79] When they recognized some of the comforts and opportunities afforded by exile, it was almost with a sense of surprise. Sir John Cheke wrote to Calvin in October 1555 that he had decided to extend his stay in Strasbourg, 'enjoying in this my exile the society of my old friends, from whose kindly intercourse I shall not willingly withdraw myself'.[80] The Genevans, however, saw their exile as a thing profitable in itself, offering

[76] Ridley, *Frendly farewel*, sig. Av[r]; Becon, *Prayers and Other Pieces*, 225.

[77] Scory, *Epistle*, sig. Biii[v]; *The Zurich Letters . . .*, ed. Hastings Robinson (Cambridge: Parker Society, 1842–6), vol. i, nos. 10, 15; Paul Christianson, *Reformers and Babylon: English Apocalyptic Visions from the Reformation to the Eve of the Civil War* (Toronto: University of Toronto Press, 1978), 41.

[78] Collinson, *Birthpangs*, 14; Bale, *Image*, vol. ii, sig. Kvii[v]; Pettegree, *Marian Protestantism*, 119; *Original Letters*, vol. i, nos. 64, 72, 77, 80.

[79] J. Hay Colligan, *The Honourable William Whittingham of Chester, ?1524–1579* (Chester: Phillipson & Golder, 1934), 51.

[80] *Original Letters*, vol. i. no. 72.

them the chance to pursue their godly ambitions. In Goodman's view, the refugees 'may be also not onely delyvered from the feare of death and the papisticall tyrannie practised without all measure in that cou[n]trie: but with great freedome of co[n]science heare the worde of God contynually preached, and the Sacraments of our Saviour Christ purely and duely ministred, without all dregges of poperie or supersticion of mans invention'.[81]

The resulting spirit of religious enterprise in the city was distinctive, and one manifestation of it was the collaboration of English and Scottish exiles in the production of the Geneva Bible. Between 1555 and 1560 a group that included Whittingham, Gilby, Kethe, Goodman, Knox, Coverdale, and John Baron, set to work on a complete translation of the scriptures. The 'arguments' which began each book and chapter, and the detailed marginal notes accompanying the text, drew on Whittingham's 1557 translation of the New Testament, as well as other sources such as Bullinger's sermons on the Apocalypse.[82] The finished work demonstrated both the extensive scholarship and the apocalyptic outlook of the exile community, in the particular importance that it attached to the Book of Revelation, the most heavily annotated of the whole work. Here, and throughout the text, attention was drawn to passages that seemed to speak directly to the exiles. The argument preceding the Book of Exodus, for instance, told them that the sharp rods and plagues of God were necessary that they might earnestly repent their former wickedness, but the introduction to the Book of Jeremiah offered the hope that God would 'ever shewe him self a preserver of his Church, and when all meanes seme to mans judgement to be abolished, the[n] wil he declare him self victorious in preserving his'.[83] The work was both a comfort to the exiles and a lasting legacy of the Anglo-Scottish integration in Geneva.

V. BRITISH PERSPECTIVES IN EXILE

Both Whittingham's New Testament and the Geneva Bible were visibly products of their time, in their especial focus on the Apocalypse, and their attempt to offer counsel and consolation to the English and Scottish exiles. Whittingham's address to his fellow brethren at the beginning of his work

[81] Goodman, *Superior Powers*, 224.

[82] Martin, *Protestants anglais*, 242; Dawson, 'Early Career of Christopher Goodman', 177; Firth, *Apocalyptic Tradition*, 122–3.

[83] Geneva Bible, *The Bible and Holy Scriptures conteyned in the Olde and Newe Testament* (Geneva: Rowland Hall, 1560; *RSTC* 2093), sigs. fiiii^r, Fffiiii^r.

set out his intention of making his text readily comprehensible to all, 'both the learned & others'. The compilers of the Bible continued this theme, describing their endeavour 'to set forthe the puritie of the worde and right sense of the holy Goste for the edifying of the brethren in faith and charitie'. The tone of the exhortations that prefaced the Bible showed a certain shift in emphasis from Whittingham's composition of 1557, since they were written more than a year into the reign of the new English queen. The exiles offered a fervent welcome to 'the moste vertuous and noble Quene Elisabet, Quene of England, France, a[n]d Ireland', though it was tempered by their appeal that she persevere in the erection of a godly kingdom, lest God's plagues come upon them once more. Their concern that complacency should not hinder the course of reform was clearly articulated. So, too, was another highly significant aspect of the thinking of the Genevan exiles: their target audience was 'our beloved in the Lord the brethren of England, Scotland, Ireland &c'.[84]

The accession of the new queen evidently fired the imagination of the exiles, who now envisioned a British community not limited to Elizabeth's own dominions, but incorporating the Protestants of three kingdoms. They dedicated their bible to the queen, offering advice that would guide her in accomplishing their vision of godly reformation in England, Wales, and Ireland. The inclusion of Scotland in their appeal to their fellow brethren showed that they hoped to extend this reform to all parts of the British Isles. This impression was borne out by many of the marginal comments in the text. The authors highlighted themes with an obvious relevance to both England and Scotland; so the introduction to the Book of Judges gave the summary, 'In this boke are manie notable points declared, but two especially: first, the battel that the Church of God hathe for the maintenance of the true religion against idolatrie and superstition: next, what great danger that commune wealth is in, when as God giveth not a magistrate to reteine his people in the purenes of religion and his true service'.[85] With the same contemporary problems in mind, the marginal notes to Revelations 2: 20 asserted, 'As that harlot Iezebel mai[n]teined stra[n]ge religion and exercised crueltie against the seruants of God, so are there amo[n]g them that do ye like'.[86] Similar comments peppered the whole text, and so the work both illustrated and fostered a sense of common struggle and shared exile culture within the Anglo-Scottish Genevan community. The same sentiments were embraced by later generations of Protestants in England and Scotland

---

[84] *The Newe Testament of our Lord Jesus Christ* (Geneva; 1557, *RSTC* 2871), fo. **ii^v; Geneva Bible, fos. ii–iiii; Dawson, 'Anglo-Scottish Protestant Culture', 93.

[85] Geneva Bible, sig. Diiii^r.

[86] Ibid., fo. 115^v.

through the enduring popularity that the Geneva Bible attained in both countries.[87]

The concern shown by the translators for the troubles affecting both Scotland and the English realm was an understandable expression of their sympathies for the suffering of fellow countrymen in the bleak years before Elizabeth's accession. The Marian exiles were a characteristically self-aware group, applying much energy to understanding the origins of their troubles, and urging constancy in the cause. In Geneva, the Anglo-Scottish complexion of the community, with its common language and pre-exile history of association in the cause of reform, took this enhanced consciousness a stage further. Its parameters were extended to include the whole island of Britain, thereby encompassing the native countries of the exiles, and, in some of their compositions, Ireland.[88] In previous decades the English and Scots had frequently played host to one another's religious refugees, but during the Marian exile the self-appointed elect of both countries shared a novel experience of mutual exile. This had a striking impact upon the ideology of the Genevan community, as witnessed in their correspondence, writings, and plans for the future of their two Churches. Their temporary detachment from their homelands and close association with each other gave a persuasive force to their vision of the reformation of the British Isles.

The singular interpretation devised by the Genevan exiles for the misfortunes of their two countries during the 1550s could be seen in a number of their publications. Their theory developed the apocalyptic framework set out by Bale and Foxe, in order to incorporate the collective experience of the English and Scottish refugees. English exiles in other congregations had, as their writings demonstrated, formulated an idiosyncratic explanation of their sufferings under Mary: their insufficient godliness during the reign of the blessed king Edward had caused them to be punished with God's scourge, their faithless queen. This construction lent meaning to their trials, while offering the promise of future deliverance, but its inadequacy as a reasoning for Scottish religious grievances was evident. The Scots had not rejected the light of the Gospel in the same way that the English had, although their avoidance of the sin of apostasy came only through their refusal to participate in the reformation at the outset. The fact that their historical experience of reform did not match that of the English therefore created a certain distance between their concerns.

The Genevans overcame this potential difficulty, and indeed made a

[87] Dawson, 'Anglo-Scottish Protestant Culture', 93–6.
[88] Geneva Bible, fo. iiii[r].

virtue of it, by their argument that the absence of any official reformation in Scotland was itself a grievous sin. It was perhaps not as heinous as the English defection from God, but Scotland's indifference to England's earlier pleas for a Protestant union of the two countries was a cause for great lamentation. It was therefore incumbent on both the English and Scots to demonstrate their repentance and, more significantly, to ensure the future commitment of both countries to the cause of reform. This idea was expressed most forcefully by Knox and Gilby, leading figures within the Genevan congregation. The fact that their publications on the subject came between 1557 and 1559, following Knox's visit to Scotland of 1555–6, suggests that news of the gathering pace of Protestant activity north of the border provided the impetus for their schemes. Knox was certainly moved by the signs of religious devotion among his countrymen, and Gilby was also inspired by their fervour, noting, 'It is bruted (to the greate comfort of all godlie that heare it) that somme of you (deare Brethren of Scotland) do desire Christ Iesus to be faithfully preached amo[n]gest you'.[89]

Knox's *First Blast of the Trumpet against the Monstrous Regiment of Women* was composed towards the end of 1557 and published early the following year. Its principal target was the iniquitous rule of Mary Tudor, which Knox condemned on the grounds that female government was not only unscriptural, but contrary to the judgements of ancient fathers, natural law, and simple reason. While focusing on England's misfortunes, however, the tract clearly attempted to address the peoples of Britain.[90] Knox's conclusion, predicting 'the day of vengeance whiche shall apprehend that horrible monstre Jesabel of England', was a specifically English one, but the main body of the work repeatedly stressed the divine connection between the present sufferings of England and Scotland. Knox's explicit warnings and appeals to both countries at intervals in the text, 'England and Scotland beware' and 'Let England and Scotland take hede', indicated that he anticipated an English and Scottish readership for his work.[91] His generalized denunciations of female government could, as contemporaries were only too aware, apply to rulers other than Mary Tudor, and so their relevance for Scotland was plain. Further, the real significance of the tract lay in its reworking of recent Anglo-Scottish history. Knox related Scotland's sinful aversion to reformation directly to the imperfect English commitment to reform under Edward, which made

---

[89] Knox, iv. 217; Anthony Gilby, *An Admonition to England and Scotland to call them to repentance* (Geneva, 1558; *RSTC* 15063), fo. 67ᵛ.

[90] Knox, iv. 351–424; Jane E. A. Dawson, 'The Two John Knoxes: England, Scotland and the 1558 Tracts', *JEH*, 42 (1991), 555–9; Mason, 'Anglo-British Imperialism', 179–80.

[91] Knox, iv. 420, 376, 414.

them unable to extend it to Scotland. Their offences were different, but inextricably bound together, and their salvation would lie in common action.

Knox's views on the negligence of the English when the possibility of perfect reformation was offered exactly matched the general exile pre-occupation with their heedless disregard for the truth, and the 'miseries and plages' which had subsequently come upon them.[92] By taking this idea further and addressing the events of the Rough Wooing, however, Knox made Scotland a part of the same explanatory framework. He attached immense significance to the 'Edwardian Moment' of the 1540s, when the possibility had arisen of uniting the two countries by the marriage of Prince Edward to Scotland's young queen. This had been a dominant theme of the Protestant unionist propaganda produced during the Anglo–Scottish war. Where the accounts of Somerset, Henrisoun, and supporters of the union in the 1540s had denounced the Scots for refusing this divine opportunity, however, the revised view of the episode focused less on who was guilty of the greater transgression, and more on how both countries could bury the memory of their past failure. The notions of English military superiority and imperial hegemony underpinning the earlier accounts were aban-doned, and the English and Scots were both reminded that, when the God-given chance came to them, 'then was the one proud and cruel, and the other unconstant and fikle of promise'.[93]

This theme was taken up by Gilby in his *Admonition to England and Scotland to call them to Repentance*, published in Geneva in 1558. His fervent appeal to both countries, 'makinge one Iland most happie, if you could know your own happines', created a powerful picture of the common Protestant destiny of England and Scotland, 'whome God hath so many waies coupled a[n]d stre[n]gthened by his worke in nature'. Gilby himself had no known Scottish connections before going into exile, but he was evidently affected by the concerns of his Scottish associates in Geneva. His account of the abortive Edwardian episode, when the island had forgone its opportunity to 'become a safe sanctuarie, as it began to be, to all the perse-cuted in all places', echoed that first expressed by Knox. Gilby illustrated the theory with an ingenious use of the parable of two brothers called to work in their father's vineyard. Scotland was the brother who refused his

[92] John Ponet, *A Shorte Treatise of politike power, and of the true Obedience which subjectes owe to kynges and other civile Governours* (Strasbourg, 1556, *RSTC* 20178; facs.edn. Menston: Scolar Press, 1970), sig. Kiii[r].

[93] Arthur H. Williamson, *Scottish National Consciousness in the Age of James VI: The Apocalypse, the Union, and the Shaping of Scotland's Public Culture* (Edinburgh: John Donald, 1979), 11–13; Mason, 'Anglo–British Imperialism', 161, 179–83; Knox, iv. 394.

father's request, while England was the brother who agreed to go, but failed to fulfil his promise. Both had transgressed, but could redeem themselves by repenting and labouring in the Lord's cause. This would mean banishing all superstition and idolatry from their boundaries, and joining with one another instead of the popish powers of France and Spain.[94] Gilby, like Knox, offered a single account of England and Scotland's difficulties, in which their current plights were innately linked together.

There was a snag to this theory in the inescapable evidence that adherents of the true religion in Scotland were not facing the same heat of persecution as their brethren in Marian England. Knox would come up against this problem when he embarked on a martyrology for Scotland, by which he had hoped to draw the English and Scottish reformations still closer together by demonstrating their shared history.[95] The usefulness of this approach was clearly limited, but in the *First Blast* Knox had found another means of connecting England and Scotland's past, present, and future. His portrayal of the three plagues affecting the countries revealed the unmistakable parallels between their sufferings: 'the Empire or Rule of a wicked woman', the 'confusion and bondage of strangiers', and 'the contempt and horrible abuse of Goddes mercies' were blights which touched both realms, a fact which Knox categorically recognized in his invocation of 'our mischevous Maryes', and 'these two cruell tyrannes', France and Spain.[96] Gilby was even more explicit in his description of their shared miseries, referring to writings 'against the regiment of wome[n], wherewith ye are both plaged, somme against unlauful obedie[n]ce, and the admitting of strangers to be your kinges', and 'that ca[n]kred poyson of papistrie' in both countries. Goodman's works also made general comments on the 'oppression and idolatrie, whiche commeth in by strangers', God's punishment in 'placeinge an infidel woman over us', and the corruptions of ungodly preachers 'moste shamefullie denying their Maister Christe'.[97]

The relevance of these complaints to England and Scotland was implicit in the marginal comments of the Geneva Bible, and through the works of the Genevans readers were left in no doubt as to the common origins of the evils afflicting Britain. All three plagues derived from the forces of Antichrist, against whom the peoples of both countries were engaged in a mutual struggle. The apocalyptic tone of this scenario was not new to the Scots. Alexander Alesius, while in England in the 1530s, had been an early

---

[94] Gilby, *Admonition*, fos. 59ᵛ, 64–5, 75–6.
[95] Dawson, 'Theatre of Martyrdom', 259; Williamson, *Scottish National Consciousness*, 4.
[96] Knox, iv. 365, 404, 412.
[97] Gilby, *Admonition*, fo. 59ᵛ; Goodman, *Superior Powers*, 52, 57, 68.

exponent of the idea that 'now is the latter time, whereof the prophets, Christ and the apostles prophesyed that there should come false prophets'.[98] The same text was used in a purely English context by Bale, to describe the Prayer Book contentions in Basle: he acknowledged the warnings they had received that 'in the latter times should come mockers, liars, blasphemers, and fierce dispisers'. The Genevan version of the historically based prophecies of Bale and Foxe, however, created a wholly new apocalyptic model applicable not just to England, but to Britain.[99] In this depiction of events, the brethren of England and Scotland were allies in the final battle between the true and false churches.

The confinement of this singularly British explanation of exile fortunes to the Genevan community was very noticeable, and the reasons for this are not immediately obvious. The atmosphere of international concord in the city, experiencing a period of settled calm after governmental difficulties during the 1540s and earlier 1550s, perhaps contributed to the broad visions of the exiles. The remarkable harmony among the English and Scottish members of the congregation may also be explained by their diligent occupation in the ambitious literary projects of the New Testament, Bible, and their own devotional tracts, as Dawson has suggested.[100] At the same time, the relatively numerous Scottish population in Geneva stimulated the exiles' interest in events throughout Britain. Knox and Gilby were not the only members of the congregation to take heart from the evidence of Scottish reforming enthusiasms after 1556. News of the St Giles's Day disturbances in Edinburgh in 1558 raised excited expectations among the Genevans, and William Cole sent to John Bale in Basle a rather exaggerated account of the fervour apparently displayed by many thousands of Protestant rioters in Scotland: his letter was later translated into lower German, and published in Geneva in 1559 as the *Truthful tidings concerning the ascendancy of the Gospel and the punishment of its declared enemies, the papist priests in Scotland*.[101] The most important source of the Genevans' British schemes, it seems, was their personal care for the Churches of the two neighbouring realms.

[98] Alesius, *Of the Auctorite*, sig. Cii[v].

[99] Strype, *Ecclesiastical Memorials*, iii(ii). 313.

[100] Dawson, 'Trumpeting Resistance', 133.

[101] Michael Lynch, 'John Knox, Minister of Edinburgh and Commissioner of the Kirk', in Mason (ed.), *John Knox and the British Reformations*, 242.

VI. RESISTANCE THEORIES AND GENEVAN RADICALISM

The originality of the British perspective in Geneva was matched by a similarly unorthodox approach to the question of what action they should take in their predicament. It was universally recognized that their self-imposed banishment and the persecution of the saints at home were the consequence of former ingratitude for the light of the true religion. All agreed that they should acknowledge their errors and shun any further contact with idolatry. They were divided, though, on how exactly their repentance should be manifested, and how, too, they might ensure their separation from the forces of popery. The conventional counsel of English exiles, in line with the opinions of their imprisoned church leaders and their spiritual advisers in Zurich, was that their immediate future lay in patient suffering for God's cause. Their spiritual imagery was often fiercely militaristic, with Ridley, for example, warning of the need to prepare for a stark battle with the grand master of darkness and the soldiers of Antichrist. The arms he recommended, however, were faith, hope, charity, truth, patience, and prayer; and he proclaimed, 'With these weapo[n]s under the banner of the Crosse of Christe we do fighte.'[102] Scory echoed this advice, advising his brethren to 'Sit stil, be quyet, and pacient, embrace & kysse the Lordes rodde.'[103] If Mary was understood to be God's instrument for their chastisement, it followed that her oppression should be borne uncomplainingly and with fortitude, following the lead of the English martyrs. The furthest that most exile authors would go was to reproach the inferior magistrates who might have counselled their queen to different courses,[104] but the essential message was one of unquestioning submission.

Initially Knox subscribed to this opinion as fully as any of the English exiles. In 1554 he addressed two epistles to his afflicted English brethren in this vein, telling them that they should patiently abide the time appointed for the correction of earthly tyrants.[105] Already, however, he seems to have been playing with the idea that it might be the duty of Christians to take a more active stand against the oppressions of their wicked rulers. On visiting Zurich in March 1554 Knox submitted a series of questions to Calvin and Bullinger on the matter. Their responses were studiously cautious, advocating nothing more than passive disobedience and patient

---

[102] Ridley, *Frendly farwel*, sigs. Bvii–Bviii.
[103] Scory, *Epistle*, sig. Bvii^v.
[104] John Olde, *A short description of Antichrist unto the Nobilitie of Englande* (?1557; *RSTC* 673), sig. Aiiii, fos. 27–31, 41.
[105] Knox, iii. 229–48.

confidence in God.[106] It was in the later 1550s, while the Anglo-Scottish perspectives were also maturing within the Genevan congregation, that ideas on the lawfulness, indeed, the Christian responsibility of resistance to tyrants, received their most forceful expression. Knox came to this opinion by degrees: his full conversion to the idea was pre-empted by the publication in 1558 of Goodman's *How Superior Powers oght to be obeyd of their subjects: and Wherin they may lawfully by Gods Worde be disobeyed and resisted.*

Goodman and Knox were not the first to urge the necessity of violent resistance to earthly authorities. In 1556 John Ponet, one of the highest ranking churchmen in exile, wrote *A Shorte Treatise of politike power, and of the true Obedience which subjectes owe to kynges and other civile Governours*, in which he set clear limits upon the freedom of action of princes. Like Goodman after him, Ponet distinguished between the office and person of the ruler, charging that princes were not exempt from God's laws, and might be lawfully deposed, even killed, if they threatened the commonwealth. Citing the historical precedents of Edward II and Richard II, and the biblical examples of Athaliah and Jezebel, Ponet urged the people of England to prepare for an immediate confrontation.[107] The motivation behind his political extremism, far removed from his conservative adherence to the religion of the Prayer Book, appears to have been his outrage at the dealing of the English government with the property of the exiles. It was in the context of parliamentary debates over the refugees' lands and goods that his tract was written, and it was a unique expression of the exiles' frustration and impotence in the matter.[108]

The Genevans, by contrast, were driven to articulate equally radical conclusions on the question of opposition by a deepening conviction that this could be the only means of atonement for their former transgressions. In their opinion, subjection by temporal rulers could be no excuse for participation in ungodly rites: instead both the ceremonies and their defenders should be resisted. It was significant that, in Knox's writings, this argument was applied with much greater force in the English context. Here, as Dawson and Mason have demonstrated, the differing histories of reform in England and Scotland were crucial.[109] Knox believed that Scotland's

---

[106] Ibid. 221–6; J. H. Burns, 'Knox and Bullinger', *SHR*, 34 (1955), 90–1.

[107] Ponet, *Short Treatise*, sigs. Gi^v–Hvii^v, Miv^r.

[108] Barbara Peardon, 'The Politics of Polemic: John Ponet's *Short Treatise of Politic Power* and Contemporary Circumstance, 1553–1556', *Journal of British Studies*, 21 (1982), 35, 41, 45.

[109] Dawson, 'Two John Knoxes', 555–8; ead., Dawson, 'Revolutionary Conclusions: The Case of the Marian Exiles', *History of Political Thought*, 11 (1990), 270; Roger A. Mason (ed.), *John Knox: On Rebellion* (Cambridge: Cambridge University Press, 1994), pp. xvi–xxii.

neglect of the Gospel could yet be remedied by persuasive counsel of the regent and the proper fulfilment of their duties by the estates. In his *Appellation from the sentence pronounced by the bishops and the clergy* of 1558, Knox directed vigorous exhortations to the nobility and commonalty to this end, ordering that they should provide for reform to the best of their ability, or 'ye shall perish in your iniquitie, as rebelles and stubborn servantes'. Knox also addressed a *Letter to the Regent*, in which he offered stern rebukes and warnings, but did not at this stage go so far as to contemplate her removal from office.[110]

In England's case, however, the sinful defection under Mary from the former godliness of Edward's reign required a more drastic remedy. The queen was an unrepentant tyrant who had disdained the nation's covenant with God, and the interests of the godly could only be served by her deposition. Knox's *First Blast* moved towards this conclusion, and Goodman's *How Superior Powers* was even blunter in its delivery of the same message. Goodman applied himself solely to the English example, contending that submission to Mary was only perpetuating England's offence. His premiss was a passage from Acts in which the apostles asserted that it was better to obey God than man, and he argued that England's failure to demonstrate this higher obedience in the past was the cause of the 'horrible slaghter of the thousandes of martyrs, which with in these few yeres in Englande alone do witnesse'. In Goodman's view the people, answerable only to God, were obliged to resist idolatrous rulers. His conclusion was unambiguous, 'this ungodlie serpent Marie, the chief instrument of all this present miserie in Englande . . . oght to be punished with death, as an ope[n] idolatres in the sight of God, a[n]d a cruel murtherer of his Sai[n]ts before me[n], a[n]d merciles traytoresse to he[r] owne native cou[n]trie'.[111]

Goodman's views were supported by Whittingham, who composed a preface for his work, and by Kethe, who appended to it a poem on the same theme.[112] A summary for Knox's proposed *Second Blast of the Trumpet* reveals that he, too, came to assimilate Goodman's forceful position on resistance. He now fully accepted the argument that 'if any manifestly wicked person has been rashly promoted and then shows himself unworthy of regiment against the people of God, the same men may justly depose and punish him'.[113] The central figures within the Genevan congregation therefore concurred in the opinion that the English queen should at the

---

[110] Dawson, 'Two John Knoxes', 558–70; Knox, iv. 467–537, 532, 431–60.
[111] Goodman, *Superior Powers*, 15, 28, 38–9, 99.
[112] Ibid. 3–8, 235–7.
[113] Knox, iv. 539–40.

very least be removed from power, and that her death would be a just punishment before God. In Knox's view the same extremes were not yet called for in Scotland. Unlike the English, the Scots had never made a covenant with God, and so Knox felt they might still be urged to embrace reform by less revolutionary counsels, although this distinction did not prevent him from occasionally slipping into covenanting language when addressing Scotland.[114] The actions that he urged on the Christian peoples of the two countries were therefore adapted to meet their different circumstances, but they were complementary aspects of what was intended to be a blueprint for a British reformation, to be effected without delay.

The Genevan congregation was highly distinctive for its combination of radicalism on the question of obedience with an Anglo-Scottish frame of reference. These peculiarities were over and above a commitment to pure Calvinist worship that was unusually marked for the Marian exile congregations. Individually, each of these tendencies had parallels in other exile churches. Extreme political theories had surfaced in Ponet's writings in Strasbourg some years earlier. Various congregations also seemed willing to explore new religious forms. The church in Emden, though unquestioningly loyal to the architects of Edwardian reform, was surprisingly unconventional in its creation of a new order of worship based on the model of John à Lasco's London Strangers' Church. Wesel, too, broke away from the constraints of the Prayer Book to institute a more thoroughly reformed rite.[115] Neither congregation, however, went so far as to dismiss England's earlier reformations as inadequate. Gilby's comparison of Henry VIII with a 'mo[n]strous bore', and assertion that even under Edward 'your religion was but an English matyns'[116] were extreme views even in Geneva: outside it they were practically heretical. In its general religious forwardness, as well as its appeals for an immediate British-wide reformation, the Genevan congregation stood out among the exiles churches.

Their Anglo-Scottish focus in particular was not found anywhere else among the Marian exiles, English or Scottish. It seems probable that Scottish ministers who had served in the Edwardian Church before joining the English in exile identified with English concerns in the same way that Knox had done in the early part of his career. Where the English refugees considered Anglo-Scottish relations at all it was frequently in narrowly Anglocentric and so wholly conventional terms. Aylmer, though a one-time colleague of Willock in the household of the marquis of Dorset, displayed

---

[114] I am grateful to Dr Wormald for pointing out Knox's tendency to revert to the language of the covenant with Scotland.

[115] Pettegree, *Marian Protestantism*, 19, 26–32.

[116] Gilby, *Admonition*, fo. 70ᵛ.

the traditional English xenophobia in his *An Harborowe*, by which he hoped to remove himself and his fellow English exiles from the taint of association with Knox's opinions on female rulers. Following a systematic rebuttal of the arguments of the *First Blast*, Aylmer resorted to crude insults to Scotland, together with France, Germany, Italy, and much of Europe. He identified the principal enemies to the English commonwealth as 'the pocky frenche man and the scorvy Scot', giving an account of English victories against Scotland in the previous fifty years. His extravagant appeals to 'good trew harted Englishe men' and to English bravery and boldness, culminated in the assertion that 'you have God, and al his army of angels on your side'.[117]

Not all the English exiles were so antagonistic towards Scotland. The Frankfurt church had a Scottish pastor in John Mackbrair, and John Willock may have performed the same service for Emden. Bale and Foxe, concerned with the sufferings of the saints throughout the universal church, included references to the Scottish martyrs in their works. Foxe's relation of the endeavours of early supporters of reform in Scotland was particularly comprehensive.[118] None of this quite matched the novel attitudes of the Anglo-Scottish group in Geneva, however. Their formation of British plans was encouraged by the liberating conditions of exile, where they, unlike Aylmer, freed themselves from the customary hostility between their realms, and the constraints of political and diplomatic obstacles. They expressed their visionary hopes in a message delivered to all exile congregations by William Kethe, shortly before they returned to England, which prayed that they 'may together reach and practise the true knowledge of God's Word; which we have learned in this our banishment, and by God's merciful Providence seen in the best Reformed Churches'. The response from Frankfurt, 'it shall lie neither in your hands nor ours to appoint what the ceremonies shall be' was disappointingly cool.[119] In their hopes to bring Scotland into an inclusive scheme for reformation, too, the Genevans would find that intentions among the English were generally more limited than their own.

The imaginative scope of the Genevans' plans for reform by the later 1550s was one product of the lively activity among English and Scottish Protestant sympathizers throughout the decade. The other notable development was the skeleton framework of reformed congregations north

[117] Aylmer, *Harborowe*, sigs. Bi–Liv, Pii^r, Qii^v, Rii^v, Piiii^v.
[118] Bale, *Image*, vol. ii, sigs. cii, iv^v; Foxe, iv. 558–80, v. 606–47.
[119] *Brief Discourse*, 224–5.

of the border. The entire period was a formative stage in the pursuit of collaborative reform, and in the conception of an island united by its Protestant faith. The Marian exile in particular brought English and Scottish reformers together in a mutual experience of invigorating religious freedom among their European hosts. In these circumstances, the Genevan refugees together engaged in a fundamental re-examination of their past, present, and future. Knox had definite ideas on how the two countries should realize this vision, his directions being tailored to take account of the variations in Protestant advancement in England and Scotland. The overriding goal that he shared with his Genevan colleagues, however, was to impress upon the English and Scots their inseparability in terms of their divinely preordained future.

The accession of Elizabeth in 1558 appeared to offer the means to fulfil this destiny. The dilemma of making active opposition to the reigning monarch appear not simply acceptable, but morally necessary, was neatly sidestepped. England's Protestant queen would reintroduce the true religion to her dominions, and, the Genevans hoped, be the means by which they would pressure Mary of Guise into extending the light of the Gospel to Scotland. Expectations were boosted by signs of solidarity among certain leading Scottish nobles: in January 1559 Sir Henry Percy had an enlightening conference with Arran, Duke of Châtelherault, during which the duke raised the possibility of an Anglo-Scottish amity based on religion. Seeing that Châtelherault seemed to be promoting such an alliance, Percy encouraged him, musing, 'how could it be better for the maintenance of God's Word to join with us of England, and we with you?'[120] In 1543 Arran had been an unpredictable and ultimately unwilling partner in an English-inspired religious alliance. His own suggestion of a renewed amity in 1559 was a significant step, and the aim appeared to have the backing of the Scottish secretary, William Maitland of Lethington. There appeared to be growing support, informed both by considered polit-ical calculation and Protestant fervour, for rejecting associations with over-bearing European powers in favour of a mutually beneficial amity.[121]

It was ironic that the Protestant rescuer lauded by Knox, Goodman, and Gilby was a female ruler, given the ferocity of their arguments against women in authority. Indeed, a good number of the exiles preferred to for-get their previous diatribes on the subject. Aylmer made desperate efforts

[120] *CSP For.*, vol. iii, no. 262.

[121] In addition to Sir Henry Percy, Châtelherault, and William Maitland of Lethington, supporters of an alliance between the Scottish reformers and the English government were known to include William Cecil, Thomas Randolph, and Sir James Croft: Alford, *Early Elizabethan Polity*, 55–6, 65; Dawson, 'William Cecil', 196–202.

to dissociate himself from these opinions, although Knox himself did not quite appreciate the delicacy with which he would have to approach Elizabeth.[122] He and his fellow exiles were, nevertheless, prepared to concede that she might be God's instrument for the reform of their kingdoms. In his *Brief Exhortation to England for the speedy embracing of the Gospel*, written in January 1559, Knox set out for the estates of England a detailed programme by which they might establish God's religion among them.[123]

The queen herself, however, was not easily persuaded of the wisdom of following Knox's schemes, and still less of taking up the Scottish Protestant cause. She was incensed by the Genevan publications, and she would throughout her reign exhibit an inherent caution in religious matters. The formation of ecclesiastical settlements for the Churches of England, Wales, and Ireland was her princely duty, but even here Elizabeth's subjects found her intentions difficult to gauge. The returning exiles and their European allies showered her with congratulatory epistles and advice as to the appropriate conduct of reform, but then proceeded to spend their first months back in England bemoaning the lack of progress in the godly cause. The realization of the ambitious British hopes of the Genevans seemed still more remote when Knox and Goodman found themselves unable even to enter England in 1559. Having made themselves 'odious' in the queen's eyes they went instead to Scotland, and it was from here that they continued to plan for a British reformation. The reformers identified a number of potential allies in the governments of both countries, but the religious alliance that they called for would not be readily achieved.

---

[122] PRO SP 52/1, fos. 123–4 (*CSP Scot.*, vol. i, no. 496); *Zurich Letters*, vol. ii, no. 15.
[123] Knox, v. 503–22.

6

'This Common Cause of Christ and Liberty?'[1]

The years between 1558 and 1561 were crucially important in redefining religious and political relations between England and Scotland. They saw the settlement of Protestant Churches in each country, and the realignment of the diplomatic stances of both governments. The Anglo-Scottish alliance which helped secure Scotland's reformation brought the confessional allegiances of the countries fully into line for the first time since 1534, when England's break with Rome introduced the doctrinal disparity to the British mainland. It would be tempting to see Scotland's official acceptance of Protestant reform in 1560 as a neat resolution of the variance created by Henry VIII and previously eliminated only during the brief Catholic resurgence of the 1550s. There was undoubtedly great excitement among English and Scottish reformers at the resolution of the mid-century disjunction, and the new prospect of fruitful collaboration in the 'furth setting of the trew word of God'.[2] The turnaround in Anglo-Scottish relations, from the mutual suspicions of the 1530s to the harmony of 1560, was truly momentous. The new Protestant consensus was not a cure-all, however, and there remained considerable grounds for uncertainty between the countries, religious and otherwise.

In the transformation of Anglo-Scottish relations, much hinged on effective collaboration in Scotland's political and religious revolution. The formulation of a workable alliance was far from straightforward, and perhaps for this reason the success of the enterprise inspired ambitious, if singularly ill-defined, hopes for a lasting union of England and Scotland. Former exiles, statesmen, and reformers of both countries engaged in eager discussions, drawing on their knowledge or personal experience of similar debates in the 1540s, their witnessing of current events, and their developing religious ideologies. Enthusiasm for the project testified to the proven tactical advantages of co-operation, and to the atmosphere of heady pos-

---

[1] *CSP Scot*, vol. i, no. 492: this phrase is used by Sir William Kirkcaldy of Grange in a letter to Cecil, 17 July 1559.
[2] Ibid., no. 673.

sibilities produced by the allies' initial success. The wide variety of opinions on forms of amity, and general lack of coherence on details, however, was a major weakness. So, too, was their failure to inspire the English queen, whose attitude towards her country's relations with Scotland probably typified that of many of her subjects: while she welcomed the strategic benefits of a Protestant alliance, Elizabeth had little independent interest in the affairs of the Kirk, or in the notion of any firmer bond between the realms. In Scotland, too, the most fervent appeals for the godly union came from a minority group, in a population more accustomed to seeing the English as hostile aggressors.

The prospects for realizing grandiose British schemes were not encouraging, and complications crowded in after 1560, notably with the return of Queen Mary to Scotland in the following year. Up to this point, however, the feat of the allies should not be diminished. For a short period, the coming together of strategic, diplomatic, and confessional aims created an alliance of potent possibilities. Certain inherent tensions in the reformers' perceptions of relations between their countries would prove impossible to ignore indefinitely: but the alliance's accomplishment by 1561 was enormous. The most productive religious collaboration between England and Scotland since 1534 established a Protestant regime in Scotland, and helped to resolve English foreign policy concerns of thirty years' standing.

I. AMBITIONS FOR A GODLY ISLE

When Protestant reformers in Scotland publicly defied the regency government in the spring of 1559, it was widely expected that their co-religionists in England would come to their assistance. The accession of Elizabeth some months previously had brought joy to the godly with the prospect of the overthrow of popery in England; and those who favoured the cause of reform in Scotland could not fail to be heartened by the idea that the tide was turning against the Catholic advance which had threatened to overtake Britain. The new queen's religious intentions were as yet somewhat obscure, but the inclinations of certain influential councillors offered grounds for hope. Secretive negotiations underway since early 1559 between English border officials and prominent Scottish politicians such as Châtelherault were reported to Cecil, who was also in contact with his counterpart in Scotland, secretary Maitland of Lethington.[3] An increasing sense of urgency informed the Scottish attitude to such deliberations since

[3] *CSP For.*, vol. iii, nos. 262, 316, 796.

the regent was showing less inclination to appease the reformers, following the grant of the crown matrimonial to the dauphin and the conclusion of peace between England and France at Cateau-Cambrésis in April. The message of English sympathy for the Scottish rebels seemed distinctly encouraging.

The preliminary events of the Scottish revolt took place independently of formal English involvement. In May 1559 a royal summons issued against the leading Protestant ministers Methven, Willock, Harlaw, and William Christison provoked a surge of popular support. This came principally from Angus and the Mearns and Fife, and the addition of Glencairn's adherents from the south-west brought as many as 7,000–8,000 to the aid of the preachers' cause. Unwilling to provoke a major confrontation with her own French forces, the regent revoked the summons, but when she later ordered that the ministers be outlawed, Protestant bands entered Perth and began a forcible reformation of the town.[4] Their challenge to the government showed a critical development from the last Protestant revolutionary endeavour in 1547, when the occupiers of the castle of St Andrews found local support, but no substantial popular or aristocratic assistance. Thanks to the religious advances and the political grievances of the intervening years, the preachers of 1559 had extensive public backing, as well as powerful noble allies in Lord James Stewart, Argyll, and Glencairn. To ensure the success of their venture, they looked once again to England to assist their cause.[5]

This was a step of immense importance. Aside from the Castilians' unsuccessful appeal for assistance in 1547, the impetus for a religious amity during the 1530s and 1540s had come almost exclusively from England. Cromwell, at Henry VIII's behest, orchestrated numerous embassies to James V, hoping to persuade the Scottish king to initiate his own Henrician-style reformation. In the 1540s the vehicle for English hopes was the unpopular dynastic alliance embodied in the Greenwich Treaties, which Henry attempted to impose by force when diplomacy failed. Somerset, too, combined coercion with his attempts to win the Scots to the idea of an island united by its faith. The notion of a Protestant league had consequently become inseparably linked to English aggression, pretensions to imperial hegemony, and a belief in evangelization by brute force. It was this that had strengthened Scotland's auld alliance with France after 1548, so helping to create the hostile diplomatic situation facing England in 1559. The increasing disaffection of the Scots with the

---

[4] Knox, i. 317–82; Leslie, *History*, 271; Kirk, *Patterns*, 101–2.
[5] Knox, i. 335, 347, 382; *CSP For.*, vol. iii, no. 878.

defiantly Catholic regime of Mary of Guise now caused them to reconsider the possible benefits of a religious amity with England, but the league they sought would be framed for their mutual benefit. As Sadler reported to Cecil, the Scots appreciated that 'the case is now moch otherwise than it was then, for then we sought of them, and now they seke of us'.[6]

The unofficial spokesmen for the Scottish Protestants, styling themselves the 'Faithful Congregation of Christ Jesus in Scotland' were figures such as William Kirkcaldy of Grange, Henry Balnaves, and inevitably John Knox, who returned from the continent in May, just in time to participate in the disturbances.[7] All three had been among the principals of the Castilian episode, and so had long-standing connections with religious sympathizers in the English government. Lethington was another politically astute supporter of the Protestants' cause who, by the time of his defection from the regent's administration in September 1559, was well known to Cecil, Sadler, Croft, and the other English officials investigating the Congregation's activities.[8] The Protestant agitators intended to bring about their liberation in religious and political terms by eliminating the hated French presence from their government. They were careful to frame their protest as one against the regent's foreign advisers, maintaining their loyalty to their absent sovereign; but the message of opposition to the Guise influence was clear. As the revolt gathered momentum they informed Cecil, 'our hole and only purpos (as knoweth God) is to advaunce the glory of Christ Jesus, the trew preaching of his evangill within this realme, to remove superstition and all sortes of externall idolatrie, to bridill to our poweris the fury of those that heirtofor have cruellie sched the blood of our brethren, and to our uttermost to mantean the libertie of this our countrey from the tyranny and thraldome of straungearis as God shall assist us'.[9]

The Congregation presented to England their ambitions for an amity that would be more than a simple alliance of necessity, born of complementary strategic objectives. Although the desire to undermine the French Catholic foothold in Scotland was undeniably the unifying factor, their agreement was presented as the manifestation of a common commitment to a more purposeful goal, that of affirming the true faith throughout Britain by defeating popery. Knox informed Cecil in July 1559, 'The tyme is now, Sir, that all that either thrist Chryst Jesus to reigne in this yle, or yett the hairtes of the inhabitantes of the same to be joyned togidder in love

[6] Marcus Merriman, 'Stewarts and Tudors in the Mid-Sixteenth Century', in Grant and Stringer (eds.), *Uniting the Kingdom?*, 121; *SSP*, i. 434.
[7] Calderwood, i. 445; *CSP For.*, vol. iii, nos. 878, 880, 907, 1030; Knox, i. 318.
[8] *CSP For.*, vol. iii, nos. 399, 559; *SSP* i. 450.
[9] *CSP Scot.*, vol. i, no. 493.

unfained, aucht rather to studie how the same mycht be brocht to passe, then vanelie to travaill for the mantenance of that, quhairof we have allreddy seine the danger, and felt the smarte.'[10] This kind of rhetoric developed the apocalyptic world-view of the Genevan exiles, while also drawing on the imagery which had formed such a central theme of 1540s unionist writings, both English and Scottish: indeed a good number of the authors had been collaborators in the 1540s, Marian exiles, or both. By reworking these earlier ideologies, the Congregation aimed to inspire the English to join them in 'an league made in the name of God', based on 'an other fundation and assuraunce then pactions made be man for warldly commoditie'. As their leaders put it, 'now we seak rather the heavn then the eartht'.[11]

English responses to their overtures made use of the same language of Protestant concord and perpetual friendship, indicating that leading figures in Elizabeth's government, if not the queen herself, were entirely in tune with the Congregation's thinking. Cecil responded to their appeals by expressing his own hope that 'this terrestryall kyngdom of Christ may be dilated through this noble Ile, and so the old great ennemyes of the trew Church of God may be kept out, and put to confusion'; while the council assured the Scottish lords of their wish that 'this famouse Ile, may be co[n]ioyned at ye last in hartes as it is in Co[n]tinent land, with one sea, and in one uniformyte of language, maners and co[n]ditions'.[12] News of the revolt also aroused sympathetic comment from English churchmen, hopeful that Scotland might be brought into the Protestant communion. John Jewel, soon to be consecrated bishop of Salisbury, apparently overlooked the insults that Knox had directed at him in Frankfurt, expressing to Martyr his concern that the Scots should succeed in their battle with the Catholic authorities. Richard Cox also set aside his exile differences with Knox to assert that the Congregation 'must be aided by the prayers of the godly'.[13] This suggests that the progress of reform in Scotland was less closely identified with Knox's personality than his *History* might indicate.

The early phases of the Congregation's activity offered hope to supporters of godly reform in England and Scotland of the realization of a British vision. So, too, did the Anglo-Scottish ministries of some returning exiles from 1559. Knox and Goodman admittedly had little choice over their destination when they settled in Scotland in May and September respectively. Knox's appeals to Cecil, Sadler, and the queen herself, however, demonstrated a heartfelt wish for 'a perpetual concord betuix these

[10] Knox, ii. 27.   [11] *CSP Scot.*, vol. i, nos. 492–3.
[12] Knox, vi. 52; PRO SP 52/1, fo. 146 (*CSP For.*, vol. iii, no. 1083).
[13] *Zurich Letters*, vol. i, nos. 9, 16, 24, 25, 28, 29.

two Realmes, the occasion wharof is now most present'. Goodman was initially bitter over his newly enforced exile, but found fulfilment in Scotland as minister to Ayr and then St Andrews, while also embarking on preaching tours of the Scottish Highlands and Isle of Man before his eventual return to England.[14] Meanwhile, William Kethe, the Scottish Genevan, made his home in England rather than his native Scotland after 1561, being appointed minister of Okeford Superior in Dorset. Another Scot, John Mackbrair (not a Genevan, but a colleague of Knox in Frankfurt), became a minister of some note in London, even preaching at St Paul's in the early months of Elizabeth's reign.[15] With these living expressions of Anglo-Scottish religious accord, hopes must have been high that the Scottish revolt would introduce an unprecedented Protestant amity between the realms.

II. THE BASIS FOR AN AMITY

The Congregation's first official request to England for aid came in December 1559, when Lethington, David Forrest, John Willock, and Robert Melville travelled to London to make their case to Elizabeth.[16] This formal suit came only after months of negotiation, with the Scots appealing in the strongest terms for assistance against the French threat. Cecil and his colleagues apparently agreed on the desirability of the proposed 'confederacie, amitie and leigue', but through the summer of 1559 were not very forthcoming in the provision of material support. Cecil's advice to Sir James Croft was that the Scots should be aided firstly with 'fair promises', secondly with money, and only lastly with arms.[17] This reluctance to make an open stand in support of the Congregation's revolt could do little to dampen the ardent zeal of the Scots, caught in the heat of their confrontation with the powers of popery and oppression. It did, however, lead to some sharp cross-border exchanges, as the Scots accused the English statesmen of coldness in their cause, describing the apocalyptic scenario that would result if the French were allowed to overrun the whole island.[18]

[14] Knox, vi. 78, 31; *CSP For.*, vol. iv, no. 145; *CSP Scot.*, vol. i, nos. 891, 1136; Kirk, *Patterns*, 105.

[15] Donaldson, 'Presbyterian Movements', 282–3; John Strype, *Annals of the Reformation and Establishment of Religion . . . during Queen Elizabeth's Happy Reign*, 4 vols. (Oxford: Clarendon Press, 1824), i. 199.

[16] Knox, ii. 4; Alford, *Early Elizabethan Polity*, 64.

[17] Knox, ii. 25; *CSP For.*, vol. iii, no. 953.

[18] *CSP For.*, vol. iii, nos. 1133, 1186; BL Cotton Calig. Bix, fo. 70 (*SSP* i. 520–2); *SSP*, i. 523; *CSP For.*, vol. iv, no. 153.

England's position, though explained and justified by sympathetic politicians such as Cecil and Sadler, was dictated by the inclinations of the queen, whose attitude was more ambivalent. A Protestant regime in Scotland would undoubtedly be a great asset to England's diplomatic position, a fact impressed forcibly upon Elizabeth by some of her most influential ministers. If England failed to make friends of the Scots, Sir Nicholas Wotton thought, 'the French shuld be lords of England and Scotland to: and what wolde ensew therof, a blynde manne can see'. His fear was that the French, 'having England, Scotland, and Yreland, no dowte, they wold looke shortlye after to be monarkes of almoste all Europe'.[19] Even such dramatic assertions, however, were in danger of being outweighed by Elizabeth's profound distaste for the revolutionary activity of the Scottish extremists, and her reluctance to spend money on their behalf. Though keenly aware of the threat which the Guise-sponsored Stuart claim posed to her realm and her own personal safety, the queen found it difficult to countenance defending the activities of seditious subjects, particularly after they went so far as to depose the regent in October 1559. More significantly, action on their behalf would constitute a breach of the recently concluded peace with France, and might also endanger England's valued Spanish alliance.[20]

The queen's advisers also recognized the incompatibility of the Congregation's religious extremism with Elizabeth's conservative ecclesiastical tastes. Her own religious settlement, the work of the parliament which sat between January and May 1559, returned the country to the Protestant religion, as anticipated: this could hardly be otherwise, given that Elizabeth was considered a bastard by the Catholic Church. The royal supremacy was restored (under the title of governor rather than head) and the Marian heresy acts repealed, but beyond this the reforming complexion of the new regime was unclear. The Prayer Book introduced by the Act of Uniformity, for instance, combined aspects of the 1549 and 1552 orders, creating a doctrinal ambiguity over the words spoken at the delivery of the consecrated bread, the very heart of the liturgy.[21] This was an intense concern to the Swiss-influenced returning exiles, and other like-minded reformers, as was the controversial ornaments proviso, retaining the Catholic-style vestments and church equipment of the second year of Edward's reign. The

[19] Patrick Forbes, *A Full View of the Public Transactions in the Reign of Queen Elizabeth* (J. Bettenham, G. Hawkins, 1740–1), i. 17, 19.

[20] Knox, i. 444–9; *CSP For.*, vol. iv, no. 483; vol. v, no. 109; *CSP Scot.*, vol. i, no. 626.

[21] Norman L. Jones, 'Elizabeth's First Year: The Conception and Birth of the Elizabethan Political World', in Christopher Haigh (ed.), *The Reign of Elizabeth I* (Basingstoke: Macmillan, 1984), 28–9, 34, 45–6; Strype, *Annals*, i. 83–105, 119–23.

hierarchical structure of the Church, too, remained unreformed, leaving the Elizabethan establishment highly conservative in its outward appearance.[22] In a period that had seen rapid and frequently contradictory religious alterations, there seemed little certainty behind the Elizabethan commitment to reform.

The majority of former exiles eventually accommodated themselves to the settlement, accepting benefices and preferment within the Church on the advice of European mentors such as Martyr, to whom they had addressed their scruples over the deficiencies in English reform.[23] Some of the more extreme exiles, however, remained deeply unhappy with the Elizabethan establishment, objecting to its unscriptural practices and the worldly privileges of the prelates. A number declined to accept high office within the Church, Coverdale and Thomas Sampson, for instance, turning down the episcopal sees of Exeter and Norwich in favour of private appointments for devout patrons. A similar reluctance to be assimilated within the establishment could be seen on the part of the twenty-eight 'godly preachers which have utterly forsaken Antichrist and all his Romish rags', according to a list presented to Robert Dudley during the early 1560s. Among them were Gilby, Whittingham, and seven more Genevans.[24] The contrast with the exiles' fortunes in Scotland could hardly have been greater. Here the Genevan veterans Knox and Goodman, together with their colleague from Emden, John Willock, were three members of the four-person religious council created by the Congregation in October 1559. In this capacity they were the spiritual leaders of the revolutionary party, as well as the ministers for Scotland's three principal burghs: Edinburgh, St Andrews, and Glasgow.[25]

Their prominence did not cause the extreme religious ideologies of the Genevans to take root throughout Scotland in 1559, despite the ambitious claims advanced in Knox's version of the revolt. The Protestant uprising was patently the work of a radical minority, seizing the opportunity afforded by the religious discontents in Perth, Dundee, and the surrounding areas, to spark a rebellion.[26] There was notable popular sympathy for

[22] Patrick Collinson, *The Elizabethan Puritan Movement* (Oxford: Clarendon Press, 1990), 32–8; Kirk, '"Politics of the Best Reformed Kirks"', 24–5, 28–9.

[23] *Zurich Letters*, vol. i, nos. 1, 4, 6, 23, 27; vol. ii, nos. 11, 14.

[24] Collinson, *Puritan Movement*, 46–50, 75, 133–4; Patrick McGrath, *Papists and Puritans under Elizabeth I* (Blandford Press, 1967), 77.

[25] *SSP* i. 509–12; PRO SP 52/5, fos. 50–3 (*CSP Scot.*, vol. i, no. 891). Alexander Gordon, bishop of Galloway, was the fourth member of the religious council.

[26] Knox, i. 351, vi. 78; Roger A. Mason, 'Covenant and Commonweal: The Language of Politics in Reformation Scotland', in Norman Macdougall (ed.), *Church, Politics and Society: Scotland 1408–1929* (Edinburgh: John Donald, 1983), 98–9.

the reformed preaching of the Congregation's ministers, both from surrounding areas and even further afield, an element crucially absent from the Protestant enterprises of 1543 and 1547; but in order to make of the revolution a more broad-based movement, the Congregation laid increasing emphasis in their public pronouncements upon their defence of the commonweal and liberties of the realm against the depredations of the French. From the assertion in May 1559 that they felt 'compelled to tak the sweard of just defence aganis all that shall persew us for the mater of religioun, and for our conscience saik', they shifted the focus towards their 'love of oure natyve cuntrey', urging their fellow Scots to 'remember your deir wyffis, children and posteratie, your ancient heretageis and houssis'.[27] This was no dilution of their religious fervour, since in their apocalyptic interpretation, the forces of their foreign oppressors were the legions of Antichrist, and their fight for freedom and for the true faith was one and the same struggle. Patriotic appeals, however, offered them a more universal rallying cry than extreme religious pronouncements.

The support Congregation activists began to receive as they moved on from Dundee and Perth to St Andrews, Edinburgh, and Stirling in the summer of 1559 therefore derived from a variety of concerns associated with the Guisian-dominated administration of the regent. Not all of the government's critics were religious radicals, but there was conspicuous Calvinist fervour among the Congregation's adherents. The devastation visited on religious buildings and houses by the rebel leaders in an eruption of iconoclasm flavoured the whole character of the revolt: as Knox admitted to Cecil, 'The Reformatioun is somwhat violent.' Many of the sites cast down by the English in the 1540s, such as the abbeys of Lindores and Balmerino, were spoiled once again. The damage was concentrated in principal centres of the south east, but its effects were also felt across the breadth of southern Scotland, and extended beyond Perth and Dundee in the north.[28] Such activity was sharply at odds with the contemporary English conservatism on ornaments and images. The queen and her council took a dim view of religious violence; indeed a proclamation of September 1560 expressly prohibited the breaking or defacing of monuments of antiquity in churches. Elizabeth herself kept a silver crucifix and candlesticks in the Chapel Royal, and so a delicate path would need to be followed in convincing her of the justice of the Congregation's cause.[29]

---

[27] Knox, i. 326, 400–7; Mason, 'Covenant and Commonweal', 106–8.
[28] Knox, vi. 32; Leslie, *History*, 272–5, 281, 288; BL Cotton Calig. Bvii, fos. 425–6 (*SSP*, i. 467–70).
[29] *TRP*, ii. 146–8; *APC*, vii. 77; *Zurich Letters*, vol. i, no. 24.

A large part of the early deliberations between Congregation representatives and English ministers bypassed the queen completely. Cecil was circumspect on her behalf in his questioning of the Scots, trying to ascertain exactly what strength they could draw on, what assistance they required, and 'what manner of amitie mighte ensue betwixte these two Realmes'.[30] His subtlety of approach was threatened by the irrepressibility of Knox, who addressed a number of hectoring letters to Elizabeth, reminding her of her defection from God during her sister's reign, and warning, 'Lett it not appeire ane small offence in your eyes, that ye have declyned from Christ Jesus in the day of his batteill'.[31] Cecil may have used some discretion over the request that he pass these messages on to the queen, as he more than anyone recognized the need for tact in approaching Elizabeth. Surprisingly, Knox too apparently came to acknowledge that diplomacy was not his strong point, recommending Balnaves as a suitable ambassador. In the end, however, it was Lethington who took the lead in framing the Congregation's petition to Elizabeth.[32] The Scottish secretary's religious, diplomatic, and strategic concerns closely matched Cecil's own, and the two were firm allies in the quest for the Anglo-Scottish amity.

III. THE DEVELOPMENT OF BRITISH STRATEGIES

The prominence of Cecil and Lethington in negotiations behind the Anglo-Scottish religious accord reflected the ability of both politicians to take into account Elizabeth's various apprehensions. By contrast, the unyielding vehemence of religious purists such as Knox and Goodman proved a positive hindrance in the tortuous process by which Elizabeth was persuaded to take action against the Guisian threat. Cecil succeeded in animating the queen by incorporating her concerns over Mary's pretensions to the English throne, the French practices in both Scotland and Ireland, and the general spectre of militant European Catholicism, into a single threat that could be countered by decisive action in Scotland. Such calculated consideration of English involvement with the Scottish rebels has in the past laid the secretary open to the charge of watering down the intense religious vision of the Congregation with worldly and secular concerns.[33] In fact it would be more accurate to see the strategy that

---

[30] PRO SP 52/1, fo. 99 (*CSP Scot.*, vol. i, no. 484).
[31] Knox, ii. 30.
[32] *CSP For.*, vol. iii, no. 1124; vol. iv, no. 229.
[33] Conyers Read, *Mr Secretary Cecil and Queen Elizabeth* (Jonathan Cape, 1965), 104–5, 143–5, 152.

emerged from the deliberations of 1559–60 as a sophisticated development of the simple British objectives of the exiles. Cecil's own vision embodied the same compelling three-kingdom religious amity, while offering a complex and many-layered programme for its realization.[34]

As Stephen Alford has argued convincingly, Cecil's approach to politics was a thoroughly providential one. Cecil's consideration of a three-sided strategy for the defence of the queen's dominions rested on his belief that concerted British action was the only means of overcoming the popish threat.[35] The idea that the Anglo-Scottish amity was a godly imperative, and far more than a simple matter of foreign policy, was shared by some of the principal negotiators from both countries. Kirkcaldy and Balnaves had long demonstrated a fervent commitment to it, and Lethington expressed himself in the same providential terms as Cecil, arguing for an alliance 'wheroff God hes offered ane good occasion to endure for ever, if it shall please her hyghnes to embrace it'.[36] On the part of England, Sir Nicholas Throckmorton was a vociferous supporter of the Scottish cause, and was not afraid to lecture Elizabeth on the apocalyptic significance of 'a perfect and everlasting amity betwixt England and Scotland'. Sadler, Randolph, and Henry Killigrew were similarly anxious to forward the matter, sharing a fundamental assurance that 'these maters of Scotland be of great importaunce for England'.[37] Their counsels revealed a thorough understanding of the political realities of the courses they were advising, permeated with a sense of the formidable Catholic international threat, and the necessity of immediate action.

This ideological perception of strategic priorities was deeply ingrained among English Protestant statesmen. It was bound up with the very origins of the reformation in England, when the break with Rome had threatened Henry VIII with diplomatic as well as religious isolation in Catholic Europe. The papal offensives against England in 1537 and 1539 failed dismally, but the existence of such immensely powerful leagues fed enduring fears of invasion. Hints of conspiracy persisted throughout the 1540s, and English suspicions were also kept alive by the unceasing French activities in Ireland.[38] If the grounds for Catholic hostility were temporarily removed during Mary Tudor's reign, they returned with a vengeance after 1559. The Scottish revolt made the problem all the more compelling. On one hand it offered England the tantalizing prospect of eliminating the Catholic

[34] Alford, *Early Elizabethan Polity*, 6–8, 43, 53–5.
[35] Ibid. 26–8, 63, 71–2.
[36] PRO SP 52/5, fos. 37–8 (*CSP Scot.*, vol. i, no. 885).
[37] *CSP For.*, vol. v, no. 503; *SSP* i. 715, 706; Forbes, *Full View*, i. 277.
[38] Collinson, *Birthpangs*, 11, 17; *SSP* i. 431; Forbes, *Full View*, i. 269.

menace in the north, but on the other it invited self-righteous and self-interested French intervention on behalf of the wronged Scottish queen. The fear of wider European interference returned to haunt the English. Sir Thomas Challoner, reporting to Cecil the rumours that Pope Pius IV would hold a general council in Germany, wrote 'Thinke what Moment this is of, and how it maye touche us . . . Themperor's Puissance, and the Kinge Catholicke's . . . ar lyke to be much avaunced by meanes of this Pope'.[39]

Elizabeth preferred to counter the possibility of Catholic aggression by temporizing in religion, and creating a settlement which was Protestant but which avoided giving overt offence to Philip II and other potential Catholic allies. When the French, as expected, charged England with aiding the seditious Congregation, strenuous attempts were made to justify to Spain and to the world Elizabeth's righteous retaliation against the French and Scottish pretensions to her realm.[40] Cecil shared the queen's concern to bolster England's position through the Spanish alliance, but his fear of multi-sided Catholic aggression produced in him a more proactive desire to secure the kingdoms of Britain for the Protestant cause. His intentions were informed by keen cartographical interests, and by his refinement of the same strategic priorities that had motivated Cromwell in the 1530s, and shaped Henrician and Edwardian policies towards Scotland.[41] The constant aim was to establish confessional agreement between the kingdoms of England, Scotland, and Ireland as a means of reducing the potential for destabilizing foreign intervention from the north and west. This had been the goal of British policies since 1534, but it had so far proved impossible to achieve. The Congregation's revolt, however, offered an opportunity for concerted Anglo-Scottish action.

Cecil was fully conscious of the significance of the Scottish Protestants' approach to England in 1559. As a member of the Marshalsea court in 1547 he had been intimately involved with Somerset's Scottish war effort, witnessing the conflict first-hand, and assisting in the production of the accompanying unionist literature. This background, and his personal contacts with men such as Knox, James Henrisoun, and William Patten, can have left Cecil in no doubt as to the disastrous impact of the English brutality in Scotland, and the alienating effects of the claim to imperial

[39] S. Haynes and W. Murdin (eds.), *Collection of State Papers . . . left by William Cecil, Lord Burghley*, 2 vols. (1740–59), i. 236–7.
[40] *CSP For.*, vol. iv, nos. 495, 629; Forbes, *Full View*, i. 402, 444, 451.
[41] Dawson, 'William Cecil', 197–9, 205; Alford, *Early Elizabethan Polity*, 50–1; *SP*, vol. ii, no. 20; *CSP For.*, vol. iii, no. 1.

hegemony.[42] Privately, Cecil appears to have shared in the traditional and deep-seated English assumption of superiority over the vassal kingdom of Scotland. His notes on the 'weighty matter' of Scotland included proofs of the homages paid by Scottish kings to the English crown, and the assertion 'the crowne of England hath a good title to the Superiorety of Scotland and ought to d[e]fend the libertyes thereof'.[43] At the same time, though, Cecil appreciated that the Scots would not turn to England for liberation from the tyranny of France, only to submit to renewed oppression: as Lethington told him, 'The feare of co[n]quest made ws to hate zow and love theym: the cais changed quhen we see theym planely attempt co[n]quest and zow schaw ws frendschip.'[44] The alliance would need to be presented as one of Protestant equals, drawn together in the struggle against idolatry and superstition.

The Scottish attachment to this version of the amity was inspired by the apocalyptic visions of the exiles, for whom the battle between the true and false churches was a very real confrontation. Although Knox, Goodman, David Lindsay, and other former Genevans were only one element of the Congregation's membership, their ideologies informed the whole tone of the official pronouncements that accompanied the revolt. In their petitions to the regent and fellow countrymen, the Congregation's descriptions of 'the insaciabill covetousnes of the Guisianeis generatioun' put their enemies on a par with 'the generation of Antichrist'.[45] Their French oppressors were not simply persecutors of their liberties and livelihoods, but threatened their spiritual survival and their very souls if they did not resist. Such apocalyptic threats gained widespread currency among Congregation activists, and laid the basis for a distinguished strain of apocalyptic thought in Scotland.[46] More importantly for the purposes of the Anglo-Scottish alliance, they powerfully reinforced an ideological English foreign policy, obsessed with the encircling threat from Catholic Europe.

An influential group of politicians and reformers from both countries was utterly committed to a Protestant amity that would extend the reformed religion throughout Britain. They recognized that such an alliance held certain complications, however. The Congregation were careful to make no public reference to it, correctly judging that the regent could use it to

---

[42] Mason, 'Anglo-British Imperialism', 181–2; Alford, *Early Elizabethan Polity*, 45–6; *CSP Dom. Edw. VI*, nos. 747, 779, 803; *CSP Scot.*, vol. i, no. 352.

[43] BL Cotton Calig. Bx, fos. 78–80 (fos. 86–8 according to alternative numbering); *SSP* i. 377–83.

[44] BL Cotton Calig. Bix, fo. 99ᵛ.

[45] Knox, i. 408, 335.

[46] Williamson, *Scottish National Consciousness*, 20–1.

ridicule their claims to be acting in defence of their native liberties. Given the experiences of the 1540s, the idea of a godly partnership with England was likely to ring hollow for many of their countrymen, and so they resorted ever more to the conventional argument that they were merely fulfilling their role as defenders of the commonweal.[47] For Elizabeth, meanwhile, the Scottish alliance was an unwelcome necessity. Her councillors, anxious to maintain her support, reminded her that the realm of Scotland was 'not onely next unto yow, but also of auncient tyme held of this crowne', and tried to tempt her with the idea that she might 'procure that Conquest of this Lande, that none of your Progenitours with all theyr Battels ever obtaynid, that is, in a Manner, the whole Harts and good Willes of the Nobilitie and People of this Land'.[48] On occasion such claims came remarkably close to the bellicose language of earlier years, but in their dealings with the Congregation, English politicians avoided these contentious associations altogether. For the sake of negotiating a mutually acceptable alliance, both the English and Scots modified their conceptions of the amity, and glossed over possible inconsistencies.

IV. THE HAMILTON MARRIAGE PROPOSAL

Even at the outset, then, there was no unanimity over the nature of the godly accord. The immediate task of confronting the menacing French threat lent a cohesive sense of purpose to the Congregation and their English supporters. Beyond this, opinions differed widely on how the Anglo-Scottish amity might be extended and reinforced. The gulf in expectations was brought to light by the suggestion, first made in June 1559, that their union should be perfected by the marriage of Elizabeth to the young earl of Arran, son of Châtelherault and heir presumptive to the Scottish throne. The unofficial overture came from Alexander Whitlaw, an experienced Scottish collaborator, held in high regard by Throckmorton and his colleagues in the English government. Whitlaw's hope that 'this may be the meane to unite England and Scotland together' became a cherished ambition of the Congregation during the upheavals of the following year. The Protestant dynastic union would, they felt, be a 'consummation' of the league now under discussion.[49] It had a distinguished precedent in the efforts of the English to effect the marriage between Prince

[47] Knox, i. 364, 368, 400–1, 427–8; Mason, 'Covenant and Commonweal', 114–15.
[48] Forbes, *Full View*, i. 393; Haynes, *State Papers*, i. 356.
[49] Forbes, *Full View*, i. 147; PRO SP 52/5, fos. 37–8 (*CSP Scot.*, vol. i, no. 885).

Edward and the Scottish queen during the 1540s. Where the earlier scheme had degenerated into recriminations and reprisals, however, the sponsors of the plan in 1559–60 believed that the English and Scottish would be willing partners in the same godly undertaking.

The Congregation's intention was that the marriage between the houses of Tudor and Hamilton should cement their political and religious alliance. It would not need to bear the whole burden of creating such an amity, as had been the case in 1543. The resonances with the earlier period powerfully illustrated a shift in balance, the Scots being transformed from reluctant allies into the prime movers of the proposition. The first opportunity for dynastic union had, according to the interpretation of the Genevans, been undermined by Scottish inconstancy, combined with English cruelty. The events of 1559, however, appeared to indicate that God in his mercy was offering the chastened realms a second chance, now that the English were delivered from their Catholic oppressor, and were assisting their Scottish brethren in the defeat of the same popish enemy. In 1543 God 'had prouided a Prince to the one, and a Princesse to the other, to be ioyned in my holy Lawes, and by the Lawe of nature', in the words of Somerset.[50] In 1559, as Whitlaw told Throckmorton, 'yow have a Quene, and we our prince the Earle of Arrayn, mariable bothe, and the chief upholders of God's religion'.[51] The new occasion for the unification of the realms in the persons of their godly princes seemed divinely ordained.

This impression gained even more persuasive effect from the fact that the very same marriage had been contemplated in 1543, alongside the better-known plans for the Tudor-Stuart alliance. In the course of his dealings with Châtelherault, who was then himself earl of Arran, Henry VIII had offered the Lady Elizabeth in marriage to Châtelherault's son. The king's rather ungodly intention was to remove the young Arran as a rival suitor to Queen Mary, but in the event Châtelherault, whose loyalty to the English alliance was then wavering, regretfully declined the offer.[52] The revival of the same marriage proposal in 1559 by a Scottish party actively in favour of the union was a significant turnaround, and the providential pattern of events seemed unmistakable. Arran himself ardently hoped that he might marry the English queen, telling Cecil that 'God hes framed hir in the Schaip of a Woman, to excell any of her Progenitors'.[53]

A notable body of English politicians and reformers also supported the

[50] Knox, iv. 394; *Complaynt of Scotlande*, 240.
[51] Forbes, *Full View*, i. 147.
[52] *LP*, vol. xviii/1, nos. 364, 391; *SSP* i. 129–31.
[53] Haynes, *State Papers*, i. 302.

proposal, making veiled references to it in their correspondence long before \
the official suit to Elizabeth was made. Hopes were raised by the queen's \
involvement in plans to escort the young earl of Arran safely to Scotland
from his father's estates in France in the summer of 1559. Following the
outbreak of hostilities in Scotland, the return of the Hamilton heir would,
it was hoped, win his father the duke to the reformed party and provide a
powerful counterbalance to the pervasive Guise influence. Arran's presence might also extend the possibilities open to the Congregation to
supplant the authority of the regent.[54] The promotion of the Hamilton
interest was a central feature of Cecil's Scottish plans. His private notes set
out his desire that the Hamiltons should safeguard the crown until the
queen had children, and during her absence from Scotland. If the French
king and queen would not agree to this Cecil believed the estates would be
justified in transferring the government 'to the next heir of the crown, binding the same also to observe the laws and ancient rights of the realm'.[55] Here
there were further parallels with 1543, when Henry VIII had promoted the
governorship of the older earl of Arran, and secured his recognition as
second person of the realm. The contemplation of the queen's removal
from power, however, was a revolutionary development, designed to serve
English interests by eliminating the Stuart threat. It was a subject that Cecil
did not broach openly with the Congregation, however, perhaps recognizing that their ambitions were essentially more conventional, resting on the
aim of directing rather than overthrowing the existing royal government.

The first step for any of these schemes was to escort Arran safely back to
Scotland, and so between May and September 1559 Elizabeth's ministers
in England, France, and Scotland conducted a complicated covert operation to this end. The earl, in disguise and accompanied by Thomas
Randolph, was conveyed from France to Geneva, and then to the Low
Countries, before sailing for England. Here he spent some time in London,
staying at Cecil's Westminster residence and being granted a private interview with the queen, before leaving for Scotland at the end of August.[56]
Rumours of his presence at the English court led to feverish speculation
among both English and Scottish supporters of the Congregation. Jewel,
describing to Martyr the meeting between Arran and Elizabeth, told
him that 'The saucy youth came to Athens, and won the good graces
of Glycerium'; while Randolph wrote to Cecil that he found many in
Scotland who 'judge that ther wolde a wondrefull benefyte insue unto them

[54] *CSP Scot.*, vol. i, no. 465; Forbes, *Full View*, i. 155, 163; *CSP For.*, vol. iii, no. 974.
[55] *SSP* i. 376–7.
[56] Forbes, *Full View*, i. 163, 166, 171; *CSP For.*, vol. iii, nos. 1274, 1290.

bothe, yf yt wolde please the Quenes heighnes timbrace the occasion offered'.[57]

The flaw in their plans, however, was that the queen was less than enthusiastic about the idea. Although convinced by her Protestant statesmen of the desirability of conducting Arran to Scotland for the benefit of the Congregation's endeavours, Elizabeth entertained no thoughts of any closer association with the earl. Her coolness was evident in carefully worded statements of sympathy for Arran. His personal sufferings, she acknowledged, bore some relation to 'the experience that we ourselves have in these and worse casees felt and yet passed, through the inestimable goodnes of almighty God'. It was out of princely concern alone, however, that she was moved to aid a distinguished suffering nobleman, and she told Throckmorton sharply, 'It semeth very strange, that the Earl of Arran maketh mention in his lettres, that he hath cause to thank us for the offres made to hym by us: wherby we be in dowt, what to thynk; and do much mislyke, that any such occasion shuld be gyven by any maner message done to hym.'[58] Elizabeth's aversion to the match was not surprising given her consistent refusal to be forced on the issue of marriage. She found the Hamilton proposal especially unattractive, moreover, since as Cecil admitted during the negotiations of 1560, 'The Queen's Majestie never liketh this matter of Scotland', sharing none of her councillors' eagerness for a British alliance.[59]

The fervent supporters of a Tudor–Hamilton union appear to have missed the clear signals that Elizabeth's pronouncements on Arran were conveying. Her complicity in his escape from France, where rumours of his imminent capture by opponents of the Congregation were rife, seemed to confirm her favour.[60] Cecil alone appears to have sensed the need for caution, accepting the implausibility of the proposal in the light of the queen's lack of interest. This realization perhaps came after his time with Arran and Elizabeth in London. During talks with the Congregation's deputies in London during December 1559, and again in Scotland the following year, Lethington noticed that Cecil 'shifted the mater as one onwillyng to talk moche in it'.[61] The marriage would in fact have served his British strategies perfectly, promising the affirmation of the Protestant alliance, together with the establishment of the Hamiltons at the expense of the Stuarts. Cecil may have retained a slim hope that it could succeed, and

---

[57] *Zurich Letters*, vol. i, no. 29; PRO SP 52/5, fo. 51ʳ (*CSP Scot.*, vol. i, no. 891).
[58] Forbes, *Full View*, i. 167.
[59] Ibid. 454.
[60] Ibid. 147, 162–3, 166.
[61] PRO SP 52/5, fo. 73ʳ (*CSP Scot.*, vol. i, no. 903).

he therefore avoided dampening the hopes of the Congregation altogether. Over the following months, therefore, expectations were raised rather than diminished, as the subject became their 'daylie, nyghtly and howerly tawlke'.[62] Their disappointment at the rejection of the proposition was only temporarily delayed.

V. SECURING A BRITISH SETTLEMENT

The most pressing business facing the English and Scottish allies was to extract a definite commitment from the queen to their informal alliance which had, by the end of 1559, brought only sporadic financial assistance to the Congregation. The embassy to Elizabeth in December marked a note-worthy advance: for the first time, the queen was persuaded to make an official show of her support for the oppressed peoples of Scotland. A sup-plication from the Scottish lords, actually composed by Elizabeth's own councillors, set out the intimidation which they were suffering at the hands of the French, and made an affecting appeal to the queen 'as the prince planted by God nexte to them, and within one land and sea', to aid them in their resistance to this intended conquest.[63] The reference to French pretensions towards Ireland as well as Scotland and England gave expres-sion to the fears of an encircling Catholic conspiracy, but the formal pronouncements of the English and Scots avoided any explicit reference to their Protestant understanding. In their responses to the proclamations and accusations that issued from the dowager and the French king and queen, the allies continued to base their defence on the traditional argument that their sole aim was the defence of the subjects of Scotland against foreign aggressors.[64]

As a result of the agreement reinforcements were sent to the border under Norfolk in January 1560, and this was followed by the despatch of a fleet under Admiral Winter. Though the action was nothing like as substantial as Cecil had wished, the arrival of the English ships in the Firth brought relief to the Scottish lords, who, following their enforced retreat from Edinburgh in November, had been fighting a losing battle against the regent's French forces around Stirling and St Andrews.[65] The boost to the Congregation's cause was timely, but England's war effort needed to be

[62] PRO SP 52/5, fo. 53ʳ (*CSP For.*, vol. v, no. 454).
[63] *SSP* i. 566–73, 572.
[64] Mason, 'Covenant and Commonweal', 115–16; *CSP For.*, vol. iv, no. 495.
[65] *CSP For.*, vol. iv, nos. 565, 585, 605, 614; *SSP*, i. 649–50, 701.

intensified in order for any substantial advance to be made. This was achieved with the February 1560 Treaty of Berwick, which formalized the Anglo-Scottish alliance. In a reversal of the events of 1548, the Scots turned to England for liberation from French domination, acknowledging 'how welthy and florisshing it sall becum yf these two kingdomes as thei be Ioyned in one Iland by creation of ye World so may be unyted in a constant and assured frendschip'. In return for English aid in Scotland, Argyll would be required to assist in the subjugation of Elizabeth's rebels in Ireland. As in December, the focus of the agreement was the unjust practices of the government, but once again the mention of Ireland reflected the desire to implement a three-kingdom strategy against the Catholic threat from Europe.[66]

Despite the agreement at Berwick it was over a month before the English land army under the command of Lord Grey finally arrived in Scotland. It could not subdue the French completely, but after some weeks of skirmishes revolving around the French occupation of Leith, the opposing parties agreed to cease their hostilities in favour of a negotiated settlement.[67] This was no easy process, as Cecil and Wotton, the English commissioners sent to Edinburgh in June, reported. With the recent outbreak of religious disturbances in Amboise, the English and Scottish allies were relatively well placed to extract favourable terms from France, but Cecil feared that the unbending Protestant zeal of certain Congregation members might still damage their cause. The discussions were also threatened by Elizabeth's revival of the demand for the return of Calais, at which Cecil almost despaired.[68] The negotiations were clearly strained, with Cecil relying heavily on Lethington and Lord James to present a more conciliatory face on the part of the Congregation. Their efforts, however, together with the weakening of their opponents following the death of the regent, helped to bring about the conclusion of the Treaty of Edinburgh on 6 July 1560.[69]

In view of the difficulties of reaching agreement between the English, Scottish, and French commissioners, it was not surprising that the treaty failed to provide a comprehensive answer to the demands of the Scottish Protestant lords. The religious question was postponed, having proved 'to whott for the French to medle withall', as Cecil told the queen.[70] In fact, the

---

[66] Knox, ii. 45–52; BL Cotton Calig. Bix, fos. 34–5 (Haynes and Murdin (eds.), *State Papers*, i. 253–5); BL Cotton Calig. Bv, fo. 38ʳ (*CSP Scot.*, vol. i, no. 786); NLS Adv. MS 33. 1. 1, vol. i; Dawson, 'Two Kingdoms or Three?', 119–20.

[67] *Diurnal*, 56–7; Knox, ii. 57–8; *CSP Scot.*, vol. i, nos. 708, 712.

[68] Leslie, *History*, 288–9; *CSP For.*, vol. v, no. 124; Haynes and Murdin (eds.), *State Papers*, i. 324, 327; *CSP Scot.*, vol. i, no. 832.

[69] Haynes and Murdin (eds.), *State Papers*, i. 333; Knox, ii. 73.

[70] Haynes and Murdin (eds.), *State Papers*, i. 352.

English and Scots themselves were far from unanimous in their opinions on the appropriate path for reform in Scotland. The reports of the English commissioners reveal their discomfort with the religious extremism of their allies, whom they found 'so depely perswaded in the Matter of Relligion, as nothing can perswade them, that maye appear to hynder it'.[71] The account of the orthodox churchman John Leslie went even further, alleging that the failure to reach a religious accord came because the Scots recoiled at England's insistence on an Elizabethan-style reformation, 'so that boith the realmes micht haif ben uniforme in religione and ceremonies'. Cecil made no mention of this specific disagreement in his accounts of the discussions, but his admission that in Scotland the reformed religion was 'freely and rather more earnestly, as I the Secretary thynk, receaved, than in England',[72] does suggest that English and Scottish differences played some part in hindering religious agreement.

The Treaty of Edinburgh remained, however, an impressive document, and was a hugely important stage in the realization of an effective three-kingdom strategy. By its terms, Cecil and Wotton triumphantly told Elizabeth, 'your Majestie's undoubted right to the Croune of Englande and Irelande, is fully confessed and acknowledged'.[73] The Stuart claim, which was the foundation of England's insecurities, was therefore rejected, while detailed arrangements were made for the government of Scotland in the continuing absence of the queen, and the removal of all foreign troops from the realm. The English may have appeared magnanimous by withdrawing their forces when in such a commanding position, but they could afford to hold back when the proposed governmental arrangements would effectively neutralize the Guise influence in Scotland. The administration would henceforth be in the hands of a council of native Scotsmen appointed by the estates and their sovereigns. A parliament was also appointed, and its consultation would be required for any matters of war or peace.[74] England was accorded no formal role in the settlement, since the Anglo-Scottish amity was the second issue that had proved too controversial for the French during the Edinburgh negotiations.[75] In practice, however, the firm understanding between the realms would allow England some hope of guiding Scottish policy on the favoured pattern of Protestant solidarity against the Guise and wider Catholic conspiracy.

The Edinburgh agreement embodied Cecil's scheme for securing

[71] Ibid. 333.
[72] Leslie, *History*, 292; Haynes and Murdin (eds.), *State Papers*, i. 352.
[73] Haynes and Murdin (eds.), *State Papers*, i. 354.
[74] Knox, ii. 73–83.
[75] Haynes and Murdin (eds.), *State Papers*, i. 329.

England from the Stuart threat by means of a closely negotiated and controlled political settlement. The basic English aim of exerting a measurable influence over Scottish policy-making in the interests of a religious alliance remained unchanged; although there had been a significant progression in Scottish attitudes towards the idea of a Protestant partnership. The means by which England sought to influence the Scottish government in 1560 bore some striking similarities to the programme set out in the Greenwich Treaties of 1543.[76] In both instances the danger that the queen might provide a focal point for orthodox loyalties was eliminated, in the first case by the requirement that she be sent to the custody of the English king, and in the second, by her absence in France. The security of a dynastic union between Mary and Edward in 1543 was also mirrored by the Congregation's plans for the Tudor–Hamilton marriage in 1559–60. Where in 1543 Henry had exerted an informal hold over the governor Arran and the Anglophile lords on the council, a similar unofficial role was contemplated by the English government following the expulsion of the French from Scotland.[77] The key difference, however, was that the heavy-handed English interventions of the earlier period, always reinforced with the threat of military intervention, were now replaced by the notion of collaboration between like-minded Protestant politicians.

This shift explained the advance from the failure of the 1540s to the initial success of the Anglo-Scottish coalition in 1559–60. Elizabeth could appear as the Protestant saviour of the Scots rather than the aggressor, their liberator and not their conqueror, thanks to judicial playing-down of England's ancient superiority claims. The fruit of this, the Congregation and their English supporters hoped, would be the extension of their political alliance to the religious sphere through the reformation of the Scottish Kirk; and dynastic union in the persons of Elizabeth and Arran would then complete their holy alliance. Their plans were threatened, however, by another fundamental difference between the circumstances of 1543 and 1560: the Scottish queen was no longer an irrelevant minor, but an adult Catholic queen, backed by the fearsome Guise connection in France. Her continued absence from the realm could not be guaranteed and, even more importantly in the short term, her ratification was required to legitimate the Edinburgh settlement. This would prove a major obstacle, over and above the hints of tension in the Anglo-Scottish religious accord.

---

[76] Ch. 3, Sect. II; *LP*, vol. xviii/1, no. 804; *APS* ii. 411–12.
[77] *LP*, vol. xviii/1, no. 22; Alford, *Early Elizabethan Polity*, 84–5.

VI. THE PROTESTANT REVOLUTION AND THE QUESTION OF
CONFORMITY

Although the Treaty of Edinburgh specified that the religious issue should be held over until the forthcoming parliament, the Scottish lords wasted no time in setting about the task of reform. The ambition for thoroughgoing Calvinist-inspired renewal in the Kirk was still far from universal, but in the course of the revolt the vigorous movement for Protestant reform had made significant progress in areas of the Congregation's activity. There was notable support throughout Fife, Angus, Argyll, Strathearn, and the Mearns, and by the end of 1559 many major burghs and centres of population had appointed their own reformed ministers.[78] English observers were reassured by the appearance that Scotland would cast off its allegiance to Rome, and by the obvious welcome that their troops received in the first part of 1560.[79] A band subscribed by the Congregation in April set out their intention to 'sett fordwart the Reformatioun of Religioun, according to Goddes word', and they pledged to take part with the English army sent for their assistance.[80] The resulting mood of religious and political concord was all the more welcome being so unprecedented in recent Anglo–Scottish relations. Hopes were raised that the alliance of 1560 would form the basis for a permanent diplomatic understanding between the realms.

It was in this spirit that the Scottish parliament, appointed in accordance with the Edinburgh agreement, opened in August 1560. The proceedings began with an oration by Lethington, praising Elizabeth in the highest terms for her gracious assistance to the Scots.[81] Randolph, attending the session, reported excitedly to Cecil on the goodwill and religious ardour he witnessed among the Scottish estates. When the alliance of the Treaty of Berwick was confirmed, some of those present, he said, 'so myche comendyd the same, that theie sayde that theie wolde be content to seale yt w[i]th ther bloode. Some exhorted all men constantly to remayne in that opinion and nev[er] to swharve from the same. Others praysed the fyrste motioners, and prayed for the lyf and welfare of her ma[jes]tie that was the performer.'[82] The talk of perpetual amity and hearty friendship between the realms produced an exhilarating contrast with earlier parliament

[78] Kirk, *Patterns*, 13, 102; *The First Book of Discipline*, ed. J. K. Cameron (Edinburgh: St Andrew Press, 1972), 5–6.
[79] *SSP* i. 511, 705; *CSP Scot*, vol. i, nos. 662, 734.
[80] Knox, ii. 61.
[81] PRO SP 52/5, fos. 12–14 (*CSP Scot.*, vol. i, no. 879).
[82] PRO SP 52/5, fo. 52ʳ (*CSP For.*, vol. v, no. 460).

debates on the necessity of defending Scottish liberties from English encroachment. All memories of centuries of animosity between the realms were swept away, at least for the time being, to be replaced by an atmosphere of lively optimism and possibilities. The Scottish devotion to England seemed as encouraging as their eagerness to embark on a religious revolution, and the two issues dominated parliamentary proceedings.

The pace of the religious transformation, beginning with acts annulling papal authority in the realm, greatly impressed Randolph, who wrote to Cecil, 'I nev[er] herde matters of so great importance, nether soner dyspached, nor w[i]th better wyll agreed unto'. The Confession of Faith adopted by the reformed Kirk was concluded and ratified in a matter of days, inspiring heartfelt declarations of support from the lords, many of whom, according to Randolph, 'offered to shiede ther blude in defence of the same'.[83] Its simple Calvinist terms produced a marked contrast with years of more tentative and conciliatory reforming activity. It expressed the reformers' single-minded espousal of reformed tenets, and of a faith consisting solely of 'hailsome and sound doctrine groundit upoun the infallibill trewth of godes word'.[84] The reformers also embarked on a wholesale revision of the ecclesiastical polity, intending to displace the entire medieval structure of the Church. A number of ministers had been working on a new discipline for the Kirk since April 1560, and the reformation parliament gave further commission to a group of reformers, the 'six Johns', to set out their conclusions in a Book of Discipline. Their revision of the work continued at the first General Assembly of the Kirk, held in December 1560, and the same meeting saw further appointments of ministers and readers to supplement those already in place.[85] The new Kirk showed impressive self-confidence and vitality.

The religious proceedings it set in train did not go unchallenged. There was a certain amount of hesitation and dissatisfaction with the tone of the confession among members of the August parliament, with the bishops of Dunblane and Dunkeld expressing outright opposition to the document. Hamilton of St Andrews was also unsure, and other prelates such as James Beaton of Glasgow had avoided the session altogether.[86] The divisions among the churchmen appeared again when a convention of the estates considered the completed Book of Discipline in January 1561. The work

---

[83] PRO SP 52/5, fos. 40ᵛ, 41ʳ (*CSP Scot.*, vol. i, no. 886).

[84] Wormald, *Court, Kirk and Community*, 120–1; *APS* ii. 526.

[85] *First Book*, 3–4, 8–9; Calderwood, ii. 44–7. The surnames of the 'six Johns' were Douglas, Knox, Row, Spottiswoode, Willock, and Winram.

[86] *CSP For.*, vol. v, nos. 418–19; Donaldson, *Scottish Reformation*, 56–8; *First Book*, 6; Leslie, *History*, 293.

defined the reformed polity of the Kirk, and set forth an ambitious scheme for the transfer of the entire patrimony of the old establishment to the hands of the reformers. The task of creating a novel church structure to replace an existing hierarchy that was never formally abolished was highly contentious and problematic. The Book contained serious deficiencies in this and other areas, and though it was subscribed by the lords of the secret council, it was never officially ratified by the estates, or accepted by the sovereign. Lethington and Erskine of Dun were two of its prominent critics, and the controversies among the reformers over its contents gave only a hint of the wider problems that they would face in communicating their doctrines to the general population.[87]

The dynamism and efficiency of the Kirk's leaders in these early stages of reform did seem to count for a great deal. Randolph's informal soundings on the issue of religious conformity between the realms rested on the hope that this energy could be channelled along a path which would accord with English reforming opinion.[88] News of the use of the second Edwardian Prayer Book in Scotland during the revolt was promising, and the English had an ally in Lethington, who hoped that 'Ernest embracing off religion will joyne ws straitly togidder'.[89] Already, however, there had been hints of friction between the versions of Protestant reform favoured by the English and Scots. The welcome, or lack of it, accorded to the returning Genevans in each realm, and the English unease at the iconoclastic outbursts of the Congregation, suggested deeper differences. During the Edinburgh negotiations Cecil had been unsettled by the Scottish rigidity on doctrinal questions, and even the optimistic Randolph now admitted to finding his contacts in the Kirk so 'severe' that he began to doubt whether they would achieve agreement.[90] If even these passionate advocates of a binding Anglo-Scottish amity were sensing the incompatibility of their devotional stances, the chances of establishing effective religious conformity seemed remote.

The Scottish reformers were themselves ambivalent over the nature of their relationship with England. They readily acknowledged their military debt to Elizabeth, and before parliament sat in 1560 the Congregation's ministers offered a prayer of thanksgiving that recognized, 'thou hes maid our conferedatis of Ingland the instrumentis be quhom we are now sett at this libertie, to quhom we in thy name have promeisit mutuall fayth agane; lett us never fall to that unkyndnes, O Lord, that ather we declair oure selfis unthankfull unto thame, or prophanaris of thy holie name'.[91] Their 'godlie

---

[87] *First Book*, 11, 51, 74; PRO SP 52/6, fos. 29–32 (*CSP Scot.*, vol. i, no. 958).
[88] PRO SP 52/5, fos. 50–3 (*CSP Scot.*, vol. i, no. 891).
[89] *CSP Scot.*, vol. i, no. 480; PRO SP 52/5, fo. 29ʳ (*CSP Scot.*, vol. i, no. 958).
[90] PRO SP 52/5, fo. 52ᵛ (*CSP Scot.*, vol. i, no. 891).   [91] Knox, ii. 86.

liegue', however, was threatened by increasingly noticeable religious differences. The Congregation had found little to admire in English reform, and the speed with which their own religious revolution was accomplished heightened the sense that they were embarking on an entirely new venture. Knox and Goodman's castigation of England's 'slack proceedings in religion', and the 'dregges of Papistrie' in the Prayer Book reflected an extreme attachment to Calvinist reform, but the idea that all elements of Catholic ritual and practice should be discarded was widely accepted among the Scottish reformers.[92] Significantly, a body of dissatisfied exile opinion in England adhered to the same view, and so looked with some envy at the thoroughness of Scots who, as Jewel told Martyr, saw to it that 'All the monasteries are everywhere levelled with the ground: the theatrical dresses, the sacrilegious chalices, the idols, the altars, are consigned to the flames; not a vestige of the ancient superstition and idolatry is left'.[93]

The distaste shown by leaders of the Kirk for the corresponding half-heartedness in England meant they showed few signs of any desire for a more exact religious conformity. They valued and wished to maintain the Anglo-Scottish alliance, but did not see any need for closer doctrinal ties with the imperfectly reformed English Church, despite Lethington and Randolph's promptings. This lack of regard was matched in England by Elizabeth's abiding disapproval of Knox, Goodman, and their Genevan associates. It was ironic, then, that these same former exiles were especially troubled by the absence of effective religious agreement, their criticisms of the English Prayer Book stemming from their desire to bring the English Church to the same purity as the Kirk. When Knox wrote to Anna Locke that the Scottish borderers in Jedburgh and Kelso were professing the word, he evidently hoped their godliness would begin to extend south of the frontier.[94] The request from both Knox and Goodman that they might preach in the English borders, together with Knox's interest in Berwick, and Goodman's mission to the Isle of Man, seem to have been first steps towards effecting a more perfect reformation throughout Britain. Goodman would also later spend time in Ireland as chaplain to Sir Henry Sidney.[95] English politicians, however, refused to countenance the idea of immoderate Genevan-style sermonizing in the north of England, while at the same time, most of Knox and Goodman's Scottish colleagues were content to maintain only a broad religious accord with England.[96]

---

[92] *CSP For.*, vol. iv, no. 145; Knox, vi. 12.
[93] *Zurich Letters*, vol. i, no. 16.   [94] Knox, vi. 78.
[95] Ibid. 47, 69; PRO SP 52/5, fos. 50–3 (*CSP Scot.*, vol. i, no. 891); *CSP Scot.*, vol. i, no. 983; *DNB* xxii, 129.   [96] *CSP Scot.*, vol. i, no. 595.

VII. DIFFERING INTERPRETATIONS OF THE AMITY

These disagreements over the form that the Anglo-Scottish Protestant
understanding should take, now that its immediate purpose had been
served, were only one aspect of significant variations in contemporary
thinking on the amity. In the months after the achievement by the allies
of their well-defined and understood strategic objectives, differences of
opinion over the future of the coalition became more visible. Lethington,
Whitlaw, and other Congregation members had made no secret of their
wish to see the union made perfect by the marriage of Elizabeth to Arran.
The same hope had gained ground among English officials such as
Throckmorton, Sadler, and Randolph, anxious that the problem of the
succession should be resolved.[97] If Cecil had tried to hold back the growing
enthusiasm of the plan's supporters he was unsuccessful, since it was very
much in the minds of the Scottish lords during the parliament of August
1560. One of the principal items on the agenda was the appointment of an
embassy to England, to return thanks for Elizabeth's military assistance,
and to make a formal suit for the marriage.[98]

In November 1560 Glencairn, Morton, and Lethington arrived at the
English court to present Elizabeth with a proposal that they considered 'the
onely mean in our sight to make the friendship constant and indissoluble'.
It also held out the enticing proposition that 'Ireland might be reformed, and
brought to perfection of Obedience', with the result that 'the Queen of
England should be the strongest Princess uppon the Seas, and establish a
certain Monarchy be it selfe in the Ocean divided from the rest of the
world'. The Congregation had fully assimilated the island imagery of 1540s
propagandists, the three-kingdom perspective of former exiles, and the
tactical concerns of Cecil. More surprising was their professed willingness to constitute the inferior kingdom of the alliance. They reassured
Elizabeth, 'You need not to feare that by marriage of a King of Scotland
unto a Queen of England the preeminence of England might be defaced, for
that should alwayes remain still for the worthines therof. And the Kings of
Scotland would ever desire to make their Residence in England, as in the
better part of the Isle.'[99] Since 1559 the English had studiously avoided
articulating their historical claims to dominion over the Scots, so this
apparently voluntary offer of submission on the part of the Scots is puzzling

[97] *CSP For.*, vol. iii, nos. 878, 888; vol. v, nos. 431, 454, 523, 759.
[98] PRO SP 52/5, fos. 37–8 (*CSP Scot.*, vol. i, no. 885); *APS* ii. 605.
[99] PRO SP 52/5, fos. 129–31 (no. 50) (*CSP Scot.*, vol. i, no. 926).

(as well as offering a startling anticipation of the actual dynastic union of 1603). It was perhaps a shrewd piece of persuasion, of the kind that Cecil and Wotton had privately used with Elizabeth, intended simply to achieve Scottish purposes. Lethington may well have persuaded his colleagues to employ the argument, his desire to win Elizabeth over being such that he confided in Cecil, 'I wishe to God I may rather dye in the voyage, then that it turne not to the union of the two realmes!'[100]

Whatever the origins of the offer, it proved unacceptable to the queen, who responded with a gracious but unequivocal rejection. She clearly hoped to retain the goodwill of the Scots, telling them of her wish to 'contynew with that Realme, and with the three Estats therof, in an unfayned and constant Amyty',[101] but her version of this amity was decidedly not a dynastic one. Generally, Elizabeth showed little sympathy with the British policy perspectives of her secretary and his Scottish counterparts. She was consistently worried about the impact of the Anglo-Scottish alliance upon her relations with Spain; and although Cecil persuaded her of the urgency of the Guise threat by way of Scotland and Ireland, she was never fully committed to a comprehensive three-kingdom strategy. Having secured Argyll's promise to assist in the subjugation of her Irish rebels, for instance, she did not pursue this important opening, and the earl was left to ask in vain for further directions.[102] Neither was the queen interested in the proceedings of the Scottish Kirk, despite the hopes of a number of her ministers that the Churches could be brought into closer conformity.

Scottish disappointment at the failure of the design for the marriage was significant. Though Elizabeth's refusal brought no open breach to the alliance, there were ominous hints that the setback might cause former supporters of England to lose heart. It was unfortunate for the English that the incident occurred just as reports began to arrive of the death of the young Francis II. The possibility that Mary's return to Scotland might be imminent was a source of great unease, and it undoubtedly caused many to rethink the purpose and long-term usefulness of the Anglo-Scottish amity.[103] Lethington warned Cecil that some in Scotland had begun to consider the advantages of reconciliation with the Scottish queen, arguing, 'that seing it hath not pleased God (our synnes deserving that ponishement) to be so beneficiall to bothe the countreys, that by receaving the ouverture lately propounded to ws, the realmes may be joyned togidder,

---

[100] PRO SP 52/5, fo. 38ᵛ (*CSP Scot.*, vol. i, no. 885).
[101] BL Cotton Calig. Bv, fo. 319 (Haynes, *State Papers*, i. 364).
[102] *CSP For.*, vol. v, nos. 438, 629, 699, 968; Dawson, 'Two Kingdoms or Three?', 122–3; Alford, *Early Elizabethan Polity*, 87–8.
[103] *CSP For.*, vol. v, no. 875.

now we must of necessite, so far as in ws lyeth, procure the Quene our Sovereane ladyis benevolence towardes ws.'[104] After the height of the Anglo-Scottish rapport earlier in 1560 a new restraint was appearing in relations between the countries.

This was only intensified by uncertainties as to Mary's likely response to the newly constituted Calvinist church discipline. Lethington hoped that the queen would 'imbrace the worde of God', though he feared 'our exactenes and singularitie in religion wyll never concurre with her judgemente'.[105] The knowledge that the queen had been living in the orthodox environment of the French court for twelve years did not encourage optimism, and the committee finalizing the Church polity quickened their proceedings in anticipation of Mary's return. While Knox and Goodman continued to cling to the belief that they could yet be united with the English in a single profession, the more general Scottish indifference to the Elizabethan establishment was eloquent. The Book of Discipline, upon completion, was translated into Latin so that Calvin, Viret, Beza, and other European divines could examine it. There was no attempt, however, to hear the opinion of Elizabethan churchmen.[106] The Book's content showed the impact of various continental reformed churches, including material based on the ecclesiastical ordinances of Geneva, the discipline of the French Church, and various works by Calvin. It had little in common with English practice, however, despite the Prayer Book's ready availability in Scotland, and the fact that the 'six Johns' between them had extensive experience of the Henrician and Edwardian Churches.[107] Influences on the Scottish Book were diverse, and it contained some unexpected legacies of English involvement, such as the humanist-inspired plans for reform of the universities, following the pattern set by John Douglas and Richard Marshall in St Andrews.[108] It showed little correspondence, however, with the officially received English religion after 1559.

The Scottish reformers, it seemed, had decided to see their alliance with England as one of broad Protestant communion in the wider reformed church. Long before the religious revolution of 1559 the Scots had shown a lively receptivity to European reformed trends in their universities and religious establishments. The ease with which they conceived of their place

[104] PRO SP 52/6, fo. 48ʳ (CSP Scot., vol. i, no. 963).
[105] PRO SP 52/6, fo. 52ʳ (CSP Scot., vol. i, no. 964).
[106] PRO SP 52/5, fo. 52ᵛ (CSP Scot., vol. i, no. 891).
[107] First Book, 16, 20, 32, 96–107, 165–73; Hewat, Makers of the Scottish Church, 25, 132–5, 282–3.
[108] First Book, 58; Hewat, Makers of the Scottish Church, 310; Durkan, 'Cultural Background', 327–8.

within the international community of the faithful was evident in the prayers offered in the Reformation parliament for France, England, and 'all prynces lyvinge in the feare of God'. The preface to their confession addressed Scotland and 'all utheris Realmeis and Natiouns, professing the samyn Christ Jesus', declaring, 'Lang have we thristit deir brethren to haue notifeit unto the warld the soume of that doctrine q[uhi]lk we profess and for the q[uhi]lk we have sustenit infamy and danger'. They had not yet had this opportunity, 'ffor how we haue bene tossit a haill zeir past the maist p[ar]te of Ewrope (as we suppois) dois understand'.[109] The architects of Scotland's reformation believed their religious decisions to have relevance for the whole of Europe, and were not afraid to say so. Their growing feeling was that the Kirk was unique among reformed churches for its absolute purity of doctrine and polity, and this self-assurance increased their distance from English reform.[110]

The altercations within the Elizabethan Church during the 1560s, on the contentious issues of vestments and ceremonies, made for a stark contrast with the reformed Scottish Kirk. The same arguments which had divided the Marian exiles in Frankfurt and Basle, focusing on what could or could not 'properly be regarded as matters of indifference' continued to trouble English churchmen long after they had been despatched by the Scottish reformers.[111] For most, the absence of exact doctrinal consensus was not a serious concern, although a minority were grieved by the obvious liturgical and structural disparities between the establishments. The variations did, however, have important implications for the future relations between the countries, particularly with the prospect of the Scottish queen's return. It was unclear how Mary's presence would impinge on the dealings of the self-confident new Kirk. The Congregation found themselves divided over how far they might seek accommodation with their queen. From England's perspective the question was whether Mary could be persuaded to support the confessional agreement between the realms, while at the same time agreeing to renounce her claim to the English throne in accordance with the Edinburgh treaty.

---

[109] Wormald, *Mary Queen of Scots*, 108–9; Knox, vi. 118; *APS* ii. 526.
[110] Wormald, *Court, Kirk and Community*, 116; Row, *Historie*, 12; Forbes, *Certain Records*, 345.
[111] *Zurich Letters*, vol. ii, no. 11; Collinson, *Puritan Movement*, 72–3.

VIII. CROSS-BORDER CONTACTS AND THE RETURN OF MARY
QUEEN OF SCOTS

Despite serious misgivings over the future of the Anglo–Scottish alliance after 1560, certain groups maintained an active interest in nourishing religious contacts between the realms, regardless of official ecclesiastical policies, and frequently in direct defiance of them. There was a considerable degree of cross-border acquaintance among the first reformed ministers in Scotland and the more extreme English Protestants, for whom the Kirk's well-publicized insistence on apostolic purity held a great attraction. In addition to their contacts during the Marian exile, a high proportion of the ministers and readers appointed by the Kirk in 1560–1 had first-hand experience of English reform. John Willock, John Spottiswoode, David Forrest, Paul Methven, and William Harlaw had all, like Knox, spent periods of exile in England.[112] Willock continued to travel between England and Scotland, maintaining his responsibilities as minister of Loughborough, superintendent of Glasgow, and occasional moderator of the General Assembly.[113] Christopher Goodman was of course an Englishman by birth, and he remained in Scotland as a minister until 1565. Knox, though firmly based in Scotland after 1559, stayed in touch with Coverdale and other former Genevans in London.[114] The simple continuation of personal friendships, and recognition of shared religious inclinations, kept alive such cross-border exchanges.

As in previous eras, the practical variations between regimes professing the same confession brought about supportive Anglo–Scottish association in the name of reform. The single-mindedness of the leaders of the Kirk, in pursuing a more radical and European path than had ever been seen in the English Church, would prove an enduring attraction to English radicals. The Scottish Kirk was held up as a model of effective discipline by extremists south of the border, and in 1566 the General Assembly endorsed their criticisms of the popish vestments of their own Church in a letter addressed to 'the Bischops and pastours of Ingland'.[115] Despite Scottish co-operation, the grievances of English radicals with the compromises of their church settlement remained unappeased, and they persisted in looking to the Kirk for inspiration. Their connection with the churchmen of Scotland would

---

[112] Knox, ii. 87; Calderwood, ii. 44–6; *SSP* i. 585.
[113] Oxford, Bodleian Library, Tanner MS 50: 10, fo. 31^r; NLS Adv. MS 19. 3. 24; Shaw, 'John Willock', 61–8.
[114] *DNB*, xxii, 129; Knox, vi. 108–9; Dawson, 'Anglo-Scottish Protestant Culture', 99.
[115] Kirk, '"Polities of the Best Reformed Kirks"', 27.

be a lasting one, fostered by the links between the famed Scottish reformer Andrew Melville and the English puritans Thomas Cartwright and Walter Travers in Geneva during the early 1570s.[116] The passage of exiles across the border in the same period continued to be a two-way process. In addition to the English refugees looking for greater purity of worship in Scotland, a significant body of Scottish presbyterian ministers and noblemen rather surprisingly sought and received sanctuary in Berwick and London, when the Kirk was subjected to a rigidly episcopalian reform programme in 1584.[117]

The dissenters within the English Church and their zealous Scottish brethren were not the only groups to seek mutual assistance in religion during the later sixteenth century. Alongside the vociferous and staunchly Calvinist reformers in Scotland were some more moderate voices, whose influence was as important, if not as conspicuous, as that of Knox and his associates. Men such as Douglas and Winram adopted a less militant approach towards the reform of the Kirk, and Lethington was even prepared to modify the tone of the Scottish confession in order to make it more acceptable in England.[118] They succeeded in silencing the combative Knox, causing him to admit to Cecil that he had been judged 'too extream' to conduct official negotiations; and they also secured the removal from the Book of Discipline of Genevan-derived passages on the lawfulness of resistance to secular authorities.[119] Those who shared their impatience with the rash and uncompromising fervour of the Kirk's leaders may have inclined towards the more temperate spirit of erastian English reform. During the 1580s Archbishop Adamson of St Andrews would attempt to replicate the royal and erastian pattern of English church government in Scotland, though his efforts were to provoke damaging controversies.[120]

There were, therefore, complementary strands of Protestant opinion of differing strengths within both Churches. The complex pattern of their relations from 1560, as Kirk has convincingly argued, bears little relation to the 'virtual unanimity on polity, and even on liturgical matters' suggested by Donaldson.[121] Despite the rhetoric of religious and political harmony at

---

[116] Kirk, *Patterns*, 92; Collinson, *Puritan Movement*, 110; Donaldson, 'Scottish Presbyterian Exiles', 67.

[117] Kirk, *Patterns*, 93; Donaldson, 'Scottish Presbyterian Exiles', 68–70; *CSP Scot.*, vol. vii, nos. 31, 79, 83, 100, 119; Calderwood, iv. 38–46, 49–61.

[118] PRO SP 52/5, fos. 71–2 (*CSP Scot.*, vol i, no. 902); PRO SP 52/5, fo. 73ʳ (*CSP Scot.*, vol. i, no. 903).

[119] Knox, vi. 105; PRO SP 52/5, fos. 71–2 (*CSP Scot.*, vol. i, no. 902).

[120] *CSP Scot.*, vol vi, no. 707.

[121] Kirk, '"Polities of the Best Reformed Kirks"', 51–3; Donaldson, 'Presbyterian Movements', 1, 71.

the outset, the Churches remained in certain important respects very distant from one another. The dissimilarity of their origins was obvious: the long process of magisterial reform in England bore no relation to the decisive proceedings that created Scotland's Protestant Kirk. In character, too, the establishments were worlds apart. England's royally governed establishment, with its highly traditional episcopal structure, was quite unlike the newly constituted Kirk, whose General Assembly intended to oversee nothing less than the total overhaul of the country's medieval dioceses in favour of a conciliar system. Although the achievement of the Kirk may have fallen short of this goal, its aim of sweeping away the pre-Reformation clerical hierarchy was revolutionary. Furthermore, the office of superintendent was not, as Kirk has shown, the continuation of bishops by another name, but was introduced as an expedient at a time when ministers were in short supply.[122] The English and Scots may have celebrated their alliance and its great achievement in 1560, but the more radical, European-influenced tendencies of Scottish reformers would only increase the distance between them.

Quite apart from the emerging distinctions in the Protestant convictions of leading reformers, it was evident that the majority of the populations remained either orthodox or uncommitted in their religious loyalties. The timing and conduct of the Scottish religious revolution owed as much to political contingencies as to the strength of popular Protestant feeling, and the remarkable advances of the reformed Kirk in the early 1560s needed to be consolidated with long-term catechization and evangelization if the alteration was to achieve a permanent status. The same was true in England and Wales, whose populations, having been subjected to numerous religious innovations, did not rush to the support of the Protestant establishment from 1559. The challenge of extending reform to Ireland was even more formidable. In each country the Churches faced parallel tasks of eradicating traditional practices, providing adequate preaching, and educating the laity in the fundamentals of the reformed faith.[123] Catholic insurgency remained a real possibility, despite the removal of the French presence from the mainland, and this raised all the old English suspicions of foreign-aided domestic instability. In 1561, moreover, Mary was still refusing to

[122] Kirk, '"Polities of the Best Reformed Kirks"', 28–31.
[123] Michael Lynch, 'Preaching to the Converted? Perspectives on the Scottish Reformation', in A. A. MacDonald, Michael Lynch, and Ian B. Cowan (eds.), *The Renaissance in Scotland: Studies in Literature, Religion, History and Culture offered to John Durkan* (Leiden: Brill Academic Publications, 1994), 306–8, 323–5, 328–30; Christopher Haigh, 'The Church of England, the Catholics and the People', in Haigh (ed.), *Reign of Elizabeth I*, 196–200, 209.

ratify the Treaty of Edinburgh. Her reluctance stemmed, so she told Throckmorton, from her wish to consult the Scottish estates, but it was evident that she rejected utterly the demand that she renounce her place in the English succession.[124] With this question hanging, any hint of Catholic activity, particularly in conjunction with Scotland, was guaranteed to cause acute disquiet.

Throckmorton warned Elizabeth of the machinations of John Elder, the Scotsman and former pensioner of Henry VIII, who had since converted to Catholicism. He was now passing on details of Pole and Bonner's religious injunctions to the French government, which made him, in Throckmorton's words, 'as great a practiser and as daungerous for the matters of England, as any that I know'.[125] Throckmorton's assessment of the risk posed by the eccentric Elder was rather exaggerated, but it illustrates the way in which isolated individuals or incidents could be woven by nervous English politicians into a pattern of insidious Catholic conspiracy. There were also signs of Catholic agitation on the Scottish frontier in 1562, when one 'Graye', otherwise known as 'Whyte', an Oxford academic and adherent of the old religion, made his way to the Benedictine abbey of Crossraguel in Ayrshire. Here he became involved in the public disputations between the Catholic apologist Quintin Kennedy and Knox. Randolph, in Edinburgh, did his best to keep Cecil informed of the movements of various English 'practisers' in Scotland, and of 'certayne wycked Friers sente owte of this countrie for feare of punyshement', who had been 'received (as yt is reported) for mynesters in Englande'. Knox's communications with Sir Henry Sidney on the subject suggest a fear of links with Catholic supporters in Ireland.[126] All this was reminiscent of the fugitive activity of rebel English friars in the 1530s, and underlines the variety of religious interchanges between all three kingdoms, even after Scotland's Protestant revolution of 1559.

The hopes of the Scottish friars, and of prominent Catholic spokesmen such as Kennedy and Ninian Winzet were undoubtedly encouraged by their queen's return from France in August 1561. Mary's presence in Scotland was, as Alford has demonstrated, a crucial point of change in the relationship between the kingdoms.[127] The common cause of the allies had been articulated in her absence, with the continual refrain that they were defending the Scottish subjects' natural allegiance to their queen.

---

[124] *CSP For.*, vol vi, nos. 108, 151, 336; Knox, ii. 169–74.
[125] Forbes, *Full View*, i. 233.
[126] *CSP Scot.*, vol. i, nos. 1152, 1136, 1139; Knox, vi. 147.
[127] Alford, *Early Elizabethan Polity*, 86–7.

England's safeguard lay in Mary's continuing absence from the realm, but in August 1561 this was removed. Mary arrived in Leith, accompanied by a modest retinue, and Scottish Anglophiles were immediately divided by a rival focus of loyalty. The strain on their allegiances was made more acute by Mary's unexpectedly ambivalent response to the recent activity of reformers: she gave her assurance to Lord James that the Protestant proceedings of the Kirk would go unchallenged, provided that she might continue to hear Mass in private.[128] Such a compromise was anathema to Knox, who would have preferred to wage an apocalyptic struggle of light against darkness. It was welcomed, however, by Protestant statesmen in Scotland who wished both to advance the reformed religion, and to uphold the lawful government of their sovereign. Knox's attempts to direct a radical, British-wide reformation therefore became increasingly futile as members of the government sought to work with the queen, leaving him to rail ineffectually against an almost mythical Catholic adversary: as Jenny Wormald says, 'Knox was insisting on resistance when there was absolutely nothing to resist'.[129]

The Anglo-Scottish amity also began to suffer as the prospect of the ratification of the Edinburgh agreement became increasingly remote. Fissures appeared in the alliance, with leading noblemen such as Morton dropping their former fidelity, and even England's most loyal supporters re-examining their allegiances.[130] Those who had been earnest advocates of co-operation found themselves particularly torn. One compromise that recommended itself to both Lethington and Lord James, was to effect an agreement between the two queens, by which Mary would renounce her disputed claim to the English throne, in return for Elizabeth's recognition of her place in the succession. Lord James's hopes for this reworking of the amity between the realms had been encouraged by his discussions with Mary, and he attempted to persuade Elizabeth of the merits of his plan to reconcile these 'tender cusines, boyth Quenes in the flour of your ages, much ressambling other in most excelleent and goodly qualiteis, on whome God hayth bestowit most liberally the gyftes of nature and fortune', asking, 'Inconvenient wer it to provyde that to the Quene my souveraine her own place wer reserved in the succession of the Crown of England?' Lethington reiterated the grounds for agreement between them, believing that 'besydes the tendernes off blood, the one off them doth so moche in all things

[128] *CSP For.*, vol. vi, no. 455; Knox, ii. 142–3; Calderwood, ii. 47, 121–2, 129.

[129] Wormald, 'Godly Reformer, Godless Monarch: John Knox and Mary Queen of Scots', in Mason (ed.), *John Knox and the British Reformations*, 231–2.

[130] *CSP Scot.*, vol. i, no. 977; Wormald, *Mary Queen of Scots*, 106–7.

ressemble the other, that whosoever loveth the one off thayr two majesties, he must also off necessite love the other'.[131]

Their references to propinquity of blood were guaranteed to alarm rather than reassure Elizabeth, however, and their appeal for an agreement to 'salve all matiers'[132] was deficient in too many respects. Elizabeth was impossible to move on the subject of the succession, continuing to insist that Mary could be accorded no recognition; while Mary herself would not abandon the argument that she was the rightful heir to the English throne. For Cecil, too, the inclusion of Mary in the succession scheme would do nothing to allay fears relating to the incessant Catholic menace to the realm. His aim of domestic security through a three-sided Protestant strategy was indivisible from that of repudiating the Stuart challenge to the English succession. With Mary's return to Scotland, therefore, the limitless possibilities sensed by the Congregation and their English supporters at the time of the Reformation parliament began to be circumscribed. Elizabeth's belated declarations of faith in a full-blown religious alliance could not hold the allies together. Only one year after the triumphant Anglo–Scottish achievement, the underlying tensions in the league were surfacing.

Before the arrival of Mary Queen of Scots subjected the Anglo–Scottish amity to its most serious test yet, the progress of the allies was remarkable. Their collaboration in 1559–60 had the desired effect of striking a blow at the menacing Catholic international, to the benefit of the European Protestant communion, not to mention the domestic and strategic interests of the principal parties. The British perspectives of those involved reflected their Protestant-inspired perceptions of foreign policy, developed since the time of England's break with Rome. The experience of the papal endeavours against England during the 1530s, together with perpetual French activity in both Scotland and Ireland, fed their belief in the necessity of a comprehensive three-kingdom policy. The religious visionaries of the Marian exile worked with providential-minded politicians in both England and Scotland to make a reality of this British imperative. In doing so they succeeded in an enterprise which English and Scottish Catholic reformers had not even attempted during the 1550s: they co-ordinated their common religious sympathies and strategic interests to their mutual benefit. The dynamic leadership of the Scottish revolt secured the permanent establishment of Protestant worship north of the border, so extending the reformed religion to the whole island of Britain.

---

[131] Alford, *Early Elizabethan Polity*, 88–9; PRO SP 52/6, fos. 115–16 (*CSP Scot.*, vol. i, no. 999); PRO SP 52/5, fo. 145 (*CSP Scot.*, vol. i, no. 935).
[132] PRO SP 52/6, fo. 31ʳ (*CSP Scot.*, vol. i, no. 958).

This was the theory at least, though in practice substantial work remained to be done in planting the reformed religion more securely. Effective co-operation among members of the political elites could not in itself guarantee the future of the Protestant Churches, and the problem of evangelization was only beginning to be addressed. In general, however, the work of reform was at least now a joint concern for the ecclesiastical authorities in England and Scotland. A shared recognition of their reformed sympathies dominated religious exchanges between the countries after 1559, although cross-border associations remained diverse, even in this new era of Protestant agreement. The fact that their official positions on reform did not coincide completely opened up a contrast between the ecclesiastical establishments, which provided a dynamic interplay between English and Scottish Protestants for years to come. Their contacts were frequently sustaining and supportive, but at the same time, the impressive self-assurance of Scottish reformers demonstrated their belief in the integrity of the Kirk, and, more significantly, a general disinclination to submit to English direction in religion.

Protestants of all persuasions were forced to rethink the amity with the presence of Mary in Scotland from 1561. Her return resurrected the various problems, now a generation old, relating to the espousal of opposing beliefs by the sovereigns of England and Scotland. The picture was complicated still further by the Mary's apparent willingness to countenance a reformed ecclesiastical establishment. This was an unexpected development, and one that offered to appease the religious and political scruples of influential members of the Scottish government. English statesmen rarely found themselves in agreement with Knox, but the return of the Scottish queen was one area in which they had some sympathy with his concerns. Mary brought the Stuart challenge directly onto British soil, and Lethington's admission to Cecil that the Scots were seeking to renew the auld alliance demonstrated how, in the space of a few months, the geographical proximity of England and Scotland, 'being by a dry marche Ioyned',[133] could appear once more as a threat rather than a divine blessing. Despite all these concerns, though, there was distinct reassurance for England in the appearance that the future of the reformed Kirk seemed secure; and even some slim hopes of establishing an understanding with the Scottish queen.[134] Even if these were to prove ill-founded, the unprecedented Protestant understanding between the two governments created a supportive bond that looked to stand some chance of surviving impending political uncertainties.

---

[133] PRO SP 52/6, fo. 48ᵛ (*CSP Scot.*, vol. i, no. 963).
[134] Wormald, 'Godly Reformer, Godless Monarch', 233–4.

Conclusion: 'To Enrich with Gospel Truth the Neighbour Realm'[1]

The picture of Protestant harmony described by Lethington, Randolph, and other observers of the Scottish reformation parliament told only part of the complex story of Anglo-Scottish religious relations, even after the revolutionary changes of 1560. In addition to underlying doubts concerning the surety of the reformed understanding between the countries, there were signs of outright opposition to official ecclesiastical policies from Catholics in both realms. Religious associations across the border continued to be diverse, unpredictable, and constantly changing. The alliance that developed from the Protestant ecclesiastical settlements in England and Scotland demonstrated an acknowledgement by their governments of the value of confessional solidarity after the troubled mid-century period; but unofficial exchanges between churchmen and laypeople recognized no formal constraints, and continued to demand the attention of the authorities in both realms.

From the time of England's break with Rome, it had become ever more apparent that the religious upheavals of one country would have an inescapable significance for the neighbouring realm. For Henry VIII this meant taking urgent action to avert the possibility of Scottish involvement in domestic sedition. The dilemma for James V lay in how he might resist Protestant encroachment, while remaining at peace with his powerful neighbour. Ongoing interactions between religious sympathizers of various persuasions throughout the 1540s brought further tension to an already difficult diplomatic relationship. The nominal Catholic consensus between the governments during the 1550s created something of a lull in cross-border affairs; but when the accession of Elizabeth at the end of the decade was followed by the arrival of Mary Queen of Scots, it seemed that the future of Protestant reform in Britain was once again under threat from a Catholic monarch. In the event, the Scottish queen's surprisingly tolerant

---

[1] NLS Adv. MS 19. 3. 24, fo. 32^r. This 20th-cent. trans. of the Latin verse by John Johnston, a professor of theology at St Andrews (1612), is in Hewat, *Makers of the Scottish Church*, 164–5.

attitude towards the Kirk's proceedings made prospects for reformers significantly better than they might otherwise have appeared. Mary's own orthodox religious loyalties, however, were an abiding source of concern to Protestants in both realms.

While the English government had been doing its best to minimize the Catholic threat from the north after 1534, the Scots, too, were attempting to counter the dangerous effects of advancing Protestant doctrines. The anxieties expressed by secular and ecclesiastical authorities, relating to heretical literature, apostate friars, and contagious influences from England, were amply borne out by the contacts between Scottish evangelicals and their co-religionists south of the border. Their collaboration in propounding reformed doctrines, from the earliest days of the English reformation, could be seen in cross-border ministries, trade in Protestant works, and the borrowing of liturgical forms. These associations, together with a combined experience of exile during the reign of Mary Tudor, helped to create a Protestant discourse between the realms. This was wide-ranging, and amounted to a broad consensus on reformed principles rather than any specific agreement, but would constitute an important bond between the allies in 1560.

This should not imply that the orthodox loyalties of the Scots were inexorably worn down by relentless exposure to Protestant influences from England after 1534. The English experience of reform was undoubtedly a source of information and inspiration for interested parties in Scotland; but the true pattern of religious interaction between the realms was more complex than one of simple encouragement from the south and gradual imitation in the north. Some of the most outspoken Protestants in the early years of the English reformation were the Scottish exiles who took up office in the Church under the patronage of Cromwell. The English, meanwhile, were far from being fervent disciples of the new learning, intent on exporting it to Scotland in the wake of their own reformation. Members of the government may have welcomed the signs that Protestant doctrines appeared to be making advances in Scotland as well as in England during the 1530s and 1540s, but many more laypeople remained indifferent to the fortunes of Protestantism in the north. A number of English churchmen even travelled to Scotland to participate in the innovative Catholic reform programme of the Kirk, actively committing themselves to the defence of the old religion against the heresies emanating from their own Church.

The religious links between the peoples of the two countries were multifaceted, confounding any pretensions by the authorities to police cross-border activity. These associations looked set to continue after 1560, since at the apex of the Protestant achievement of that year, differing opinions on the right course of reform prevented absolute religious agreement between the realms. The confidence of Scottish reformers in rejecting both the doctrines and structure of the old religion demonstrated a vitality of expression and a refusal to compromise which set them apart from English churchmen. While some radical English Protestants stood back in admiring awe at the Kirk's ruthlessness, other members of the conservative Elizabethan establishment found it more disconcerting. These differences did not remove the basis for religious intercourse between the realms, but ensured that contacts would persist between moderates on the one hand and the extremists of the presbyterian and puritan parties on the other. The nature of the religious dialogue between England and Scotland was constantly evolving, and in this sense 1560 was simply one moment, albeit a highly significant one, in a much longer process.

By the same token, the associations between Catholics of the two countries were not eliminated by the Protestant accord of 1560. Despite emotive accounts of the reformers' victory in the Scottish reformation parliament, with ageing lairds repenting their lifetime of errors,[2] it was clear that in the country at large, as in England, there had been no wholesale repudiation of orthodox teachings. Large sections of the populations of both realms either resisted the new doctrines, or at least were yet to be convinced of the need for Protestant reform. Among them, a number of militant supporters of the Roman religion attempted to combine forces in defence of their faith. Their involvement with one another during the early 1560s, and their contacts with possible associates in Ireland, demonstrated the continuing relevance of a three-kingdom dimension to reforming considerations. From the time of the Kildare rebellion, the activities of Irish rebels had never been absent from English considerations. In its own right the kingdom presented the English with intractable problems of governance: in conjunction with domestic religious unrest and Scottish interference, Ireland's disruptive potential was immeasurably increased, giving rise to serious security fears.

The Anglo–Scottish amity could not provide an answer to all the problems of the preceding decades, but it nevertheless offered an important source of strength and security to the reformed regimes of England and Scotland. Their awareness of one another had been greatly sharpened by the events of the reformations in both countries, as their simple geographical proximity made religious contacts between them inevitable. In

[2] PRO SP 52/5, fo. 41ʳ (*CSP Scot.*, vol. i, no. 886).

determining the theological character of their religious settlements, the varied influences of the reformed churches of Europe were undoubtedly of fundamental importance. Their immediate island context, however, shaped all the basic processes of reform in England and Scotland, demonstrating beyond any doubt that the doings of one country were impossible for the other to ignore.

Well-established interactions between Protestant sympathizers in the two realms played a vitally important part in securing a reformed settlement for the Kirk in 1560. The combination of political activism and significant popular backing helped to carry through the religious rebellion in defiance of the crown. At the same time, though, the Congregation's actions were entirely dependent on a succession of contingencies. England's loss of Calais in 1558, bringing an end to its continental interests, underlined a focus upon the island form of Britain, which highlighted the advantages of a Scottish alliance. Mary Tudor's failure to produce an heir and her death in November 1558 then cleared the path for a Protestant successor to the English throne. The entirely unforeseen death of Henry II in July 1559, by which the French dauphin and Mary Queen of Scots became king and queen of France, heightened Scottish and English anxieties over the pervasive Guise influence in Scotland, and hastened their readiness to take combined action against the threat. With Mary absent in France, and an ambitious party of Scottish Protestant nobles receiving the necessary encouragement from England, the circumstances were created for the successful Scottish coup.

The historiography of these years rightly stresses the crucial significance of the coincidence of all these events in assuring the Congregation's victory.[3] It would be wrong to imply, however, that Anglo-Scottish collaboration in 1559–60 was a mere matter of luck and timing. While it was essential for the joint action that the right combination of factors should be in place, the will to make it succeed depended on more than simple chance. This can be demonstrated by the contrasting events of the earlier 1550s, when England's return to Rome meant that the two countries shared the same Catholic faith. By 1553 the strains of living with the confessional difference between the realms had become obvious to all. The activity of religious rebels troubled the governments of both realms, threats of religious-inspired foreign leagues aggravated domestic insecurities, and the effectiveness of reform in each country was compromised. Their common espousal of Catholicism would appear to have offered a timely

---

[3] J. H. Burns, 'The Political Background of the Reformation, 1513–1625', in McRoberts (ed.), *Essays*, 16–17; Morrill, 'British Problem', 22–3.

opportunity for an Anglo-Scottish agreement, to ensure political as well as religious harmony and the maintenance of a united front against Protestant heresies. The grounds for religious co-operation between the two Catholic governments were compelling, and the programmes for orthodox reform in the two Churches remarkably similar, but in the event there was no attempt to make of them a co-ordinated campaign.

Associations between Catholics of the two realms, paradoxically, were more active when the regimes were of differing confessions, and the traditional religion seemed especially threatened. Aside from a handful of energetic reforming churchmen such as Richard Marshall, the Catholics of one realm seemed barely aware of those in the other between 1553 and 1558: their collaboration would only begin to gather pace once more in the early 1560s. The most obvious explanation for this seeming indifference was the outward pull of their opposing diplomatic ties. The strength of the Guise position in Scotland, together with the unshakeable bond between Tudor and Spanish interests, made the idea of an Anglo-Scottish Catholic alliance impossible to contemplate. The overall effectiveness of the reform schemes of the English and Scottish Churches was clearly not dependent on securing cross-border approval and assistance: if other factors had worked in their favour, the Catholic Church in each country might have coexisted quite comfortably without any reference to the other. Co-operation between the churchmen of the two countries, however, could potentially have fortified their efforts to withstand the challenge from Protestant reformers. Its absence removed an important line of defence in 1559.

The English and Scottish Protestant parties may have been assisted by political accident and opportunity in 1559, therefore, but their effective conjunction was due to more than this. It could not have come about without a will to take action on the part of prominent figures in both countries, an element crucially lacking among Catholics. The political and religious ambitions of Scottish activists such as Balnaves, Kirkcaldy, Glencairn, and Knox dated back to the 1540s, when English interventions had stimulated the Protestant aspirations of certain nobles and reformers. Many of the same assured Scots who had worked with the Henrician and Edwardian governments involved themselves with the efforts of the Congregation from 1559, drawing on their long experience of collaboration, and their personal contacts in England. On the English side, statesmen such as Cecil, Randolph, Percy, and Throckmorton, were willing supporters of the Scottish endeavours, being advocates of a religiously motivated foreign policy whose priority was the defence of the Protestant cause against Catholic intrigues. The queen may have been less interested in taking action on behalf of the Scottish rebels, but the combined advice of her ministers was able to overcome her reluctance.

The broad identity of aims within the Anglo-Scottish political community contributed significantly to their effective action in 1560: that a British Protestant culture was taking shape has been recognized in several recent studies.[4] The shaping influences of religious interactions from the time of the 1534 religious differentiation between England and Scotland, however, have not previously been closely examined. These associations were not always amicable, but their impact upon political and religious discourse was profound. Sponsors of Protestant reform shared a sense of the powerful Catholic international menace that was bound up with the English religious revolution of the 1530s, and was constantly reinforced by the practices of Catholic rebels and foreign powers in the following decades. In 1559 the grounds for concern seemed greater than ever, with the Guises asserting their dominance in Scotland, while laying claim to the English throne. The theories lately set forth by the Marian exiles contributed to the idea that common action was required against the popish enemy, and the vision of the godly isle of Britain had a captivating appeal for Protestants of the two countries. The image had been used to good effect by reformers and propagandists since the early 1540s: it recalled historical interpretations of the original unity of the island, and offered a healing of the religious breach of recent years.[5] The Protestant isle that the allies aspired to seemed geographically, historically, and divinely ordained. It both fitted into, and fed, the providential interpretations of the activists of both realms.

The sense of euphoria surrounding the establishment of the reformed Kirk in Scotland stemmed from a belief among participants in the events of 1559–60 that they were fulfilling a divine destiny. England had played a central role in the reformation drama by providing the Scots with the means of overthrowing their foreign oppressors. Their fateful collaboration inspired some of the allies to consider that their diplomatic partnership might be the basis for a more complete bond between the realms. The pace of events in recent years encouraged such speculation, as both countries had experienced a series of revolutionary developments. The shape of their ecclesiastical establishments, the religious sympathies of leading figures in government, and their political alliances had all been transformed. Even more striking was the imperceptible and yet unmistakable alteration in English and Scottish thinking on the peoples of the two realms, and the

[4] Dawson, 'Anglo-Scottish Protestant Culture', 87–8; Alford, *Early Elizabethan Polity*, 8, 45.
[5] *Complaynt of Scotlande*, 212–14; Mason, 'Anglo-British Imperialism', 164, 171–2.

nature of the relationship between them. The psychological shift that occurred during this relatively short period seemed immense. Inherited medieval hostilities had been very much in evidence during the 1530s and 1540s, and further frictions arose from England's imperial pretensions in Scotland. By the time that the Congregation came into being, however, it was possible to speak of fruitful collaboration between the English and Scots in a jointly identified godly cause.

The magnitude of this change was continually demonstrated to those who had played any part in the events of the period. In 1543 Sir Ralph Sadler and his servants had feared for their lives among the hostile people of Edinburgh, causing him to write to Suffolk, 'God help me, I had lever be among Turks'. By 1560, however, he was actively engaged in Scottish service once more, and was, according to Norfolk, 'best esteemed by the Scots of any Englishman'.[6] Meanwhile, the same city that had been violently hostile to all things English during the early 1540s became, in 1560, a place of Anglo-Scottish harmony, where prayers were offered for Queen Elizabeth, and for the eternal surety of the bond between the realms. The Scottish parliament that had railed in 1548 against the 'mortall weiris crudeliteis depredatiounis and intollerabill inuiris done be our auld enimeis of Ingland', acknowledged in 1560, 'how profitable thare amyte may be to us, quhat welth and commodite we may obtene thairthrou'.[7]

The transformation in Scottish attitudes, then, was particularly pronounced. During the years immediately after England's break with Rome, the Scots had presented themselves as staunch defenders of orthodoxy. This position was dropped briefly in 1543, but the short-lived reformation of that year was followed by a return to the more usual animosity between the realms. Through the greater part of their dealings with the governments of Henry VIII and Edward VI, the Scots attempted to hold England at arm's length, reluctantly assenting to dynastic union when this seemed inevitable, but nervily insisting on safeguards to their own laws and liberties, and to the native governance of the realm. After 1559, then, their utter dedication to the Protestant cause, and equally to their English partners, showed a complete reversal in their thinking. Their former allies, the French, were now the enemies to their freedom, while the English were their godly associates, and the deliverers of their suffering countrymen. For their part, the English, although characteristically more sluggish in their changing attitudes, also managed to move away from the customary antagonisms of earlier years. A notable body of politicians and reformers

---

[6] *SSP*, i. 347; *CSP Scot.*, vol. i, no. 733.
[7] *APS*, ii. 481, 605.

shared in the infectious spirit of unity that followed on from the successful action by the Congregation.

It was evident, however, that outside this small group, neither the English nor the Scots had entirely let go of the older tensions between their realms. Lord Wharton's assertion, during his time as warden of the marches, that 'the naturall enclynaton of that Reallme haithe ever beyne agaynst this Reallme . . . sithens the Reallmes hadd thar names of Englande and Scotlande',[8] was a conviction which some found hard to abandon. The supporters of reform in Scotland were not necessarily inclined to favour a closer religious alliance, or indeed any form of amity with England. The English reputation for xenophobia, meanwhile, remained well deserved, even among promoters of the Congregation's cause. A casual reference by Cecil to the 'slights and finesses' of the Scottish nation, which made him 'loath to commit trust to any word or promise',[9] gave a small hint of the prejudices which had been ingrained by centuries of hostile warfare. These were impressively set aside, but not completely erased in 1560.

Anglo-Scottish relations remained full of contradictions, but the continuing speculation over a more substantive form of amity between the realms gave a telling indication of the changed atmosphere of recent years. Having been assisted by the English queen, Scottish reformers now hoped that they might convince her to agree to a more lasting alliance. It was ironic that Elizabeth, coaxed so unwillingly into action in the north, found herself lauded as the Protestant saviour of the godly in both realms, when Henry VIII's desperate efforts to secure a Protestant union had evoked such widespread resentment in Scotland. This was, perhaps, the key difference between the failures of the 1530s and 1540s, and the initial success of the later Anglo-Scottish conjunction: Elizabeth's disinclination to involve herself in the affairs of the Congregation, indeed, her positive distaste for the complications faced by her government on the northern border, allowed the Scots to project their own expectations and desires onto the alliance of 1560. Their hopes were articulated in their project for dynastic union, and Elizabeth's rejection of the proposal was a grievous disappointment to men such as Lethington, who lamented to Cecil, 'God hath by tymes offred many meanes off a godly conjunction—by what providence it hath chansed that none hath taken effect as yet, I cannot tell!'[10] Lethington was evidently frustrated that the union had once again eluded them, but this was a revealing comment on his attitude towards the hoped-for con-

---

[8] PRO SP 15/2, fo. 27ᵛ (*CSP Dom. Add.*, p. 366).
[9] *CSP For.*, vol. iii, no. 973.
[10] PRO SP 52/6, fo. 162ʳ (*CSP Scot.*, vol. i, no. 1037).

junction: a complete accord between the realms had not been accomplished 'as yet', but its eventual realization would only be a matter of time.

A readiness among contemporaries to contemplate the possibility of closer union, if not always to welcome it as Lethington did, was one of the most important consequences of Anglo-Scottish religious interactions in the mid-sixteenth century. By 1560 the Scots had overtaken the English in their consideration of the subject, even if any consensus on the matter remained very distant. The processes of reformation from the 1530s prompted the peoples of England and Scotland to reconsider all aspects of the relations between the countries: religious, diplomatic, historical, and physical. The exigencies of promoting or resisting reform created a heightened sensitivity to the affairs of the neighbouring realm, and the result was a concentrated focus upon the island form of Britain, with all its dangers and its potentialities. In 1561 the two realms were entering a difficult new phase in their relations with one another, as a result of Mary's pretensions to the English throne. Elizabeth would spend more than half of her reign working through the implications of the continuing Scottish threat to her crown. The underlying inconsistencies in Anglo-Scottish perceptions of one another would be still more difficult to resolve. The Protestant alliance of 1560 testified to a degree of understanding between the realms that would have been incredible only a few years earlier. As the Congregation were the latest to realize, however, the problem of defining a satisfactory relationship between the kingdoms defied simple solutions. The resonances of the same contentious debate remain with us to this day.

Bibliography

MANUSCRIPT SOURCES

Edinburgh, National Library of Scotland

MS 1746	Adam Abell's chronicle, 'The Roit or Quheill of Time', written 1533–7
Advocates MS 19. 3. 24	Notebook of John Johnston (?1570–1612), prof. of theology at St Andrews
Advocates MS 29. 2. 1–5	Balcarres Papers: state papers and correspondence from the administration of Mary of Lorraine
Advocates MS 33. 1. 1	Denmilne Papers: state papers of the reigns of James VI and Charles I, collected by Sir James Balfour of Denmilne

Edinburgh, Scottish Record Office

CC 8/8/13	Register of testaments, Edinburgh, 1515–32, 1567–1829
GD 1/371/3–5	Warrender Papers: miscellaneous papers relating to Scottish history, mainly 1542–1625
GD 149/264	Caprington MS: royal letter book, 1525–49
GD 249/2/2	Tyninghame MS: royal letter book, 1529–32
SP 1/2	Elphinstone MS: inventory of royal letters, 1525–46
SP 2/1–4	Correspondence of Mary of Lorraine, 1543–1588

Edinburgh, University Library

Dc. 4. 83/1	Draft of a document regarding marriage of Mary Queen of Scots with the Dauphin, 1549
Dd. 3. 16	Material from Edinburgh council book, concerning library of Clement Little

London, British Library

Additional 4734–6	Larger MS of David Calderwood's History of the Church of Scotland 1514–1586, 3 vols.
Additional 32 649–54	Official correspondence and state papers relating to transactions between England and Scotland during the latter part of the reign of Henry VIII, 1532–45

Additional 33 531	Scottish state papers and correspondence, 1449–1594
Cotton Caligula Bi–Bx	Transactions between England and Scotland, 1509–70
Cotton Cleopatra Eiv–Evi	Papers and letters from the reign of Henry VIII, relating to the dissolution of the monasteries, the power of the king in ecclesiastical councils, and other matters concerning the reformation of the church
Cotton Galba Bx	Transactions between England and the Low Countries, 1531–47
Cotton Titus Bi	State papers and letters, 1485–1547
Cotton Vespasian Cxiii	Transactions between England and Spain, 1559–1625
Cotton Vitellius Bxxi	Transactions between England and Germany, 1526–45
Cotton Vitellius Bxiv	Transactions between England and Rome, 1527–39
Harleian 289	A collection of papers, mostly sixteenth century, relating to the affairs of Scotland, or to transactions between England and Scotland
Royal 7C xvi no. 27	Papers received by Thomas Cromwell from Sir William Eure, Captain of Berwick
Royal 18A xxxviii	Address to Henry VIII by John Elder

London, Public Record Office

E36/153	Inventories, surrenders, valuations, and correspondence (of Thomas Cromwell) concerning friaries
SP 1/74–1/246	State papers of the reign of Henry VIII, general series, 1533–47
SP 15/1–3	State papers, Domestic, addenda 1547–51
SP 50/1–5	State papers, Scotland, Edward VI
SP 51	State papers, Scotland, Mary
SP 52/1–6	State papers, Scotland, Elizabeth I (1558–61)

Oxford, Bodleian Library

Tanner MS 50: 10	Collection of letters and papers 1559–69: short and summary notes of some sermons preached at Paul's Cross, 1565–6

PRINTED PRIMARY SOURCES

Place of publication is London unless otherwise stated.

Public records

Accounts of the Lord High Treasurer of Scotland, ed. T. Dickon and Sir James Balfour, 12 vols. (Edinburgh: General Register House, 1877–1916).

The Acts of the Parliaments of Scotland 1124–1707, ed. T. Thomson and C. Innes, 12 vols. (Edinburgh, 1814–75).

Acts of the Privy Council of England, ed. J. R. Dasent *et al.*, 46 vols. (HMSO, 1890–1964).

Calendar of State Papers, Domestic, Edward VI, Philip and Mary, Elizabeth, ed. R. Lemon, M. A. E. Green, *et al.*, 9 vols. (HMSO, 1856–72).

Calendar of State Papers, Domestic, of the Reign of Edward VI, ed. C. S. Knighton (HMSO, 1992; replacing older Calendar for 1547–53).

Calendar of State Papers, Domestic, of the Reign of Elizabeth 1601–1603; with Addenda 1547–1565, ed. Mary Anne Everett Green (HMSO, 1870).

Calendar of State Papers, Foreign, ed. W. B. Turnbull, J. Stevenson, *et al.*, 23 vols. (HMSO, 1836–1950).

Calendar of the State Papers relating to Scotland and Mary Queen of Scots, 1547–1603, ed. J. Bain *et al.*, 14 vols. (Edinburgh: General Register House, 1898, 1969).

Calendar of State Papers, Spanish, ed. P. de Gayangos, G. Mattingly, M. A. S Hume, and R. Tyler, 15 vols. in 20 (HMSO, 1862–1954).

Calendar of State Papers, Venetian, ed. R. Brown, C. Bentinck, and H. Brown, 9 vols. (HMSO, 1864–98).

The Hamilton Papers: Letters illustrating the Political Relations of England and Scotland in the Sixteenth Century, ed. Joseph Bain, 2 vols. (Edinburgh: General Register House, 1890–2).

Haynes, S., and Murdin, W., (eds.), *Collection of State Papers . . . left by William Cecil, Lord Burghley*, 2 vols. (1740–59).

Hughes, P. L., and Larkin, J. F., (eds.), *Tudor Royal Proclamations*, 2 vols. (New Haven: Yale University Press, 1964, 1969).

Letters and Papers, Foreign and Domestic, of the Reign of Henry VIII 1509–1547, ed. J. S. Brewer *et al.*, 21 vols. and 2 vols. addenda (HMSO, 1862–1932).

Register of the Privy Council of Scotland, 1545–1625, ed. J. Hill Burton and D. Masson, 14 vols. (Edinburgh: General Register House, 1877–98).

Sadler, Ralph, *The State Papers and Letters of Sir Ralph Sadler, Knight-Banneret*, ed. Arthur Clifford, 2 vols. (Edinburgh: A. Constable, 1809).

State Papers Published under the Authority of His Majesty's Commission, King Henry VIII, 11 vols. (Record Commission, printed by G. Eyre and A. Strahan, 1830–52).

Source collections, narrative and literary works, tracts and religious formulas

Alesius, Alexander, *Of the Auctorite of the Word of God agaynst the bisshop of London, wherein are conteyned certen disputacyons had in the parlament howse betwene the bisshops a bowt the number of sacrame[n]ts and other things very necessary to be known* (?Leipzig, ?1537; *RSTC* 292).

Aylmer, John, *An Harborowe for Faithfull and Trewe Subiectes, agaynst the late blown Blaste concerninge the Gouerme[n]t of Wemen, wherin be confuted all such reasons as*

a straunger of late made in that behalfe, with a breife exhortation to obedience
(Strasbourg, 1559; *RSTC* 1005).

Bale, John, *The Image of both Churches after the moste Wonderful and heauenly
Reuelacion of Sainct John The Eua[n]gelist* (I. Daye and W. Seres, *c.*1550; *RSTC*
1298).

——*Dramatic Writings of John Bale*, ed. J. S. Farmer (Early English Drama
Society, 1907).

——*King John*, ed. J. H. P. Pafford (Oxford: Malone Society, 1931).

Becon, Thomas, *A Confortable Epistle too Goddes faythfull people in Englande*
(Strasbourg, 1554; *RSTC* 1716).

——*Prayers and Other Pieces of Thomas Becon*, ed. John Ayre (Cambridge: Parker
Society, 1844)

Bonner, Edmund, *A profitable and necessarye doctryne, with certayne homelies
adioyned hereunto* (Ihon Cawodde, 1555; *RSTC* 3282).

The Book of Common Order, ed. G. W. Sprott (Edinburgh: William Blackwood &
Sons, 1901).

*A Brief Discourse of the Troubles at Frankfort, 1554–1558 AD; attributed to William
Whittingham, Dean of Durham, 1575 AD*, ed. Edward Arber (1907).

Buchanan, George, *The History of Scotland*, trans. with notes and continuation by
James Aikman, 2 vols. (Edinburgh: Blackie, Fullarton & Co., 1827).

Bullinger, Heinrich, *A hundred Sermons upon the Apocalyps of Jesu Christe* (I. Day,
1561; *RSTC* 4061).

Calderwood, David, *The History of the Kirk of Scotland*, ed. T. Thomson and
D. Laing, 8 vols. (Edinburgh: Wodrow Society, 1842–9).

Cardwell, Edward (ed.), *Documentary Annals of the Reformed Church of England,
1546–1716*, 2 vols. (Oxford: Oxford University Press, 1839–44).

Chronicle of the Grey Friars of London, ed. John Gough Nichols (Camden Society,
53; 1852).

*Collectanea Anglo-Minoritica, or, A Collection of the Antiquities of the English
Franciscans, or Friers Minors, commonly call'd Gray Friers, compiled and collected
by A.P.* (Thomas Smith, 1726).

*A Compendious Book of Godly and Spiritual Songs, commonly known as 'The Gude and
Godlie Ballatis'*, ed. A. F. Mitchell (Edinburgh: STS 39; 1897).

*The Complaynt of Scotlande vyth ane Exhortatione to the thre Estaits to be vigilante in
the Deffens of their Public Veil*, ed. J. A. H. Murray (Early English Text Soc., extra
ser. 17; 1872).

Cranmer, Thomas, *Miscellaneous Writings and Letters of Thomas Cranmer*, ed. J. E.
Cox (Cambridge: Parker Society, 1846).

Cranstoun, James (ed.), *Satirical Poems of the Time of the Reformation*, 4 vols.
(Edinburgh: STS, 1889–93).

Dalyell, John (ed.), *Fragments of Scottish History* (Edinburgh, 1798).

*A Diurnal of Remarkable Occurrents that have passed within the country of Scotland,
since the death of King James the Fourth, till the year 1575*, ed. T. Thomson
(Edinburgh: Bannatyne Society, 1833).

Elder, John, *The Copie of a Letter sent in to Scotlande* (J. Waylande, 1555; *RSTC* 7552).

The First Book of Discipline, ed. J. K. Cameron (Edinburgh: St Andrew Press, 1972).

Foley, Henry (ed.), *Records of the English Province of the Society of Jesus . . . in the Sixteenth and Seventeenth Centuries*, 7 vols. (Burns and Oates, 1875–83).

Forbes, John, *Certaine records touching the estate of the Church of Scotland*, ed. D. Laing (Edinburgh: Wodrow Society, 1846).

Forbes, Patrick, *A Full View of the Public Transactions in the Reign of Queen Elizabeth: or a particular account of all the memorable affairs of that Queen*, 2 vols. (J. Bettenham, G. Hawkins, 1740–1).

Foreign Correspondence with Marie de Lorraine from the Originals in the Balcarres Papers, ed. Marguerite Wood, 2 vols. (Edinburgh: SHS, 3rd ser. 4 and 7; 1923–5).

Foxe, John, *Acts and Monuments*, ed. S. R. Cattley, 8 vols. (R. B. Seeley, W. Burnside, 1837–41).

Gau, John, *The Richt Vay to the Kingdom of Heuine*, ed. A. F. Mitchell (Edinburgh: STS, 1888).

Geneva Bible, *The Bible and Holy Scriptures conteyned in the Olde and Newe Testament* (Geneva: Rowland Hall, 1560; *RSTC* 2093).

Gilby, Anthony, *An Admonition to England and Scotland to call them to repentance* (Geneva, 1558; *RSTC* 15063).

Goodman, Christopher, *How Superior Powers oght to be obeyd of their subjects* (Geneva: Iohn Crispin, 1558; *RSTC* 12020; facs. edn., Amsterdam, 1972).

Hamilton, John, *The Catechisme* (St Andrews: J. Scot, 1552; *RSTC* 12731).

——— *The Catechism set forth by Archbishop Hamilton, together with the Twopenny Faith*, ed. A. F. Mitchell (Edinburgh, 1882).

Hooper, John, *A declaration of the ten holy commandements* (Zurich, 1548, 1550; *RSTC* 13746–50).

James V, *Letters of James V*, ed. R. K. Hannay (Edinburgh: HMSO, 1954).

Keith, Robert, *History of the Affairs of Church and State in Scotland, from the Beginning of the Reformation to the Year 1568*, ed. J. P. Lawson and C. J. Lyon, 3 vols. (Edinburgh: Spottiswoode Society, 1844).

Ketley, Joseph (ed.), *The Two Liturgies AD 1549 and AD 1552 of the Reign of Edward VI* (Cambridge: Parker Society, 1844).

Knox, John, *The Works of John Knox*, ed. D. Laing, 6 vols. (Edinburgh: Bannatyne Society, 1846–64).

Lamb, William, *Ane Resonyng of ane Scottis and Inglis Merchand betuix Rowand and Lionis*, ed. R. J. Lyall (Aberdeen: Aberdeen University Press, 1985).

Leslie, John, *History of Scotland from the Death of James I in the Year 1436, to 1561* (Edinburgh Bannatyne Society, 1830).

Lindsay, David, *The Works of Sir David Lindsay of the Mount 1490–1555*, ed. Douglas Hamer, 2 vols. (Edinburgh: STS, 3rd ser. 1; 1931).

The Liturgical Portions of the Genevan Service Book: Used by John Knox while a

Minister of the English Congregation of Marian Exiles at Geneva, 1556–1559, ed. William D. Maxwell (Faith Press, 1965).

Livre des Anglois à Genève, ed. J. S. Burn (1831).

Livre des Habitants de Genève, 1549–1560, ed. P. Geisendorf (Geneva, 1957).

Livre du Recteur de l'Académie de Genève, ed. S. Stelling-Michaud (Geneva, 1959).

Machyn, Henry, *The Diary of Henry Machyn*, ed. John Gough Nichols (Camden Society, 1 ser. 42; 1848).

Mason, Roger A. (ed.), *John Knox: On Rebellion* (Cambridge: Cambridge University Press, 1994).

Merriman, R. B. (ed.), *Life and Letters of Thomas Cromwell*, 2 vols. (Oxford: Clarendon Press, 1902).

Miscellany of the Bannatyne Society, ed. D. Laing (Edinburgh: Bannatyne Society, 1827).

Miscellany of the Wodrow Society, ed. D. Laing (Edinburgh: Wodrow Society, 1844).

A Necessary Doctrine and Erudition for any Christen man (T. Berthelet, 1543; *RSTC* 5168).

The Newe Testament of our Lord Jesus Christ (Geneva, 1557; *RSTC* 2871).

Olde, John, *The acquital or purgation of the moost catholyke Prince Edwarde VI* (Emden, 1555; *RSTC* 18797).

——*A short description of Antichrist unto the Nobilitie of Englande* (? 1557; *RSTC* 673).

Original Letters relative to the English Reformation, ed. Hastings Robinson, 2 vols. (Cambridge: Parker Society, 1846–8).

Pitcairn, Robert (ed.), *Ancient Criminal Trials in Scotland*, 3 vols. (Edinburgh: Bannatyne Society, 1833).

Pitscottie, Robert Lindsay of, *The History and Chronicles of Scotland*, ed. A. E. J. G. Mackay, 3 vols. (Edinburgh: STS, 42, 43, 60; 1899–1911).

Pollard, A. F. (ed.), *Tudor Tracts 1532–1588* (A. Constable, 1903).

Ponet, John, *A Short Treatise of politike power, and of the true Obedience which subjectes owe to kynges and other civile Governours* (Strasbourg, 1556; *RSTC* 20178; facs. edn. Menston: Scolar Press, 1970).

Raikes, Henry (trans.), *The Reform of England by the Decrees of Cardinal Pole . . . translated from the original aldine edition, as published at Rome, 1562* (Chester, 1839).

Registres de la Compagnie des pasteurs de Genève, ed. R. M. Kingdom and J. F. Bergier (Geneva: Droz, 1962).

Rentale Sancti Andree 1538–1546, ed. R. K. Hannay (Edinburgh: SHS, 2nd ser. 4, 1913).

Ricart, Robert, *The Maire of Bristowe is Kalendar*, ed. L. Toulmin Smith (Camden Society, NS 5; 1872).

Richardinus, Robertus, *Commentary on the Rule of St Augustine*, ed. G. Coulton (Edinburgh: SHS, 3rd ser. 26, 1935).

Ridley, Nicholas, *A frendly farewel, which Master Doctor Ridley, late Bishop of*

London did write beinge prisoner in Oxeforde, unto all his true Lovers and frendes in God, a little before that he suffred for the testimony of the truthe of Christ his Gospell (I. Day, 1559; *RSTC* 21051).

—— *The Works of Nicholas Ridley, DD*, ed. H. Christmas (Cambridge: Parker Society, 1843).

Row, John, *The Historie of the Kirk of Scotland*, ed. D. Laing (Edinburgh: Wodrow Society, 1842).

St Andrews Formulare 1514–1546, ed. G. Donaldson and C. Macrae (Edinburgh: Stair Society, 1942).

Sandys, Edwin, *The Sermons of Edwin Sandys, DD*, ed. John Ayre (Cambridge: Parker Society, 1841).

Scory, John, *An epistle written vnto all the faithful that be in pryson in Englande* (Emden, 1555; *RSTC* 21854).

Scot, William, *An Apologetical Narration of the State of the Kirk*, ed. D. Laing (Edinburgh: Wodrow Society, 1846).

The Scottish Correspondence of Mary of Lorraine, 1543–1560, ed. Annie I. Cameron (Edinburgh: SHS, 3rd ser. 10; 1927).

Smith, Richard, *The Assertion and Defence of the sacramente of the aulter* (J. Herforde, R. Toye, 1546; *RSTC* 22815).

Spottiswoode, John, *History of the Church of Scotland*, ed. M. Russell and M. Napier, 3 vols. (Edinburgh: Spottiswoode Society, 1847–51).

Statutes of the Scottish Church, ed. David Patrick (Edinburgh: SHS, 1st ser. 54; 1907).

Stuart, John, *Records of the Monastery of Kinloss* (Edinburgh: Edinburgh Society of Antiquaries, 1872).

Teulet, J. B. A. T. (ed.), *Correspondance diplomatique: Recueil des dépêches, rapports des ambassadeurs de France en Angleterre et en Écosse pendant le XVI siècle*, 4 vols. (Paris, 1840)

—— (ed.), *Papiers d'état, pièces et documents inédits ou peu connus relatifs à l'histoire de l'Écosse au XVI siècle*, 3 vols. (Edinburgh 1852–60).

Von Wied, Hermann, *A Simple and Religious consultation of vs Herman by the grace of God Archbishop of Colone, and prince Electoure* (J. Daye and W. Seres, 1548; *RSTC* 13214).

Wriothesley, Charles, *A Chronicle of England during the Reigns of the Tudors from AD 1485 to 1559*, ed. W. D. Hamilton, 2 vols. (Camden Society, 2nd ser., 11 and 20; 1875–7).

The Zurich Letters, comprising the correspondence of several English bishops and others, with some of the Helvetian reformers during the early part of the reign of Queen Elizabeth, ed. Hastings Robinson, 2 vols. (Cambridge: Parker Society, 1842–6).

SECONDARY SOURCES

Place of publication is London unless otherwise stated.

Books

Alford, Stephen, *The Early Elizabethan Polity: William Cecil and the British Succession Crisis, 1558–1569* (Cambridge: Cambridge University Press, 1998).

Armstrong, R. B., *The History of Liddesdale, Eskdale, Ewesdale, Wauchopedale and the Debatable Land* (Edinburgh: David Douglas, 1883).

Ayris, Paul, and Selwyn, David (eds.), *Thomas Cranmer: Churchman and Scholar* (Woodbridge: Boydell Press, 1993).

Baskerville, Geoffrey, *English Monks and the Suppression of the Monasteries* (Jonathan Cape, 1949).

Bauckham, Richard, *Tudor Apocalypse: Sixteenth Century Apocalypticism, Millenarianism and the English Reformation, from John Bale to John Foxe and Thomas Brightman* (Abingdon: Sutton Courtenay Press, 1978).

Bellesheim, Alphons, *A History of the Catholic Church of Scotland from the Introduction of Christianity to the Present Day*, trans. D. Oswald Hunter, 4 vols. (Edinburgh: William Blackwood, 1887).

Blake, W., *William Maitland of Lethington 1528–73: A Study of the Policy of Moderation in the Scottish Reformation* (Lampeter: Edwin Mellen Press, 1990).

Bradshaw, Brendan, and Morrill, John (eds.), *The British Problem, c.1534–1707: State Formation in the Atlantic Archipelago* (Basingstoke: Macmillan, 1996).

Bridgett, T. E., and Knox, T. F., *The True Story of the Catholic Hierarchy deposed by Queen Elizabeth* (1889).

Brown, A. D., *Popular Piety in Late Medieval England: The Diocese of Salisbury, 1250–1550* (Oxford: Clarendon Press, 1995).

Brown, Andrew. J., *Robert Ferrar: Yorkshire Monk, Reformation Bishop and Martyr in Wales, c.1500–1555* (Inscriptor Imprints, 1997).

Bryce, W. M., *The Scottish Grey Friars*, 2 vols. (Edinburgh: W. Green, 1909).

Burns, J. H., *The True Law of Kingship: Concepts of Monarchy in Early Modern Scotland* (Oxford: Clarendon Press, 1996).

Bush, M. L., *The Government Policy of Protector Somerset* (E. Arnold, 1975).

—— *The Pilgrimage of Grace: A Study of the Rebel Armies of October 1536* (Manchester: Manchester University Press, 1996).

Cameron, Euan, *The European Reformation* (Oxford: Clarendon Press, 1991).

Cameron, Jamie, *James V: The Personal Rule, 1528–1542*, ed. Norman Macdougall (East Linton: Tuckwell Press, 1998).

Christianson, Paul, *Reformers and Babylon: English Apocalyptic Visions from the Reformation to the Eve of the Civil War* (Toronto: University of Toronto Press, 1978).

Colligan, J. Hay, *The Geneva Service Book of 1555* (Manchester: Aikman, 1931).

Colligan, J. Hay, *The Honourable William Whittingham of Chester, ?1524–1579* (Chester: Phillipson & Golder, 1934).

Collinson, Patrick, *The Birthpangs of Protestant England: Religious and Cultural Change in the Sixteenth and Seventeenth Centuries* (Basingstoke: Macmillan, 1988).

——— *The Elizabethan Puritan Movement* (Oxford: Clarendon Press, 1990).

Cowan, Ian B., *The Scottish Reformation: Church and Society in Sixteenth Century Scotland* (Weidenfeld & Nicolson, 1982).

——— and Easson, David E., *Medieval Religious Houses: Scotland, with an appendix on the houses in the Isle of Man*, 2nd edn. (Longman, 1976).

Cross, Claire, *The Puritan Earl: The life of Henry Hastings, Third Carl of Huntingdon 1536–1595* (Macmillan, 1966).

Cuming, G. J., *A History of the Anglican Liturgy* (Macmillan, 1969).

——— *The Godly Order: Texts and Studies relating to the Book of Common Prayer* (Alcuin Club Collections, 65; SPCK, 1983).

Dickson, Robert, and Edmond, J. P., *Annals of Scottish Printing* (Cambridge: Macmillan & Bowes, 1890).

Dictionary of National Biography, ed. Leslie Stephen and Sidney Lee, 63 vols, with suppl. (Smith Elder, Oxford University Press, 1885–1990).

Dilworth, Mark, *Scottish Monasteries in the Late Middle Ages* (Edinburgh: Edinburgh University Press, 1995).

Dodds, Madeleine Hope, and Dodds, Ruth, *The Pilgrimage of Grace 1536–1537 and the Exeter Conspiracy 1538*, 2 vols. (Frank Cass, 1971).

Donaldson, Gordon, *The Scottish Reformation* (Cambridge: Cambridge University Press, 1960).

——— *Scottish Church History* (Edinburgh: Scottish Academic Press, 1985).

Dowling, Maria, *Humanism in the Age of Henry VIII* (Routledge Press, 1986).

Duffy, Eamon, *The Stripping of the Altars: Traditional Religion in England c.1400–c.1580* (New Haven: Yale University Press, 1992).

Dunbar, John G., *Scottish Royal Palaces: The Architecture of the Royal Residences during the Late Medieval and Early Renaissance Periods* (East Linton: Tuckwell Press, 1999).

Durkan, John, and Ross, Anthony, *Early Scottish Libraries* (Glasgow: John S. Burns & Sons, 1961).

Dwyer, John, Mason, Roger A., and Murdoch, Alexander (eds.), *New Perspectives on the Politics and Culture of Early Modern Scotland* (Edinburgh: John Donald, 1982).

Eadie, John, *The English Bible*, 2 vols. (Macmillan, 1876).

Easson, D. E., *Gavin Dunbar, Chancellor of Scotland, Archbishop of Glasgow* (Edinburgh: Oliver & Boyd, 1947).

Edington, Carol, *Court and Culture in Renaissance Scotland: Sir David Lindsay of the Mount 1486–1555* (Amherst, Mass.: University of Massachusetts Press, 1994).

Ellis, Steven G., *Tudor Frontiers and Noble Power: The Making of the British State* (Oxford: Clarendon Press, 1995).

Ellis, Steven G., and Barber, Sarah (eds.), *Conquest and Union: Fashioning a British State 1485–1725* (Longman, 1995).

Elton, G. R., *England under the Tudors* (Methuen, 1965).

——*Policy and Police: The Enforcement of Reformation in the Age of Thomas Cromwell* (Cambridge: Cambridge University Press, 1972).

Fawcett, Richard, *The Architectural History of Scotland: Scottish Architecture from the Accession of the Stewarts to the Reformation, 1371–1560* (Edinburgh: Edinburgh University Press, 1994).

Ferguson, William, *Scotland's Relations with England: A Survey to 1707* (Edinburgh: Saltire Publications, 1994).

Firth, Katharine R., *The Apocalyptic Tradition in Reformation Britain, 1530–1645* (Oxford: Oxford University Press, 1979).

Fox, Alistair, and Guy, John, *Reassessing the Henrician Age: Humanism, Politics and Reform 1500–1550* (Oxford: Blackwell Publishers, 1986).

Garrett, Christina, *The Marian Exiles 1553–1559: A Study in the Origins of Elizabethan Puritanism* (Cambridge: Cambridge University Press, 1966).

Gasquet, Francis, *Cardinal Pole and his Early Friends* (G. Bell & Sons, 1927).

——*Henry VIII and the English Monasteries*, 2nd edn., 2 vols. (Hodges, 1888–9).

Grant, Alexander, and Stringer, Keith J. (eds.), *Uniting the Kingdom? The Making of British History* (London: Routledge Press, 1995).

Green, M. A., *Life of Mr William Whittingham, Dean of Durham* (Camden Society Miscellany, 6; 1871).

Griffiths, Ralph A., *Sir Rhys ap Thomas and his Family: A Study in the Wars of the Roses and Early Tudor Politics* (Cardiff: University of Wales Press, 1993).

Gunn, S. J., *Charles Brandon, Duke of Suffolk* (Oxford: Blackwell Publishers, 1988).

Hadley Williams, Janet (ed.), *Stewart Style 1513–1542: Essays on the Court of James V* (East Linton: Tuckwell Press, 1996).

Haigh, Christopher, (ed.), *The Reign of Elizabeth I* (Basingstoke: Macmillan, 1984).

——(ed.), *The English Reformation Revised* (Cambridge: Cambridge University Press, 1987).

Haller, William, *Foxe's Book of Martyrs and the Elect Nation* (Jonathan Cape, 1963).

Hannay, R. K., *The Scottish Crown and the Papacy, 1424–1560* (Edinburgh: Historical Association of Scotland, 1931).

Herkless, John, and Hannay, R. K., *The Archbishops of St Andrews*, 5 vols. (Edinburgh, 1907–15).

Hewat, Kirkwood, *Makers of the Scottish Church at the Reformation* (Edinburgh: MacNiven & Wallace, 1920).

Hotle, C. Patrick, *Thorns and Thistles: Diplomacy between Henry VIII and James V, 1528–1542* (Lanham, Md: University Press of America, 1996).

Hutton, Edward, *The Franciscans in England, 1224–1538* (Constable, 1926).

Inglis, John A., *Sir Adam Otterburn of Redhall, King's Advocate, 1524–1538* (Glasgow: Jackson, Wylie, 1935).

Jarrett, Bede, OP, *The English Dominicans* (Burns, Oates & Washbourne, 1937).

Kirk, James, *Patterns of Reform: Continuity and Change in the Reformation Kirk* (Edinburgh: T. & T. Clark, 1989).

—— (ed.), *Humanism and Reform: The Church in Europe, England and Scotland, 1400–1643* (Studies in Church History, subsidia 8; Oxford: Blackwell Publishers, 1991).

Knowles, David, *The Religious Orders in England*, 3 vols. (Cambridge: Cambridge University Press, 1959).

Lake, Peter, and Dowling, Maria, (eds.), *Protestantism and the National Church in Sixteenth Century England* (Routledge Press, 1987).

Lau, Franz, and Bizer, Ernst, *A History of the Reformation in Germany to 1555* (A. & C. Black, 1969).

Lorimer, Peter, *Patrick Hamilton, the First Preacher and Martyr of the Scottish Reformation* (Edinburgh: Constable, 1857).

Lynch, Michael, *Edinburgh and the Reformation* (Edinburgh: John Donald, 1981).

—— *Scotland: A New History*, 2nd edn. (Pimlico, 1992).

MacCulloch, Diarmaid, *Thomas Cranmer: A Life* (New Haven: Yale University Press, 1996).

MacDonald, A. A., Lynch, Michael, and Cowan, Ian B. (eds.), *The Renaissance in Scotland: Studies in Literature, Religion, History and Culture offered to John Durkan* (Leiden: Brill Academic Publications, 1994).

Macdougall, Norman, (ed.), *Church, Politics and Society: Scotland 1408–1929* (Edinburgh: John Donald, 1983).

McGrath, Patrick, *Papists and Puritans under Elizabeth I* (Blandford Press, 1967).

McNeill, John T., *The History and Character of Calvinism* (New York: Oxford University Press, 1967).

MacQueen, John, (ed.), *Humanism in Renaissance Scotland* (Edinburgh: Edinburgh University Press, 1990).

McRoberts, David (ed.), *Essays on the Scottish Reformation, 1513–1625* (Glasgow: John S. Burns & Sons, 1962).

Martin, Charles, *Les Protestants anglais réfugiés à Genève au temps de Calvin, 1555–1560* (Geneva, 1915).

Mason, Roger A. (ed.), *Scotland and England, 1286–1815* (Edinburgh: John Donald, 1987).

—— (ed.), *Scots and Britons: Scottish Political Thought and the Union of 1603* (Cambridge: Cambridge University Press, 1994).

—— (ed.), *John Knox and the British Reformations* (Aldershot: Ashgate Publishing, 1998).

Merriman, Marcus, *The Rough Wooings: Mary Queen of Scots 1542–1551* (East Linton: Tuckwell Press, 2000).

Mews, Stuart, (ed.), *Religion and National Identity* (Studies in Church History, 18; Oxford: Blackwell Publishers, 1982).

Mitchell, A. F., *The Wedderburns and their Work, or, The Sacred Poetry of the Scottish Reformation in its Historical Relation to that of Germany: A Lecture* (Edinburgh: William Blackwood & Sons, 1867).

Monter, E. William, *Studies in Genevan Government, 1536–1605* (Travaux d'Humanisme et Renaissance, 62; Geneva: Librairie E. Droz, 1964).

Moorhouse, Geoffrey, *The Pilgrimage of Grace* (Weidenfeld & Nicolson, 2002).

Nicolson, J., and Burn, R., *History and Antiquities of the Counties of Westmoreland and Cumberland*, 2 vols. (W. Strahan and T. Cadell, 1776–7).

Olsen, V. N., *John Foxe and the Elizabethan Church* (Berkeley and Los Angeles: University of California Press, 1973).

Palmer, M. D., *Henry VIII*, 2nd edn. (Longman, 1983).

Pettegree, Andrew, *Marian Protestantism: Six Studies* (Aldershot: Scolar Press, 1996).

Phillipson, Nicholas, and Skinner, Quentin (eds.), *Political Discourse in Early Modern Britain* (Cambridge: Cambridge University Press, 1993).

Prestwich, Menna (ed.), *International Calvinism 1541–1715* (Oxford: Clarendon Press, 1985).

Rae, Thomas I., *The Administration of the Scottish Frontier, 1513–1603* (Edinburgh: Edinburgh University Press, 1966).

Read, Conyers, *Mr Secretary Cecil and Queen Elizabeth* (Jonathan Cape, 1965).

Reid, Rachel R., *The King's Council in the North* (Wakefield: EP Publishing, 1975).

Ridley, Jasper, *John Knox* (Oxford: Clarendon Press, 1968).

Ritchie, Pamela E., *Mary of Guise in Scotland, 1548–1560: A Political Career* (East Linton: Tuckwell Press, 2002).

Robbins, Keith (ed.), *Religion and Humanism* (Studies in Church History, 17; Oxford: Blackwell Publishers, 1981).

Sanderson, Margaret H. B., *Cardinal of Scotland, David Beaton c.1494–1546* (Edinburgh: John Donald, 1986).

——*Ayrshire and the Reformation: People and Change, 1490–1600* (East Linton: Tuckwell Press, 1997).

Scarisbrick, J. J., *Henry VIII* (Harmondsworth: Penguin, 1972).

Scott, John, *Berwick-on-Tweed: The History of the Town and Guild* (1888).

Shaw, Duncan, (ed.), *Reformation and Revolution: Essays Presented to the Very Rev. Principal Emeritus Hugh Watt on the 60th Anniversary of his Ordination* (Edinburgh: St Andrew Press, 1967).

A Short Title Catalogue of Books printed in England, Scotland, and Ireland and of English books printed abroad before the year 1640, ed. A. W. Pollard and G. R. Redgrave, rev. W. A. Jackson and F. S. Ferguson, completed K. F. Pantzer, 3 vols. (Bibliographical Society, 1967–91).

Simpson, M. A., *John Knox and the Troubles begun at Frankfurt* (West Linton: the author, 1975).

Skeeters, Martha C., *Community and Clergy: Bristol and the Reformation, c.1530–c.1570* (Oxford: Clarendon Press, 1993).

Slavin, Arthur Joseph, *Politics and Profit: a study of Sir Ralph Sadler, 1507–1547* (Cambridge: Cambridge University Press, 1966).

Strype, John, *Historical Collections of the Life and Acts of John Aylmer, Lord Bishop of London in the Reign of Queen Elizabeth* (1701).

——*Memorials of the Most Reverend Father in God Thomas Cranmer, sometime Archbishop of Canterbury*, 2 vols. (Oxford: Clarendon Press, 1812).

——*Ecclesiastical Memorials; Relating Chiefly to Religion, and the Reformation of it . . . under King Henry VIII, King Edward VI and Queen Mary*, 3 vols. (Oxford: Clarendon Press, 1822).

——*The Life and Acts of John Whitgift*, 3 vols. (Oxford: Clarendon Press, 1822).

——*Annals of the Reformation and Establishment of Religion . . . during Queen Elizabeth's Happy Reign*, 4 vols. (Oxford: Clarendon Press, 1824).

Thompson, E. M., *The Carthusian Order in England* (SPCK, Macmillan, 1930).

Tittler, Robert, and Loach, Jennifer (eds.), *The Mid-Tudor Polity, c.1540–1560* (Totowa, NJ: Rowman & Littlefield, 1980).

Wendel, François, *Calvin: The Origins and Development of his Religious Thought*, trans. Philip Mairet (Collins, 1965).

Whatmore, L. E., *The Carthusians under King Henry the Eighth* (Salzburg: Institut für Anglistik und Amerikanistik Universität Salzburg, 1983).

White, Helen C., *The Tudor Books of Private Devotion* (Madison: Greenwood Press, 1951).

Wilks, Michael, (ed.), *Prophecy and Eschatology* (Studies in Church History, subsidia 10; Oxford: Blackwell publishers, 1994).

Williams, Glanmor, *Recovery, Reorientation and Reformation: Wales c.1415–1642* (Oxford: Clarendon Press, 1987).

Williamson, Arthur H., *Scottish National Consciousness in the Age of James VI: The Apocalypse, The Union and The Shaping of Scotland's Public Culture* (Edinburgh: John Donald, 1979).

Wood, Diana, (ed.), *Martyrs and Martyrology* (Studies in Church History, 30; Oxford: Blackwell Publishers, 1993).

Wooding, Lucy E. C., *Rethinking Catholicism in Reformation England* (Oxford: Clarendon Press, 2000).

Wormald, Jenny, *Mary Queen of Scots: A Study in Failure* (George Philip, 1988).

——*Court, Kirk and Community: Scotland 1470–1625* (New History of Scotland, 4; Edinburgh: Edinburgh University Press, 1991).

Articles

Barrow, G. W. S., 'The Anglo-Scottish Border', *Northern History*, 1 (1966), 21–42.

Baxter, J. H., 'Alesius and Other Reformed Refugees in Germany', *RSCHS* 5 (1933–5), 93–102.

——'Dr Richard Hildyard in St Andrews, 1540–1543', *St Andrews Alumnus Chronicle* (June 1955), 2–10.

Beckingsale, B. W., 'The Characteristics of the Tudor North', *Northern History*, 4 (1969), 67–83.

Bernard, G. W., 'The Making of Religious Policy, 1533–1546: Henry VIII and the Search for the Middle Way', *HJ* 41 (1998), 321–49.

Bradshaw, Brendan, 'Cromwellian Reform and the Origins of the Kildare Rebellion, 1533–1534', *TRHS*, 5th ser. 27 (1977), 69–93.

Burleigh, J. H. S., 'The Scottish Reforming Councils, 1549–59', *RSCHS* 11 (1953), 189–211.

Burns, J. H., 'Knox and Bullinger', *SHR*, 34 (1955), 90–1.

Burrell, S. A., 'The Apocalyptic Vision of the Early Covenanters', *SHR* 43 (1964), 1–24.

Bush, M. L., 'The Problem of the Far North: A Study of the Crisis of 1537 and its Consequences', *Northern History*, 4 (1971), 40–63.

Cameron, James K., ' "Catholic Reform" in Germany and in the Pre-1560 Church in Scotland', *RSCHS* 20 (1979), 105–17.

—— 'The Cologne Reformation and the Church of Scotland', *JEH* 30 (1979), 39–64.

Collinson, Patrick, 'The Authorship of *A Brief Discourse*', *JEH* 9 (1958), 188–208.

Cowell, Henry, 'English Protestant Refugees in Strasbourg, 1553–1558', *Proceedings of the Huguenot Society*, 15 (1933–7), 69–120.

—— 'The Sixteenth Century English-Speaking Refugee Churches at Strasbourg, Basle, Zurich, Aarau, Wesel and Emden', *Proceedings of the Huguenot Society*, 15 (1933–7), 612–55.

Currie, David R., 'The Order of Friars Preacher in Scotland', *RSCHS* 9–10 (1945–50), 125–39.

Davidson, Donald, 'The Influence of the English Printers on the Scottish Reformation', *RSCHS* 1 (1926), 75–87.

Davies, C. S. L., 'The Pilgrimage of Grace Reconsidered', *Past and Present*, 41 (1968), 54–76.

Dawson, Jane E. A., 'William Cecil and the British Dimension of Early Elizabethan Foreign Policy', *History*, 74 (1989), 196–216.

—— 'Revolutionary Conclusions: The Case of the Marian Exiles', *History of Political Thought*, 11 (1990), 257–72.

—— 'The Two John Knoxes: England, Scotland and the 1558 Tracts', *JEH* 42 (1991), 555–76.

Donaldson, Gordon, 'The Scottish Episcopate at the Reformation', *EHR* 60 (1945), 349–64.

—— 'Scottish Presbyterian Exiles in England, 1584–1588', *RSCHS* 14 (1960–2), 67–80.

Durkan, John, 'George Wishart: His Early Life', *SHR* 32 (1953–4), 98–9.

—— 'Scottish "Evangelicals" in the Patronage of Thomas Cromwell', *RSCHS* 21 (1982), 127–56.

—— 'The Observant Franciscan Province in Scotland', *Innes Review*, 35 (1984), 51–7.

Ellis, Steven G., 'Thomas Cromwell and Ireland, 1532–1540', *HJ* 23 (1980), 497–519.

—— 'England in the Tudor State', *HJ* 26 (1983), 201–12.

Head, David M., 'Henry VIII's Scottish Policy: A Reassessment', *SHR* 61 (1982), 1–24.

Kirk, James, '"The Polities of the Best Reformed Kirks": Scottish Achievements and English Aspirations in Church Government after the Reformation', *SHR* 59 (1980), 22–53.

Lang, A. (ed.), 'Letters of Cardinal Beaton, 1537–1541', *SHR* 6 (1909), 150–8.

Lee, Maurice, Jun., 'John Knox and his *History*', *SHR* 45 (1966), 79–88.

Loach, Jennifer, 'Pamphlets and Politics, 1553–1558', *Bulletin of the Institute of Historical Research* 48 (1975), 31–44.

—— 'The Marian Establishment and the Printing Press', *EHR* 101 (1986), 135–48.

Lynch, J., 'Philip II and the Papacy', *TRHS* 5th ser. 2 (1961), 23–42.

Mackenzie, W. Mackay, 'The Debateable Land', *SHR* 30 (1951), 109–25.

Martin, J. W., 'The Protestant Underground Congregations of Mary's Reign', *JEH* 35 (1984), 519–38.

Merriman, M. H., 'The Assured Scots: Scottish Collaborators with England during the Rough Wooing', *SHR* 47 (1968), 10–34.

—— 'The Forts of Eyemouth: Anvils of the British Union?', *SHR* 67 (1988), 142–55.

Newns, Brian, 'The Hospice of St Thomas and the English Crown, 1474–1538', *Venerabile*, 21 (1962), 145–92.

Parks, George B., 'The Reformation and the Hospice, 1514–1559', *Venerabile*, 21 (1962), 193–217.

Peardon, Barbara, 'The Politics of Polemic: John Ponet's *Short Treatise of Politic Power* and Contemporary Circumstance, 1553–1556', *Journal of British Studies*, 21 (1982), 35–48.

Pearson, A. F. Scott, 'Alexander Alesius and the English Reformation', *RSCHS* 9–10 (1945–50), 57–87.

Pocock, J. G. A., 'British History: A Plea for a New Subject', *Journal of Modern History*, 47 (1975), 601–29.

—— 'The Limits and Divisions of British History', *American History Review*, 87 (1982), 311–36.

Reid, W. Stanford, 'The Scottish Counter-Reformation before 1560', *Church History*, 14 (1945), 104–25.

Southgate, W. M., 'The Marian Exiles and the Influence of John Calvin', *History*, 27 (1942), 148–52.

Stewart, Alisdair M., 'Adam Abell's "Roit or Quheill of Tyme"', *Aberdeen University Review*, 44 (1972), 386–93.

Walker, Greg, 'Sir David Lindsay's *Ane Satire of the Thrie Estaitis* and the Politics of Reformation', *Scottish Literary Journal*, 16 (1989), 5–17.

White, D. G., 'Henry VIII's Irish Kerne in France and Scotland, 1544–1545', *Irish Sword*, 3 (1957–8), 213–25.

Wiedermann, Gotthelf, 'Alexander Alesius' Lectures on the Psalms at Cambridge, 1536', *JEH* 37 (1986), 15–41.

Williams, W. Llewelyn, 'A Welsh Insurrection', *Y Cymmrodor*, 16 (1903), 1–94.
Wormald, Jenny, 'James VI and I: Two Kings or One?', *History*, 68 (1983), 187–209.
—— 'The Creation of Britain: Multiple Kingdoms or Core and Colonies?', *TRHS*, 6th ser. 2 (1992), 175–94.

Unpublished Theses

Alford, Stephen, 'William Cecil and the British Succession Crisis of the 1560s', Ph.D. thesis (St Andrews, 1996).
Brown, K., 'The Franciscan Observants in England, 1482–1559', D.Phil. thesis (Oxford, 1987).
Dawson, J. E. A., 'The Early Career of Christopher Goodman and his Place in the Development of English Protestant Thought', Ph.D. thesis (Durham, 1978).
Donaldson, Gordon, 'The Relations between the English and Scottish Presbyterian Movements to 1604', Ph.D. thesis (London, 1938).
Höllger, C., 'Reginald Pole and the Legations of 1537 and 1539: Diplomatic and Polemical Responses to the Break with Rome', D.Phil. thesis (Oxford, 1989).
Ritchie, Pamela, 'The Political Career of Mary of Guise in Scotland, 1548–1560', Ph.D. thesis (St Andrews, 1999).
Wooding, Lucy, 'From Humanists to Heretics: English Catholic Theology and Ideology, *c.*1530–*c.*1570', D.Phil. thesis (Oxford, 1994).

INDEX

Aarau, exile congregation in 159
Abell, Adam 24, 34, 44, 52, 75
Aberdeen 80, 84
Adamson, Patrick, Archbishop of St
    Andrews 214
Advancement of True Religion, Act for the
    (1543) 85
Alen, John 21
Alesius (Alane), Alexander 27, 37–9, 40, 56,
    80, 117–18, 175–6
Alford, Stephen 2, 194, 216
Alnwick 36, 43
Amboise 202
Ancrum Moor, battle of (1545) 97
Angel, John 129
Anglo-Scottish relations 4, 6–12, 46, 55, 69,
    142–3, 225–8
    alliance (1559–60) 184–5, 189, 194–7,
        201–4, 208–11, 217–18, 222–8
    confessional difference and 3, 8–12, 31,
        44, 77, 86, 130, 155, 184, 220, 223–4
    geographical conjunction and 5–6, 222–3
    medieval background to 6–8, 226
    peace treaty (1534) 51
    peace treaty (1551) 111
Angoulême, Henri, Duke of 48
Angus, Earl of, see Douglas
Angus 107, 151–2, 186, 205
Anne Boleyn, Queen of England 14
Anne of Cleves, Queen of England 37
Antwerp 24, 57–8
apocalypticism 38, 150, 157, 172–3, 175–6
    of Geneva Bible compilers 170
    in pronouncements of Congregation 188,
        192, 196
    in writings of Bale 38, 163–4, 172, 176
Argyll, Earl of, see Campbell
Argyll 205
'Arkryges' (Cartmell friar) 73
Armstrongs 13
Arran, Earls of, see Hamilton
Asche (Ashton), Edward 34, 72
Ashley, Thomas 163
Askew, Anne 100
assured Scots 95–100, 108
    oaths taken by 97
    reasons for assuring 96
    religious motivations 96–100

Attainder, Act of (1539) 66
Augsburg Interim 115
Augustinians, Scottish 80
Axholme 25
Aylmer, John, Bishop of London 1 n. 2, 40,
    180–2
    An Harborowe for Faithfull and Trewe
        Subiectes 157, 181
Ayr 27, 32, 100, 151, 189
Ayrshire 26, 100, 152

Bale, John 38, 163–4, 167, 176, 181
    Image of bothe Churches 169
Balkesky, Martyne 32
Balmerino 92, 192
Balnaves of Halhill, Henry 81–2, 89, 187,
    193–4, 224
    as client of James V 30
    imprisoned by Beaton 90
    reconciled with government of Mary of
        Guise 140
    sponsors Scottish bill for vernacular Bible
        84
Bamborough 70
Banks, John 156
Barlow, William, Prior of Bisham, Bishop of
    St David's 52–5, 67, 106
Barnes, Robert 154
Baron, Anne 159
Baron, John 158–9, 163, 170
Barton, Elizabeth ('Mayde of Kent') 23
Barton, William 72
Basle:
    exile congregation in 157–60, 163, 212
    University of 158–9
Baynton, Edward 17
Beaton, David, Archbishop of St Andrews
    28, 31–2, 58, 60–1, 63, 70, 73–4, 79, 82,
    89–95, 136
    appointed cardinal 63
    appointed chancellor 91
    assassination 101–3, 109, 113
    imprisonment and release (1543) 83–4, 88
    as protector of English Catholic exiles
        43–4, 72
Beaton, James, Archbishop of Glasgow 142,
    206
Beauvale 25

Becon, Thomas 115, 154, 168
Bell, Andrew 72
Bellahoe 65
Bellay, Cardinal Jean du 49
Bellenden, John 30
Bellenden, Thomas 69–70, 82
Berwick 27, 35, 107, 117–18, 208, 214
  defensive preparations in 66
  Treaty of (1560) 202, 205
Beverley 36
Beza, Theodore 211
Bible, English 32, 80, 84–5, 127, 137
  Scottish act sanctions reading of 84
'Bishops' Book' (1537) 38
Blackfriars, *see* Dominicans
Blackness 88
Bodrugan, Nicholas:
  Epitome of the title that the Kynges
    Maiestie of Englande hath to the
    souereigntie of Scotlande 106
Boece, Hector 80
Bonespoir, Jane 167
Bonner, Edmund, Bishop of London 40, 85,
  216
  A profitable and necessarye doctrine 134–5
  London visitation of (1554) 129, 131–3
Book of Common Order 165
Book of Common Prayer:
  (1549) 117–19, 124
  Black Rubric 119
  (1552) 127, 139, 154, 160, 165, 207, 211
  (1559) 190
Book of Discipline, First (1561) 206–7, 214
border, Anglo-Scottish 3–5, 13, 15, 23–4,
    31, 33, 44–5, 66, 78, 113, 145, 155, 208,
    227
  borderers 3, 13, 28, 72, 96, 99, 118
  cross-border associations 3–9, 15–16, 28,
    86, 113, 117, 149, 155, 213–14, 219–22
  disputes 47, 75–6, 143
Borthwick, John 32, 81, 98, 167
Bothwell, John 27
Boulogne, Treaty of (1550) 111
Bowes, Elizabeth 153
Bowes, Robert 76
Bradgate (Leicestershire) 40
Brandon, Charles, Duke of Suffolk 36, 85,
  226
Brechin 151
Bretton, Henry 43–4
Bristol 39
'British history' 4
  see also Morrill; Canny

Brittany 111
Broughty Craig 107
Brunstone, *see* Crichton
Brussels 57
Bucer, Martin 116, 121
Buchanan, George 23, 36, 53, 81
  Franciscanus 80
Buckenham, Robert 26, 58, 66
Bukkery, Henry 35
Bullinger, Henry 116, 138, 156, 164, 167,
    170, 177
  Decades 117

Calais 21, 49, 100, 138, 145, 202, 223
Calvin, John 115–16, 138, 153, 162, 164–5,
    177, 211
Calvinism 1, 164, 180, 205–6, 208, 211, 214
Cambridge 26, 37, 58
  University of 37, 116, 123
Cambuskenneth 28, 40, 80
Campbell, Archibald, 4th Earl of Argyll
    140, 146
Campbell, Archibald, Lord Lorne and 5th
    Earl of Argyll 153, 186, 202, 210
Campeggio, Cardinal Lorenzo, Bishop of
    Salisbury 61
Canny, Nicholas 5
Carlisle 66, 72, 108, 117
Carmelites, Scottish 30
Carthusians 24–5
  Scottish 28
  see also Mountgrace
Cartwright, Thomas 214
Cassillis, Earl of, *see* Kennedy
Castilians 102–3, 152, 186
  see also Norman Leslie of Rothes; John
    Leslie of Parkhill; William Kirkcaldy
    of Grange; Alexander Crichton of
    Brunstone
Castillon 66
Cateau-Cambrésis, Treaty of (1559) 186
Catherine of Aragon, Queen of England 14,
    22, 24
Catholic league, *see* papal legations (1537,
    1539)
Cawe Mylles 51
Cecil, William, Baron Burghley 146, 182 n.
    121, 185, 187–8, 199, 209–10, 224, 227
  British thinking of 21–2, 193–6, 218
  and negotiations with Congregation 189,
    193–4, 200, 202–3, 207
  and plans for government of Scotland
    199–201, 203–4

Celsus, Maximilian 167
Challoner, Thomas 146, 195
Chapuys, Eustace 19, 53, 60, 62
  urges imperial invasion of England 49,
    58–9
Charles V, Holy Roman Emperor 12, 20, 50,
  53, 58–9, 115, 143
  and Henry VIII 48–9, 62, 65, 94
  and Mary I 139, 143
  and papal legations 59–63
  and relations with Scotland 48–51
Charltons 72
Charteris, Andrew 28
Châtelherault, Duke of, *see* Hamilton
Cheke, John 169
Cheshire 33
Chisholm, James, Bishop of Dunblane (d.
  1545) 28
Chisholm, William, Bishop of Dunblane
  (d. 1564) 206
Christian III, King of Denmark 48
Christison, William 186
Church of England 31, 45, 119, 136, 147
  conservatism of (1540s) 40, 85, 100, 123
  Protestant complexion of 1, 11, 113–14,
    117, 184, 190–1
  vestment and ceremony controversies
    within (1560s) 212–13
Cistercians 25
Clement VII, Pope 28–9, 56, 68
Cleutin, Henri, sieur d'Oysel 144
Clifford, Henry, Earl of Cumberland 15
Clinton, Edward Fiennes de, Earl of
  Lincoln 109
Cochlaeus, John 56
Cockburn, Alexander 158–9
Cockburn, Ninian 97
Cockburn of Ormiston, John 97, 99–102,
  140
Cocklaw, Thomas 28
Coldingham Abbey 92
Cole, Thomas 165
Cole, William:
  *Truthful tidings concerning the ascendancy
    of the Gospel* 176
College of Justice (Edinburgh) 106
Cologne 80
  reforms of Hermann von Wied in 121–3
Colville, James 72
Confession of Faith, Scottish (1560) 206
Congregation, Lords of the 187–97, 207,
  212, 223, 228
  common bond (1557) 153

embassies to Elizabeth I (1559, 1560) 201,
  209–10
  and pledge to further religious reform
    (1560) 205
  and Tudor–Hamilton marriage plan
    197–201, 204, 209–10, 227
Constantine the Great, Emperor 97
Cooper, Thomas, Bishop of Lincoln 40
Council of the Marches 15, 16
Council of the North 25, 34, 35, 68, 118
Coverdale, Miles, Bishop of Exeter 38, 154,
  167, 170, 191, 213
Cox, Richard, Bishop of Ely 162–3, 188
Craig, John 36
Cranmer, Thomas, Archbishop of
  Canterbury 27, 38, 82, 113, 117–19,
  154
  Book of Homilies 125–7, 134–5
  and the example of Cologne 121–2
  execution 138
  and plans for Edwardian Church 113–16,
    121, 124–5, 128, 130
  religious views 85, 113, 115, 118–19, 125,
    127
Crépy, Peace of (1544) 95
Crichton, Robert, Bishop of Dunkeld 206
Crichton of Brunstone, Alexander 99–101,
  140
Croft, James 182 n. 121, 187, 189
Crome, Edward 100
Cromwell, Thomas, Earl of Essex 13,
  17–18, 20, 23, 27, 34, 64, 82, 89, 186,
  195
  as patron of Scottish exiles 37, 40, 119,
    221
  fall from power 40
  and plans to extend royal government 14,
    21
  policy towards Scotland 20–2, 41–2,
    50–2, 66–7
  reformed convictions 20
  'three kingdom' mentality 21–2
Crosiers 96
Crossraguel Abbey 216
Crystall, Thomas 80
Cumberland, Earl of, *see* Clifford
Cumberland 33–4
Cunningham, William, 4th Earl of
  Glencairn (d. 1548) 83, 87, 90–1, 97
Cunningham, Alexander, 5th Earl of
  Glencairn (d. 1574) 137, 140, 153, 186,
  209, 224

Dacre, Thomas, 2nd Lord Dacre of
  Gilsland 13
Dacre, William, 4th Lord Dacre of Gilsland
  13, 36
  dismissal from office (1534) 14
Dalkeith 17
Dalyvell, Robert 35
Danyell, Thomas 35
Darcy, Thomas Lord 33, 49
Dawson, Jane 2, 21–2, 137, 176, 178
Debatable lands 13, 111
Desmond, Earl of, *see* Fitzmaurice
Dieppe 64, 153
'Dodd, a Scotchman' 100
Dominicans 26, 155
  Scottish 26, 27, 155
Donaldson, Gordon 2, 214
Doria, Andrea 49
Dorset, Marquis of, *see* Grey
Douglas, Archibald, 6th Earl of Angus 72,
  83, 87, 90–1, 94, 97
Douglas, George 72, 83, 86–7, 91
Douglas, James, 4th Earl of Morton 209, 217
Douglas, John 151–2, 206 n. 85, 211, 214
Douglas of Longniddry, Hugh 102
Douglas of Parkhede, James 72
Douglases 52
Drogheda 17
Dryburgh Abbey 92
Dudley, Andrew 107
Dudley, John, Baron and Viscount Lisle,
  Earl of Warwick, Duke of
  Northumberland 115
  as patron of Knox 118
Dudley, Robert, Earl of Leicester 191
Duguid, Laurence 159
Dumbarton 111
Dumfries 107, 110
  Greyfriars of 92
Dunbar, Gavin, Archbishop of Glasgow 17,
  31–2, 34–5, 43, 58, 69, 84
Dunbar 100
Dunblane, Bishops of, *see* Chisholm
Dundee 27, 32, 80, 89–90, 92, 100, 107, 110,
  151, 191–2
Dunkeld, Bishop of, *see* Crichton
Durham, Henry 98
Durham, Michael 98, 141
Durham 33

Eadie, John:
  The English Bible 158
East Friesland, Duchess of 159

Eccles 92
Edinburgh 17, 35, 54, 63–4, 80, 90, 151–2,
  191–2, 201–2
  anti-English feeling in 90, 226
  Castle Hill 137
  English assault on (1544) 91
  heresy trials in 32, 137
  reports of English exiles in 75
  St Giles Day disturbances (1558) 176
  Treaty of (1560) 202–5, 212, 216–17
Edward II, King of England 178
Edward VI, King of England 92, 97, 114,
  156–7, 172, 179–80
  accession 103, 114
  betrothal to Mary Queen of Scots 78, 111,
  174, 198, 204
Elder, John 98, 140, 216
Elizabeth I, Queen of England 183, 185,
  188, 193, 197, 202–5, 208, 218, 227–8
  accession 146–8, 171, 182, 185, 220
  foreign policy 22, 190, 195–6, 210, 224–5
  and marriage 48, 85, 197–201, 209–10,
  227
  religious conservatism of 183, 190–2
  and religious settlement (1559) 190–1,
  195
  and the succession 217–18
Ellis, Steven 14
Elston, Henry 24
Emden, exile congregation in 139, 157, 159,
  180–1
Erasmus, Desiderius 30
  Paraphrases on the New Testament 122
Eriksson, Gotskalk 52
Erskine, Thomas 17
Erskine of Dun, John 152–3, 207
Essé, Jean d', Seigneur de Montalembert
  110
Essex 37
Eure, William 15, 68–9
Exeter, bishopric of 191
exiles, cross-border 8, 24–8, 45, 55–6, 71–6,
  155–6, 214
  English Catholics in Scotland 24–6, 33,
  41–4, 57, 75, 221
  English Protestants in Scotland 151, 155
  Scottish Protestants in England 26–8,
  36–41, 69, 96, 117–18, 139, 221
exiles, Marian 149, 155–83, 221
  historiography and 158, 168
  resistance theories of 177–80
  Scottish presence among 149–50,
  157–60, 166–7

see also under individual entries for
congregations in Aarau; Basle; Geneva;
Emden; Frankfurt; Strassburg; Wesel;
Zurich

Faenza, Bishop of, *see* Pio
Fagius, Paul 114
Farnese, Cardinal Alexander 94
Ferdinand I, Holy Roman Emperor 48, 57
Ferrar, Robert, Bishop of St David's 54
Fife 102, 107, 186, 205
Fisher, John, Bishop of Rochester 57, 59
Fitzgerald, Gerald, 9th Earl of Kildare
    14–15, 19
Fitzgerald, Gerald, 11th Earl of Kildare 64,
    95
Fitzgerald, Thomas, Lord Offaly, 10th Earl
    of Kildare 19–20
Fitzmaurice, Thomas, 10th Earl of
    Desmond 58
Fitzwilliam, Sir William, Earl of
    Southampton 23
Flanders 18
Fleming, Malcolm, 3rd Lord 17, 83
Forme of prayers and ministration of the
    sacraments 165
Forrest, David 189, 213
Forty-two Articles (1552–3) 119
Foxe, Edward, Bishop of Hereford 38
Foxe, John 114, 128, 138–9, 163–5, 172,
    176, 181
    Acts and Monuments ('Book of Martyrs')
    157, 169
France 8, 22, 86, 103, 149, 175, 181, 196,
    199–200, 204, 212
    Church in 211
    Franco-Scottish ties 31, 48–9, 50, 60,
        70–1, 75, 89–91, 94, 109–12, 142–4,
        148, 186, 219
    and links to Irish rebels 65, 95, 143, 146,
        193–4, 201, 218
    and military presence in Scotland 110,
        143–4
    and relations with England 47, 61, 94,
        102, 111, 145–6, 186, 190, 202
    and role in papal legations 60, 62–3
Francis I, King of France 12, 71, 95
    and Henry VIII 48, 56, 61–2, 65, 73
    and papal legations 59–63
    and Scotland 50, 66
Francis II, King of France and Scotland
    110, 146, 201, 223
    and crown matrimonial 145, 186

death 210
Frankfurt, exile congregation in 139, 157–8,
    163–5, 167, 169, 181, 212
    establishment 161
    Prayer Book disputes of 160–4
Fulbeck, rectory of 36
Fullarton, Adam 154

Garrard, Thomas 25
Garrett, Christina:
    The Marian Exiles 158
Gateshead 43
Gau, John 81
    The Richt Vay to the Kingdom Of Heuine
    81
General Assembly of the Kirk 213, 215
    (1560) 206
    (1566) 213
Geneva 119, 139, 199, 211, 214
    Academy 166
Geneva Bible 170–2, 175
Geneva, exile congregation in 150, 157–9,
    162–83
    and ambitions for British reformation
        150, 171–6, 178–83
    Anglo-Scottish composition of 166–7,
        170, 172
    formal establishment 165
    liturgy of, see *Forme of prayers*
Geraldine League 64–5
Germany 18, 28, 39–40, 48, 56, 58, 149, 181,
    195
Giberti, Gian Matteo, Bishop of Verona 63
Gilby, Anthony 165, 170, 173, 180, 182, 191
    Admonition to England and Scotland to call
    them to Repentance 174–5
Giovenale, Latino 63
Glasgow 32, 191, 213
Glastonbury, Strangers' Church in 115, 161
Glencairn, Earls of, *see* Cunningham
Glenluce 117
Goldwell, Thomas, Bishop of St Asaph 138
Goodman, Christopher 139, 175, 182–3,
    188–9, 208, 211, 213
    and the Congregation 191, 193, 196
    as exile in Geneva 164–5, 167, 170
    How Superior Powers oght to be obeyd of
    their subjects 178–9
Gordon, Alexander 112
Grahams 13
Gray, Patrick 4th Lord 90
'Graye' (alias 'Whyte') 216
Greenwich 24

Greenwich Treaties (1543) 88, 91, 95, 105, 108, 143, 186, 204
Grey, Henry, Marquis of Dorset, Duke of Suffolk 40, 107, 116–17, 180
Grey, Lord William, Baron Grey de Wilton 202
Grierson, John 27
Grimani, Marco 94
Grindal, Edmund, Archbishop of Canterbury 161
Gropper, John:
    Enchiridion 121, 123
Gruffydd, Rhys ap 14, 16–17
    execution of 14, 16
Gruffydds 13
Guilliame, Thomas 84
Guisborough 40
Guise, Claude, Duke of 66
Guises 22, 203–4, 225

Habsburg–Valois relations 47, 65, 130, 143, 145
Haddington 92, 107, 110
Haddon Rigg 76
Haller, William:
    Foxe's Book of Martyrs and the Elect Nation 168
Hamilton, James, 2nd Earl of Arran, Duke of Châtelherault 82, 93, 102, 120, 145, 198–9
    appointed regent (1543) 78
    defects to Beaton's party (1543) 89, 94
    gives up regency to Mary of Guise 137
    and Henry VIII 82–8, 90, 92–3, 100, 204
    religious views 78–9, 83, 85, 89
    support for Anglo-Scottish alliance (1559) 182, 185
Hamilton, James, 3rd Earl of Arran 85
    as suitor to Elizabeth I 197–201
Hamilton, John, Abbot of Paisley, Archbishop of St Andrews 42, 82, 87–9, 113, 135–7, 151–2, 206
    appointed archbishop 120, 142
    and the example of Cologne 121–2
    and plans for reform of Kirk 113–14, 120–1, 124–8, 130–1, 136–8, 141–2; *see also* Hamilton *Catechisme*; provincial councils
    religious views 88, 120
Hamilton, Patrick 26–7, 37–8, 80, 82
Hamilton of Linlithgow, James 37, 56
Hamilton *Catechisme* (1552) 42, 124–7, 131–5
Harlaw, William 151, 154, 186, 213

Head, David 86
Henderson, Henry 28
Henrisoun, James 104–5, 174, 195
    Exhortacion to the Scottes 104–5
    Godly and Golden Book 104
    reconciled with government of Mary of Guise 108–9, 140–1
    taken into English pay 98
Henry II, King of France 110, 143
    death 223
Henry VIII, King of England 6, 11, 68–9, 82, 89, 93, 123–4, 180, 186, 194, 198–9, 220
    and concerns over cross-border exiles 26, 28, 33–5, 56–8, 72–5
    death 103
    Declaration of the just causes of the warre with the Scottes 74, 105–6
    and eagerness for religious understanding with Scotland 9, 46–8, 50–1, 66–9, 77, 86, 227
    foreign policy 21–2, 47–8, 61, 66–7, 75, 86–7
    and involvement in Beaton assassination plot 101–3
    marriage to Anne Boleyn 11
    and plans for dynastic union with Scotland 78, 84, 86–7
    and reaction to papal legations 62–3, 65
    religious views 4, 32, 85
    and Scottish noble allies 82–3, 87–8, 91, 95, 97–100, 104, 204
Hepburn, John, Bishop of Brechin 44, 80
Hepburn, Patrick 27
heresy:
    acts, Marian 190
    in England 39, 128, 130, 132–3, 137, 139; *see also* Mary I, religious persecution under
    laws, Scottish (1525, 1535, 1543) 29, 56, 80, 91
    in Scotland 32, 56, 80, 94, 109, 132–3, 137–8
    trials, Scottish (1538–9, 1544, 1550) 32, 80, 91
Hertford, Earl of, *see* Seymour
Highlands, Scottish 3, 12, 189
Hilliard, Richard:
    protected by Beaton 43–4, 72
    in Rome with Pole 58
    in St Andrews 43
    sought by English government 43, 71–2
Holcroft, Thomas 52–4, 67
Holgate, Robert, Bishop of Llandaff 68

Holst, Duke of 18
Holy Land 23
Holyrood Abbey 73, 92
Holyrood Palace 70
Hooper, Anne 167
Hooper, John, Bishop of Gloucester 105,
  115, 119, 138, 154, 167
  Declaration of the ten holy commandements
  127
Hooper, Rachel 167
Houghton, John 25
Howard, Thomas, 2nd Earl of Surrey, 3rd
  Duke of Norfolk (d.1554) 27, 34, 76, 85
Howard, Thomas, 3rd Earl of Surrey, 4th
  Duke of Norfolk (d. 1572) 201, 226
Howard, William, Lord Howard of
  Effingham 52, 54, 67, 138
Hubert, Conrad 114
Hull 36, 117
humanist reform, Scottish 31, 44, 79–80, 95,
  114, 120, 127
Hunters 72
Hussey, John, Lord 49
Hutton, John 57
Hywel, Alice Gruffydd ap 17
Hywel, James Gruffydd ap 16–20, 44, 66
  and connection with Kildare rebellion 19
  and meetings with James V 17–18, 35
  in Rome with Pole 58
  sought by English government 18
Hywel, Sage Gruffydd ap 17

Inch Colm Abbey 92
injunctions, English religious:
  (1536, 1538) 122, 131
  (1547) 122–4, 131
Ireland 5, 11–17, 21, 49, 78, 183, 190, 195,
  202–3, 208–10, 215–16, 222
  English sovereignty over, asserted by
  Henry VIII (1541) 87
  French involvement with rebels in 65, 95,
  143, 146, 193–4, 201, 218
  Pale 15, 65
  in plans of Genevan exiles 150, 171–2
  and religious links with Highlands 5, 12
  Scottish troops in 19–20, 58, 64–5, 146
  see also Kildare rebellion
Isle of Man 14, 17, 189, 208
Italy 23, 143, 149, 181

James IV, King of Scotland 8
James V, King of Scotland 9, 11, 17, 26–8,
  36, 44, 57, 68–73, 82, 89, 186, 220

and dealings with papacy 29–31, 46–50,
  55, 59–63, 67–8
death 76–8
foreign policy 46, 48–50, 62
implicated in conspiracies against Henry
  VIII 17, 23, 35–6, 71
and marriage to Madeleine of France 51,
  60–1
as subject of English kidnap scheme 74
suspected of involvement with Irish
  rebels 19–20, 64–5
religious views 4, 12, 29–32, 65, 70, 76
and response to English embassies 46–7,
  50, 52–4, 61, 70–1, 76–7
Jaquemayne, Katheryne 167
Jedburgh 24, 208
  Abbey 34, 92
Jervaulx 25
Jewel, John, Bishop of Salisbury 154, 188,
  199, 208
Jobbe, John 41
Johnston, John 39
justification, doctrine of 125–6

Kelso 208
  Abbey 92
Kendall 40
Kennedy, Gilbert, 3rd Earl of Cassillis
  82–3, 91, 97
Kennedy, Quintin 216
Ker of Cesford, Walter 99
Kethe, William 158–9, 163, 170, 179, 181,
  189
Kildare, Earls of 13
  see also Fitzgerald
Kildare rebellion 15, 19, 58–9, 143, 222
Killigrew, Henry 194
'King's Book' (1543) 40, 86, 89, 122, 124–7,
  134–5
Kinloss 80
Kirk, James 2, 214–15
Kirk, Scottish 1, 29, 42–5, 56, 79–82, 113,
  120, 136, 147, 210, 214
  admired by English extremists (1560s)
  213–14, 222
  and attitude to Elizabethan Church 208,
  211, 214, 219
  Henrician reformation as threat to 24,
  28–9, 32, 44, 55, 70, 93, 221
  notion of singularity of 1–2, 211–12, 219
  Protestant settlement of (1560) 184, 204,
  206–8, 218–19, 223, 225
  see also General Assembly

Kirkcaldy of Grange, James 30
Kirkcaldy of Grange, William 101, 140, 187, 194, 224
Knox, Eleezer 167
Knox, John 27, 128, 136, 141, 156–8, 182–3, 188, 195, 206 n. 85, 208, 211, 213–14, 216, 224
    Appellation from the sentence pronounced by the bishops and clergy 179
    Brief Exhortation to England 183
    and the Congregation 153–4, 187, 191–3, 196
    and the Edwardian Church 118–19
    Faithful Admonition 162
    First Blast of the Trumpet 173–5, 179
    in Frankfurt 139, 158, 161–3
    History 188, 191
    Letter to the Regent 179
    and Marian resistance theories 177–80
    and Mary Queen of Scots 217, 219
    as minister to Genevan exiles 152, 163, 165, 167, 170
    and ministry in Berwick and Newcastle 107, 118
    preaching career begins in St Andrews 102–3
    Scottish preaching tour of (1555–6) 152–3, 173
    Second Blast of the Trumpet 179
Knox, Nathaniel 167
Kyle, Lollards of 80

Lamb, William 75
    Ane Resonyng of ane Scottish and Inglis Merchand betuix Rowand and Lionis 106
Lancashire 33
Lasco, John à 115, 119, 180
Lassigny 66
Latimer, Hugh, Bishop of Worcester 38
    execution 138
Lauder 107
Laurence, Robert 25
Layton, Brian 92
Lazenby, George 25
Learmonth, James 30, 89
Learmonth, William 37, 119
Leche, William 34, 66, 72, 76
Lee, Edward, Archbishop of York 38
Lee, Rowland, Bishop of Coventry and Lichfield 15–16
Leicester 35
    Earl of, *see* Dudley

Leicestershire 22
Leipzig 117
Leith 17, 32, 80, 100, 202, 217
Lennox, Earl of, *see* Stewart
Leslie, John, Bishop of Ross 110, 203
Leslie of Parkhill, John 101
Leslie of Rothes, Norman 90, 101, 103
Lethington, *see* Maitland
Lever, Thomas 156
Liddesdale (Scotland) 13
Lincoln, Bishop of, *see* Cooper
Lincolnshire 33
Lindores 192
Lindsay of the Mount, David 42, 81, 102, 108, 129
    The Complaynt (1529–30) 82
    and the Congregation 196
    at court of James V 30, 70
    diplomatic background of 82
    Epiphany play (1540) 69
    The Monarche (1548–53) 82, 136
    at St Andrews 81
    Ane Satyre of the Thrie Estaitis (1552) 150
    The Testament (1530) 82
Linlithgow 44, 88
Lisle, Viscount, *see* Plantagenet
Little, Clement 154
Llandaff, Bishop of, *see* Holgate
Lloyd, Edward 16
Locke, Anna 208
Lockhart of Bar, John 100
Lockhart of Bar, Robert 152
Logie, Robert 28
London 27, 28, 38, 72, 103, 141, 155, 199–200, 213–14
    All Hallows, Bread Street, benefice of 118
    Charterhouse 25, 37
    diocese of 129, 131
    Fleet Prison 41
    Islington underground congregation 139, 155
    Marshalsea court 105, 195
    merchant community 40, 117
    Newgate Prison 139
    Paul's Cross 23, 37, 41
    St Katherine Coleman, parish of 41
    St Paul's Cathedral 189
    Strangers' Church 115, 180
    Tower of London 14, 16, 24, 100
    Westminster 16, 199
    Windsor 119
Longland, John, Bishop of Lincoln 38
Loretto, shrine of, Musselburgh 92

Lorne, Lord, *see* Campbell
Lothians 99–100, 151
Loughborough 117, 213
Louvain 26, 80
Low Countries 19, 28, 58, 143, 199
Lutheran princes 8, 48, 50
  see also Schmalkaldic League
Lutheranism 29, 31–2, 37, 46, 56, 80–1, 121
  literature 56, 80
  in Scotland 26–7, 155
Luttrell, John 92, 109
Lynch, Michael 2
Lyne, John 28

MacAlpine, John 27, 37–8, 40, 154
MacDowell, John 27, 37–9, 117, 139, 159
Machyn, Henry 117
Mackbrair, John 117, 139, 157–8, 161, 163, 181, 189
Madde, Thomas 25
Madeleine, Queen of Scotland 48
Magnus, Thomas 18
Mainz, Peter of 41
Maitland, David 96
Maitland of Lethington, William 182, 185, 187, 205, 211, 214, 219–20
  and Congregation's negotiations with England 189, 193, 196, 200, 202, 209
  and desire for closer Anglo-Scottish alliance 194, 207–10, 227–8
  succession scheme of 217–18
Marches 13, 111
  wardens 13, 15
  see also Council of the Marches; Debatable lands
Margaret Tudor, Queen Dowager of Scotland 8, 52, 54
Marillac, Charles de 28, 71, 74
Marshal, Richard (Carthusian friar) 25
Marshall, Richard (Dominican prior of Newcastle) 26, 42, 44, 126, 211, 224
Martin, Charles 158
Martyr, Peter 115–16, 164, 167, 191
Mary of Guise, Queen Dowager of Scotland 90, 94, 109, 136, 142, 147, 182, 187, 196, 201
  becomes regent 137, 144
  conciliatory government of 138, 140–2, 149–52, 155, 186
  deposed as regent 190
  French advisers of 112, 140, 144, 192
  religious views 150
Mary I, Queen of England 9, 17, 48, 136,

139, 162, 172–3, 177, 179, 221, 223
  accession 4, 114, 130, 156, 158
  Catholic reform under 114, 128–36, 147
  death 146, 223
  foreign policy 130, 142–3, 145–6
  marriage to Philip of Spain 143
  religious persecution under 128, 130, 137–9, 147–8
Mary Queen of Scots 83, 85, 88–9, 105, 143, 195, 198, 201, 215, 223
  accession 77–8
  betrothal and marriage to dauphin 110–11, 144–6
  betrothal to Prince Edward 78, 111, 174, 198, 204
  and claim to English throne 146, 190, 203, 216–19, 225, 228
  religious beliefs 221
  and response to Scottish reforming activity 217, 219–20
  return to Scotland (1561) 185, 210–12, 216–20
Mason, Roger 2, 178
Maxton, Henry 26, 44
Maxwell, Robert, 5th Lord 75, 83–4, 90
Mearns 151–2, 186, 205
Melanchthon, Philipp 18–19, 27, 116, 121, 164
Melrose Abbey 92
Melville, Andrew 214
Melville, James 56
Melville, John 109, 139
Melville, Robert 189
Merriman, Marcus 96
Merse 97
Methven, Henry 1st Lord 99
Methven, Paul 151, 154, 186, 213
Middleton, Edward 34
Milan, Christina, Duchess of 48
Milan, duchy of 61
Mirapoix (Mirepoix), Cardinal of, *see* Beaton, David
Montmorency, Anne de, Constable of France 50, 66
Montrose 100, 151
Monymele 44
Moorhouse, Geoffrey 33
Moray, Earl of, *see* Stewart
More, Robert 64
More, Thomas 57, 59
Morpeth 43
Morrill, John 4
Morton, Earl of, *see* Douglas

Mountgrace Priory, Yorkshire 25, 43
Musgrave, Nicholas 73
Myln, Alexander 80

Necessary Doctrine and Erudition for any
Christian Man, see 'King's Book'
Nevilles 13
Newark, Scottish friar preaching in 23
Newbattle Abbey 73, 92
Newcastle 26, 34, 107, 117–18
   mayor of 118
Neweye, James 25
Nice, Truce of (1538) 62
Nixsons 96
Norfolk, Dukes of, *see* Howard
Norham, Treaty of (1551) 113
Normandy 111
Northern Conspiracy (1541) 71
Northumberland 33
Northumberland, Duke of, *see* Dudley
Northumberland, Earl of, *see* Percy
Norwich, bishopric of 191

O'Brien, Cornelius 59
Observant Franciscans:
   exiled in Europe 24, 57
   exiled in Scotland 24–6, 33–4, 41, 44, 52,
      72
   linked to Kildare rebellion 19–20
   Scottish 24, 30, 34
   suppression of 24
O'Donnell, Calvagh 146
O'Donnell, Manus 64
O'Donnells 146
Offaly, Thomas Lord, *see* Fitzgerald
Okeford Superior, Dorset 189
Olde, John:
   Acquital or purgation of the moost catholyke
     Prince Edwarde VI 161
Oliphant, Andrew 70
Ollyvers 96
O'Neill, Conn 64–5
Order of Communion (1548) 124, 128
Orkney 96
Ormiston, *see* Cockburn
Otterburn, Adam 47, 51–2, 103–4
Ottoman Turks 86
Oxford 168
   Alban Hall 42
   University of 116, 123
Oysel, d', *see* Cleutin

Padua 80, 164

papacy 46, 48–9, 52, 58, 93–4, 145
   authority of 3, 11, 30–1, 64, 68, 70, 73, 85,
     127, 135, 206
   grants made by 9, 29–30
   papal legation (1537) 59–62, 194
   papal legation (1539) 62–3, 67, 93, 194
   see also Clement VII; Paul III; Pius IV
Paris 63–4, 80, 164
parliament, Scottish:
   (1541) 31
   (March 1543) 84
   (December 1543) 91
   (1546) 102
   (1548) 110–11, 226
   (1554) 145
   (1558) 145
   (1560) 1, 205–6, 209, 212, 220, 222, 226
Patenson, John 35–6
Patten, William 92, 105, 195
Paul III, Pope 28–9, 49–50, 56, 58–64, 68,
   93
Penrith 40
Percies 13
Percy, Henry, 6th Earl of Northumberland
   15
Percy, Henry (brother of Thomas, 7th Earl
   of Northumberland) 182, 224
Perth 27–8, 32, 90–1, 151, 167
   reformation of (1559) 186, 191–2
Peto, William 24, 57
Philip, King of Spain and England 145, 162,
   195
   anti-Spanish feeling towards 144–5
Pilgrimage of Grace 33–6, 40, 59, 66, 71, 76
   causes of 33
   and flight of rebels to Scotland 33–6, 72
Pinkie, battle of (1547) 92, 105, 107
Pio, Rodolfo, Bishop of Faenza 49, 60–2
Pius IV, Pope 195
Plantagenet, Arthur, Viscount Lisle 21
Pole, Cardinal Reginald, Archbishop of
   Canterbury 57–8, 64–6, 93–4, 101,
   130, 143, 216
   De Unitate Ecclesiae 53, 57
   legatine synod of (1556) 129, 133
   and Marian Catholic reform 129, 136–8
   and papal legations 59–60, 62, 67
   as superintendent of the English hospice,
     Rome 58
Ponet, John, Bishop of Winchester 126–7,
   154, 164, 180
   A Shorte Treatise of politike power 178
Pontefract 71

Poullain, Valérand 115–16, 161
Prayer Book, see *Book of Common Prayer*
Priestman, John 73, 76
Privy Council, English 118–19, 140
privy kirks, Scottish 149, 150–5
  geographical extent of 151
Proctor, John 129
Protestant culture, Anglo-Scottish 2, 221,
  225
Protestantism 80–1, 84, 104
  character of, in Scotland 120, 155
  growth in adherence to in England 40,
    215, 221–2
  penetration into Scotland 11, 55–6,
    79–80, 90–1, 95–6, 107, 111–12, 116,
    152–3, 191–2, 205, 221–2
  see also Calvinism; Lutheranism
provincial councils of the Scottish Kirk
    120–2, 127, 130
  (1549) 42
  (1552) 124
  (1559) 142
  statutes of 120–4, 131–3, 137, 141–2

Rainsford, John 37
Randolph, Thomas 154, 182 n. 121, 194,
    199, 205–9, 216, 220, 224
Redesdale 13
reformation, English 7, 9, 11–12, 38, 45, 82,
    97, 175, 194
  enforcement of 11, 15, 21
  historiography of 2–3, 128, 147
  nature and timing of 1, 4, 215
  popular responses to 12, 22–3
  see also Rome, break with; supremacy,
    royal; Protestantism, growth in
    adherence to in England
reformation, Scottish 175, 184, 212
  historiography of 2–3, 141–2
  nature and timing of 1, 4, 215
  rebellion (1559–60) 1, 120, 186–8, 191–2,
    205, 215, 223
  reforms of 1543 83–6, 89–90, 226
  see also Kirk, Scottish, Protestant
    settlement of; Protestantism,
    penetration into Scotland
Reforming of Kirks and Kirkmen, Act for
    the (1541) 30
Reid, Robert 80
Renard, Simon 143–4
Restraint of Appeals, Act in (1533) 11
Richard II, King of England 178
Richardson, Robert 40, 80, 117, 139

Ridley, Nicholas, Bishop of London 154,
    161, 168, 177
  execution 138
  A frendly farewell 160–1
Robsons 72
Rochester, John 37
Rochester, bishopric of 118
Roger, Marjorie 154
Rogers, John 137
Rome 43–4, 58–9, 63–4, 70, 80, 94, 102,
    164
  English Hospice in 58
Rothes, *see* Leslie
Roubay, Yves du 144
Rough, John 117–18, 154
  and Castilians 102
  in Emden 139, 159
  execution of 159
  and Islington congregation 139, 155
  as minister with English armies 107
  appointed preacher at Scottish court 84
Rough Wooing 79, 99, 111, 113, 116, 166,
    174
Row, John 206 n. 85
Roxburgh 92, 99, 107
Russell, Jerome 32
Rutherford, George ('Cokbanke') 72

Sadler, Ralph 84–5, 87–8, 90, 101, 187–8,
    190, 194, 209, 226
  and embassies to James V 67, 70–1
St Andrews 25, 27, 32, 44, 58, 90, 93, 107,
    110, 189, 191–2, 201
  Castle of 88, 101–2, 186
  convention of clergy in (1543) 88
  Holy Trinity parish church 102
  reforming activity of Castilians in 102
  St Leonard's College 80
  University of 42–3, 81, 126, 211
saints, intercessory prayer and 42, 126–7
Salisbury 37–9
Sampson, Richard, Bishop of Chichester
    38
Sampson, Thomas 191
Sandys, William Lord 49
Scarborough 36
Schmalkaldic League 66
Scory, John, Bishop of Hereford 161, 177
Scot, John 23
Scot of Branxholme, Walter 99
Scrimger, Henry 158
Seton, Alexander 27, 36, 40, 96
Seton, George Lord 88, 93

Seymour, Edward, Earl of Hertford, Duke of
    Somerset 95, 99, 103, 108–9, 174, 186
    appointed Protector 103
    downfall 115
    Epistle or Exhortacion to Unitie and Peace
        104–6
    foreign policy 104, 115
    garrison strategy of 107–8
    religious views 85, 104, 115
    and Scottish military campaigns 91–3,
        104–5, 195
Shaxton, Nicholas, Bishop of Salisbury 37,
    38
Shrewsbury, *see* Talbot
Sidney, Henry 208, 216
Simpson, William 72
Simson, David 159
Sinclair, John, Dean of Restalrig 142
Six Articles, Act of (1539) 40, 117
'six Johns' 206, 211
    see also Douglas; Knox; Row;
        Spottiswoode; Willock; Winram
Skea, James 96
Skeffington, William 15
Smith, Richard 42
    *Assertion and Defence of the sacramente of
        the aulter* 129
Solway Moss:
    battle of (1542) 76
    prisoners 82–3
Somerset, Duke of, *see* Seymour
Somerset Herald 34, 76
Somerville, Hugh 4th Lord 90
South Shields 64
Spain 59–60, 142–3, 175, 190
Spottiswoode, John 206 n. 85, 213
Stafford, Jane 167
Stafford, Thomas 145
Stewart, Lord James, Earl of Moray 86, 140,
    142, 186
    and the Congregation 153, 202
    succession scheme of 217–18
Stewart, Matthew, 4th Earl of Lennox 91,
    94, 97, 99
Stewart, William, Bishop of Aberdeen 17,
    52
Stirling 32, 151, 192, 201
    Greyfriars' house in 89
Stockton 43
Stokesley, John, Bishop of London 38
Strasbourg 114, 165
    exile congregation in 157, 159–61, 164,
        167, 169

Strathearn 205
Strype, John 157
Stumphius, John Rodolph 116
Suffolk, Dukes of, *see* Brandon, Grey
superintendent, office of 215
Supremacy, Act of (1534) 11
supremacy, royal 11, 25–6, 37–8, 45, 54,
    127, 190
Sweden 27, 81
Switzerland 149

Talbot, Francis, Earl of Shrewsbury 99
Ten Articles (1536) 38
Teviotdale 96–7
Throckmorton, Nicholas 194, 197–8, 200,
    209, 216, 224
Tillbodie (Scotland) 28
Toledo 63
    Treaty of (1539) 62
Travers, Walter 214
Treason Act (1534) 16, 25
Trent, General Council of 116, 120, 127–8,
    132–3
Tunstall, Cuthbert, Bishop of Durham 35,
    43, 118
Turner, William 115
'Twopenny Faith', Scottish (1559) 128
Tyndale, William 154
Tynedale 13

Ulmis, John ab 116
Ulster 12, 146
Uniformity, Act of (1559) 190
Union, Act of, *see* Wales
Uses, Statute of (1536) 33

Venice 164
Villemore, Bartholomew de 144
Viret, Pierre 211

Wales 5, 13–16, 20, 183
    Act of Union (1536–43) 16, 87
    enforcement of reformation in 21, 215
    Henrician government of 13, 15–16, 21
    and links with Irish rebels 20, 49
    in plans of Genevan exiles 171
Wallace, Adam 137
Wallop, John 47, 57
warfare, Anglo-Scottish:
    (1542) 6, 76
    (1543–50) 91–3
    religious dimension to 92–3, 95, 101, 107,
        109, 112

Watson, Robert 154
Watson, Thomas 129
Watts, Friar 38
Webster, Augustine 25
Wedderburn, James 81
Wedderburn, John 81
   Gude and Godlie Ballatis 81, 106
Wedderburn, Robert:
   The Complaynt of Scotlande vyth ane
   Exhortatione to the thre Estaits 106
Wesel, exile congregation in 159, 180
Westmoreland 33
Wharton, Lord Thomas, Baron Wharton
   15, 18, 74, 92, 96, 108–9, 227
Whitgift, John, Archbishop of Canterbury 1
   n. 2
Whitbarn 36
Whithorn (Scotland) 17
Whitlaw, Alexander 197–8, 209
Whittingham, William 179, 191
   in Frankfurt 161
   in Geneva 162–3, 165, 167, 170
   marriage 167
   translation of New Testament by (1557)
   170–1
Wied, Hermann von, Archbishop of
   Cologne 121
   Simplex et Pia Deliberatio 121–2
Wigtown 27
Willock, John 27, 39, 117, 119, 180, 186, 206
   n. 85, 213
   and the Congregation 189, 191
   in Emden 139, 159, 181
   imprisoned in Fleet by Bonner 41, 96

as minister with English troops 107
   and the privy kirks 151, 154
Wilson, John 43
Winram, John 142, 206 n. 85, 214
Winter, Admiral William 201
Winzet, Ninian 216
Wishart, George 96, 102
   in Bristol 39, 41
   execution 100–1
   preaching tour of (1544–5) 100, 152
Wittenberg 27, 56
Wolsey, Cardinal Thomas, Archbishop of
   York 20, 63
Wooding, Lucy 128, 135
Woodmansey, William 34
Wormald, Jenny 217
Wotton, Nicholas 190, 202–3, 210
Wriothesley, Thomas, Earl of Southampton
   24, 62, 85, 115
Wyatt, Thomas 145
Wyatt rebellion 137, 144

xenophobia, Anglo-Scottish 7, 9–10, 34, 39,
   45, 90, 109, 180–1, 227

York 40
   proposed meeting between Henry VIII
   and James V in 52, 73–5
Yorkshire 33
Young, Peter 166

Zurich 105, 119–20
   exile congregation in 159–60, 164, 167,
   177